y W. Scott

Eastern States

al Park Lodges

Praise for previous editions of

Guide to the National Park Areas:
WESTERN STATES

"Will tell you how to get there, what to see, and what camping and
recreational facilities are available. Like our national parks themselves,
a bargain for motorhomers!"

—*Motorhome Life* magazine

"The Scotts did a lot of traveling, and their firsthand research has paid off."

—*Kliatt Paperback Book Guides*

"Offers excellent encouragement for leaving the beaten paths of overcrowded
tourist areas and getting back to America's treasures."

—*Hudson Valley* magazine

"The information the authors pass on in their book will help
many travelers prepare a wonderful vacation."

—*Camp-orama*

"The Scotts have a winner here . . . good basic information."

—*Pike County* (Pa.) *Dispatch*

Help Us Keep This Guide Up to Date

Every effort has been made by the authors and editors to make this guide as accurate and useful as possible. However, many changes can occur after a guide is published—establishments close, phone numbers change, facilities come under new management, and so on.

We would love to hear from you concerning your experiences with this guide and how you feel it could be made better and be kept up to date. While we may not be able to respond to all comments and suggestions, we'll take them to heart, and we'll make certain to share them with the authors. Please send your comments and suggestions to the following address:

The Globe Pequot Press
Reader Response/Editorial Department
P.O. Box 480
Guilford, CT 06437

Or you may e-mail us at: editorial@GlobePequot.com

Thanks for your input, and happy travels!

Also by David L. Scott and Ka

Guide to the National Park Areas:

The Complete Guide to the Nation

Text photographs and Facilities and Activities Chart a
courtesy of the National Park Service.

Text and map design by Nancy Freeborn

ISSN 1537-3339
ISBN 0-7627-2989-9

Manufactured in the United States of America
Eighth Edition/First Printing

CONTENTS

*Map reference numbers correspond with locations on the map on pp. viii–ix.

Alaska

157
158
159
160
161
162
163
164
165
166
167
168
169
170
171
187

Hawaii

Niihau
Kauai
Oahu
172
Molokai
173
174
Maui
Hawaii
175
176
177
178

1
2
3
4
5
6
7
8
9
Washington
12
10
13
11
38
14
Oregon
15
16
17
18
39
19
20
California
21
22
25
23
26
24
27
Nevada
28
29
31
30
42
32
43
56
34
35
33
36
37
69

American Samoa
Ofu
Olosega
179
63 miles
Ta'u
179
179
Tutuila

Northern
Mariana
Islands
Garapan
180
Saipan

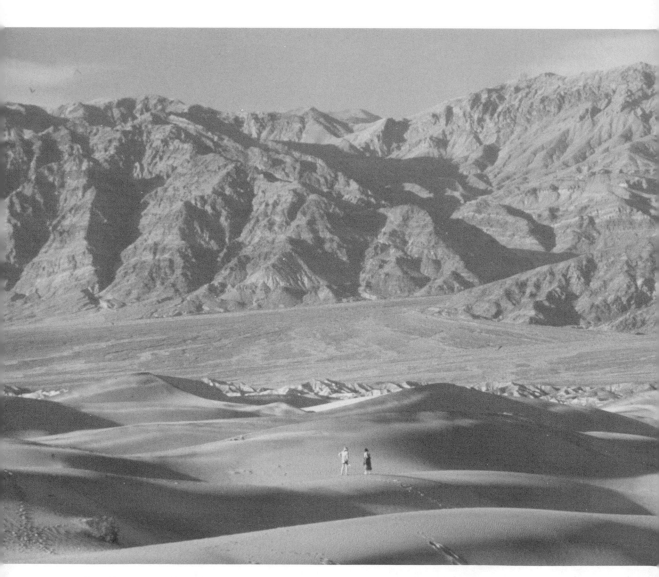

Death Valley National Park

PREFACE

Any discussion of America's national parks is likely to cause most people to think instinctively of one or more well-known national parks such as Acadia, Grand Canyon, Grand Teton, Olympic, Rocky Mountain, Great Smoky Mountains (by far the most visited NPS area), Yellowstone, and Yosemite. These are eight of our most spectacular and frequently visited and photographed national parks. Literally hundreds of other beautiful and interesting areas are included in the National Park System, however, even though they are not all officially designated as national parks. The system of parks also includes national monuments, historical parks, military parks, historic sites, reserves, lakeshores, battlefields, and recreation areas. The National Park Service (NPS) administers areas that include seashores to walk, parkways to drive, rivers to float, and majestic redwoods to admire. Each area offers something special that is worth seeking out. How about a visit to a restored fort on the historic Oregon Trail? Have you tried camping in the midst of a field of cinders and volcanic rock? Perhaps you would enjoy a visit to the reconstructed fort in Oregon where Lewis and Clark camped during the winter of 1805–1806 following their epic journey to the Pacific Ocean. How about a stroll around the Missouri birthplace and home of educator George Washington Carver?

Of the 388 areas administered by the National Park Service, only about 15 percent are officially designated as national parks. Most national parks are relatively large and contain a variety of resources. Other areas administered by the National Park Service, designated as national monuments, battlefields, historic sites, and historical parks, are more limited in size and scope. The different designation doesn't make these areas any less rewarding to visit. In fact, you are likely to discover that these other areas are less well known and less crowded and offer much to see and do. Several times we were the only members on ranger-guided walks, and we once experienced a wonderful campfire program with only six other visitors. These experiences frequently become a trip's most memorable events.

As these books are written, we have spent twenty-seven summers touring the national parks. We have visited all the states and have seen nearly all of the park areas administered by the National Park Service. We have spent a week hiking Canyonlands National Park and a day strolling through Fort Laramie National Historic Site. We took a ferry to Klondike Gold Rush National Historical Park in Skagway, Alaska, and a plane to Hawaii Volcanoes National Park on the Big Island of Hawaii; and we drove the Alaska Highway to spend a week at Denali National Park. We have seen the sights, walked the trails, talked with the park rangers, and visited with other campers. We have loved it all and in virtually every case would like to be able to go back and visit the same places again. In many instances that is exactly what we have done.

The idea for this series of books occurred to us about the fifth summer of our travels. Each time we headed in a new direction, we found ourselves trying to decide which areas of the National Park Service to visit and, once there, attempting to determine which particular points of interest and activities held the most promise for our limited time. We discovered that we often delayed trips to areas we should have visited earlier and spent time driving to parks that held less interest for us. In addition, after arriving at a park, we were often unsure of which campgrounds to use or what activities and facilities were available.

Our hope is that the contents of these books will assist others in avoiding these same pitfalls. We have tried to include enough information to allow readers to decide which parks to visit as well as how long to allow to adequately discover the major features of each park. For most areas we have tried to provide information on why the area was set aside, a summary of the history and/or geology of the area, activities for visitors, facilities such as availability of food service and overnight accommodations, campgrounds and their facilities, and possibilities for those who fish. In the limited space allotted to each area, we believe that this information is most useful to the majority of visitors.

The material in these books is believed to be accurate. The Park Service is constantly altering the areas under its jurisdiction, however, and no doubt there will be changes before you buy this book. Budget limitations have resulted in the closing of certain facilities as funds for maintenance and personnel have been cut or at least have not kept up with visitation growth. In some cases, the closings are temporary; in other instances, they appear permanent. Regardless of the changes, we can assure you that you will enjoy yourself. The people are nice, the scenery is breathtaking, and the history is real.

We want to express our thanks to park personnel who took the time to read and correct the written material we sent. In addition, we appreciate the time that rangers have spent with us on our annual tours. We hope these books can help you have some of the wonderful times in our national parks that we have enjoyed.

David L. Scott
Kay W. Scott
Valdosta, Georgia

The information in this guidebook was confirmed at press time. We recommend, however, that you call establishments before traveling to obtain current information.

INTRODUCTION

SOME BASICS FOR VISITING AMERICA'S NATIONAL PARKS

Preparation

Each of the 388 areas administered by the National Park Service offers something special. Learning as much as possible about what is special before you visit a park helps you appreciate what you are likely to experience. You will also waste less of your limited time after arrival. Why wait until you arrive to find out what you will be seeing? Most park officials are good about responding to requests for information.

Each of the park write-ups in this book provides a telephone number, address, and, in some cases, an e-mail address to use in requesting information. You will also find park Web addresses that allow access to basic information including opening and closing times, facilities, and activities. If you plan to drive thousands of miles on a vacation of several weeks, take some time to bone up on what you are likely to see, both along the way and at your destination.

What to do when you arrive

The first order of business should be to stop at the park visitor center, especially when you are planning to spend a half day or less in a park area. With a short stay you need to make every minute count. Ask someone at the visitor center information desk about the activities and sights he or she recommends for the time you have available. Most visitor centers offer exhibits and an orientation film or slide presentation to introduce you to the park. The video presentations are generally excellent at providing a better appreciation of what you will experience in the park. Visitor centers generally operate sales areas with pamphlets and paperback guides relevant to the park and nearby areas. You may want to ask someone at the information desk which publications are likely to prove most helpful. Also check for a listing of the day's ranger-led interpretive programs. Guided walks, living history programs, and ranger presentations are nearly always worthwhile.

It is our opinion that, with a limited amount of time, you are better off taking time to really experience a few park areas than trying to visit as many park areas as possible. Why miss some of the worthwhile things a park has to offer when you are already there and may not return?

Fees

Most areas operated by the National Park Service levy entrance fees that range from $3.00 to $5.00 per vehicle at the low end to $20.00 per vehicle at very popular parks such as Yosemite, Grand Canyon, and Yellowstone. Separate fees apply to bikers and hikers. The initial entrance fee is generally good for several days, although this varies by park. Many individual parks also offer annual entrance passes at a higher charge. You may discover that certain activities inside a park such as a cave tour or a guided tour of a building will require a separate charge. Fees for entrance and activities have increased in both amount and frequency in recent years. Many park areas that once offered free entrance now impose a fee. In addition, nearly a hundred park areas, including most of the national recreation areas, are participating in a new program for fee demonstration areas. Most of the fees collected under this program are retained by the parks that collect them.

Four types of passes are available for individuals and families who expect to be visiting several parks. The National Parks Pass and Golden Eagle Passport are each valid for one year from the month of purchase. Purchase either of these passes on June 10, and the pass will be valid through the end of June in the following year. The Golden Age Passport is a lifetime pass available only for seniors age sixty-two or older; the Golden Access Passport is a lifetime pass for the disabled. The National Parks Pass and Golden Eagle Pass both cover entrance fees but are not good for reductions on charges for facilities or tours. For example, the fees charged for the guided cave tours at Carlsbad Caverns National Park in New Mexico are not covered by either of these passes. The Golden Age Passport and Golden Access Passport are lifetime passes that cover entrance fees and are also good for reductions on many other fees including camping, parking, and tours. Additional information about the various passes applicable for national park entrance is available on the Internet at www.nps.gov/fees_passes.htm.

The **National Parks Pass** costs $50 and provides entrance for one year to national parks, national monuments, national historical parks, and all other areas operated by the National Park Service. For parks that charge a vehicle entrance fee, the pass provides free entrance for one private vehicle and its passengers. For parks with a per-person entrance fee, the pass provides free entrance for the pass holder, spouse, children, and parents. This pass does not usually cover fees charged for tours, campgrounds, shuttles, and the like. The National Parks Pass is available at most national park entrance stations and visitor centers or by calling (888) GOPARKS, and on the Internet at www.nationalparks.org. The pass is also available by sending a check or money order to National Parks Pass, 27540 Avenue Mentry, Valencia, CA 91355. A shipping charge of $3.95 applies to passes purchased by mail, phone, or the Internet.

The **Golden Eagle Passport** costs $65 and provides one year's entrance to all federal lands, including areas operated by the National Park Service, the USDA Forest Service, and the Bureau of Land Management. Like the National Parks Pass discussed above, the Golden Eagle Passport applies to one private vehicle and its passengers as well as to the pass holder and immediate family when a per-person fee is assessed. The $50 National Parks Pass can be upgraded for $15 at most federal areas that allow free entrance with the Golden Eagle Passport. The holder of a Golden Eagle Passport does not receive discounts on activities such as tours, parking, camping, and boat launching.

The **Golden Age Passport** costs $10 and provides lifetime entrance to all areas operated by the National Park Service. This pass is available only to citizens and permanent residents of the United States who are sixty-two years of age and older. The pass must be purchased in person, and proof of age is required. The Golden Age Passport applies to one private vehicle and its occupants or to the pass holder and his or her immediate family. Unlike the National Parks Pass and Golden Eagle Passport, the Golden Age Passport also provides for a 50 percent discount on many activities, such as parking, camping, and tours. This reduction is sometimes limited to the pass holder. This pass is available at entrance stations and visitor centers of areas managed by the National Park Service. This is the best deal going if you are sixty-two or older.

The **Golden Access Passport** is a lifetime pass that is issued without charge to individuals who show proof of medically determined disability and eligibility for receiving benefits under federal law. This pass provides free entrance and a 50 percent discount for many activities, such as camping, tours, and parking. Some activities are available at a discount only to the holder of the Golden Access Passport. This pass must be obtained in person and is available only to citizens and permanent residents of the United States.

Crowds

Most of America's national park areas are heavily visited, especially during summer months, when the weather is good and children are out of school. If possible, try to plan your trip during the spring or fall, when crowds are smaller, prices are sometimes reduced, and the weather is still enjoyable. In fact, the weather at many of the western parks is delightful during the spring, when flowers are blooming, and in the fall, when leaves are turning. We had an enjoyable visit to Yosemite National Park just after Christmas, when the air was crisp, the valley was covered with snow, and visitors were a fraction of the normal crowds this busy park experiences during June, July, and August.

Crowds are less of a problem at some of the smaller parks, especially in early mornings and late afternoons. Parks near urban areas are nearly always less crowded during weekdays, when nearby residents are working and children are in school. Try to plan trips to eating establishments before or after the most popular hours.

Programs for children

Nearly all national park areas offer special programs and activities for children. The majority are designed for children ages six to twelve, although some park areas also offer special activities for kids ages six and under. Most park areas sponsor a Junior Ranger program that typically incorporates an activity booklet with questions, puzzles, scavenger hunts, and other activities to help young people learn about the natural and human history of a particular park. Children who complete a required number of activities that may include ranger-led walks and collecting trash are awarded a badge, pin, patch, certificate, or some other form of recognition. Young visitors who complete Junior Ranger requirements are sometimes given public recognition in the visitor center. We have been in a visitor center when a ranger announced that a child had just become a Junior Ranger. The glowing smile and look of pride made the day for all who were fortunate enough to be there. Be certain to ask at the visitor center about a Junior Ranger program when you first enter the park, because required activities must often be completed during the visit. In other words, don't ask about the program when you are ready to leave the park. Parks may also offer ranger-led activities designed specifically for children.

Some parks have Web-based Junior Ranger programs. Check individual park Web sites for information. The National Park Service offers a WebRanger program for children who are unable to visit a national park. The site allows participants to print a membership card and become involved in educational activities related to our national parks. The program, available at www.nps.gov/webrangers, is for ages six through nine, ten through twelve, and thirteen and up.

Campgrounds

Although many National Park Service areas, especially those with primarily a historical theme, do not have campgrounds, a number of areas in the western states administered by the National Park Service do provide camping facilities. Multiple campgrounds are in the bigger national parks, such as Yosemite, Sequoia, Olympic, Mount Rainier, Glacier, Yellowstone, Big Bend, Rocky Mountain, and Grand Teton, which serve as popular vacation destinations. Campgrounds are also at some less heavily visited areas, including Lava Beds National Monument, Natural Bridges National Monument, Devils Tower National Monument, and Theodore Roosevelt National Park.

Most National Park Service campgrounds offer similar facilities, including picnic tables, fire grates, water, a dump station, and rest rooms with flush toilets. Hookups for water, electricity, and waste disposal are generally unavailable except for a few instances when a campground is operated by a private concessioner rather than the Park Service itself. Likewise, showers are not

NPS Areas, Western States, with Campgrounds that Accept Reservations

Channel Islands National Park (CA)

Death Valley National Park (CA)

Glacier National Park (MT)

Grand Canyon National Park (AZ)

Joshua Tree National Park (CA)

Katmai National Park (AK)

Kings Canyon National Park (CA)

Mount Rainier National Park (WA)

Rocky Mountain National Park (CO)

Sequoia National Park (CA)

Whiskeytown National Recreation Area (CA)

Yosemite National Park (CA)

Zion National Park (UT)

offered at most Park Service campgrounds. Concessioners sometimes provide pay showers near a visitor center or store, but this is the exception rather than the rule.

National parks with and without campgrounds are often surrounded by national forests that offer numerous camping opportunities. USDA Forest Service campgrounds often provide relatively rustic facilities, including pit toilets, although this is certainly not always the case. Many USDA Forest Service campgrounds are quite nice, with paved parking pads and modern rest rooms. Because National Park Service campgrounds tend to be heavily used, you may wish to settle in at a Forest Service campground the night before entering one of the busy parks, especially if you arrive in the late afternoon.

Most National Park Service campgrounds are operated on a first-come, first-served basis, so the earlier in the day you arrive, the more likely you are to locate a vacant campsite. Approximately two dozen park areas managed by the National Park Service have campgrounds with sites that can be reserved. Campgrounds at each of the parks listed above can be reserved through the National Park Reservation Service. Reservations (except for Yosemite, which has a separate reservation service at 800–436–7275) can be made via the Internet (reservations.nps.gov), by phone (800–365–2267), or through the mail (National Park Reservation Service, P.O. Box 1600, Cumberland, MD 21501). Reservations can be made beginning on the fifth of each month (the fifteenth for Yosemite), up to five months in advance. Not all campgrounds in each of the listed parks are always subject to reservation.

Lodging

A limited number of national park areas (most of which are in the western states) offer overnight lodging facilities. Private accommodations are often available outside or near a park's entrance. Most national park lodges are owned by the federal government but operated under long-term lease by private concessioners who must have their charges approved by park superintendents. A limited number of park lodges are privately owned, including Furnace Creek Inn and Panamint Springs Resort in Death Valley National Park. Park lodging is subject to wide variation in both price and quality, from Yosemite's luxurious Ahwahnee, which charges approximately $360 per night, to tent cabins and dorm-style buildings at Grand Teton that rent for $30 to $40 per night. Most lodging facilities with a private bath are in the $90 to $120 range. Despite the relatively steep cost, park accommodations are often fully booked months in advance, so you should seek a reservation early if you plan to stay overnight at a park facility during a busy period. Reservations are easier to obtain in the off-season.

Facilities

Facilities available in national park service areas vary widely. A large and busy park such as Yosemite or Yellowstone offers nearly anything you can find in a small town, including groceries, museums, restaurants, snack bars, medical centers, service stations, and hotels. Smaller park areas may offer little other than a visitor center and a picnic area, one of which will generally have drinking water and rest rooms. The visitor center may even have a soft drink machine, but don't count on it. Most of these smaller park areas don't have a small store, place to eat, or vending machines. They certainly don't have a place to stay the night, except, perhaps, a campground. Plan to pick up the fixings for a picnic before you enter one of the smaller parks.

Volunteers in parks

The National Park Service offers opportunities for men and women to serve as volunteers in individual park areas. Volunteers can fill a wide variety of jobs, depending on the needs of the particular parks to which applications are sent. Individuals who serve as volunteers are not paid by the federal government but are sometimes reimbursed for personal expenses such as meals, uniforms, and local travel costs. Park housing is generally not available for volunteers, although many volunteers live on park property in their own motor homes or trailers. Volunteers can work several hours a week, seasonally, or full-time, depending on the agreement that is reached with a park supervisor. Applications for the Volunteer in Parks program can be obtained from the National Park Service office in Washington, D.C., or from individual parks. The application brochure lists the address and phone number for each area operated by the National Park Service. Applications request an applicant's interests such as geology, natural history, desktop publishing, and visitor programs in order to determine if a particular park has a need that matches the interest of the potential volunteer. Two references and dates of availability are also required on the application form that is sent directly to individual parks in which the applicant is interested.

NPS Areas, Western States, with Lodging Facilities

Badlands National Park (SD)

Big Bend National Park (TX)

Bryce Canyon National Park (UT)

Buffalo National River (AR)

Canyon de Chelly National Monument (AZ)

Crater Lake National Park (OR)

Death Valley National Park (CA/NV)

Glacier Bay National Park (AK)

Glacier National Park (MT)

Glen Canyon National Recreation Area (AZ/UT)

Grand Canyon National Park (AZ)

Grand Teton National Park (WY)

Hawaii Volcanoes National Park (HI)

Kings Canyon National Park (CA)

Lake Chelan National Recreation Area (WA)

Lake Mead National Recreation Area (NV)

Lassen Volcanic National Park (CA)

Mesa Verde National Park (CA)

Mount Rainier National Park (WA)

Olympic National Park (WA)

Oregon Caves National Monument (OR)

Ozark National Scenic Riverway (MO)

Ross Lake National Recreation Area (WA)

Sequoia National Park (CA)

Voyageurs National Park (MN)

Yellowstone National Park (WY)

Yosemite National Park (CA)

Zion National Park (UT)

KEY FOR
MAP SYMBOLS

———————— Roads

---------- Dirt Roads

··················· Trails

—·—·—·— State Border

Park Area

Rivers / Water

Visitor Center

Camping

Lodge

Building

Locator / Town

Picnic Area

Ruins / Historic Site
(as noted on individual maps)

Parking

ALASKA

STATE TOURIST INFORMATION
(907) 929–2200
www.travelalaska.com

The national parks of Alaska are immense. With a cumulative total of more than 50 million acres, or more than twenty times the area of Yellowstone, the sixteen Alaska parks include ten units authorized in 1978 that actually doubled the size of the National Park System. Many of the parks are so remote that it is necessary to charter transportation to reach them. Even for more developed and accessible parks such as Denali (formerly Mount McKinley), it is difficult to do much more than scratch the surface. Regardless, the parks of Alaska are superb, unspoiled areas and true national treasures.

Alaska may seem rather remote for most travelers, but transportation to the state is not difficult to arrange. For first-time visitors, tours involving air or a combination of air, bus, and ship are probably desirable, especially for those individuals with limited time. For visitors with more time who plan to drive, it is best to take the Alaska Marine Highway on one leg of the trip and drive the Alaska Highway on the other leg. The trip along the inland passage is spectacular. In addition, it is the only way to visit cities in the panhandle (as well as Sitka National Historical Park). Ferries leave Seattle, Washington, and Prince Rupert, British Columbia, regularly. For information on the ferry system, write Alaska Marine Highway, Kodiak Terminal, P.O. Box 703, Kodiak, AK 99615; call (800) 382–9229; or visit their Web site at www.akmhs.com.

Another method of visiting Alaska is to drive the Alaska Highway from Dawson Creek, British Columbia, to Fairbanks, Alaska. Most of the highway is now paved, so the drive is not nearly as difficult and hard on a car or camper as it once was. In fact, any adventure-seeking traveler should try the drive at least once. Anyone considering the drive should pick up a copy of *Milepost* at a local bookstore (or on the Web at www.milepost.com).

Because of the difficulty in reaching many of the Alaskan parks, we have allotted less space to these generally undeveloped areas. Individuals contemplating a trip to one or more of these parks will need more information than we can hope to provide in a book such as this. Readers will find a brief description of each park and an address to write to for more detailed information. Descriptions of the five older parks are more complete.

1. Bering Land Bridge National Preserve

2. Cape Krusenstern National Monument

3. Noatak National Preserve

4. Kobuk Valley National Park

5. Gates of the Arctic National Park and Preserve

6. Yukon–Charley Rivers National Preserve

7. Denali National Park and Preserve

8. Lake Clark National Park and Preserve

9. Kenai Fjords National Park

10. Katmai National Park and Preserve

11. Aniakchak National Monument and Preserve

12. Wrangell–St. Elias National Park and Preserve

13. Glacier Bay National Park and Preserve

14. Sitka National Historical Park

15. Klondike Gold Rush National Historical Park

16. Aleutian World War II National Historic Area

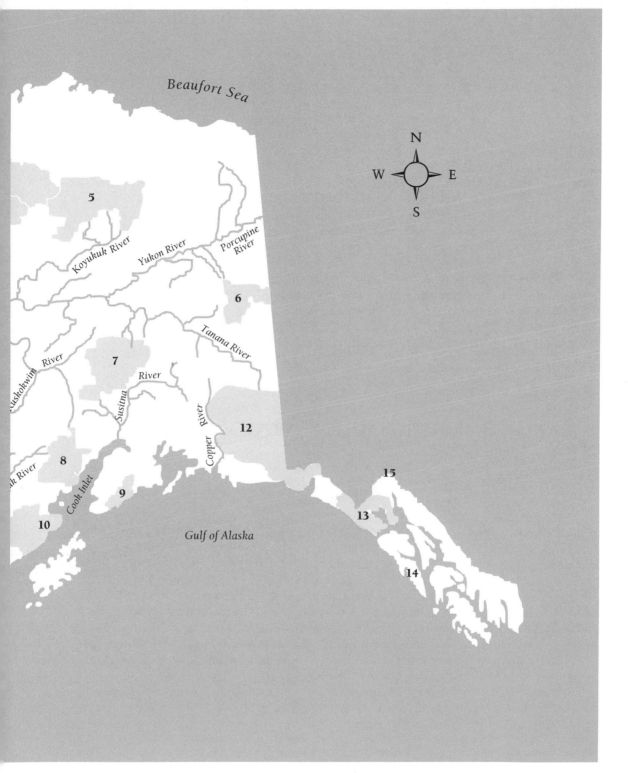

Beaufort Sea

5

Koyukuk River

Yukon River

Porcupine River

6

Tanana River

Kuskokwim River

7

River

Susitna

8

Copper River

12

Cook Inlet

9

15

13

10

Gulf of Alaska

14

N
W · E
S

ALEUTIAN WORLD WAR II NATIONAL HISTORIC AREA

P.O. Box 149
Unalaska, AK 99685
(907) 581–1276
www.nps.gov/aleu

These eighty-one nonfederal acres were designated a national historic area in 1996 to help interpret the history of the Aleut people and the role they and the Aleutian Islands played in the defense of the United States in World War II. The Japanese occupied portions of the Aleutian Islands for nearly a year beginning in June 1942. Battles between the Japanese and Americans were affected as much by unpredictable Aleutian weather as by military might. The national historical area includes the remnants of U.S. Army Fort Schwatka, one of four coastal defense posts constructed in 1942 and 1943 to protect the Dutch Harbor Naval Operating Base.

Most of Fort Schwatka's bunkers and wooden structures have collapsed, although the gun mounts and lookouts remain. The park is open year-round, and visitors are free to explore the remaining structures and ruins. Summer access to the national historic area is via an unimproved gravel switchback road from Unalaska. The Aleutian World War II National Historic Area is located on Amaknak Island in the Aleutian Islands, 800 miles west of Anchorage. It can be reached by commercial and charter flights from Anchorage or via ferries that are part of the Alaska Marine Highway. From June through August the spongy subarctic tundra is covered with wildflowers. These islands are a paradise for bird lovers and sport fishermen.

ENTRANCE FEE: No charge.

ANIAKCHAK NATIONAL MONUMENT AND PRESERVE

P.O. Box 7
King Salmon, AK 99613-0007
(907) 246–3305
www.nps.gov/ania

Aniakchak comprises slightly more than 600,000 acres, including the Aniakchak Caldera, which covers 30 square miles and is one of the great dry calderas of the world. The caldera, which remained undiscovered until 1922, has a floor of cinder cones, debris, and formations formed by volcanic activity, all surrounded by 2,000-foot walls. The volcano last erupted in 1931.

The Aniakchak Wild River begins at Surprise Lake in the caldera, passes through The Gates in the caldera wall, then flows 30 miles to Aniakchak Bay on the south coast of the peninsula. Over the first 15 miles, the river drops 60 feet per mile as it runs through the tundra- and shrub-covered foothills. This rock-strewn section contains class 2 through class 4 white water. The final 15 miles are a much more gentle class 1. It is not uncommon for river runners to see brown bears, caribou, bald eagles, and, on the coast, sea otters.

Access to the park is difficult and expensive. Inclement weather often makes it impossible. Peninsula Airways (800–448–4226) flies between Anchorage and Port Heiden. From Port Heiden, a very difficult 15-mile hike is necessary to reach the caldera. Access is also possible by charter plane from King Salmon or one of the towns in the lower Alaska Peninsula. The nearest lodging is in King Salmon. The King Salmon Visitor Center (907–246–4250) at the King Salmon Airport provides information about the monument and other locations and services in southwest Alaska.

ENTRANCE FEE: No charge.

BERING LAND BRIDGE NATIONAL PRESERVE

P.O. Box 220
Nome, AK 99762-0220
(907) 443–2522
www.nps.gov/bela

Bering Land Bridge National Preserve, 2.7 million acres on the Seward Peninsula of northwest Alaska, is a remnant of a land bridge that connected North America with Asia during the last ice age. The bridge was once a migration route for people, animals, and plants but is now covered by the Chukchi and Bering Seas.

Most visitors arrive during summer months, when temperatures are relatively mild (40 to 60 degrees Fahrenheit), plants burst into color, and wildlife becomes active. One hundred seventy species of birds and over 400 species of plants have been found in the preserve. Reindeer, wolf, moose, grizzly bear, and musk ox are some of the animals found there. Fishing for Dolly Varden char and grayling is excellent.

Access to the isolated preserve is difficult. Summer access is usually by bush planes and small boats; winter access is by small planes on skis, by snowmobile, or by dog sled. Airplanes may be chartered at Nome and Kotzebue. The nearest lodging and meals are also in these two towns.

ENTRANCE FEE: No charge.

CAPE KRUSENSTERN NATIONAL MONUMENT

P.O. Box 1029
Kotzebue, AK 99752
(907) 442–3890
www.nps.gov/cakr

Cape Krusenstern National Monument, located in northwest Alaska, comprises 560,000 acres and has been the site of seasonal marine mammal hunting by Eskimo peoples for more than 5,000 years. Eskimos continue to hunt seals along Cape Krusenstern's outermost beach.

The monument has no facilities of any kind, and visitors generally come only to kayak along the coast, or to hike, camp, and backpack in this very primitive area. Insect repellent is recommended for summer months. A variety of wildlife inhabits the monument, including black and grizzly bears, caribou, lynx, moose, musk ox, and wolves. Offshore, seals or whales may be seen on occasion.

Access to Cape Krusenstern is by chartered boat or plane from Kotzebue. The monument, at its nearest point, is approximately 10 miles from Kotzebue, where lodging is available. The town also has small stores. The best areas for visiting are along the monument's west coast and in the hills running north to south through the park.

ENTRANCE FEE: No charge.

DENALI NATIONAL PARK AND PRESERVE

P.O. Box 9
Denali Park, AK 99755-0009
(907) 683–2294
denali_info@nps.gov
www.nps.gov/dena

Denali (formerly Mount McKinley) National Park and Preserve comprises 6,028,924 acres of mountains, alpine glaciers, and rolling lowlands with wide rivers. The park can be reached via the Parks Highway, which connects Fairbanks and Anchorage. This road is open all year. Denali may also be reached during the summer from Paxson via the gravel Denali Highway. The Alaska Railroad provides daily service from late May to mid-September and reduced service during the remainder of the year. The train ride from Anchorage (237 miles) requires five hours; the train ride from Fairbanks (122 miles), two hours. For information, write Alaska Railroad Corporation Passenger Services, P.O. Box 107500, Anchorage, AK 99510 (Continental U.S. and Hawaii 800–544–0552; Anchorage 907–265–2494; Fairbanks 907–465–4155). Several companies provide transportation service in summer, including Alaska-Denali Transit (907–276–6443); Alaska Sightseeing Tours (Anchorage 907–276–1305, Fairbanks 907–452–8518); and Gray Line of Alaska/Westours (Anchorage 907–277–5581, Fairbanks 907–456– 7741). A 3,000-foot airstrip is maintained at the park for light aircraft.

Most of Denali is covered with alpine tundra, rock, and ice. Wet tundra contains dense brush and shrubs, while dry tundra along slopes and hills is characterized by small plants and wildflowers. The park contains a wide variety of wildlife, including more than 167 species of birds. Caribou, Dall sheep, moose, and grizzly bears are commonly seen in open spaces around the park.

Detailed information on the park and its visitor activities is available at the visitor center near the park entrance. During summer months, park personnel conduct theater programs in the visitor center, campfire programs at the campgrounds, and 1/2- to 6-mile hikes. They also conduct sled-dog demonstrations at the park kennels, a twenty-five-minute bus ride (free) from the visitor center. In the summer of 2005 a new visitor center will have a 299-seat theater, large exhibit area, bookstore, food court, rest rooms, and transit station.

An 87-mile park road parallels the Alaska Range from the park entrance to Wonder Lake. Only the first 15 miles are paved, and the road is generally open from early June until mid-September. Driving beyond Savage River (mile 15) is restricted. At the closest point, the 20,320-foot summit of Mount McKinley is 27 miles from the road. Buses run regularly from the Denali Visitor Center to Eielson Visitor Center and Wonder Lake. Scheduled stops are at Savage River, Teklanika River, Polychrome Pass, Toklat River, Eielson Visitor Center, and Wonder Lake. A wildlife scenic tour and a Denali natural history tour leave in the early morning and midafternoon and go to the central area of the park. The driver interprets park features. The park shuttle is operated for the National Park Service under a concession contract. The shuttle provides visitors with access to backcountry units, campgrounds, and day-trip excursion areas. Reservations are generally required for seats on all westbound buses (907–272–7275 in the Anchorage area and outside the United States; 800–622–7275 outside

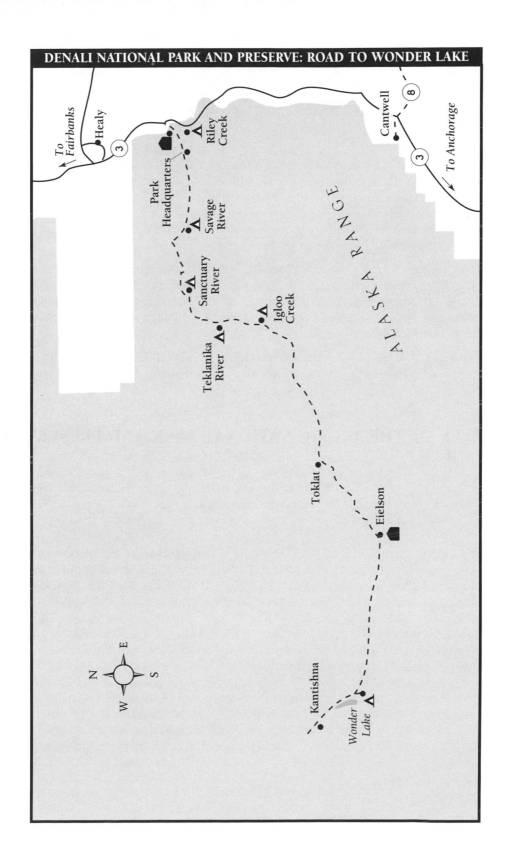

DENALI NATIONAL PARK AND PRESERVE: ROAD TO WONDER LAKE

Anchorage). Fees vary depending on age and destination. Full details on the shuttle service are available at park headquarters, or visit the Web site (www.nps.gov/dena). Air tours are available through Denali Air (907–683–2261).

ENTRANCE FEE: $10.00 per vehicle or $5.00 per person; good for seven days. Shuttle bus and tour fees are additional.

FACILITIES: A service station, located just outside the park entrance, has gasoline and oil. Pay showers are located at Riley Creek Mercantile, just inside the park entrance. Groceries and supplies are available at the adjacent store, but no vehicle or food services are available after leaving the entrance area. (Check your gas.) The only lodging facilities within the park boundaries are on private land. They are located near Wonder Lake: Kantishna Roadhouse (800–942–7420) and Denali Backcountry Lodge (907–683–1650 summer). Additional lodging is available immediately outside the park entrance.

CAMPING: Improved campgrounds with flush toilets, tap water, tables, and grills are available at Riley Creek (267 spaces, dump station), Savage River (33 spaces), Teklanika (53 spaces), and Wonder Lake (28 spaces, tents only). Campgrounds with chemical toilets are located at Igloo Creek (seven spaces) and Sanctuary River (seven spaces). Only Riley Creek is open year-round, but no services are available in winter.

FISHING: Fishing is generally poor because rivers are silty and ponds are shallow. Arctic grayling are caught in a few mountain streams and lake trout in Wonder Lake.

GATES OF THE ARCTIC NATIONAL PARK AND PRESERVE

201 First Avenue, Doyon Building
Fairbanks, AK 99701
(907) 456–0281
GAAR_Visitor_Information@nps.gov
www/nps.gov/gaar

Gates of the Arctic comprises 8.2 million acres, including the heart of the spectacular Brooks Range. The entire park lies north of the Arctic Circle, where shrubs and tundra but few trees are found. Visitors will find long, magnificent valleys, rivers, lakes, and a few glaciers. Black bears, caribou, Dall sheep, eagles, grizzlies, marmots, moose, wolverines, and wolves are found in the park.

This wilderness park has no facilities, roads, or trails. Most visitors to the park backpack the valleys or float the rivers. Rock and mountain climbing are available in the Arrigetch Peaks and Mount Igikpak areas. Fish include grayling, lake trout, and char.

Access to Gates of the Arctic is via scheduled airline from Fairbanks to Bettles, Coldfoot, and Anaktuvuk Pass. Bush charters are available from Bettles and Coldfoot into the park and preserve boundaries. Information on flights is available on this park's Web site. The nearest facilities are a general store in Bettles and Anaktuvuk Pass and a lodge in Bettles. Rangers may be contacted in Fairbanks or Bettles; ranger stations in Coldfoot and Anaktuvuk Pass are periodically staffed.

ENTRANCE FEE: No charge.

GLACIER BAY NATIONAL PARK AND PRESERVE

P.O. Box 140
Gustavus, AK 99826-0140
(907) 697–2230
glba_administration@nps.gov
www.nps.gov/glba

Glacier Bay was established as a national monument in 1925 (changed to a national park and preserve in 1980) and comprises nearly 3.3 million acres, including some of the world's most impressive examples of tidewater glaciers. The park is located in southeastern Alaska, approximately 65 miles northwest of Juneau. No roads lead to the park, and entrance must be gained by either plane or boat. A small airport is located about 9 miles from park headquarters in Gustavus.

Much of the snow that falls in the mountains around Glacier Bay does not completely melt. As it grows deeper, lower layers change into small grains of ice and gradually fuse into solid ice. When an icefield fills its basin, it begins flowing downhill. The glaciers eventually flow to the sea and are called tidewater glaciers. Glaciers advance and retreat as an area's climate changes.

The glaciers that can be seen in the park today are the remains of what was formed during the "Little Ice Age" about 4,000 years ago. The glaciers reached maximum size around 1750, before a milder climate brought about a general melting. When Captain George Vancouver sailed through Icy Strait in 1794, Glacier Bay was little more than a mere 5-mile indentation in a huge wall of ice extending more than 100 miles to the north. By 1916, Grand Pacific Glacier was 65 miles from the mouth of Glacier Bay. Today glaciers continue to retreat on the bay's east side. Glaciers on the west side, however, stabilized by 1929, and many are even growing again. The bay includes twelve tidewater glaciers that calve icebergs into Glacier Bay.

Glacier Bay National Park is rich in both plant and animal life. Brown and black bears, mountain goats, seals, humpback whales, and porpoises are frequently seen. More than 200 species of birds are found here.

Park rangers are in the park year-round, with headquarters at Bartlett Cove. In summer, naturalists lead hikes, and a concessioner-operated tour boat (eight to nine hours) leaves from the Glacier Bay Lodge. Overnight boat trips are also available. The park is best seen by boat. A permit is required for entry (via private boat) into the park during June, July, and August. Applications are available on the Web site (www.nps.gov/glba) or by calling (907) 697–2627. Navigating the bay presents special problems, and appropriate precautions should be observed.

ENTRANCE FEE: No charge.

FACILITIES: Glacier Bay Lodge provides rooms and meals from mid-May to mid-September. For reservations, write Glacier Bay Lodge, P.O. Box 199, Gustavus, AK 99826 in summer and Park Concessions Inc., 226 Second Avenue, Seattle, WA 98119 in winter (800–451–5952 for reservations). Food and lodging facilities are available in the town of Gustavus. Air excursions, charter boats, and kayak rentals are also available in Gustavus. Temporary docking facilities, gasoline, and #2 diesel fuel are available at Bartlett Cove. No other public facilities for boats are located within the park.

CAMPING: A campground (thirty-five spaces) at Bartlett Cove has bear-resistant food caches, a fire pit, and firewood. Limited camping supplies and food are available in nearby Gustavus, while Juneau offers many shopping possibilities.

FISHING: Silver, pink, chum, sockeye, and king salmon can be caught in the park. Halibut are found nearly everywhere in the park's salt water. Cutthroat and steelhead trout and Dolly Varden char are in lakes and streams. An Alaska fishing license is required.

KATMAI NATIONAL PARK AND PRESERVE

P.O. Box 7
King Salmon, AK 99613-0007
(907) 246-3305
www.nps.gov/katm

Katmai National Park and Preserve occupies 4.1 million acres of rugged wilderness on the Alaska Peninsula. The interior wilderness of forests and lakes is bounded on the east by 100 miles of ocean bays, fjords, and lagoons. Katmai has no rail or road approaches. Commercial boat service is available from King Salmon. Scheduled jets fly to King Salmon Airport on the Bristol Bay side of the peninsula. Daily commercial flights connect King Salmon and Brooks Lodge from June through Labor Day. Private float planes can be chartered for flights to scenic lakes within Katmai.

In 1912 the area that is now contained within the park was the site of one of the greatest volcanic eruptions in history. Novarupta Volcano sent forth an explosion of pumice and white-hot ash. Within a few hours 2½ cubic miles of ash flowed into the Ukak River valley, and 40 square miles of the valley floor were covered to depths as great as 700 feet. Hot gases and water vapor percolating up through the ash as it settled gave rise to the name Valley of Ten Thousand Smokes. At the same time or soon after Novarupta was erupting, Mount Katmai, 6 miles to the east, was collapsing. A conduit under Mount Katmai allowed a transfer of magma and resulted in a loss of support for the mountain's top.

Katmai National Park and Preserve has a wide variety of plant and animal life. Woodlands of spruce, poplar, and birch are interspersed with alder thickets, marshes, and grassland on the southern and western parts of the mountains. At higher elevations only plants typical of the Arctic tundra can survive the cold, high winds and short growing season. Brown bears and moose are fairly common, and bald eagles are seen frequently. The Steller sea lion and the hair seal are commonly observed on rock outcroppings. Much of the wildlife in the park at any one time depends on the runs of migrating salmon.

Park rangers give illustrated evening talks at Brooks Camp, and guided nature walks are conducted from the same location. A ³/4-mile trail leads to Brooks Falls, where there is an elevated platform from which visitors can, at certain times of the summer, watch brown bears try to catch salmon as the fish jump the falls. A concessioner-operated scenic bus tour (23 miles one-way) to the Valley of Ten Thousand Smokes begins at the lodge. Good views of the valley

Glacier Bay National Park and Preserve (opposite page)

and surrounding mountains may be enjoyed from the shelter located at the end of the trip. In addition, a short trail from the Brooks River Ranger Station leads to the site of a prehistoric dwelling. A pit house built around A.D. 1300 has been excavated and restored for public inspection.

ENTRANCE FEE: No charge.

FACILITIES: A concessioner provides accommodations and services at four points in the park. Brooks Camp has modern cabins with plumbing and family-type meals. Fishing equipment and canoes may be rented, and limited camping and food supplies are sold. Guide service is available. Overnight packages are also available for Grosvenor Camp and Kulik Lodge. A privately owned lodge is operated at Enchanted Lake. In addition, there are a number of lodges outside the park that cater to park visitors. Information may be obtained by writing to the King Salmon Visitor Center (P.O. Box 298, King Salmon, AK 99613).

CAMPING: A single campground (18 spaces) at Brooks River is open from June 1 through September 17. Piped-in treated water is provided from early June through early September. The camp contains pit toilets, weather shelters, and elevated food caches. It is a park regulation that campers' food must be stored in the elevated caches to secure it from the bears. Meals and showers can be purchased at Brooks Lodge. Campers who are not camping at Brooks Camp may camp anywhere in the park and preserve as long as it is at least 1½ miles outside the radius of Brooks Camp. Reservations are required and can be made by calling (800) 365–CAMP or on the Web at reservations.nps.gov. There is a charge of $8.00 per person, per night.

FISHING: Rainbow and lake trout, Dolly Varden char, grayling, northern pike, and sockeye salmon are plentiful. An Alaska fishing license is required, and fishing in any way other than with hook and line (with rod or line held in hand) is not allowed. Coho, chinook, and pink salmon are occasionally seen in the streams, and one of the most magnificent sights is that of the sockeye salmon fighting upstream to its spawning ground. Brooks River is a fly-fishing-only river (catch-and-release for rainbow trout). Any salmon-spawning stream is likely to have a number of brown bears in attendance. Park rangers can provide information on how to minimize conflicts with bears while fishing.

KENAI FJORDS NATIONAL PARK

P.O. Box 1727
Seward, AK 99664-1727
(907) 224–3175
www.nps.gov/kefj

Kenai Fjords' 650,000 acres on the Kenai Peninsula, 125 miles south of Anchorage, include the 300-square-mile Harding Icefield, a Quaternary icefield that radiates thirty-two named glacial arms. In addition to long glaciated valleys and mountain peaks, the peninsula supports temperate rain forests. Wildlife includes bald eagles, sea lions, seals, whales, sea otters, moose, bear, mountain goats, and both horned and tufted puffins. Commercial tour boat companies located in Seward's small boat harbor provide daily half-day and all-day tours into the bay and fjords. Three public-use cabins located in the fjords are available for rental (three-day maximum, with reservations made through the Alaska Public Lands Office, 907–271–2737).

Twelve miles north of Seward is Exit Glacier, the most accessible section of the park, which is reached by a paved road and then a short walk. Here visitors can stop by the new nature center, participate in ranger-led walks during summer, walk right up to a valley glacier, and hike several trails, including the 7-mile round-trip (3,200 feet) Harding Icefield Trail, which ends with a spectacular view of the icefield. Tent camping (twelve sites) is available at Exit Glacier, and one public-use cabin is available during winter. Park headquarters and a visitor center are located in Seward, which can be reached by road, rail, and air.

ENTRANCE FEE: No charge. There is a user fee for Exit Glacier: $5.00 per vehicle or $3.00 per person, good for seven days.

KLONDIKE GOLD RUSH NATIONAL HISTORICAL PARK

P.O. Box 517
Skagway, AK 99840
(907) 983–2921
KLGO_Ranger_Activities@nps.gov
www.nps.gov/klgo

Klondike Gold Rush National Historical Park comprises more than 13,000 acres and was established in 1976 to commemorate the 1897–1898 Klondike gold rush. The park's main unit is located in the Skagway area of the Alaska panhandle. Access is via the Alaska Marine Highway from Bellingham, Washington, or Prince Rupert, British Columbia, or by driving south from Whitehorse, Yukon, approximately 110 miles on State Highways 2 and 8. Other Alaska units include the White Pass and the Dyea–Chilkoot Trail. A separate unit of this park is in Seattle and is listed under the Washington section of this book.

The Klondike gold rush went into high gear after the arrival of the steamer *Portland* in Seattle with 2 tons of gold aboard. The event that started this flood of people into the wilderness area of Canada's Yukon River was a large gold strike in August 1896 on Rabbit Creek by two Indians and a white man. When other prospectors saw the gold these three brought to the settlement of Fortymile, they headed into the same area to make their own claims. It was this group that arrived in Seattle during the summer of 1897. Located at the confluence of the Yukon and Klondike Rivers, the town of Dawson, created in the fall of 1896, had grown substantially larger following the second influx of people in 1897 and 1898.

As word of the riches spread, people began a stampede to the Klondike. Although several routes were used, the quickest, cheapest, and most practical was over the Coast Mountains, then 550 miles down the Yukon River to Dawson. Skagway quickly grew to a population of 8,000 to 10,000 as it became the gateway city to the Klondike goldfields. From Skagway, most stampeders went to nearby Dyea, the beginning of the infamous Chilkoot Trail that led into the interior. Other stampeders briefly attempted the White Pass Trail into the interior from Skagway, but this trail disintegrated after a few months, winning the name Dead Horse Trail for the 3,000 animals that perished on it. Construction of the narrow-gauge White Pass and Yukon Route Railway from Skagway to Whitehorse eventually eliminated the need for both trails. Dyea, which once boasted a population of 5,000 to 8,000, was scavenged for building materials, and today only ruins remain.

The park's visitor center in the old White Pass and Yukon Route Railway depot at Broadway and Second Avenue has displays and artifacts from the gold rush. The National Park Service provides information, films, talks, and guided walks through the town. The Skagway Historic District has over one hundred historic buildings and wooden boardwalks that retain the flavor of the gold rush days. The National Park Service has restored fifteen of these structures for public use as museums and exhibits, offices, and housing. Featured are the visitor center, museum, Mascot Saloon, and Moore Homestead.

Dyea, at the start of the Chilkoot Trail, is 12 miles from Skagway via a paved, then graded dirt, road. The drive is beautiful. Most of the Dyea buildings were torn down for use as firewood or as materials for buildings in Skagway. All that is left now are scattered remains of foundations and a mile-and-a-half row of piling stubs from the old wharf. The town fell into disuse after an 1898 avalanche and the completion of the railroad from Skagway to the White Pass Summit in February 1899. Visitors may hike the 33-mile Chilkoot Trail (three to five days) to Bennett Lake. Permits are required for overnight hikes on this trail (800–661–0486 and Parks Canada, www.parkscanada.gc.ca/lhn/yt/chilkoot). The trail offers historic ruins and artifacts along the way. These are not to be disturbed.

ENTRANCE FEE: No charge. A $50 permit is required for those who plan to camp on the Chilkoot Trail. This covers both the United States and Canada.

FACILITIES: Lodging and food services are not provided by the Park Service, but both are available in downtown Skagway. No facilities are in Dyea.

CAMPING: A Park Service campground (twenty-six sites) with tables and pit toilets (no water) is in Dyea (fee). Skagway has several campgrounds. The Dyea site is much nicer.

FISHING: Fishing is available at both Skagway and Dyea.

KOBUK VALLEY NATIONAL PARK
P.O. Box 1029
Kotzebue, AK 99752
(907) 442–3890
www.nps.gov/kova

Kobuk Valley National Park comprises approximately 1.75 million acres in northwestern Alaska above the Arctic Circle. The park lies along the valley surrounding the Kobuk River and includes a boreal forest, sand dunes, and archaeological sites from 10,000 years of human occupation. Wildlife includes caribou, grizzly and black bears, lynx, moose, and wolves. Fishing can yield arctic char, grayling, salmon, and sheefish.

Most visitors take the regularly scheduled small plane from Kotzebue to Ambler in order to float through the park and exit at Kiana. Other visitors, especially fishermen, access the river by chartered floatplane. An easy hike from the river provides access to the Great Kobuk Sand Dunes that cover 25 square miles, reach heights of 100 feet, and experience summer temperatures that can exceed 100 degrees Fahrenheit. There are no facilities within the park. Lodging is available in Kiana, Ambler, and Kotzebue. All three towns have small stores with staples.

ENTRANCE FEE: No charge.

LAKE CLARK NATIONAL PARK AND PRESERVE

4230 University Drive, Suite 311
Anchorage, AK 99508
(907) 271–3751
www.nps.gov/lacl

Lake Clark National Park and Preserve comprises more than 4 million acres in the heart of the Chigmit Mountains, where the Alaska and Aleutian ranges join. The park lies along the western shore of Cook Inlet. The eastern side of the park has majestic mountains with glaciers and two active, steaming volcanoes. The rocky coastal cliffs above Cook Inlet serve as home for puffins, cormorants, and other seabirds. Seals and whales may be seen offshore. On the western side of the park and preserve, at the base of the mountains, are tundra-covered foothills, a boreal forest, beautiful glacially carved lakes, and wild rivers. Activities center around backpacking, camping, river running, and fishing. Lake trout, northern pike, arctic grayling, Dolly Varden char, and five species of salmon inhabit streams in the park.

Access to Lake Clark National Park and Preserve is by chartered aircraft from Anchorage, Kenai, or Homer. The trip takes one to two hours.

ENTRANCE FEE: No charge.

Lake Clark National Park and Preserve

NOATAK NATIONAL PRESERVE

P.O. Box 1029
Kotzebue, AK 99752
(907) 442–3890
www.nps.gov/noat

Noatak National Preserve comprises more than 6.5 million acres, including the largest undeveloped river basin in the United States. The Noatak River flows more than 425 miles, carrying Mount Igikpak's glacial melt to Kotzebue Sound through boreal forest and treeless tundra.

There are no Park Service facilities within the preserve. Most visitors enter to float the Noatak or to backpack. A variety of wildlife, including bears, caribou, and wolves, inhabit the park. Fish include arctic char, grayling, whitefish, and several species of salmon.

Access is by chartered plane or boat from Kotzebue or by air charter from Bettles. Kotzebue may be reached by commercial flights from either Anchorage or Fairbanks.

ENTRANCE FEE: No charge.

SITKA NATIONAL HISTORICAL PARK

106 Metlakatla Street
Sitka, AK 99835
(907) 747–6281
SITK_Interpretation@nps.gov
www.nps.gov/sitk

Sitka National Historical Park comprises 107 acres. It was set aside as a federal reserve in 1890 and designated a national monument in 1910 to commemorate the site of the last major Tlingit Indian resistance to Russian colonization. The park is located in the town of Sitka in Alaska's southeastern panhandle. Sitka is reached by scheduled airline or by boat. The town is a stop on the Alaska Marine Highway, but the park is 7 miles from the ferry terminal.

An 1804 battle between the Russians and the Tlingit Indians resulted in an important "victory" for the Russians (the Tlingit claim the Russians won by default because of a Tlingit withdrawal caused by lack of ammunition), who strengthened their hold on the northwest coast of the American continent. The Russians were able to continue using the area as an important source for furs and established Sitka as the busiest port in the North Pacific. Although the Tlingit lost the battle and their homes, they returned to trade after several years and settled just outside the Russian stockade. In 1806 Sitka became the headquarters of the Russian American Company. In 1867 the Russians sold their overseas empire for $7.2 million, and Alaska became an American possession.

The park's visitor center is open daily from 8:00 A.M. to 5:00 P.M. from mid-May through September. It is open Monday through Saturday from 8:00 A.M. to 5:00 P.M. from October through mid-May. The visitor center includes exhibits, native craft workshops, and an audiovisual room for slide presentations and movies. Exhibits include displays of Tlingit history and culture. A self-guided trail begins behind the visitor center and leads into the rain forest to the 1804 battleground and fort site. Fourteen totem poles are located in the park. The visitor center can supply visitors with a map of a walking tour of Sitka. The town is especially interesting, and the tour is a must.

A second section of the park, the 1842 Russian Bishop's house, is 1/4 mile from the visitor center on Lincoln Street. The house is open daily from 9:00 A.M. to 5:00 P.M. from mid-May through September. It is open the remainder of the year by appointment only. The Park Service completed a restoration of this historically important building in 1988. The first floor contains exhibits about Russian America, the Russian American Company, and the efforts of the Russian Orthodox Church in Alaska. The second floor is restored to its 1842–1853 appearance with many of the original furnishings.

ENTRANCE FEE: $3.00 per person entrance fee, and $3.00 per person for tour of the Russian Bishop's House; children age twelve and under free for both entrance and tour.

FACILITIES: A picnic area with tables and a shelter is located near the impressive visitor center. Rest rooms and drinking water are available in the building. The park is within walking distance of the town of Sitka, where complete facilities are available.

CAMPING: No camping is available at the park, but a U.S. Forest Service campground with tables and pit toilets is a short distance north of the ferry terminal on Halibut Point Road.

FISHING: The park is surrounded by the Indian River and Sitka Sound, where saltwater fishing is available with an Alaska fishing license. Salmon fishing is not permitted in the Indian River.

WRANGELL–ST. ELIAS NATIONAL PARK AND PRESERVE

P.O. Box 439
Mile 106.8 Old Richardson Highway
Copper Center, AK 99573
(907) 822–5234
wrst_interpretation@nps.gov
www.nps.gov/wrst

Wrangell–St. Elias is the largest park area in the National Park System, with 13.2 million acres of mountains, remote valleys, massive glaciers, and wild rivers. The park has the United States' second-highest mountain, 18,000-foot Mount St. Elias, and North America's largest collection of peaks above 16,000 feet in an area where four mountain ranges converge. More than one hundred glaciers exist in a landscape dominated by mountains and snowfields.

Visitors to the park engage in backpacking, camping, cross-country skiing, mountain climbing, and river running. The park can provide a list of licensed operators for air taxis, river trips, backpacking, big game hunting, and mountaineering. Summers are often cloudy with rain, although clear, relatively hot days occur especially in June and early July.

The Wrangell–St. Elias Visitor Center, at mile 106.8 Old Richardson Highway, Nabesna District Visitor Center, at mile 0.2 Nabesna Road, and Yakutat Visitor Center, in the town of Yakutat, are open year-round. During summer months the visitor centers are open daily from 8:00 A.M. to 6:00 P.M., and during winter months, Monday through Friday, from 8:00 A.M. to 4:30 P.M. The Kennecott Visitor Center, in the Depot Building in Kennecott, and the Chitina Visitor Center, at mile 33 Edgerton Highway, are open only during the summer.

No lodging within the park is provided by the park service. Lodging on private property within park boundaries is available. Modern motels and cabins are found in Glennallen and along the Richardson Highway and Tok cutoff. Private and state campgrounds are located near the park. A small National Park Service day camp is located near the end of McCarthy Road between Chitina and McCarthy.

Wrangell–St. Elias is one of the few new Alaska parks with road access. A 61-mile gravel-surface road follows an old railroad route from the community of Chitina to McCarthy. This is not your typical gravel road; sharp rocks and railroad spikes may cause flat tires (a full-size spare tire is recommended), narrow bridges make it difficult to maneuver large vehicles (not recommended beyond mile 17), and heavy rain makes driving very difficult. The 61 miles can take three or more hours. Parking areas are at the end of the mining road. From there, access to the historic communities of McCarthy and Kennecott is by foot or by shuttle. Private lodging facilities are in both communities. Outstanding hiking and fishing are available in this area. In the northern section of the park, a 42-mile secondary road, which is also gravel, extends from Slana to the privately owned mining community of Nabesna. This road remains in approximately the same condition as when it was constructed in 1934 to transport gold to the port in Valdez. Four-wheel drive is recommended, especially past mile 29. This road leads to wetlands, boreal forest, and the Mentasta and Wrangell mountains. Campgrounds are scattered along the road. A private bed-and-breakfast is at the end of the road.

ENTRANCE FEE: No charge.

YUKON–CHARLEY RIVERS NATIONAL PRESERVE

201 First Avenue
Doyon Building
Fairbanks, AK 99701
(907) 547–2233
YUCH_Eagle_office@nps.gov
www.nps.gov/yuch

Yukon–Charley Rivers National Preserve comprises 2.5 million acres along the Canadian border in central Alaska. The park incorporates all of the 120-mile Charley River and 135 miles of the 1,800-mile Yukon River, including old cabins and relics of the gold rush.

The primary activity in the preserve is floating the rivers. The Yukon is most popular and provides particularly good kayaking, canoeing, or rafting from June through September. It takes approximately a week to float between Eagle, at the preserve's upper end, and Circle, at the lower end. The towns of Eagle and Circle both provide interesting sights for visitors. The Charley, a particularly scenic clear-water river, is class 2 water that requires river experience. The best time to float this river is June and July. It is common to see Dall sheep, caribou, moose, bears, peregrine falcons, eagles, and waterfowl along both rivers. Fishing for grayling, northern pike, and whitefish is available on side tributaries. Grayling fishing is excellent on the Charley.

Access to the preserve is by way of Eagle and Circle. Both are served by scheduled air taxis, and both may be reached via a gravel road from the Alaska Highway. It takes approximately five hours to drive either of these gravel roads in good weather. Air access is also available from Tok and Fairbanks. Call the preserve or check this park's Web site for air taxi information. There are no roads within the park. Both Eagle and Circle offer food service, gas, groceries, campgrounds, and limited lodging. The preserve maintains an information center in Eagle, which is open daily from 8:00 A.M. to 5:00 P.M. from mid-May to mid-September. The remainder of the year it is open Monday through Friday from 8:00 A.M. to 5:00 P.M. The headquarters in Fairbanks is open Monday through Friday from 8:00 A.M. to 4:30 P.M. year-round.

ENTRANCE FEE: No charge.

AMERICAN SAMOA

TOURIST INFORMATION
(684) 633–1093

NATIONAL PARK OF AMERICAN SAMOA

Pago Pago
American Samoa 96799
(684) 633–7082
NPSA_Administration@nps.gov
www.nps.gov/npsa

National Park of American Samoa comprises 10,500 acres, including sections of three islands and approximately 2,500 acres that are underwater. The park was authorized in 1988 and established in 1993 to protect cultural and natural resources on and surrounding three volcanic islands in the South Pacific. This remote national park is 2,600 miles southwest of Hawaii and 4,800 miles from the U.S. mainland. Access is via scheduled flights from Honolulu, Hawaii, to Pago Pago International Airport on the island of Tutuila.

American Samoa (meaning "sacred earth") is a U.S. territory comprised of five highly eroded volcanic islands and two coral atolls that are part of the Samoan chain that stretches south of the equator for 300 miles. The five islands are extinct volcanoes surrounded by narrow coral reefs. With a land area of 76 square miles and a population of approximately 60,000, American Samoa lies east of the independent nation of Samoa (formerly Western Samoa). The three islands of National Park of American Samoa offer secluded villages, nearly 8,000 acres of mixed-species Old World rain forests, coral reefs, unique tropical plants and animals, and white-sand beaches. The park is home to over thirty-five species of birds, but bats are the only

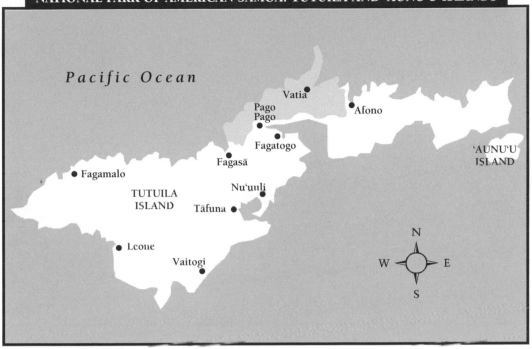

native mammals. All the land comprising the park is leased for fifty years from native villages and the American Samoa Government.

Pago Pago on the main island of Tutuila is the arrival point for park visitors. This island has a major expanse of undisturbed mixed-species rain forest. Visitors can take a scenic drive to the island's northern coast with its sheer cliffs and sheltered coves. Either park headquarters or the American Samoa Office of Tourism (684–633-1092) can help make arrangements for overnight stays in a Samoan home. Information on the park homestay program can be found at this park's Web site at www.nps.gov/npsa/homestay. Another activity is hiking to the top of 1,610-foot Mount Alava for a view of the harbor. The volcanic island of 'Aunu'u, 1 mile southeast of Tutuila's eastern tip, can be reached via boat and explored by foot in a day. Visitors should also consider visits to the eastern and western ends of Tutuila, where ocean vistas and local culture can be enjoyed. Local buses travel Tutuila from dawn to dusk, and taxi service and rental cars are available.

The islands of Ta'ū and Ofu, which contain the other two units of the park, are 60 miles east of Tutuila and are reached via a thirty-minute plane ride. Ta'ū, with the largest of the three park units, is mostly rain forest. It is also the home island of Saua, the Samoan legendary birthplace of Polynesia. Tufu Point, on the island's south coast, provides a spectacular view of steep cliffs that drop from the top of Lata Mountain to the rugged coastline. The island of Ofu, 9 miles from Ta'ū, has white-sand beaches and a magnificent coral reef. This unit offers the park's best snorkeling.

ENTRANCE FEE: No charge.

National Park of American Samoa (opposite page)

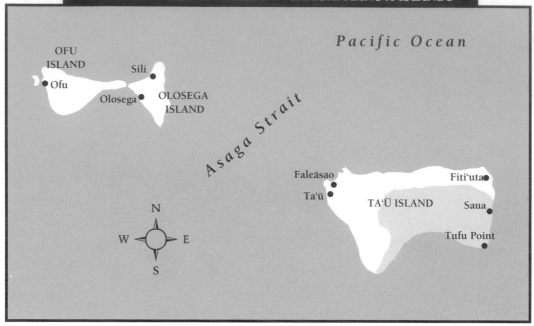

NATIONAL PARK OF AMERICAN SAMOA: MANU'A ISLANDS

FACILITIES: No lodging is available in the park. Lodging and food are available at various locations on Tutuila and also on Ofu. There are currently no commercial lodging facilities on Ta'ū. Park visitors may want to consider staying with local families in their homes to experience firsthand the culture and lifestyle of the Samoan people.

CAMPING: Camping is not permitted in the park.

ARIZONA

STATE TOURIST INFORMATION
(888) 520-3434
www.arizonaguide.com

CANYON DE CHELLY NATIONAL MONUMENT

P.O. Box 588
Chinle, AZ 86503
(928) 674-5500
ailema_benally@nps.gov
www.nps.gov/cach

Canyon de Chelly (pronounced "d'Shay") National Monument comprises 83,840 acres. It was authorized as part of the National Park System in 1931 to preserve ruins of Indian villages built in steep-walled canyons between A.D. 350 and 1300. The monument is located in northeastern Arizona, approximately 85 miles northwest of Gallup, New Mexico, near Chinle, Arizona. Monument headquarters is 2 miles east of U.S. 191. Highway 7, connecting South Rim Drive with Fort Defiance, is dirt between the monument boundary and the town of Sawmill. It is virtually impassable during bad weather.

Following an uplift of the Defiance Plateau, Rio de Chelly cut through sandstone and left canyon walls in Canyon de Chelly 30 to 1,000 feet high. Typically, the streams of this region are dry except during the rainy seasons and the spring thaw of mountain snow.

The canyons contain the ruins of several hundred prehistoric Anasazi villages, most of which were built between A.D. 350 and 1300. The earliest known Indians lived in pithouses, grew crops of corn and squash, and made intricate baskets. Centuries later, the Anasazi began making pottery and constructed rectangular houses of stone masonry above the canyon walls.

Canyon de Chelly National Monument

The canyon dwellers (now known as Pueblos) built most of the large cliff houses between A.D. 1100 and 1300.

During the 1200s occupants of the Four Corners region left their homes and scattered throughout the Southwest. In later years the canyons were occupied sporadically by the Hopi, a Pueblo group culturally related to the Anasazi, and later the Navajo, who continue to inhabit Canyon de Chelly today. The Navajo began to move into this area around 1700. They brought domesticated animals acquired from the Spanish and used the canyons to grow corn and raise peaches.

Except for a trail to White House Ruin, travel in the canyons is permitted only with a park ranger or other authorized guide. The park ranger on duty at the visitor center will help to arrange guides for those interested in hikes or four-wheel-drive vehicle trips. Horseback-riding tours are also available. Thunderbird Lodge near monument headquarters offers group trips to the canyon floors.

The first order of business upon entering the monument should be to stop at the visitor center, where exhibits help explain the history of the canyon and the cultures of its inhabitants. A Navajo silversmith is sometimes in the center demonstrating crafts. Here you may obtain guidebooks for driving both the north and south rims. These books are quite helpful in interpreting the drives. From Memorial Day through Labor Day, talks are presented at the visitor center, and guided walks begin at various places around the monument. During the summer season, nightly campfire programs are provided in the National Park Service campground.

Twenty-two-mile Rim Drive, along the south rim of Canyon de Chelly, provides access to six scenic overlook points and the trailhead of White House Trail. Even though the 500-foot

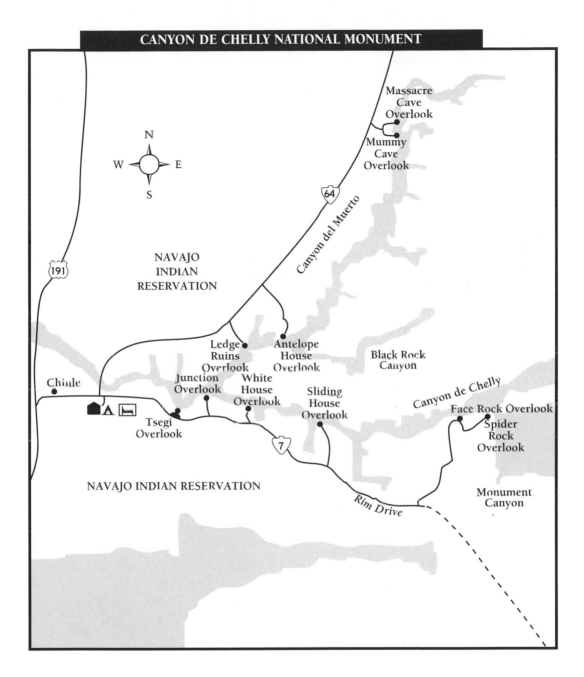

CANYON DE CHELLY NATIONAL MONUMENT

Massacre Cave Overlook

Mummy Cave Overlook

64

Canyon del Muerto

NAVAJO INDIAN RESERVATION

191

Ledge Ruins Overlook

Antelope House Overlook

Black Rock Canyon

Chinle

Junction Overlook

White House Overlook

Sliding House Overlook

Canyon de Chelly

Face Rock Overlook

Spider Rock Overlook

Tsegi Overlook

7

Rim Drive

Monument Canyon

NAVAJO INDIAN RESERVATION

climb back up the trail from White House Ruin (2 1/2 miles, one and a half to two hours, round-trip) will leave you breathless, the hike is worthwhile. Not only does it afford a close viewpoint of the impressive ruin and some pictographs, but unless you take a guided trip, this will be your only chance to see this beautiful canyon from its floor. Spider Rock, an 800-foot sandstone spire, can be viewed from an overlook at the junction of Canyon de Chelly and Monument Canyon. Mummy Cave Ruin, in Canyon del Muerto, is one of the larger ruins and features a three-story tower house. Pictographs may be seen at many places in the canyons, with some dating from prehistoric Basketmaker and Pueblo periods.

ENTRANCE FEE: No charge.

FACILITIES: Food, lodging, gifts, and tours are available at the Thunderbird Lodge near the monument entrance. Reservations and information may be obtained by writing Thunderbird Lodge, Box 548, Chinle, AZ 86503 (928–674–5841). Two other restaurants, lodging, and a supermarket are within 3 miles of the visitor center.

CAMPING: Cottonwood Campground (ninety-six spaces), set in a grove of cottonwood trees, is located near the park entrance. The campground is open year-round and has grills, tables, and, during the summer season, water and flush toilets. Individuals are limited to a five-day stay. Two group camps are available by reservation only. Recreational vehicles and trailers are not permitted in the group camping sites. No camping is permitted in the canyons without a guide.

FISHING: No fishing is available in Canyon de Chelly National Monument. Fishing for trout is permitted in Wheatfields Lake, near where the North Rim Drive intersects Highway 12. A tribal fishing license is required.

CASA GRANDE RUINS NATIONAL MONUMENT

1100 Ruins Drive
Coolidge, AZ 85228-3200
(520) 723–3172
www.nps.gov/cagr

Casa Grande Ruins National Monument comprises 472 acres. The land was set aside in 1892 as Casa Grande Reservation (changed to a national monument in 1918) to preserve ruins of a massive four-story building constructed by the prehistoric Hohokam culture more than 650 years ago. The monument is about midway between Phoenix and Tucson, in the town of Coolidge on Arizona Highway 87.

The Hohokam farmed the Gila Valley for more than a thousand years, eventually digging up to 1,000 miles of irrigation canals, many measuring from 8 to 10 feet in width and 7 to 10 feet in depth. Crops of cotton, corn, beans, and squash were grown with the use of these canals.

Approximately 650 years ago the Hohokam constructed the four-story Casa Grande. The building was given its Spanish name (meaning "Big House") by the Jesuit priest Father Kino when he visited it in 1694. The purpose of the structure is uncertain. The Casa Grande was probably built around the early 1300s and used for a relatively short period. This type of village in the Gila Valley had generally been abandoned by the mid-1400s.

The monument is open from 8:00 A.M. to 5:00 P.M. throughout the year (closed Christmas). The visitor center has a collection of artifacts made and used by the Hohokam. Park rangers in the visitor center answer questions and conduct periodic tours from Thanksgiving to early spring. In addition, a self-guided trail leads visitors through the ruins. Summer temperatures are very high; as a result, the monument's heaviest visitation occurs between Thanksgiving and Easter.

ENTRANCE FEE: $3.00 per person. Children ages sixteen and under are free.

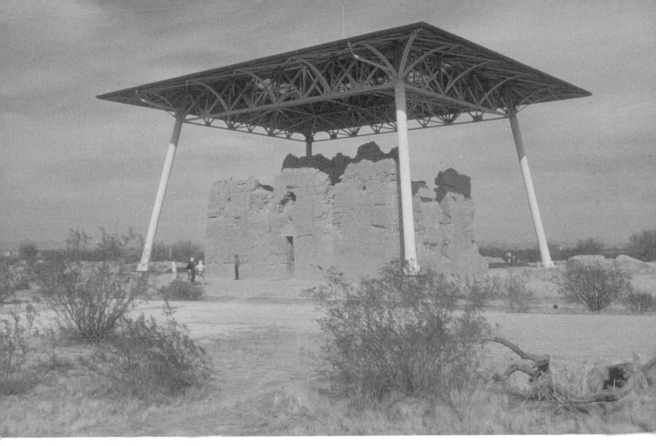

Casa Grande Ruins National Monument

FACILITIES: Lodging and food service are not available in the monument, but several restaurants and motels are located in Coolidge. A picnic area with tables, water, and shade is available at the monument. Flush toilets and drinking water are located in the visitor center.

CAMPING: No camping is permitted at the monument. Two mobile home parks in Coolidge accept overnighters.

CHIRICAHUA NATIONAL MONUMENT

13063 East Bonita Canyon Road
Willcox, AZ 85643-9737
(520) 824–3560, ext. 104
CHIR_Superintendent@nps.gov
www.nps.gov/chir

Chiricahua National Monument comprises 11,985 acres (including 10,290 acres of wilderness) and was established in 1924 to preserve varied rock formations created by volcanic activity millions of years ago. The monument is located in south-eastern Arizona, 36 miles southeast of Willcox, Arizona, off State Highway 186.

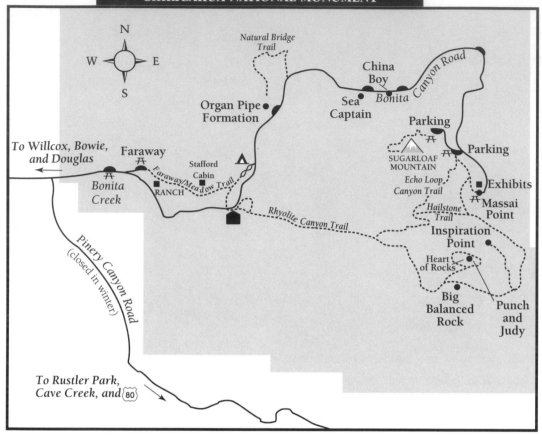

An area of pinnacles and balanced rocks, Chiricahua stands out from the surrounding dry grasslands. The monument's range in elevation from 5,124 to 7,563 feet results in many species of shrubs and trees. The shady glens are alive with various types of birds. Arizona white-tailed deer are frequently seen, and dense vegetation grows in the shaded canyon bottoms and on the north slopes at higher elevations. Temperatures are generally moderate, ranging from summer highs of more than 90 degrees in May and June to freezing temperatures from November through March. Annual precipitation is 18 inches and falls mostly in July and August, when afternoon thunderstorms are common. Light snows fall during winter months.

The area's present geologic features began forming millions of years ago, when the region was subject to extensive volcanic activity. Explosions covered the area with many layers of volcanic ash. Later, the earth's crust was slowly lifted, and cracks developed in the land. These gradually grew larger as water and winds used the openings to work at erosion.

A visitor center is located 2 miles inside the park's entrance. It contains exhibits describing the area's history and geography. Rangers are present to answer visitors' questions. A single 6-mile paved road winds through the monument, ending at Massai Point. The turn at the road's end provides an excellent view of the monument. Faraway Ranch is a pioneer homestead that once served as a working cattle ranch and guest ranch. Tours of the main house are conducted by park rangers. Check at the visitor center for tour information.

More than 17 miles of trails are provided for hikers. A self-guided loop trail, located at Massai Point, takes about thirty minutes to walk. Features along the trail include a balanced rock and a lookout point with view finder. One of the highest points in the monument can be reached via the 1-mile Sugarloaf Trail, which begins at the end of a side road. Round-trip walking time is eighty minutes. One of the most scenic hikes is a 3½-mile loop trail through Echo Canyon and Echo Park. Round-trip time is two hours. A longer hike (four to five hours round-trip) leads to Big Balanced Rock and Punch and Judy.

ENTRANCE FEE: $5.00 per person.

FACILITIES: No overnight accommodations or food services are available within the monument. Motels, restaurants, groceries, and gasoline are available at Willcox. Modern rest rooms and drinking water are located at the visitor center and the campground. Picnic facilities are also available at designated areas.

CAMPING: A single campground (twenty-four spaces) is located ½ mile from monument headquarters in Bonita Canyon. Flush toilets, drinking water, tables, and grills are available, and the campground is open all year. The monument is nearly surrounded by Coronado National Forest, where a dozen USDA Forest Service campgrounds are located.

CORONADO NATIONAL MEMORIAL

4101 East Montezuma Canyon Road
Hereford, AZ 85615
(520) 366-5515
CORO_interpretation@nps.gov
www.nps.gov/coro

Coronado National Memorial comprises 4,750 acres. It was established as a national memorial in 1952 to commemorate the Hispanic heritage and initial European exploration of the American Southwest. The memorial is located in southeastern Arizona on the Mexican border. It is 26 miles west of Bisbee, Arizona, and 21 miles south of Sierra Vista, Arizona, off State Highway 92.

Coronado National Memorial overlooks the valley through which Francisco Vásquez de Coronado first entered what is now the United States. The Coronado expedition was viewed as a failure at the time it was completed because no riches were discovered. Perhaps more important, however, the explorers brought back information about both the land and the people and opened the way for subsequent Spanish explorations and colonization.

The Coronado expedition began from Compostela, Mexico, in February 1540, with a party of approximately 1,100 Spanish soldiers and Mexican-Indian allies. The expedition moved north and east before crossing New Mexico through present-day Albuquerque. By spring 1541 the group had crossed through northern Texas, the Oklahoma panhandle, and into central Kansas. Disillusioned with the discoveries, Coronado returned to Mexico in the spring of 1542.

Memorial headquarters contains a visitor center and museum and is located near the east entrance, 5 miles west of State Highway 92. It is open daily from 8:00 A.M. to 5:00 P.M., except on Thanksgiving and Christmas Day. Montezuma Pass, a 3-mile scenic drive from the visitor center, provides access to viewpoints and to the beginning of a foot trail that leads to Coronado Peak. From this point the visitor has a panoramic view of the country through which Coronado and his party marched. The 3-mile Joe's Canyon Trail leads from Montezuma Pass to the headquarters and picnic area. One-mile-long Yaqui Ridge Trail leads from Joe's Canyon Trail to the

CORONADO NATIONAL MEMORIAL

United States–Mexico boundary. This is the southern terminus of the Arizona trail, which, when completed, will run the length of the state from Mexico to Utah.

Visitors may tour Coronado Cave, which is ¾ mile from the visitor center. The 600-foot-long cave contains stalactites, stalagmites, and flowstones. The Park Service recommends that visitors bring water, hiking shoes, and a flashlight (two flashlights when traveling alone). Permits are required and may be obtained free at the visitor center. The park's climate is relatively warm (high 80s) and rainy during summer months and mild during winter (low 30s).

ENTRANCE FEE: No charge.

FACILITIES: No food service or lodging is available in the memorial. The nearest places for meals and overnight accommodations are Bisbee, 26 miles east, and Sierra Vista, 21 miles north. A picnic area near the visitor center has tables and grills. Rest rooms and water are also available at the visitor center.

CAMPING: No camping is available within the park. A USDA Forest Service campground is located at Parker Canyon Lake, 18 miles west of the memorial. In addition, open camping is permitted in Coronado National Forest, which abuts the memorial to the north and west.

FORT BOWIE NATIONAL HISTORIC SITE

3203 South Old Fort Bowie Road
Bowie, AZ 85605-0158
(520) 847–2500
FOBO_Operations@nps.gov
www.nps.gov/fobo

Fort Bowie National Historic Site was authorized by Congress in 1964 to preserve the Apache Pass Stage Station, Apache Spring, the Fort Bowie complex, and a portion of the Butterfield Overland Mail Route. The 1,000-acre park is 12 miles south of Interstate 10 at Bowie on a mostly paved road. From Willcox, on Interstate 10, Fort Bowie is 22 miles southeast on Arizona Highway 186, then east on a graded dirt road to Apache Pass. The major portion of the historic site can be reached only by a 1½-mile foot trail that begins at a parking area on Apache Pass Road.

The spring located at Apache Pass has drawn a procession of Indians, immigrants, prospectors, and soldiers. Apaches made this their homeland sometime around the sixteenth century but were unable to protect it during the westward expansion of the nineteenth century. In 1857, the postmaster general awarded an overland mail contract to John Butterfield, and the Apache Pass Station was constructed in 1858 as a stop along the St. Louis–San Francisco route.

After years of relative peace between Apaches and white settlers, the early 1860s saw sporadic fighting. In 1862 Fort Bowie was built to keep Apache Pass open to Union troops coming from and going to New Mexico during the Civil War. Peace was made by Cochise and his people in 1872. The Apaches were given a reservation of about 3,000 square miles, but two years later Cochise died, and soon hostilities resumed under the leadership of Geronimo and

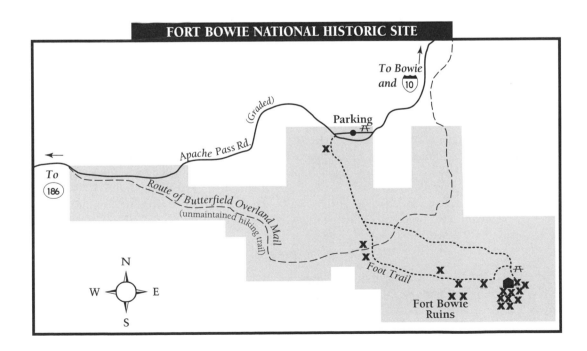

others. After years of intense fighting, a final surrender in 1886 resulted in the remaining Indians being shipped to forts in Florida and later Alabama. Fort Bowie was officially abandoned on October 17, 1894.

The ruins and historic trail are open to the public from sunrise to sunset. Access to the fort ruins is only by a moderately strenuous, 1½-mile foot trail that begins at the parking lot. Summer visitors need to be aware that temperatures can reach over 100 degrees Fahrenheit, and summer storms may suddenly flood the washes. High water generally recedes quickly, so just waiting it out is usually the best option.

The trail passes the Apache Spring, the ruins of the Apache Pass Stage Station of the Overland Mail Company, the post cemetery, and the site of the first Fort Bowie. A ranger is normally on duty at a small ranger station/museum next to the ruins of the second Fort Bowie. The museum is open from 8:00 A.M. to 5:00 P.M. daily, except Christmas.

ENTRANCE FEE: No charge.

FACILITIES: There are no lodging or eating facilities within the park. There is a picnic area at the site, and overnight accommodations and food are available in Willcox. Drinking water and rest rooms are located at the ranger station near the ruins of the fort. Handicap access to Fort Bowie is available by appointment by contacting the historic site either by phone or mail.

CAMPING: No camping is permitted within the park, but a campground is located at Chiricahua National Monument, 25 miles southwest of Fort Bowie. Private campgrounds are located in Bowie and Willcox.

GLEN CANYON NATIONAL RECREATION AREA

P.O. Box 1507
Page, AZ 86040-1507
(928) 608–6200
betsy_scroggs@nps.gov
www.nps.gov/glca

Glen Canyon National Recreation Area comprises 1.25 million acres (most of which are in Utah). It is the result of the Glen Canyon Dam built by the Bureau of Reclamation between 1956 and 1964. Lake Powell, formed from the Colorado River in back of the dam, is 186 miles long with nearly 2,000 miles of shoreline. The southern portion of the park—the most accessible part—is intersected by U.S. 89 through Page, Arizona. Page is 129 miles east of Zion National Park and 132 miles north of Flagstaff. The park also may be crossed at Hite Crossing via Utah Highway 95, and via Utah Highway 276, which is connected by a ferry (carrying both cars and people) that runs from Halls Crossing to Bullfrog and back, every other hour from 8:00 A.M. to 7:00 P.M. during the summer season and four times a day during the winter. For up-to-date ferry information, call (435) 684–7000.

The name Glen Canyon was given to a long stretch of the Colorado River by John Wesley Powell, who led exploration trips through the canyons in 1869 and 1871. Around 1900, the area attracted prospectors looking for gold, but the particles were too fine to be economically recovered. The Navajo Nation borders Glen Canyon to the south. According to anthropologists, Navajo arrived in the Southwest sometime in the 1600s and perhaps as early as the 1500s. Prior to that time ancestral Puebloans (Anasazi) lived in the region. Archaeological sites of these Indians exist throughout the park.

The canyons themselves are the result of a general uplifting of the region that occurred about sixty million years ago. As the uplift progressed, streams of the ancient, low-lying Colorado Basin ran faster, cutting the deep scars that remain today.

Most of the activities at Glen Canyon National Recreation Area are water-related. These include boating, fishing, and waterskiing. Guided tours through the dam are discontinued until further notice. Call for current status of tours. Below the dam, U.S. Highway 89A leads to Lees Ferry, roadside exhibits, and relics of the gold mining days. U.S. 89 North leads to Kanab, Utah, where many western movies have been filmed. Numerous locations, including the beach at Wahweap, are good for swimming.

ENTRANCE FEE: $10.00 per vehicle or $3.00 per person; good for seven days. There is a boating fee of $10.00.

FACILITIES: All concession facilities listed are available through ARAMARK Lake Powell Resorts and Marinas, 2916 North 35th Avenue, Suite 8, Phoenix, AZ 85017 (800–528–6154; 602–278–8888 in Phoenix). The main lodging facility is at Wahweap.

Bullfrog: Visitor center (open April through October), launching ramp, and picnic area. Concessioner-operated campground, lodging, service station, restaurant, camp store, marina, and trailer village with hookups. Write Bullfrog Resort and Marina, P.O. Box 4055, Bullfrog, Lake Powell, UT 84533 (435–684–3000).

Dangling Rope Floating Marina: Ranger station, water, rest rooms, emergency communications, fuel service, and camp supplies. Accessible only by boat.

Halls Crossing: Ranger station (open intermittently), launching ramp, concessioner-operated campground, lodging, boat rental, marina, boat excursions, boating and camping supplies, and trailer village with hookups. Write Halls Crossing Marina, P.O. Box 5101-Halls, Lake Powell, UT 84533 (435–684–7000).

Hite: Ranger station (open intermittently), concessioner-operated boat rental, marina, camp store, service station, and small primitive camping facilities. Write Hite Marina, Inc., Box 501-Hite, Lake Powell, UT 84533 (435–684–2278).

Lees Ferry: Ranger station, launching ramp, and campground. A store, motel, restaurant, and service station are 3½ miles away at Marble Canyon.

Page: Motels, restaurants, and stores. Scenic flights are available from Page airport. Carl Hayden Visitor Center is at Glen Canyon Dam (open year-round). Write Chamber of Commerce, Box 727, Page, AZ 86040.

Wahweap: Ranger station, campground (see camping section), picnic shelters, and launching ramp. Concessioner-operated boat rental, boat tours, boating supplies and repairs, marina, restaurant, lodge, trailer village with hookups, and service station. Write Wahweap Lodge and Marina, P.O. Box 1597, Page, AZ 86040 (520–645–2433; www.visitlakepowell.com).

CAMPING: The major camping area is at Wahweap, 7 miles northwest of Page. A concessioner-operated campground (300 spaces) offers sites with full hookups and sites without hookups, water, a dump station, flush toilets, tables, grills, and pay showers. Campgrounds are also located at Lees Ferry (fifty-eight spaces with flush toilets), Halls Crossing (sixty-five spaces with flush toilets), and Bullfrog (seventy-five spaces with flush toilets). Concessioner-operated trailer parks are at the latter two locations as well as at Wahweap. There is also vehicle-accessible primitive camping allowed at Hite in Farley Canyon, Dirty Devil area, White Canyon, and Blue Notch Canyon; and in Bullfrog at Bullfrog North, Bullfrog South, and Stanton Creek. Some of these areas are accessible only by four-wheel-drive vehicles. Farley, Dirty Devil, Bullfrog North, Bullfrog South, and Stanton Creek have pit toilets and charge a nominal fee for camping.

Anyone camping within ¼ mile of the shoreline of Lake Powell must have and use some device for containing solid human wastes, unless they are camped within 200 yards of a toilet. Use of plastic bags as receptacles for human waste is prohibited. Also, any vessel equipped with a marine sanitation device (toilet) capable of overboard discharge must be sealed in a way that makes overboard discharge impossible. All wastes must be disposed of properly—in portable toilet dump stations or boat pumpout stations.

FISHING: Striped bass, largemouth bass, and black crappie have been stocked in Lake Powell. Catches of striped bass frequently include specimens of up to 10 pounds. Native catfish are also plentiful. Below the dam, the clear, cold river makes Lees Ferry famous for trout fishing. An appropriate state fishing license (Arizona or Utah) is required.

GRAND CANYON NATIONAL PARK

P.O. Box 129
Grand Canyon, AZ 86023-0129
(928) 638–7888
www.nps.gov/grca

Grand Canyon National Park comprises nearly 1.2 million acres of land where the forces of erosion have unveiled a variety of spectacular formations that illustrate vast periods of geological history. The park is located in northwestern Arizona. The South Rim is approached from Flagstaff via U.S. 180 (80 miles to Grand Canyon Village) or by U.S. 89 and Arizona Highway 64 (82 miles to Desert View). The North Rim is 45 miles south of Jacob Lake via Arizona Highway 67.

About 1,700 million years ago, volcanic islands were pushed against the North American continent's edge. After these island-based layers were eroded away, movements within the earth created a basin in which sediments and volcanic rocks collected. About 800 million years ago, these layers were pushed upward to form a new, uplifted plateau that, in turn, eroded away. Between 225 and 570 million years ago, the region was an intercontinental sea similar to today's Gulf of Mexico. The sandstones, shales, and limestones that collected in the basin make up today's upper three-fourths of the canyon walls. About sixty-five million years ago the region began to rise above sea level. Moisture falling on the newly created Rocky Mountains created the Colorado River, which began cutting the canyon some six million years ago.

The river divides the park into two separate sections—the North Rim and the South Rim—with the inner canyon accessible from either side. There are several concessioners licensed by the National Park Service offering three- to nineteen-day trips down the Colorado River. Information may be obtained at the park visitor centers or by mail from the park. (Write Trip Planner, Grand Canyon National Park, P.O. Box 129, Grand Canyon, AZ 86023.)

Although an average of 10 miles separates the developed areas of the North and South Rims, the distance by road is 220 miles. By foot, the Kaibab Trail (20½ miles) leads from Yaki Point on the South Rim down to the river, across to Phantom Ranch, then up to the North Rim, ending 2 miles from Grand Canyon Lodge. Campgrounds in the canyon, accessible only by foot or by mule, require reservations. Phantom Ranch, north of the river on Kaibab Trail, offers meals and accommodations. Reservations (888–297–2757) are required and should be made well in advance.

NORTH RIM

The road to the less-developed North Rim winds through forests of pine, spruce, and aspen on the Kaibab Plateau. This area of the park is at elevations of 7,800 to 8,800 feet and has a cooler and wetter climate than the South Rim. The North Rim is closed by heavy snowfall from mid-November to mid-May. Facilities close by mid- to late October.

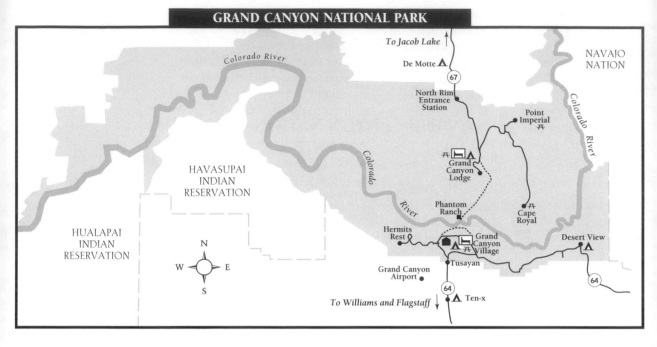

The main information station is located beside the Bright Angel Point parking area. Park rangers are available to answer questions, and publications concerning the park are for sale. The entrance station is located 13 miles north of Bright Angel Point. A USDA Forest Service information station is located at Jacob Lake, 32 miles north of the North Rim Entrance Station.

A 23-mile paved road connects Grand Canyon Lodge to Cape Royal. This latter point provides an eastward view of the canyon toward the Painted Desert. Point Imperial, on a 3-mile spur off the Cape Royal Road, offers the best eastward view across the canyon. Point Sublime is 17 miles south of the park entrance via a four-wheel-drive dirt road. Ask at the NPS Information Desk for directions. Evidence of a fire that occurred in 2000 can be seen along the North Rim road.

Various ranger-guided walks are scheduled during summer months. Bright Angel Point Trail is a 1/4-mile self-guided nature trail that begins near the lodge. Transept Trail (1 1/2 miles) provides a leisurely walk along the canyon rim from Grand Canyon Lodge to the North Rim store and campground. Uncle Jim Trail (2 1/2 miles) starts at the Kaibab trailhead and winds through the forest, ending at a point overlooking the canyon. Cape Royal Trail is a 1/3-mile self-guided nature trail from the Cape Royal parking lot. The inner canyon is reached via the North Kaibab Trail (9 miles round-trip to Roaring Springs) by foot or mule. Information on mule trips may be obtained by writing Grand Canyon Trail Rides, P.O. Box 1638, Cedar City, UT 84720, or calling (435) 679–8665.

ENTRANCE FEE: $20 per vehicle or $10 per person; good for seven days on either rim. There is a fee for a backcountry permit.

FACILITIES: Meals and lodging are available from mid-May to mid-October at Grand Canyon Lodge, which provides cabins and motel-type units. For information or reservations, write Grand Canyon National Park Lodges, Xanterra Parks and Resorts, 14001 East Iliff Avenue, Suite 600, Aurora, CO 80014. Call (888) 297–2757; fax (303) 297–3175. A general store, post office, showers, and laundry are also located near the campground, 1 mile north of Bright Angel

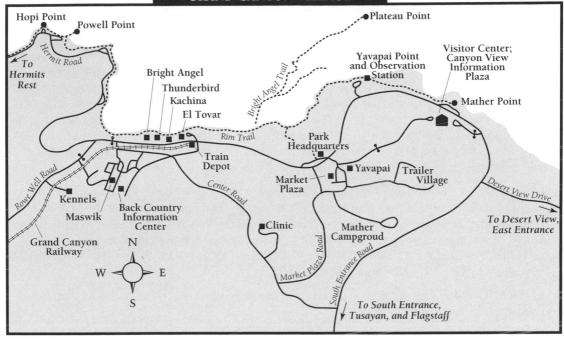

GRAND CANYON VILLAGE

Point. Additional food services and accommodations are located at Kaibab Lodge (5 miles north of the entrance station) and at Jacob Lake.

CAMPING: North Rim Campground (eighty-two spaces), 12 miles south of the entrance station and 1 mile north of Grand Canyon Lodge, has tables, grills, water, flush toilets, and a dump station. A campground store sells groceries, sandwiches, soft drinks, wine, and beer. This is a very attractive campground that is full virtually all summer, so advance reservations are necessary and can be made by calling (800) 365–2267, or on the Web at reservations. nps.gov. De Motte Campground (5 miles north of the entrance station) and Jacob Lake Campground (32 miles north of the entrance station) are operated by the USDA Forest Service and provide water and rest rooms.

FISHING: Access to fishing is very difficult, and catches are generally poor. Brown and rainbow trout live in the bottom of the canyon in Bright Angel Creek near Phantom Ranch. Channel catfish are very rarely taken from the nearby Colorado River and rainbows from Thunder River and Tapeats Creek. An Arizona fishing license is required.

SOUTH RIM

The South Rim is open year-round, and temperatures during summer months range from the mid-40s at night to the mid-80s in daytime. The visitor center is located in Canyon View Information Plaza, 7 miles north of the South Entrance Station. Rangers are available to answer questions, and a schedule of activities is posted. The visitor center has exhibits to help you plan your visit to the park. Additional museums are the Yavapai Observation Station (on Yavapai Point) and Tusayan Museum (3 miles west of Desert View), with displays describing prehistoric inhabitants of the area.

A free shuttle system operates three routes in the park and is the easiest way to explore the South Rim. One route provides transportation throughout Grand Canyon Village and to Canyon View Information Center. A second shuttle route provides service from Canyon View Information Center to scenic points to the east. These two routes are operated year-round. A third shuttle route, operating from March through November, uses Hermit Road to access points to the west. This latter road (8 miles) offers several scenic viewpoints of the canyon on the way from Grand Canyon Village to Hermits Rest. Desert View Drive to Desert View (26 miles and not on the shuttle bus route) offers an excellent view of the canyon at several viewpoints. The Watchtower at Desert View overlooks the canyon and the Painted Desert.

A number of self-guided nature trails, paths, and undeveloped trails lie along the rim between Mather Point and Hermits Rest. Ranger-guided walks are presented year-round on a scheduled basis at Grand Canyon Village, at Desert View, and at Tusayan Ruins.

LODGING: The South Rim of the Grand Canyon has six lodges. Accommodations range from the historic El Tovar (completed in 1905), which sits near the edge of the South Rim, to motel-type units at Yavapai, Maswik, Thunderbird, and Kachina, to rustic cabins at Bright Angel Lodge. Reservations for all six lodging units are available by writing Grand Canyon National Park Lodges, Xanterra Parks and Resorts, 14001 East Iliff Avenue, Suite 600, Aurora, CO 80014. Call (888) 297–2757; fax (303) 297–3175.

ENTRANCE FEE: $20 per vehicle or $10 per person; good for seven days on either rim. A fee is charged for backcountry permits.

FACILITIES: Nearly anything the heart desires, with the exception of a service station, can be found in Grand Canyon Village. This includes a bank, general store, post office, laundry, restaurants, gift shops, bookstores, showers, pet kennel, and lost-and-found facility. A general store, bookstore, snack bar, and service station are located at Desert View.

CAMPING: The park's most developed campground is Mather Campground (310 spaces and 7 group camps) at Grand Canyon Village. It provides tables, grills, water, flush toilets, pay showers, laundry facilities, and a dump station. Reservations for Mather are available by calling (800) 365–2267, or check out the Web site at reservations.nps.gov. Nearby, Trailer Village (eighty-two spaces) is operated by Grand Canyon National Park Lodges and provides hookups. Write Xanterra Parks and Resorts, 14001 East Iliff, Suite 600, Aurora, CO 80014; (888) 297–2757. Desert View Campground (fifty spaces) is located 1/2 mile west of the east entrance station and has tables, grills, water, and flush toilets. Ten X Campground (seventy sites, pit toilets), operated by the USDA Forest Service, is located 10 miles south of Grand Canyon Village, outside the park. Ten X is a pleasant campground with lots of shade. Desert View and Ten X campgrounds are open seasonally from mid-May to October. Both are first-come, first-served.

FISHING: Access to fishing is difficult, and catches are generally poor. See fishing section under the North Rim section for details.

HUBBELL TRADING POST NATIONAL HISTORIC SITE
P.O. Box 150
Ganado, AZ 86505-0150
(928) 755–3475
hutr_ranger_activities@nps.gov
www.nps.gov/hutr

Hubbell Trading Post was authorized as a national historic site in 1965 to preserve an active trading post. The site is on the Navajo Nation, $1/2$ mile west of Ganado, Arizona, and 55 miles from Gallup, New Mexico.

Hubbell Trading Post is the oldest continuously operating trading post on the Navajo Nation. The post was established in 1871. Trader John Lorenzo Hubbell purchased the post from William Leonard in 1878. Hubbell eventually established a network of trading posts, a wholesale warehouse in Winslow, and a stage and freight line. A personal friend of men such as Theodore Roosevelt and General Lew Wallace, Hubbell was instrumental in early Arizona history and statehood. His death in 1930 was mourned by his Navajo friends, and his body lies overlooking the trading post on Hubbell Hill. The Hubbell family operated the post for eighty-nine years, until it became a national historic site.

Visitors may participate in the experience of a living, active post. Here members of the Navajo, Hopi, Zuni, and other tribes still come to sell and trade such crafts as hand-woven rugs, jewelry, baskets, and pottery. Ranger-led interpretive programs are available. Weaving demonstrations are offered in the visitor center. A booklet for a self-guided tour of the site may be borrowed at the visitor center.

The site is open daily except Thanksgiving, Christmas, and New Year's Day. Hours are 8:00 A.M. to 5:00 P.M. October through April, 8:00 A.M. to 6:00 P.M. the rest of the year. Note: Daylight savings time is observed.

ENTRANCE FEE: No charge.

FACILITIES: The trading post continues traditional operation under the direction of the Western National Parks Association, a nonprofit organization operating the post for the National Park Service. Many fine Navajo, Hopi, Zuni, Apache, and other Indian arts are offered for sale. Groceries and snacks may also be purchased here. A half mile east, in the town of Ganado, visitors will find three cafes, a gas station, and a market. Rest rooms and drinking water are available at the visitor center.

CAMPING: No camping is allowed at the site. Canyon de Chelly National Monument, 40 miles north on Highway 191, offers 104 sites at Cottonwood Campground (flush toilets).

MONTEZUMA CASTLE NATIONAL MONUMENT

2800 Montezuma Castle Road
Camp Verde, AZ 86322
(928) 567–3322
MOCA_Administration@nps.gov
nps.gov/moca

Montezuma Castle National Monument was established in 1906. It contains one of the best-preserved prehistoric cliff dwellings in the Southwest. The five-story, twenty-room castle is 90 percent intact. The monument is located in central Arizona, just off Interstate 17, 55 miles south of Flagstaff and 4 miles northeast of the town of Camp Verde. The monument is approximately 90 miles north of Phoenix.

Several million years ago the Verde River was dammed by lava, forming a lake 35 miles long and 18 miles wide. Later, after tributaries had deposited large quantities of lime-filled mud in the lake, overflows wore down the lava dam and the lake drained. The Verde River and its tributaries then cut deep channels through the sediments, and further erosion caused a broadening of the valleys.

Although there is little evidence of the earliest inhabitants of the Verde Valley, Indians are known to have lived in the Southwest for several thousand years. About A.D. 600, the Hohokam came into the valley from the south. About 450 years later, these farming Indians moved north to the fertile lands produced by the eruption that created Sunset Crater in the mid-1060s. Around 1100, a group of dry-farming Indians entered the valley from the north, and around 1150, they began erecting large dwellings on hilltops or in cliffs. The limestone cliff along the north bank of Beaver Creek was an ideal place to build house clusters because it had good cropland on the creek terrace nearby. Two of the clusters (including Montezuma Castle) eventually became five-story apartment houses that were occupied for about two centuries. By about 1450, Montezuma Castle appears to have been abandoned.

The visitor center is in the Montezuma Castle section of the park. It contains exhibits describing the culture of the people who lived here. Examples of weaving, basketry, jewelry, and pottery-making tools are on display.

Additional prehistoric Indian work can be seen at Montezuma Well, 11 miles northeast of Montezuma Castle. This part of the monument has a limestone sink 470 feet in diameter with water 55 feet deep. Indians diverted the well water into irrigation ditches that are still visible today. This section also contains the remains of a Hohokam pithouse and Sinagua dwellings.

ENTRANCE FEE: $3.00 per person; good for seven days. Children ages sixteen and under free.

FACILITIES: No food or lodging is available within the monument's boundaries, but both can be found nearby. Limited picnic facilities are located in each of the two sections of the park.

Drinking water and modern rest rooms are available in the visitor center. There is easy wheelchair access to rest rooms, the visitor center, and the trail at the Montezuma Castle section.

CAMPING: No camping is permitted in the monument. Forest service campgrounds are located in Coconino National Forest, and other private campgrounds are located nearby.

NAVAJO NATIONAL MONUMENT

HC 71 Box 3
Tonalea, AZ 86044-9704
(928) 672–2700
NAVA_Superintendent@nps.gov
www.nps.gov/nava

Navajo National Monument comprises 360 acres, surrounded by Navajo Nation land. It was established in 1909 to preserve the spectacular cliff dwellings built by the Anasazi Indian farmers who lived in the canyons more than 700 years ago. Park headquarters, located on the Navajo Nation in northeastern Arizona, can be reached by following U.S. 160 east 50 miles from Tuba City or west 29 miles from Kayenta. At Black Mesa, a 9 mile paved road (Highway 564) leads to the monument.

American Indian people have been intimately tied to the Kayenta Region for over a thousand years. The Zuni and Hopi Pueblos of today have cultural and religious ties to Keet Seel and Betatakin, the two large Indian village archaeological sites in the Navajo National Monument. Farming was the main occupation of the villagers who grew corn, squash, and beans using desert-adapted crops, dry-land farming techniques, and various methods of irrigation, including flood farming. Seeds, nuts, greens, fruits, and berries were gathered for food, as well as for medicinal and ceremonial uses. Limited hunting supplemented the largely agricultural diet. By the thirteenth century, the occupants were able to create beautifully decorated pottery vessels they traded across large distances for turquoise, cotton, seashells, parrots, and macaws. The Navajo who followed the Pueblo people into this region called the builders of these villages *Anasazi,* meaning "The Ancient Ones." The villages are on the Navajo Reservation, and Navajo residents continue to farm and herd livestock through the canyons.

Anglo-Americans first saw the larger of the two villages, Keet Seel (Navajo for "empty dwellings"), in 1895. The dwelling has more than 155 masonry rooms and is believed to have been occupied from approximately A.D. 950 to 1300. It is the largest such village in Arizona and considered one of the best-preserved prehistoric villages in existence. Betatakin (Navajo for "alcove dwelling") was occupied for a much shorter period and not discovered until August 1909, five months following the establishment of the Navajo National Monument, when local Navajo residents informed archaeologists of the site. Betatakin has 135 rooms and was constructed inside an enormous Navajo Formation alcove of massive pale reddish brown cliffs of sandstone. Rooms for sleeping, food storage, and ceremonies were constructed of sandstone blocks using sand and mortar. Rooms were built onto the natural ledges beneath the shelter of the alcove. The Navajo Formation is a natural aquifer with many seeps and springs that provided the canyon's inhabitants with convenient sources of water

The monument's visitor center is open daily from 8:00 A.M. to 5:00 P.M. except on Thanksgiving, Christmas, and New Year's Day. Here you will find exhibits about Anasazi and Navajo culture, a twenty-minute video, books for sale, and an American Indian arts and crafts shop. A Navajo hogan, sweat lodge, and nineteenth-century wagon are behind the visitor center. Two self-guided hiking trails behind the visitor center include 1-mile round-trip Sandal Trail, which leads to an overlook that offers a cross-canyon view of Betatakin. The more strenuous 0.8-mile round-trip Aspen Forest Overlook Trail descends 300 feet to view a surviving ancient forest of aspen and fir. This latter trail does not offer a view of the ruins. Signs along the trails identify plants used by the Hopi and Navajo. Betatakin may be visited only with a park ranger. Five-hour guided hikes to the village are limited to twenty-five people and leave once each day at 8:15 A.M. The trail to Betatakin is fairly strenuous and requires a canyon climb that is equivalent to walking up the steps of a 70-story building. Visits to Keet Seel along an 8½-mile primitive trail are limited to twenty persons daily from Memorial Day weekend through Labor Day. Visitors wishing to hike to Keet Seel must obtain a backcountry permit at the visitor center. Hikers to Keet Seel are permitted to camp one night at a primitive campground. Visitors to the monument are required to stay within designated trail markers.

ENTRANCE FEE: No charge.

FACILITIES: Rest rooms and drinking water are in the visitor center. Black Mesa Trading Post at the intersection of Highways 160 and 564 has gasoline, a laundromat, and a small convenience store. A motel and gift shop are on Highway 160, 10 miles east of the Black Mesa Trading Post. Twenty-eight miles northeast of the monument, Kayenta offers motels, restaurants, service stations, and a supermarket.

CAMPING: A campground (thirty-one spaces, picnic tables, flush toilets) in a juniper-piñon forest is open year-round. Stays are limited to seven days, and vehicles are limited to 27 feet in length or less. Overflow camping is permitted in a primitive campground 1 mile from the main campground. No open-flame fires are permitted.

ORGAN PIPE CACTUS NATIONAL MONUMENT

10 Organ Pipe Drive
Ajo, AZ 85321-9626
(520) 387–6849
orpi_information@nps.gov
www.nps.gov/orpi

Organ Pipe Cactus National Monument comprises 330,689 acres. This park was established as a national monument in 1937 to preserve and protect unique Sonoran Desert plants and animals, including the rare cactus for which the park is named. The monument is located in southwestern Arizona on the Mexican border, 141 miles south of Phoenix and 144 miles west of Tucson. From Phoenix, take Interstate 10 to Arizona 85 South. From Tucson, take Arizona 86 (Ajo Way) West and then Arizona 85 South. The monument visitor center is 34 miles south of Ajo.

Organ Pipe Cactus National Monument was designated to protect the natural features and life contained in this segment of the Sonoran Desert. The stark and rough landscape of the monument includes mountains, plains, canyons, and dry washes. Summer days can be quite warm—temperatures of 95 to 115 degrees Fahrenheit are most common. Of the 9¼ inches of annual rainfall, nearly two-thirds results from summer thunderstorms. Winter weather is generally mild, with sunny days. Temperatures can hover just above freezing during winter nights, with occasional dips below that mark.

A visitor center with exhibits explaining the monument and desert is located 17 miles south of the northern entrance. The visitor center is open year-round (except Christmas) from 8:00 A.M. to 5:00 P.M. Evening programs are presented in the campground amphitheater during the busy winter months from mid-December through mid-March.

A single paved road (Arizona 85) through the park connects Why, Arizona, with Sonoyta, Mexico. Two graded loop drives through remote areas begin at the visitor center, where guide booklets are available. Puerto Blanco Drive is 53 miles long, with two-way traffic on the first 5 miles of the road, and one-way traffic on the rest. It takes approximately a half day to drive the entire road. This route circles the Puerto Blanco Mountains and parallels the Mexican border. Side roads lead to a stand of senita cactus at Senita Basin and to a human-made oasis at Quito-baquito Springs. Ajo Mountain Drive is a 21-mile road that takes approximately two and a half hours to drive and provides outstanding views of the desert. Various species of cactus can be seen as the road circles the Ajo Mountains.

A number of trails are located in the park. A 1½-mile trail connects the campground and visitor center, and a 1¼-mile self-guided Desert View Nature Trail leads from the group campground to a nearby ridge overlooking the desert. Victoria Mine Trail (4½ miles round-trip) leads to what was once one of the area's most productive silver mines. O'Odham Day, a celebration of native culture, is celebrated on the third Saturday of March. Demonstrations include pottery, dancing, storytelling, native plant use, and dry-land farming.

ENTRANCE FEE: $5.00 per vehicle or $3.00 per person; good for seven days. A fee is charged for overnight backcountry permits.

FACILITIES: Lodging and food service are not available within the monument. A motel, post office, grocery store, cafe, and service station are located in Lukeville, 5 miles south of the visitor center. Motels and restaurants are located in Ajo, Gila Bend, and Sonoyta. A cafe and service stations are located in Why, near the park's northern entrance. Modern rest rooms and drinking water are available at the visitor center, at the 5-mile mark on Puerto Blanko Drive, and at the campground.

CAMPING: A single campground (208 spaces) is open all year and is located 1½ miles southwest of the visitor center. The campground has tables, grills, flush toilets, and a dump station. There is a 35-foot limit on trailers and motorhomes. A drive-in primitive campground with four sites is at Alamo Canyon. A permit from the visitor center is required. No trailers or motorhomes are allowed.

PETRIFIED FOREST NATIONAL PARK

P.O. Box 2217
Petrified Forest National Park, AZ 86028-2217
(928) 524–6228
pefo_superintendent@nps.gov
www.nps.gov/pefo

Petrified Forest National Park was proclaimed a national monument by President Theodore Roosevelt in 1906 and was legislated as a national park by Congress in 1962. The park protects 93,533 acres of Late Triassic Period plants, animals, and trees that fossilized to multicolored stone. Early Puebloan dwelling sites, petroglyphs (pictures and designs chiseled on rock faces), and the Painted Desert are also found within the park. The park is located in northeastern Arizona, 46 miles from the New Mexico border on Interstate 40. It is 119 miles east of Flagstaff, Arizona. The park is accessed via a 28-mile paved road that runs north/south between Interstate 40 on the north and U.S. Highway 180 on the south. The road is adequate for large RVs and trailers.

The Painted Desert of northern Arizona is a landscape of various colors and shapes. Within the eroded badlands of Petrified Forest National Park, visitors will find a multitude of logs brilliant with jasper and agate. Long before modern visitors came to the park, early Native Americans used the fossilized wood for tools and as building material for some of their pueblos. Some dwellings and petroglyphs can still be seen at Agate House, Puerco Pueblo, and Newspaper Rock.

The fossils of Petrified Forest tell of a very different place and time. This region was crossed by many streams as part of a vast tropical floodplain 225 million years ago. On drier upland areas and near the streams' headwaters, large coniferous trees grew. As trees fell, many were carried downstream and buried by mud. While they were buried, a lack of oxygen slowed the decaying process. The overlying sediment was rich in silica from volcanic ash. Silica, carried by groundwater, was absorbed by the waterlogged trees. The silica gradually crystallized into quartz. Today these hardened remains of the Triassic are found among the badlands in the sedimentary layers of mudstone, silts, clays, and sandstones known as the Chinle Formation.

At the Interstate 40 exit near the north end of the park, Painted Desert Visitor Center offers books, brochures, information, and an excellent twenty-minute video that explains how this area came to be so special. The visitor center is adjacent to a nice gift shop and a cafe with a Route 66 theme. At the park's south entrance off Highway 180, Rainbow Forest Museum has specimens of petrified wood, fossils of plants and animals, and exhibits about the Triassic period. A short paved trail behind the museum provides access to some of the largest and most colorful fossilized logs in the park. Numerous trails and exhibits are between the north and south entrances. Ranger programs are conducted throughout the year, and program locations and times are posted at the Painted Desert Visitor Center and Rainbow Forest Museum. The park is open year-round; however, hours vary with the season. For park hours and information, call (928) 524–6228. The park is closed on Christmas Day. Be aware that winter storms may close the park or delay the opening. Use yellow phones to report emergencies or threats to park resources.

Nearly thirteen tons of petrified wood are stolen from this park each year. The collection or destruction of any natural or cultural resource is prohibited. Violators may be fined, imprisoned, or both. Do your part to protect your park. Petrified Forest is now on the "Ten Most Endangered Parks" list due to the theft of its resources.

Some of the major points (numbers keyed to those found on map) are:

1. Painted Desert Visitor Center—The first stop upon entering the park from Interstate 40. A free, twenty-minute park film, *Timeless Impressions,* is shown every half hour. A restaurant, gift shop, gas station, and travel store are located next to the visitor center; rest rooms are available year-round.

2. The Painted Desert and Painted Desert Inn—A particularly colorful portion of the Painted Desert can be viewed from a series of eight overlooks scattered along the northern loop of the road. The Painted Desert Inn, a National Historical Landmark that now serves as a museum and visitor center, once provided food and rooms to travelers along Route 66. Originally built in 1924, it was extensively modified in the 1930s by the Civilian Conservation Corps and later operated by the Fred Harvey Company. The firm's architect and interior designer, Mary Elizabeth Jane Colter, directed renovations of the building. Drinking water, information, and rest rooms are available here. A picnic area and seasonal rest rooms are a short distance away at Chinde Point.

3. Puerco Pueblo—The remains of a 1,000-year-old pueblo and some outstanding petroglyphs are a short walk from the parking area. Rest rooms are available year-round. An emergency phone also is available.

4. Newspaper Rock—Excellent petroglyphs may be viewed on the surface of a massive sandstone block at the base of the overlook. Free spotting scopes are on the viewing platform.

5. The Tepees—Colorful mounds that resemble tepees or haystacks are examples of erosion of the soft-layered clay deposits of the Chinle Formation.

6. Blue Mesa—A 3-mile loop road leads travelers to several excellent viewpoints. A 1-mile self-guided trail meanders through an area of badlands and petrified logs. An emergency phone is available.

7. Agate Bridge—A huge petrified log lies partially exposed across a gully. Both ends of the log are encased in sandstone, with a 40-foot ravine beneath that has been carved by erosion. This unusual feature was reinforced by concrete in 1917. Rest rooms are available only during summer months.

8. Jasper Forest Overlook—Masses of log sections litter the valley floor below.

9. Crystal Forest—These fossil logs were once filled with clear and amethyst quartz crystals. Before the turn of the twentieth century, most of the crystals were removed by souvenir hunters and gem collectors. A 3/4-mile trail leads through an impressive area of large fossil logs.

10. Long Logs and Agate House—The 1/2-mile Long Logs loop trail is an area of exceptionally long logs that are only partially uncovered. Another 3/4-mile trail leads to Agate House, a partially restored eight-room pueblo made of petrified wood sections.

11. Rainbow Forest Museum and Giant Logs Trail—The museum displays sections of petrified wood, as well as geology and paleontology exhibits. The 1/2-mile self-guided Giant Logs Trail begins behind the museum. Rest rooms are available year-round.

ENTRANCE FEE: $10.00 per vehicle or $5.00 per person; good for seven days.

FACILITIES: No overnight lodging is available in the park, but accommodations can be found in nearby communities. Food, gifts, and gasoline can be obtained all year at the Painted Desert Oasis next to the Painted Desert Visitor Center at the north entrance. Rainbow Forest Curios, near the south entrance, has refreshments and gifts. Picnic areas are located at Chinde Point and near the Rainbow Forest Museum.

CAMPING: No campgrounds are in the park. Backcountry camping is allowed by wilderness permit only and requires backpacking into the Painted Desert Wilderness Area (43,020 acres). Travel is cross-country, and there are no trails, facilities, or water. The nearest public campgrounds are in national forests to the southeast and west, nearly 100 miles away. Private campgrounds are in both Holbrook and Winslow. A county park near Joseph City has limited camping. Two state parks in the area are Lyman Lake and Homolovi Ruins.

PIPE SPRING NATIONAL MONUMENT

HC 65 Box 5
Fredonia, AZ 86022
(928) 643–7105
pisp_interpretation@nps.gov
www.nps.gov/pisp

Pipe Spring National Monument comprises forty acres. It was established in 1923 to preserve a historic fort and other structures built by Mormon pioneers. Pipe Spring is located in northwestern Arizona near the Utah border. The monument is 15 miles southwest of Fredonia, Arizona, on Arizona Highway 389. It is located 66 miles from Zion National Park, 89 miles from the North Rim of the Grand Canyon, and 45 miles from Hurricane, Utah.

Located on the Arizona Strip (the northern part of Arizona separated from the rest of the state by the Grand Canyon), the water of Pipe Spring has allowed plants and animals to thrive in this dry, desert region. Humans have also taken advantage of this water for at least 1,000 years. Ancestral Puebloans (Anasazi) grew crops near the springs. Paiute Indians gathered seed from abundant grasses, hunted animals that used the springs, and raised crops in the area. In the late 1850s Mormon missionaries en route to the Hopi lands camped at the spring. The name of Pipe Spring supposedly originated when one of the men shot the bottom out of a smoking pipe to demonstrate his marksmanship.

In 1863 Mormon cattleman James Whitmore established a claim at Pipe Spring. Because of the presence of water and abundant forage, he built a dugout, cultivated a small piece of land, and started a livestock ranch. At the same time the Mormons were migrating into the region, the U.S. Army was waging a war against the Navajo south of the Colorado River. Navajo who raided his livestock presumably killed Whitmore on January 8, 1866. Pipe Spring and the surrounding region were subsequently abandoned until the area found use by the Utah Territorial Militia as a base of operations against the Navajo. By 1868 a peace treaty was signed with the Navajo, and pioneers began to return to the Arizona Strip area.

In 1870 Brigham Young bought the Pipe Spring claim from Whitmore's widow. A fortified ranch house called Winsor Castle (after the first ranch superintendent) was constructed directly over the main spring to secure the water supply and provide protection from the Indians. Winsor Castle was never attacked and became the headquarters of a large tithing ranch for the Mormon church. In the early days a dairy was operated from Pipe Spring. It always served as a way station for travelers, and in the 1880s and 1890s, Pipe Spring was a refuge for the wives and children of polygamists sought by the federal marshals. In the mid-1890s Pipe Spring passed into private hands but continued to serve as a ranch until its purchase by the National Park Service in 1923.

The climate at Pipe Spring is fairly temperate because the area is nearly 1 mile above sea level. Plant and animal life are typical for a semidesert area. Small rodents live among the cactus and sagebrush, and coyotes are occasionally seen. Water from the spring provides a perfect habitat for the flora and fauna of this oasis. Birds are abundant in this monument.

The monument is open from 8:00 A.M. to 5:00 P.M. year-round, with the historic buildings open from 8:30 A.M. to 4:00 P.M. The monument is closed Thanksgiving, Christmas, and New Year's Day. Guided tours are offered on the hour and half hour year-round. Ranger talks and living history programs, representative of pioneer and Paiute life, are offered during the summer months. The monument grounds include a re-created historic orchard and garden, Winsor Castle, other historic buildings, a juniper-log corral, and a ½-mile loop trail, with markers noting the natural and cultural history of the area. The visitor center contains displays and an introductory video.

ENTRANCE FEE: $4.00 per person; good for seven days; children ages sixteen and under are free.

FACILITIES: A gift shop/bookstore is operated by the Zion Natural History Association. The nearest town with accommodations is Fredonia, 15 miles to the northeast. Similar facilities are also available in Hurricane and Kanab, Utah.

CAMPING: No camping is permitted at Pipe Spring. A campground operated by the Kaibab-Paiute Indian tribe is located ¼ mile north of the monument. Full hookups and tent sites are available. Zion National Park (66 miles) and Utah's Coral Pink Sand Dune State Park (45 miles) both have complete camping facilities. Commercial camping is available in Fredonia, Arizona (15 miles), and Kanab, Utah (25 miles).

SAGUARO NATIONAL PARK

3693 South Old Spanish Trail
Tucson, AZ 85730-5601
(520) 733–5100
SAGU_Information@nps.gov
www.nps.gov/sagu

Saguaro National Park comprises 91,000 acres in two sections near Tucson, Arizona. It was established as a national monument in 1933 to preserve giant saguaro cacti. The park's largest part, Rincon Mountain District, is east of the Tucson city limits on Old Spanish Trail. A smaller part, Tucson Mountain District, is west of the city limits. This part can be reached by driving west to Kinney Road on either Gates Pass Road or Ajo Way. The distance between the districts is about 30 miles, but it takes about an hour to drive from one to the other.

Saguaro National Park was named after a large cactus in the Sonoran Desert that averages a height of 30 feet and lives up to 150 years. The seed of the saguaro sprouts and survives in the shade of another desert plant. After five years it has grown only a few inches and at thirty years is only a few feet tall. At seventy-five years the plant may reach 15 or 20 feet and begin developing its first branch.

The saguaro is well suited to the area's dry climate. The root system is widespread and lies just below the ground surface so as to absorb as much of the infrequent rain as possible. A mature plant weighing 6 to 10 tons may absorb as much as a ton of water. During long dry periods, the saguaro consumes its stored moisture and shrinks in girth. During May and early June, clusters of white flowers appear on the saguaro's branch ends. These are Arizona's state flower.

Variations in elevation from 2,800 to 8,700 feet within the park make it the home of numerous types of plant and animal life. The saguaro cactus itself serves as home for several species of birds. Gila woodpeckers and gilded flickers bore holes that are later used by elf and screech owls, purple martins, and cactus wrens.

A visitor center, located at the west entrance of Rincon Mountain District, contains exhibits describing the history and geology of this area of the country. Ranger-guided walks are conducted from here during winter months. An 8-mile paved road that begins near the visitor center takes the motorist on a scenic drive through the stands of large, old saguaros found in the eastern section of the park. Pullouts are located along the drive so that visitors can walk along some short trails. A number of longer trails lead into the wilderness of the Rincon Mountains, where there are woodlands of scrub oak and pine and forests of ponderosa pine and Douglas fir. Horseback riding is permitted on most trails in the park, but bicycles and dogs are not.

Tucson Mountain District contains stands of young and old saguaros. The main unpaved 9-mile loop drive through this district leads to hiking trails and scenic overlooks. Short and long trails are also available in this section of the park. The longer trails lead high into the Tucson Mountains. At the south entrance, a visitor center has exhibits, audiovisual programs, and trail and drive guides. Ranger-guided hikes are also conducted here during winter months.

The nearby Arizona-Sonora Desert Museum contains exhibits of living plants and animals of the Sonoran Desert. Mild temperatures from fall through spring turn uncomfortably hot (more than 100 degrees Fahrenheit) during summer months.

ENTRANCE FEE: $6.00 per vehicle or $3.00 per person; good for seven days in the Rincon Mountain District. There is no entrance fee for the Tucson Mountain District.

FACILITIES: Modern rest rooms and drinking water are available at the visitor centers of both districts. Four picnic areas with tables, shelters, and rest rooms (but no water) are located in Tucson Mountain District. Two picnic areas are also located on Cactus Forest Drive in Rincon Mountain District. Other facilities can be found in nearby Tucson.

CAMPING: No developed campgrounds are in the park. Walk-in camps are in the Rincon Mountain District only, along backcountry trails. Permits are required. Tucson Mountain County Park, on the southern border of the Tucson Mountain District, has camping with electrical hookups.

SUNSET CRATER VOLCANO NATIONAL MONUMENT

6400 North Highway 89
Flagstaff, AZ 86004
(928) 526–0502
flag_information@nps.gov
www.nps.gov/sucr

Sunset Crater Volcano National Monument was created in 1930 to preserve 3,040 acres containing a magnificent volcanic cinder cone formed around A.D. 1064. The monument is 15 miles north of Flagstaff, Arizona, off U.S. 89 on FS 545. It is a convenient stop for motorists traveling from Flagstaff to or from the South Rim of Grand Canyon National Park (approximately two hours away). Wupatki National Monument is a short drive north of Sunset Crater.

North-central Arizona is covered with cinder cones, volcanic peaks, and lava flows representing about ten million years of volcanic activity. The eruptive phase that started in A.D. 1064–1065 resulted in the symmetrical cinder cone and black lava and cinder area of Sunset Crater. Lava, cinders, and ash were blown from a volcanic vent, creating a 1,000-foot-high cone-shaped volcano. Prevailing southwesterly winds caused most of the material to fall on the northeast side. As eruptions slackened, lava outpourings occurred from vents near the cinder cone's base. Later, hot springs and vapors seeped out from fumaroles near the vent. Minerals from these vapors stained the cinders and make the summit seem to glow with the hues of a perpetual sunset.

A visitor center is located along the 36-mile Sunset Crater–Wupatki Loop Road, 2 miles east of Highway 89. The visitor center hours vary during the year, with the longest hours (8:00 A.M. to 6:00 P.M.) in June, July, and August. The center contains exhibits, an audiovisual program, and other information concerning the monument and should be your initial stop. Rangers are on duty year-round (except Christmas) to answer questions. During summer months a variety of activities are available, including evening programs (in the campground) and guided walks.

Some excellent views of lava flows resulting from the eruption of Sunset Crater are a short distance east of the visitor center on the road to Wupatki National Monument. Approximately 1 1/2 miles east of the visitor center, be sure to stop and hike the self-guided Lava Flow Nature Trail, a short paved loop that offers views of dormant volcanoes and lava flows. A cinder trail off the main loop leads across some of the lava flow, around part of the volcano base, and alongside the opening to an ice cave. Trail guides are inside a metal box at the beginning of the paved loop trail.

Roads are kept open year-round, although the summer tourist season is most popular. Daytime temperatures during the summer are generally pleasant, and evenings can be quite cool because the monument is located at an elevation of 7,000 feet. July and August can also be quite damp.

ENTRANCE FEE: $5.00 per person; children ages sixteen and under are free. This fee also covers Wupatki National Monument.

FACILITIES: No facilities are available within the monument. Drinking water and modern rest rooms are located at the visitor center and the Lava Flow Trail parking area. Gas stations, motels, and food service are located along Highway 89 toward Flagstaff.

CAMPING: The USDA Forest Service Bonito Campground is open from May through mid-October and offers forty-four individual camping spaces across from the National Park Service visitor center. Pull-through sites are available, and the campground can handle motor homes and trailers of up to 41 feet. Each individual site has a grill, fire pit, and table. Water and flush toilets are available, but no dump station is at the campground. Sites at Bonito Campground are nicely spaced on a field of volcanic cinders, with scattered pine trees providing some shade. This is one of our favorite campgrounds. Three group sites are available by reservation only.

TONTO NATIONAL MONUMENT

HC102 Box 4602
Roosevelt, AZ 85545
(928) 467–2241
TONT_Superintendent@nps.gov
www.nps.gov/tont

Tonto National Monument comprises 1,120 acres. It was established in 1907 to preserve prehistoric cliff dwellings. The monument is located just off Arizona 88/188, 28 miles northwest of Globe. From Phoenix, take U.S. 60 east approximately 70 miles, and turn left on Arizona 88/188 toward Roosevelt.

The area occupied by Tonto National Monument was once the home of the Salado (Spanish for "salty") Indians. The newest archaeology in the area suggests that the earliest identifiable Salado sites date from approximately A.D. 1100. No one really knows for sure where the Salado came from, but by 1100 they were here. They lived in small villages along the river edges until the 1200s, when the population expanded to include the ridgetops. In the early 1300s, a move to caves commenced, and cliff dwellings built in natural caves remain preserved in the monument. The Upper Cliff Dwelling contains about forty rooms, and the Lower Cliff Dwelling has nineteen rooms. The villages are constructed of stone and mud, and some sections are two stories high. As was the case with most Pueblo cultures in the Southwest, the Salado abandoned the Tonto Basin around 1450. Where they went and why they left is uncertain.

The monument's visitor center, 1 mile from the park turnoff, is open from 8:00 A.M. to 5:00 P.M. daily. The building contains items made and used by the Salado. A ranger is on duty to answer visitors' questions. A self-guided trail to the Lower Cliff Dwelling that begins at the visitor center closes to uphill travel each day at 4:00 P.M. Along the trail, the hiker will see many of the same species of desert plants that were used by the Salado—barrel cactus, saguaro, jojoba, sotol, cholla, yucca, and others. The strenuous 3-mile, three-hour round-trip hike to the Upper Cliff Dwelling is by guided tour only. Advance reservations are required, and space is limited.

ENTRANCE FEE: $3.00 per person.

FACILITIES: Picnic facilities, drinking water, and modern rest rooms are available in the monument. Food and lodging are not provided in the park, but both can be found in Roosevelt, at Roosevelt Lake Resort, and in the Globe-Miami area.

CAMPING: No camping is permitted in the monument, but several campgrounds with modern rest rooms and dump stations are located along Highway 88 in Tonto National Forest.

TUMACÁCORI NATIONAL HISTORICAL PARK

1891 East Frontage Road
Tumacácori, AZ 85640-0067
(520) 398–2341
tuma_interpretation@nps.gov
www.nps.gov/tuma

Tumacácori National Historical Park comprises forty-seven acres and was initially established as a national monument in 1908 by order of President Theodore Roosevelt. Two additional units were added to the park in 1990, when its designation was changed to national historical park. Tumacácori NHP commemorates the introduction of European civilization into present-day Arizona with typical frontier mission churches that illustrate Spanish colonial endeavor. It also tells the story of the native people encountered by the Spanish. The historical park comprises three units, although only one unit is currently open to the public.

More than 500 years ago, Spain sent soldiers and missionary priests into Central America and Mexico to bring Christian civilization to the Indian tribes of the frontier areas. Missions established among friendly tribes served as both churches and centers of European culture. The churches at Los Santos Angeles de Guevavi, San Jose de Tumacácori, and San Cayetano de Calabasas were northern outposts of a mission chain constructed by Franciscan priests in the late 1700s on sites previously established by Jesuits in what was then the Mexican province of Sonora. The Jesuits had been expelled from all Spanish dominions in 1767.

After Mexico won independence from Spain in 1821, many frontier missions were abandoned because the new government was unable to provide a defense against hostile Indians. In addition, Mexican law tended to weaken the power of the church, and missions were required to become parish churches. In 1844 Mexico sold some of the Tumacácori mission lands to a private citizen. The mission community was abandoned in December 1848.

The park visitor center and museum (open from 8:00 A.M. to 5:00 P.M.) are next to the parking area. Exhibits in the museum depict early Indian and Spanish history. Craft demonstrations take place on weekends. A self-guided walk leads through the church, and a park employee is on duty to help visitors. In addition to the church, which still stands, a cemetery and unfinished mortuary chapel are just north of the church. A special two-day fiesta takes place on the first full weekend in December. Weather at the monument favors winter visits because of high summer temperatures.

ENTRANCE FEE: $3.00 per person; good for seven days.

FACILITIES: No food service or accommodations are available in the park. Both can be found in nearby communities. Drinking water and rest rooms are located at the visitor center, and picnic grounds are nearby.

CAMPING: No camping is permitted in the park, but private campgrounds are in close proximity on Interstate 19. Patagonia Lake State Park provides more than 200 camping sites (with flush toilets) 15 miles northeast of Nogales on Highway 82. Coronado National Forest, 13 miles off Interstate 19, approximately 18 miles north of Tumacácori, has campsites (pit toilets).

Tumacácori National Historical Park

TUZIGOOT NATIONAL MONUMENT

P.O. Box 219
Camp Verde, AZ 86322
(928) 567–5276
MOCA_Administration@nps.gov
www.nps.gov/tuzi

Tuzigoot National Monument is comprised of forty-three acres and was established in 1939 to protect a prehistoric Indian town built between A.D. 1000 and 1400. Tuzigoot is located in north-central Arizona, 55 miles south of Flagstaff via U.S. 89A (an exceptionally beautiful drive). The monument is approximately 25 miles off Interstate 17 connecting Flagstaff and Phoenix. See the area map under Montezuma Castle National Monument in this section.

The Verde Valley's first permanent settlers were the Hohokam Indians, a farming people who moved into this area around A.D. 600. The Hohokam, who used irrigation techniques to grow a variety of crops, were later joined by the Sinagua, who had inhabited and dry-farmed the foothills and the plateau beyond the valley. The Sinagua borrowed the agricultural techniques of the Hohokam and began constructing aboveground masonry dwellings that eventually evolved into large pueblos constructed on hilltops and cliffs. By the early 1400s, the Sinagua had abandoned the Verde Valley. In 1583, Spanish soldiers entered the valley and found the pueblos, which then lay undisturbed for nearly two centuries.

Tuzigoot is a remnant of a Sinaguan village that began as a small cluster of rooms inhabited by about fifty persons. More than a century later, the village population expanded as farmers surrendered the drought-parched land and moved to the irrigated valley.

The monument and visitor center are open daily from 8:00 A.M. to 5:00 P.M. in winter and from 8:00 A.M. to 7:00 P.M. in summer, with a ranger on duty. The visitor center contains exhibits, and a short self-guided trail to the ruins begins near the center.

ENTRANCE FEE: $3.00 per person; good for seven days. Children ages sixteen and under free.

FACILITIES: There are no accommodations or food service available in the monument. Both can be found 2 miles away in either Clarkdale or Cottonwood. Water and rest rooms are located at the visitor center.

CAMPING: No camping is permitted in the monument, but Dead Horse Ranch State Park (45 sites), with flush toilets, showers, hookups, and a dump station, is located north of nearby Cottonwood.

WALNUT CANYON NATIONAL MONUMENT

6400 North Highway 89
Flagstaff, AZ 86004
(928) 526–3367
flag_information@nps.gov
www.nps.gov/waca

Walnut Canyon is a 3,541-acre national monument established in 1915 to protect the remains of Sinagua Indian cliff dwellings that were constructed nearly 900 years ago. The park is located at the end of a 3-mile paved road that begins 7 1/2 miles east of Flagstaff on Interstate 40. (Take exit 204.)

Nearly 900 years ago the inhabitants of Walnut Canyon made their homes in the natural recesses of the limestone cliff faces. These creative people, who are known today as the *Sinagua* (Spanish for "without water"), existed in this relatively dry region through a combination of gathering, hunting, and farming. The Sinagua occupied the cliff dwellings at Walnut Canyon for approximately one hundred years before departing and building new villages a few miles to the southeast. Most historians believe the Sinagua were the ancestors of modern-day Puebloan Indians. The homes in Walnut Canyon remained relatively undisturbed until the late nineteenth century, when souvenir hunters arrived on the railroad.

The visitor center contains exhibits detailing the history of the Walnut Canyon area. Park employees are present to answer visitors' questions. A paved footpath at the rear of the center leads to Island Trail, which provides a close view of twenty-five cliff dwelling rooms and allows observation of many others across the canyon. Interpretive signs are located along the trail, which closes an hour before the park. The round-trip hike of slightly less than 1 mile is fairly strenuous and requires many steps while first descending and later ascending 200 feet in elevation (equivalent to an 18-story building). Also keep in mind that the visitor center is at 6,700 feet and that you will be breathing oxygen that is 20 percent thinner than at sea level. On the positive side, hiking the trail allows you to view the ruins up close, which is the main reason for visiting Walnut Canyon. The trail is generally wide enough so that you can stop and rest if you become winded. A second and much easier walk begins just outside the front of the visitor center. This ¾-mile paved trail winds along the rim and provides views of cliff dwellings across the canyon. The trail includes interpretive signs and is a very pleasant walk. A cutoff from this trail to the parking lot takes visitors past some surface ruins. Allow at least two hours to visit the museum, hike down to see the cliff dwellings, and walk the Rim Trail.

ENTRANCE FEE: $5.00 per person; good for seven days. Children ages sixteen and under free.

FACILITIES: No accommodations or food services are available in the monument, but full facilities are available a short distance away in Flagstaff. Water and modern rest rooms are located at the visitor center. A shaded picnic area is located near the parking lot. Three smaller picnic areas are on the entrance road. A Flagstaff visitor center is at 101 West Santa Fe Avenue. Call (928) 774–9541 or (800) 842–7293.

CAMPING: No camping is permitted in the monument, but a number of private facilities are found near Flagstaff, and Forest Service campgrounds are located to the south, near Lake Mary and Oak Creek Canyon. Another Forest Service campground (with flush toilets) is located at Sunset Crater Volcano National Monument, 15 miles north of Flagstaff and about 21 miles from Walnut Canyon. It is open from late spring through early fall. For additional information on camping, write Supervisor's Office, Coconino National Forest, 2323 Greenlaw Lane, Flagstaff, AZ 86004. Call (928) 527–3491.

WUPATKI NATIONAL MONUMENT

6400 North Highway 89
Flagstaff, AZ 86004
(928) 679–2365
flag_information@nps.gov
www.nps.gov/wupa

Wupatki National Monument comprises 35,000 acres. It was established in 1924 to preserve ruins of red sandstone pueblos built by farming Indians about A.D. 1100. The monument is located in north-central Arizona, approximately 35 miles north of Flagstaff via U.S. 89. It may also be reached by exiting U.S. 89 at Sunset Crater Volcano National Monument (15 miles north of Flagstaff) and driving over a good 35-mile paved loop road. See the map of both areas under Sunset Crater in this section.

After the eruptions of Sunset Crater Volcano to the south of Wupatki ceased about 900 years ago, the land was covered with black ash. The improved farmland drew farming Indians into the area, which became an Indian cultural frontier as word of the rich farmland spread.

Of the villages that were established in the area, one of the longest inhabited is now called *Wupatki*, the Hopi word for "long cut house." From its location near one of the region's few springs, Wupatki grew to three stories and contained one hundred rooms during the 1100s.

Near the pueblo are the remains of an open-air amphitheater and a stone-masonry ball court. By 1225, after a decade of drought, all the Indians had left the area, perhaps because continuous farming and winds had stripped the land of volcanic ash.

The visitor center, with books and exhibits of the area's cultures, is near the south entrance to the monument, 14 miles from U.S. 89 and 18 miles north of Sunset Crater Volcano National Monument. Self-guided trails to the Nalakihu-Citadel Pueblos and the Wupatki Pueblo begin from the main park road. Wupatki Pueblo is just behind the visitor center, and guidebooks are available for loan at the visitor center and the trailhead. Paved roads lead to pueblos at Wukoki and Lomaki. Wayside exhibits are on both the Citadel and Lomaki trails. With limited time you should at least stop at the visitor center, pick up a trail guide, and walk the trail to Wupatki Pueblo.

ENTRANCE FEE: $5.00 per person; children ages sixteen and under are free. The entry fee is good for both Wupatki and Sunset Crater Volcano National Monuments.

FACILITIES: Rest rooms and drinking water are available at the visitor center. Picnic areas are located about 5 miles north of the visitor center and on the road between Sunset Crater and Wupatki. All other facilities are available along U.S. 89 and in Flagstaff.

CAMPING: No camping is available at Wupatki. A USDA Forest Service campground (with modern rest rooms) is located near the visitor center at Sunset Crater Volcano National Monument. Contact the Peaks Ranger Station of the Coconino National Forest (928–526–0866) for more information.

ARKANSAS

STATE TOURIST INFORMATION

(800) 628–8725

www.arkansas.com

ARKANSAS POST NATIONAL MEMORIAL

1741 Old Post Road

Route 1, Box 16

Gillett, AR 72055

(870) 548–2207

ARPO_Historian@nps.gov

www.nps.gov/arpo

Arkansas Post comprises 389 acres that were incorporated into the National Park Service in 1960 to commemorate the site of the first permanent European settlement in the Lower Mississippi Valley. The site is located in eastern Arkansas on the banks of the Arkansas River between Gillett and Dumas. It is on Arkansas Highway 169, 7 miles south of Gillett via U.S. 165 (Great River Road) and about 20 miles northeast of Dumas via U.S. 165.

While the French were the first European settlers in this area beginning in 1686, Arkansas Post passed through a number of hands as a strategic military and commercial center on the frontier. The reason for its importance is its location near the confluence of the Arkansas and Mississippi Rivers. In 1763 France ceded Louisiana (which included the Arkansas Territory) to Spain following the British victory in the French and Indian War. The Spanish recognized the area's value in controlling British influence and Indian trade in the region. The Quapaw Indian tribe played an important role in the history of this area by offering trade and protection to the French and, later, the Spanish. The Quapaw were forced to leave their traditional homeland in 1824 by the U.S. government.

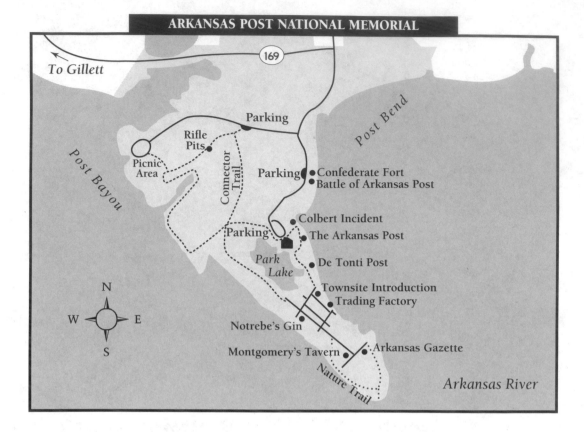

Following the American Revolution, frontiersmen moved into the Mississippi Valley and settled on the rich river-bottom land. In addition to provoking more Indian raids, this caused Spain to strengthen the post. In 1800 the Spanish ceded Louisiana back to France after Napoleon Bonaparte rose to power. Pressed for money, Napoleon sold Louisiana to the United States in 1803.

As the first capital of the territorial government for Arkansas, Arkansas Post became a typical frontier village. In 1821, however, the capital was moved to Little Rock, and Arkansas Post began its downhill slide. The area was temporarily revived when Confederate forces constructed a fort here during the Civil War.

Today this post, which has contained at least five different forts and settlements, has few visible remains. The national memorial has 2½ miles of paved trails that connect the town site, nature trail, and rifle pits; wayside exhibits along the way help interpret the post's history. An additional unpaved trail follows the edge of Post Bayou along a bluff bank. A visitor center is open daily (except Thanksgiving, Christmas, and New Year's Day) from 8:00 A.M. to 5:00 P.M. and offers exhibits and an audiovisual program to help explain the events that occurred here. Special programs and events are scheduled throughout the year. Check the Web site or call for information.

ENTRANCE FEE: No charge.

FACILITIES: No food or lodging is available in the park, but both can be found in nearby Gillett. Rest rooms with flush toilets are located in the visitor center and near the shaded picnic area, which has tables and grills. The visitor center, rest rooms, and picnic facilities are accessible to wheelchairs.

CAMPING: No camping is permitted in the park. The nearest camping facilities are at Pendleton Bend, 20 miles southwest of the park off Highway 165, and Merrisach Lake Park, 25 miles northwest of the park off Highway 44. Both facilities are operated by the U.S. Army Corps of Engineers.

FISHING: Fishing is permitted with an Arkansas license. Catches are best in spring and fall and include largemouth bass, channel catfish, bream, crappie, and shad. No boat launching is allowed at the park, but a ramp is available at Moore Bayou, a short distance outside the Arkansas Post entrance.

BUFFALO NATIONAL RIVER

402 North Walnut, Suite 136
Harrison, AR 72601
buff_information@nps.gov
(870) 741-5443
www.nps.gov/buff

The Buffalo National River, which winds 135 miles through 95,700 acres, was authorized as part of the National Park Service in 1972. It is one of the most scenic, unpolluted, and undeveloped free-flowing rivers remaining in the lower forty-eight states. The park is located in northwestern Arkansas in the Ozarks, across a three-county area. The nearest sizable community is Harrison, population 13,000, located 13 miles away.

Buffalo National River flows eastward through forested hill country dominated by oaks and hickories. Along its course, the river has cut through limestone and sandstone, leaving bluffs as tall as 400 feet. The area boasts a wide variety of fish, plants, and wildlife along the river, which drops from a level of 2,300 feet in the Boston Mountains to 400 feet at its confluence with the White River. A side canyon at Hemmed-In Hollow features a 204-foot waterfall, one of the highest between the Rockies and the southern Appalachians.

Information may be obtained at Tyler Bend Visitor Center, the park's main visitor center, at Buffalo Point Ranger Station, at Pruitt Ranger Station, and at park headquarters in Harrison. Centrally located in the park is Tyler Bend Visitor Center, where exhibits and auditorium programs help to tell the park story. Guided walks and campfire programs are offered at or near all three contact stations between Memorial Day and Labor Day. At Tyler Bend and Buffalo Point, interpretive programs about the history and flora and fauna of the area are presented daily throughout the summer, with more extensive program offerings on weekends. Interpretive programs at Buffalo Point are the most extensive in the park.

On the west side, several campgrounds offer spectacular scenery. These sites are extremely popular in spring, when higher water flows allow for canoeing in the area. The Tyler Bend campground has hiking trails, a boat launch, and swimming and picnic areas. On the east side, Buffalo Point is a popular destination area, with hiking trails, a canoe-launch area, swimming areas, a picnic area, and the most developed campground, including hookups and showers.

One of the most popular activities in the park is canoeing or floating the river. Visitors may enjoy anywhere from a half-day to a ten-day, 120-mile trip. Environments vary along the river, with wilderness-like areas between Carver and Woolum and Rush Landing to Buffalo City, and a developed setting around Buffalo Point. Fourteen concessionaires along the river rent canoes

Buffalo National River

and related items and provide shuttle services to various points along the river. A list of concessionaires may be obtained by writing to the park superintendent or visiting the park Web site at www.nps.gov/buff.

There are three congressionally designated wilderness areas within the park. Two of the three, the Ponca Wilderness and the Lower Buffalo Wilderness, have trails.

ENTRANCE FEE: No charge.

FACILITIES: Books and theme-related items may be purchased at all three contact stations and at park headquarters. The only food service or lodging provided in the park is at Buffalo Point. At Buffalo Point eight modern and five rustic concession-operated cottages are available for rent from March 1 to November 30. A restaurant, open Memorial Day through Labor Day, is also available. For information, write to Buffalo Point Concession, 2261 Highway 268 East, Yellville, AR 72687 (870–449–6206).

CAMPING: A total of thirteen campgrounds are scattered along the river. Most have flush toilets. All but Hasty, Mt. Hersey, Woolum, and Maumee have drinking water. The most developed campgrounds are Tyler Bend (38 spaces, 5 group camps) and Buffalo Point (103 spaces, 5 group camps), which offer tables, grills, a dump station, flush toilets, and showers. Buffalo Point also has electrical hookups. There is a camping fee at all campgrounds except Hasty, Mt. Hersey, Wollum, and Maumee South.

FISHING: Smallmouth and other varieties of bass, perch, suckers, and gar are the most common fish caught. An Arkansas fishing license is required. Keeper bass are limited to 14 inches, two per day. Hunting is permitted in the park, in accordance with Arkansas Game and Fish regulations.

CENTRAL HIGH SCHOOL NATIONAL HISTORIC SITE

2125 Daisy L. Gatson Bates Drive
Little Rock, AR 72202
(501) 374–1956
CHSC_Visitor_Center@nps.gov
www.nps.gov/chsc

Central High School National Historic Site was designated a unit of the National Park Service in 1998 to commemorate the site of one of the country's major battlegrounds for school desegregation. The historic site is located at the intersection of Daisy L. Gatson Bates Drive and Park Street in the city of Little Rock, Arkansas. From Interstate 630, exit south on either 3A or 2B, and turn on Fourteenth Street. From Fourteenth Street, turn south on Park Street.

The U.S. Supreme Court ruled in 1954 that segregation in public education was unconstitutional. By 1957 the city of Little Rock had desegregated its parks and public transportation, and its school board had voted in favor of a plan to begin desegregating the high school. The night prior to the opening of school on September 3, 1957, Arkansas Governor Orval Faubus ordered state National Guard personnel to surround the high school and prevent black students from entering. He justified use of the National Guard on the basis of protecting citizens and property from possible violence. A federal judge granted an injunction against using the National Guard, and the troops were withdrawn on September 20. After an unsuccessful attempt to have nine black students attend class on September 23, President Dwight Eisenhower federalized the National Guard on September 24, and the nine students entered the school the following day under the protection of 1,000 members of the U.S. Army.

The national historic site visitor center is in a restored Mobil service station across the street from Central High School. The visitor center is open from 8:00 A.M. to 4:00 P.M. Monday through Saturday, and from 1:00 P.M. to 4:00 P.M. on Sunday. It is closed Thanksgiving, Christmas, and New Year's Day. Visitors will find an interpretive exhibit about the 1957 class of Central High School. Park rangers are available to give tours of the visitor center exhibit, commemorative garden, and the exterior of Central High School. The high school, considered one of the country's most beautiful when it was built in 1927, is still in use.

ENTRANCE FEE: No charge.

FACILITIES: Rest rooms and drinking water are available in the visitor center. Food and lodging are nearby in Little Rock.

FORT SMITH NATIONAL HISTORIC SITE

P.O. Box 1406
Fort Smith, AR 72902-1406
(501) 783–3961
fosm_interpretation@nps.gov
www.nps.gov/fosm

Fort Smith National Historic Site embraces the remains of two frontier forts and the nineteenth-century federal court for the Western District of Arkansas. The site commemorates a significant phase of America's westward expansion and stands today as a reminder of eighty turbulent years in the history of federal Indian policy. The 35-acre park was established in 1961 and is located in downtown Fort Smith, along the Arkansas River. The parking lot is reached from U.S. 64 (Garrison Avenue) by turning south on Fourth Street, then west on Parker Avenue.

The first Fort Smith was established in 1817 to maintain peace between local Osage and emigrating Cherokee, many of whom had been forced to leave their lands in the southeastern United States—a relocation known as the Trail of Tears. Construction on the second fort commenced in 1838, twelve years after the first fort was abandoned. As the frontier continued to move westward, Fort Smith became an important supply depot for forts in Indian Territory and the Southwest. During the Civil War both Confederate and Union troops occupied the fort.

The U.S. Army closed the fort in 1871, and the next year the former soldiers' barracks was converted into a courtroom and jail for the Federal Court for the Western District of Arkansas. This court had criminal jurisdiction over western Arkansas and the vast Indian Territory, a haven for outlaws in the aftermath of the Civil War. The court, supported by U.S. deputy marshals, was the only buffer between this lawless element and the territory's peaceful citizens.

The man who presided over this court from 1875 to 1896 was Judge Isaac C. Parker, who possessed a sound legal background, total honesty and dedication to the job, and a sense of fair play toward the Indians. Parker heard more than 12,000 criminal cases during his twenty-one years on the bench. He sentenced 160 persons to hang, the penalty demanded by U.S. law for the capital offenses of rape and murder, and 79 were executed on the grounds. With the help of both dedicated lawmen and citizens, Parker began to bring order to Indian Territory. Gradually, as more settlers moved into the region, additional federal courts took over much of his jurisdiction. Parker died in 1896 and is buried in the Fort Smith National Cemetery.

The park completed a major restoration of the historic buildings and grounds in 2000. The visitor center, located in the historic barracks/courthouse/jail building, includes Judge Parker's restored courtroom, the "Hell on the Border" jail, a partial reconstruction of 1888 jail cells, and new exhibits and videos on military history, Native Americans, the Trail of Tears, the Federal Court's impact on Indian Territory, and U.S. deputy marshals and outlaws. The visitor center is open daily except Thanksgiving, Christmas, and New Year's Day. Visitors can also tour the reconstructed gallows, restored commissary building, and grounds of the two forts. A ½-mile paved walking trail follows the Arkansas River. An overlook has exhibits on the Trail of Tears. Ranger-led activities and demonstrations are regularly scheduled during summer months. A minimum of one hour is recommended to view the orientation film and examine exhibits in the visitor center. Three to four hours are recommended if you plan to walk the river trail and participate in interpretive programs.

ENTRANCE FEE: $6.00 per family or $3.00 per person; good for seven days. Children ages sixteen years and under are free.

FACILITIES: Food and lodging are available in the city of Fort Smith. Rest rooms and drinking water are available in the visitor center.

CAMPING: No camping is permitted at the site. A U.S. Army Corps of Engineers' campground with tables, grills, water, and flush toilets is on the Arkansas River, 2 miles north of Barling.

FISHING: Fishing in the Arkansas River is permitted with an Arkansas license.

HOT SPRINGS NATIONAL PARK

P.O. Box 1860
Hot Springs, AR 71902-1860
(501) 624–3383, ext. 640
(501) 624–2308 TDD
hosp_interpretation@nps.gov
www.nps.gov/hosp

Hot Springs National Park, which was designated a reservation in 1832 and added to the park system in 1916, comprises 5,500 acres. It is famous for the forty-seven hot springs that provide nearly a million gallons of water a day for thermal bathing. The park is located in central Arkansas, approximately 50 miles southwest of Little Rock via Interstate 30 and U.S. 70. It may also be reached on Arkansas Highway 7 and U.S. 270.

The hot springs of Arkansas were used by local Indians long before Europeans came into the region. Permanent settlement began after the United States purchased the Louisiana Territory from France in 1803. In 1832 the springs were made into a federal reservation.

The rainwater that soaks through fractured rocks northwest of the springs is heated as it comes into contact with hot rock deep beneath the earth's crust. Each day, approximately 850,000 gallons of water heated to 143 degrees Fahrenheit flow from the park's forty-seven springs. The water—which is colorless and entirely free of bad odors and taste—is collected, cooled, and piped to central reservoirs for bathhouse use. Two springs, accessible from Bathhouse Row or the Grand Promenade, are open for display to visitors, in addition to a larger display at the Tufa Terrace, where the flow of the upper springs built up a thick mineral deposit. The remainder of the springs have been covered to prevent contamination.

The park's visitor center, in the restored Fordyce Bathhouse, provides exhibits of the history and geology of the area and is open for touring. A seventeen-minute movie is presented in the auditorium. Nearby—on Reserve Avenue, Bathhouse Row, and the Grand Promenade—drinking fountains provide free thermal water. Water from natural cold-water springs is available on Fountain Street and on Whittington Avenue. During spring and fall scheduled activities that include guided walks are offered, and during the summer the list of interpretive activities is expanded.

Visitors may take baths, sit in a whirlpool, or have a massage at a number of bathhouses operated by concessioners and permittees in accordance with National Park Service regulations. A list of facilities and locations is available at the visitor center.

Numerous trails wander around the park's mountains and through its dense oak-hickory-pine forests. Many of these begin from the scenic paved road that climbs Hot Springs Mountain and North Mountain. Conducted walks and evening programs take place in the summer. The Hot Springs National Park Visitor Center is open year-round, except for Thanksgiving, Christmas, and New Year's Day.

ENTRANCE FEE: No charge.

FACILITIES: No food service or lodging is provided in the park, but nearly any type of facility can be found in the city of Hot Springs, which adjoins the park. Modern rest rooms are provided in the visitor center, on Bathhouse Row and the Grand Promenade, and at the campground.

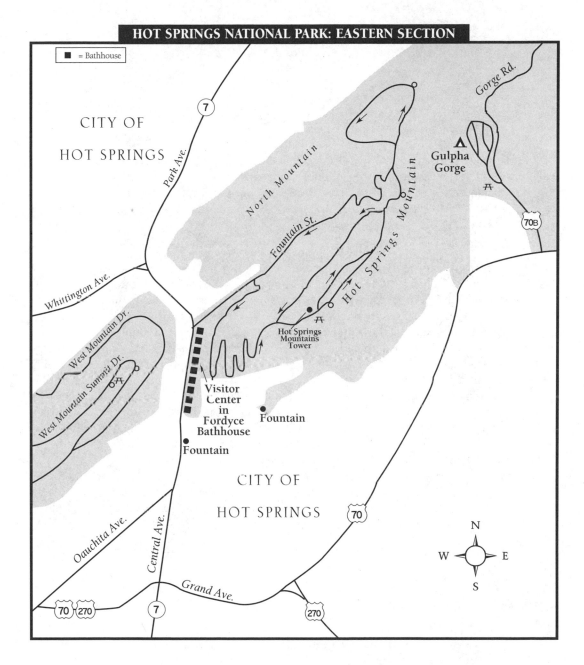

CAMPING: A single campground (forty-three spaces) is located at Gulpha Gorge in the northeast corner of the park. Although the sites are fairly close together, the campground is quite nice. Tables, pedestal grills, water, flush toilets, and a dump station are provided. The campground is open year-round.

FISHING: No fishing is available in the park, but nearby Lakes Catherine, Hamilton, and Ouachita provide good possibilities. Boats and sporting supplies are available at the lakes.

PEA RIDGE NATIONAL MILITARY PARK

P.O. Box 700
Pea Ridge, AR 72751
(501) 451–8122
PERI_Interpretation@nps.gov
www.nps.gov/peri

Pea Ridge National Military Park, which comprises 4,300 acres, was authorized in 1956 to memorialize the site of one of the major Civil War military battles that took place west of the Mississippi River. The park is located in northwestern Arkansas, 10 miles northeast of Rogers and 30 miles northeast of Fayetteville via U.S. Highway 62.

During the first year of the Civil War, a prime objective for both the Confederate and Union forces was control of Missouri. That was one of the reasons the battle of Pea Ridge was fought during a two-day period in March 1862. Late in the previous year, the new commander of federal forces in southwest Missouri initiated an aggressive policy of pushing pro-Confederate forces out of the state. Many of these men moved south near Fayetteville and joined a large force of Confederate soldiers. The combined group of 16,000 marched northward with an eventual goal of St. Louis. Between their position and St. Louis, the new federal commander stood with 10,500 soldiers at Pea Ridge.

The Confederate commander decided to circle the area and attack from the north. After two days of fighting, the Confederates ran short of ammunition while located near the Elkhorn Tavern and retreated eastward down the Old Huntsville Road. By noon the battle was ended with an overall Federal victory. Reported casualties were 203 Union troops and an estimated 250 Confederates killed. The state of Missouri was saved for the Union.

A visitor center near the park entrance contains exhibits to help visitors interpret the park. Personnel are on duty from 8:00 A.M. to 5:00 P.M. to answer questions. A terrace at the back of the building affords visitors a sweeping view of the battlefield. Near the visitor center is a short (7-mile) self-guided auto road to significant battlefield sites.

ENTRANCE FEE: $5.00 per vehicle or $3.00 per person; good for seven days. Children ages sixteen and under are free.

FACILITIES: No lodging or food service is available at the park, but both can be found in Rogers. Water and rest rooms are located in the visitor center. A picnic area with tables is located nearby.

CAMPING: No camping is permitted in the park, but public campgrounds are available at Beaver Reservoir, 20 miles away.

CALIFORNIA

STATE TOURIST INFORMATION
(800) 862–2543
www.gocalif.com

CABRILLO NATIONAL MONUMENT
1800 Cabrillo Memorial Drive
San Diego, CA 92106-3601
(619) 557–5450
(619) 222–8211 TTY
CABR_Administration@nps.gov
www.nps.gov/cabr

Cabrillo National Monument comprises 160 acres and was established in 1913 to commemorate Juan Rodriguez Cabrillo, the Portuguese explorer who in 1542 led a Spanish expedition of three ships up the west coast of what is now the United States. The monument is at the south end of Point Loma in the city of San Diego. It can be reached by driving south on Rosecrans Street to Canon Street, following Canon west to Catalina Boulevard, and driving south on Catalina to the end of Point Loma.

Juan Rodriguez Cabrillo, a Portuguese explorer and conquistador, arrived in the Americas by 1519. Active in various military actions in what is now Mexico, Guatemala, and San Salvador, Cabrillo was to become a wealthy landowner and shipbuilder. In 1542 the viceroy of New Spain gave Cabrillo command of three vessels and sent him north to explore the west coast of New Spain. The fleet set sail on June 27, 1542, and after exploring the west coast of what is now Baja California, Cabrillo and his ships landed on September 28 at a port he named San Miguel—today's San Diego. Cabrillo and his men remained here for six days while taking on supplies and trading with native people living around the bay. The ships left October 3 to continue their voyage north. On January 3, 1543, Cabrillo died of complications from an accident he is believed to have suffered during a visit to one of the Channel Islands. Despite Cabrillo's death, the ships continued on their journey and reached as far north as the northern coast of California or the Rogue River area of Oregon before turning around and returning to their home base in present-day Mexico. Although he didn't complete the epic journey, Cabrillo is considered a major figure in Spain's great era of exploration.

The monument is open daily from 9:00 A.M. to 5:15 P.M., with slightly longer hours during summer months. Your first stop should be at the visitor center, which offers films and an interactive exhibit about Juan Cabrillo. Rangers present talks and give demonstrations of sixteenth-century arms and armor. A short walk leads to the Old Point Loma Lighthouse, constructed in 1854 and abandoned in 1891 because the light was often obscured by fog and low clouds. The lighthouse has been restored to its 1880s appearance, when lightkeepers and their families lived here. Visitors are permitted inside the lighthouse, which contains period furnishings. A new lighthouse exhibit was completed in 2004. On clear days the lighthouse area offers terrific views of the Pacific Ocean, Mexico, and the harbor of San Diego. An exhibit about the history of Fort Rosecrans and the coastal defenses of Point Loma is in a nearby building that once housed an army radio station.

Self-guided Bayside Trail (2 miles round-trip), which begins near the lighthouse, winds through a coastal sage scrub forest, and offers views of the harbor and the city of San Diego. A little south of the lighthouse is the Whale Overlook, which offers a vantage point for views of the Pacific Ocean and the New Point Loma Lighthouse. From December through February, thousands of gray whales migrate from the Arctic Ocean to the lagoons of Baja California. Ten- to 15-foot spouts may be seen from the whale-watching station, where a recorded message explains the migration. A beautiful coastal area on the west side of Point Loma is accessible only

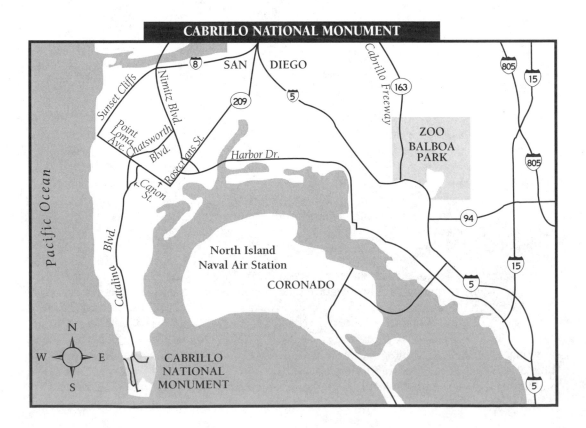

by car. Winter is the best time to visit the tide pools, which contain sea life such as sea anemones, crabs, and sea hares. The monument is a preferred destination for veteran bird-watchers, who search for migrant birds that stop here on their long journeys during the spring and fall.

ENTRANCE FEE: $5.00 per vehicle or $3.00 per person; good for seven days.

FACILITIES: No food or lodging is available at the monument, but both are located nearby. Water and modern rest rooms are provided at the visitor center. The monument's bookstore is also located at the visitor center.

CAMPING: No camping is permitted in the monument. Private campgrounds are on Mission Bay north of the monument and at Mission Trails Regional Park off California Highway 52.

FISHING: Surf fishing is allowed on the west side of the monument off Gatchell Road. A California fishing license is required, and bait must be brought to the monument. Only fin fish may be taken. Fishing is fair, with catches of bass, halibut, opaleye, and shark. A bit of scrambling is required to reach the shoreline. Extreme care is necessary because of unstable sandstone cliffs and slippery rocks.

CHANNEL ISLANDS NATIONAL PARK

1901 Spinnaker Drive
Ventura, CA 93001-4354
(805) 658–5730
chis_interpretation@nps.gov
www.nps.gov/chis

Channel Islands National Park was established in 1980 and comprises approximately 249,000 acres of land and water, with large rookeries of sea lions, nesting seabirds, and unique plants and animals. The park preserves a record of over 10,000 years of human use and occupation. The Channel Islands are from 10 to 70 miles off the coast of California, extending about 150 miles from the latitude of San Diego to that of Ventura. They are reached only by private boat or public transportation via boat or plane.

Millions of years ago, mountains rose from the sea and large areas along the continent cracked. Land masses rose above the ocean, then slowly sank back beneath the water. A great land mass along the western edge of North America eventually submerged, leaving only the mountaintops now known as the Channel Islands.

For many thousands of years, the islands were inhabited by the Chumash and other tribes of Indians. These people were skilled in making ornaments out of shells. They also built large seagoing canoes of planks lashed together with thongs and caulked with native asphalt. The ancient Indian burial and village sites on some of the Channel Islands possess considerable archaeological information covering the past 13,000 years.

Anacapa Island, at the eastern end of Santa Barbara Channel, is 11 miles from the mainland. It is actually a chain of three closely linked islets combining to a length of approximately 5 miles. Anacapa's rocky shoreline is highlighted by sheer cliffs, and the only beach not submerged at high tide is at Frenchy's Cove. Here, a day-use area is located near tide pools containing a variety of marine life. On East Anacapa Island are found the ranger station, the campground, nature trails, and a small visitor center—all within the setting of an old Coast Guard station. Neither Frenchy's Cove nor East Anacapa Island has docking facilities, and a small craft is required to go ashore. There is no safe anchorage at East Island, and public transportation is advised for those wishing to visit this portion of Anacapa.

Santa Barbara Island (630 acres), 42 miles off the coast, is surrounded by kelp beds abounding in marine life. The island is composed of rolling, grass-covered hills that are edged by high cliffs from the sea. Anchorage is rough, and landing in the rocky cove is hazardous. A National Park Service ranger is stationed throughout the year on both Anacapa and Santa Barbara Islands.

Santa Cruz, at ninety-six square miles, is the largest island in the park and is especially important for its diversity of habitat. The island contains two mountain ranges, a large central valley, deep canyons, tide pools, beautiful beaches, and one of the world's largest and deepest sea caves, Painted Cave. The National Park Service owns and manages the eastern 25 percent of Santa Cruz; the western 75 percent is owned and managed by The Nature Conservancy. A permit (fee charged) that is required to land on The Nature Conservancy's property can be obtained by contacting the Santa Cruz Island Preserve, P.O. Box 23259, Santa Barbara, CA 93121; (805) 664–7839. The National Park Service portion of the island is accessible by boat without a permit. There are no buoys available to the general public at any of the landing areas, but a small pier is available at Scorpion Harbor, where you will find a ranger station, rest rooms, a campground, and an easy 1/2-mile trail leading to the historic Scorpion Ranch complex. Other more difficult trails also start near Scorpion Harbor. Campgrounds and rest rooms are available in Scorpion Canyon, and rest rooms are at Prisoners Harbor. This is a great island for hiking, swimming, camping, snorkeling, diving, kayaking, and bird-watching.

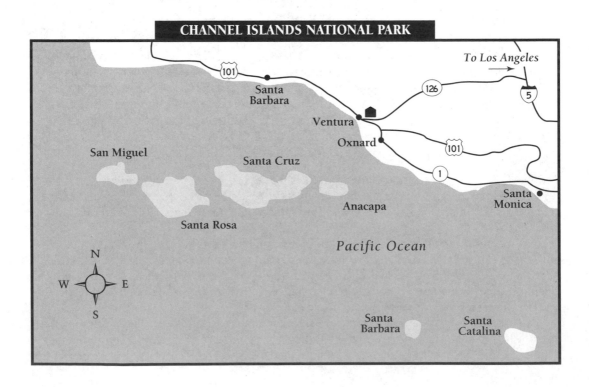

CHANNEL ISLANDS NATIONAL PARK

Santa Rosa is the park's second largest island and exhibits a variety of natural features, including cliffs, high mountains, fossil beds, grasslands, rolling hills, beaches, and a marsh. Harbor seals breed on the island's beaches. No permit is required for landing at Bechers Bay or Johnson's Lee (day-use only).

San Miguel has outstanding natural and cultural features, including the best examples of caliche (a mineral sand casting). The island hosts large numbers and varieties of seals and sea lions, and the island's largest mammal, the island fox, can be seen here. San Miguel has more than 500 relatively undisturbed archaeological sites, some dating back thousands of years. Visitors may land on the beach at Cuyler Harbor without a permit for day-use only. Contact park headquarters for information on guided hikes.

The park's main visitor center is at the harbor in the town of Ventura. From U.S. Highway 101, exit on Victoria Drive (northbound) or Harbor Boulevard (southbound). Turn east on Olivas Park Drive from Victoria or Spinnaker Drive from Harbor Boulevard. The visitor center is open daily (closed Thanksgiving and Christmas) from 8:30 A.M. to 5:00 P.M. It has an observation deck, artificial tide pool with marine aquatic life, exhibits, a twenty-three-minute video about the islands, and a bookstore. A small visitor center at the harbor museum building in Santa Barbara offers exhibits and an observation area but is staffed by volunteers and open intermittently.

Public transportation to the Channel Islands is available by boat and plane. Boat transportation to all five islands from Ventura is offered by Island Packers. The same company also offers departures from Channel Islands Harbor in Oxnard (805–642–1393; ipco@isle.net; www.islandpackers.com). Boat transportation from Santa Barbara is offered by Truth Aquatics (805–962–1127 or 805–963–3564; taqua@tx.netcom.com; www.truthaquatics.com). Both companies offer a variety of island tours. Channel Islands Aviation offers air transportation to Santa Rosa Island from Camarillo and Santa Barbara (805–987–1301; cia@flycia.com; www.flycia.com). Round-trip boat transportation ranges from $35 to $65 per person, depending on destination. Campers are generally charged extra. Day trips by plane cost a little over $100 per person.

ENTRANCE FEE: No charge.

FACILITIES: No accommodations, concessioner facilities, fuel, or other services are available on the islands managed by the National Park Service. Pit toilets, but no drinking water, are located at the primitive campgrounds on Anacapa, Santa Barbara, and San Miguel Islands. Santa Rosa and Santa Cruz Islands have water available in the campgrounds.

CAMPING: Five established campgrounds, one each on Anacapa, Santa Barbara, Santa Cruz, San Miguel, and Santa Rosa Islands, offer pit toilets and picnic tables. These campgrounds are very primitive and, with the exception of Santa Cruz, offer no trees or shade. High winds are not uncommon. No campfires are permitted except on eastern Santa Cruz. Reservations required (800–365–2267; reservations.nps.gov), and transportation to the island must be secured before camping reservations can be made. Campers need to take camping gear, food, water, cooking equipment, and fuel for cooking. (Santa Rosa and Santa Cruz Islands have water available in the campgrounds.) Gear must be packed well, as it may get wet during loading or off-loading, and it must be carried some distance to the campground. Campers must pack out their own trash.

FISHING: Fishing is permitted in accordance with California regulations, unless further restricted by federal law. Sea bass, barracuda, bonito, and yellowtail are among the varieties of fish living in the surrounding Pacific waters.

DEATH VALLEY NATIONAL PARK

P.O. Box 579
Death Valley, CA 92328-0579
(760) 786-3200
DEVA_Superintendent@nps.gov
www.nps.gov/deva

Death Valley National Park, which comprises 3.3 million acres, was established as a national monument in 1933 to preserve a large desert containing the lowest point in the Western Hemisphere. The major part of the park is located in southeastern California, with the remaining portion in southern Nevada. Four paved roads enter the park from the east, and two enter from the west. The major road through the park is California Highway 190. The visitor center is approximately 120 miles from Las Vegas, Nevada.

Death Valley is a special place. The harsh environment, with an average annual rainfall of less than 2 inches, requires hardy varieties of plants, animals, and humans. Most life revolves around permanent water sources such as springs. Higher elevations have cooler temperatures and more moisture, resulting in a greater variety of plants and animals. In spite of hordes of prospectors seeking precious metals over the years, most humans have been unable to establish much of a life in this area, with the exception of the Timbisha Shoshone people, who have lived in Death Valley for thousands of years.

The focal point of the park is the Furnace Creek Visitor Center. Here visitors may view exhibits and obtain information on self-guided trails. An illustrated slide program is available, and ranger-conducted programs are scheduled daily during winter months. Activity schedules are posted.

Seeing the park requires a considerable amount of driving. Some of the more interesting places (with numbers keyed to the map) are:

1. Scotty's Castle, a desert mansion built by Albert Johnson and enjoyed by Death Valley Scotty (the area's most famous resident). A fifty-minute tour of the castle is provided frequently during the day.

2. Ubehebe Crater, 1/2 mile across and 500 feet deep.

3. Titus Canyon, with colorful mountains, a ghost town, petroglyphs, and deep narrows. This is located on a one-way, high-clearance road.

4. The ruins of Rhyolite, an old mining town, a short distance outside the park boundary.

5. Sand dunes that are the easiest to visit (on the main road) in the park.

6. Keane Wonder Mine, an old mine site dating to the early 1900s.

7. Mosaic Canyon, a small canyon containing interesting rock foundations.

8. The site of Skidoo, an old mining town. (High-clearance vehicles are recommended for the dirt road.)

9. Aguereberry Point, provides a grand view of the valley and mountains. (High-clearance vehicles are recommended for the dirt road.)

10. Charcoal Kilns built in 1877 for fuel for Hearst's silver-lead smelters.

11. Harmony Borax Works, an old borax-processing plant.

12. Zabriskie Point, which presents a view of colorful and dramatically eroded hills.

13. Dantes View, which provides views of the Panamint Range and the western hemisphere's lowest point.

14. Badwater, which at 280 feet below sea level, is the lowest point to which a motorist can drive in the Western Hemisphere.

15. Father Crowley Point, which overlooks the colorful depths of Rainbow Canyon and northern Panamint Valley.

ENTRANCE FEE: $10.00 per vehicle or $5.00 per person; good for seven days. An $8.00 fee is charged to tour Scotty's Castle.

FACILITIES: Furnace Creek Inn and Ranch Resort provides rooms, food service, a store, service station, and swimming year-round. Horseback riding is available from early November through Easter. The inn is an unusual and wonderful (and expensive) hotel, while the ranch is composed of motel-type accommodations. For information or reservations, write Furnace Creek Inn and Ranch Resort, P.O. Box 1, Death Valley, CA 92328. Call (800) 236–7916 or visit their Web site, www.furnacecreekresort.com. Stovepipe Wells Village has motel rooms, food, a store, service station, and swimming pool available year-round. For information or reservations, write Stovepipe Wells Village, Death Valley, CA 92328. Call (760) 786–2387, or visit the Furnace Creek Resort Web site. Scotty's Castle offers food service, gasoline, and souvenirs, but not lodging. Panamint Springs Resort on the western edge of the park provides motel-type rooms and meals. Write P.O. Box 395, Ridgecrest, CA 93556, for information and reservations. Call (775) 482–7680, or visit their Web site, www.deathvalley.com.

CAMPING: Nine NPS-operated campgrounds are located within the park. Furnace Creek (136 spaces), Mesquite Spring (30 spaces), and Texas Spring (92 spaces, October–April) each offer tables, grills, water, flush toilets, and a dump station. Campsites at Furnace Creek and two group campsites may be reserved. Call (800) 365–2267, or visit the Web site, reservations.nps.gov. Emigrant (10 sites, tent only), Sunset (1,000 sites, October–April), and Stovepipe Wells (200 sites, October–April) offer water and flush toilets. Wildrose (thirty sites) offers tables, grills, and pit toilets. Thorndike (ten sites) and Mahogany Flat (ten sites) are open from March to November and offer tables, grills, and pit toilets. The roads to these last three are not passable for trailers, campers, or motor homes. Private or concession-operated campgrounds are at Stovepipe Wells and Panamint Springs.

DEVILS POSTPILE NATIONAL MONUMENT

P.O. Box 3999
Mammoth Lakes, CA 93546
(760) 934–2289
DEPO_Superintendent@nps.gov
www.nps.gov/depo

Devils Postpile National Monument (opposite page)

Devils Postpile National Monument is nearly 800 acres in size and was established in 1911 to preserve two natural features: the formation of columnar basalt known as Devils Postpile and 101-foot Rainbow Falls. The monument is located on the east side of the Sierra in east-central California. From Bishop, drive 39 miles north to the junction of U.S. 395 and S.R. 203, then west 17 miles on S.R. 203. A shuttle bus (fee charged) operates over the last 8 miles of the narrow mountain road that connects Minaret Summit with the monument. Day-use visitors are required to use the shuttle bus from early morning to early evening.

Less than 100,000 years ago, basalt lava, which was to become Devils Postpile, erupted in the already-glaciated valley of the Middle Fork San Joaquin River. The cooling lava cracked horizontally and vertically in a specialized way, forming the columns. About 10,000 years ago a glacier flowed through the area and overrode the solidified lava. The moving ice removed much of the fractured lava mass, leaving the more-resistant parts, such as Devils Postpile. The glacier also quarried away one side of the Postpile, exposing a sheer wall of columns 40 to 60 feet high.

The monument closes mid- to late October, due to snow, and reopens sometime in June, depending on the snow removal. Access to the monument is by shuttle bus (fee) from opening day to late September. A ranger station by the parking area and shuttle stop has booklets about the monument. A short, steep hike along a well-used trail leads visitors to the top surface of the Postpile. Here the columns have been worn level and polished by the grinding of the glacier. Exposed cross sections of the three- to seven-sided columns have the appearance of a mosaic.

Devils Postpile National Monument has numerous short trails and is one of the key points on the 211-mile John Muir Trail, which stretches between Yosemite and Sequoia/Kings Canyon National Parks. The Pacific Crest Trail passes through the monument en route from Mexico to Canada. Two miles down the river trail from the Postpile, Rainbow Falls makes a drop of 101 feet into a deep green pool. During the middle of the day, a rainbow forms to add to the beauty. A short, steep trail leads to the bottom of the falls, where a garden of trees, flowers, and grasses is found. A bubbling hot spring at Reds Meadow is evidence of regional volcanic activity.

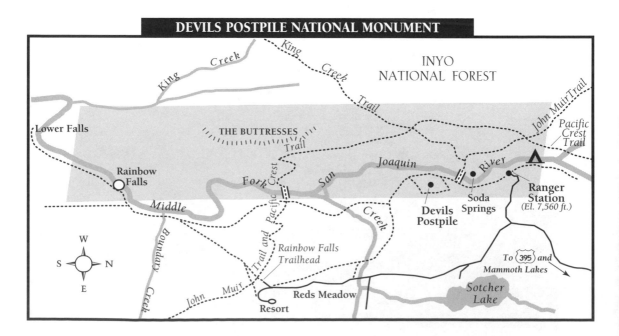

DEVILS POSTPILE NATIONAL MONUMENT

The shuttle bus stops at a number of locations in addition to the Postpile, including Reds Meadow and Sotcher Lake. Visitors are free to ride the shuttle as much as they desire so long as they don't leave the valley. The narrow access road combined with the valley's traffic congestion make the shuttle an excellent way to see the monument and the surrounding scenery.

ENTRANCE FEE: No charge. Inyo National Forest charges an access fee for shuttle bus users and overnight campers.

FACILITIES: Outside monument boundaries, about 2 miles from the campground, are the Reds Meadow Resort and Store, where groceries, meals, cabins, a telephone, and saddle and pack horses are available. Water and flush toilets are provided at the monument's campground. Full services are available 13 miles away in the town of Mammoth.

CAMPING: A campground (twenty-one sites) with tables and flush toilets is open from mid-June to October 15. Campers may ride the shuttle to Reds Meadow for supplies or meals. A number of USDA Forest Service campgrounds are located outside the monument in Inyo National Forest. Additional Forest Service campgrounds are located at Mammoth Lakes.

FISHING: The Middle Fork San Joaquin River contains rainbow, brook, and brown trout. Fishing is only a short walk from the campground and from several of the shuttle stops. A California license is required for persons over sixteen years of age.

EUGENE O'NEILL NATIONAL HISTORIC SITE

P.O. Box 280
Danville, CA 94526-0280
(925) 838-0249
EUON_interpretation@nps.gov
www.nps.gov/euon

Eugene O'Neill National Historic Site was established in 1976 to commemorate the contribution of America's only Nobel Prize–winning playwright to literature and drama. The park is located in Danville, California, 30 miles east of San Francisco. Visits are by reservation only and include a guided tour.

Nestled in the Corduroy Hills above the San Ramon Valley is an unusual house of Chinese and California Monterey–style architecture. The site at one time provided playwright Eugene O'Neill with a sanctuary in which to create masterpieces of American drama.

Built in 1937, the home today serves as a memorial to O'Neill's contribution to our country's vast cultural heritage. Named Tao House (referring to the Chinese philosophy) by O'Neill and his wife, Carlotta, it served as their home for six years. While residing at Tao House, Eugene O'Neill completed the last five plays of his successful career, including his best-known work, *Long Day's Journey into Night*.

Free visits to the site, scheduled Wednesday through Sunday at 10:00 A.M. and 12:30 P.M., include a free shuttle to the site and a guided tour. Reservations are required, and the Park Service recommends making reservations about two weeks prior to the desired date (925–838–0249). The ninety-minute tours allow visitors a glimpse into the personal and professional life of an internationally famous playwright. The tour of Tao House focuses on O'Neill's work and life. A visitor center provides displays, and a self-guided grounds tour is available. Comfortable walking shoes are recommended. On-site plays are performed in the spring and fall.

ENTRANCE FEE: No charge.

FACILITIES: No overnight accommodations are available within the park, but food and lodging are available in nearby communities. Rest rooms and drinking water are available in the visitor center.

CAMPING: No camping is permitted at the site.

FORT POINT NATIONAL HISTORIC SITE

P.O. Box 29333
Presidio of San Francisco, CA 94129
(415) 556–1693
goga_wr_information@nps.gov
www.nps.gov/fopo

Fort Point National Historic Site comprises twenty-nine acres and was established as a national historic site in 1970 to preserve a classic brick-and-granite mid-nineteenth-century coastal fortification. The fort sits just under the south end of the Golden Gate Bridge. From U.S. 101 going south, take the Twenty-fifth Avenue exit at the tollgate. Northbound on 101, take the exit marked VIEW AREA, PRESIDIO, GOLDEN GATE NRA. From there, turn right to Lincoln, go left on Lincoln, and turn left again at Long Avenue.

San Francisco became a major West Coast harbor after the discovery of gold at Sutter's Mill, California, in 1849. Following California's statehood the next year, the U.S. Army decided to protect the bay by building fortifications at Alcatraz, Fort Mason, and Fort Point. Construction of Fort Point commenced in 1853 and continued until the first cannons were mounted in 1861. The three-story brick structure, with walls 5 to 12 feet thick, was designed for 600 soldiers and 126 cannons. Although the fort was manned during the Civil War, no attacks materialized.

While Fort Point's effectiveness against attack was never tested, similar forts on the East Coast suffered considerable damage during the Civil War, as their masonry walls proved unable to withstand rifled artillery. The U.S. Army never again continuously occupied the fort after troops were moved out in 1886. From 1933 to 1937 the fort was used as a base of operations during the building of the Golden Gate Bridge. Initial plans for construction of the bridge called for the fort's removal, but the chief engineer redesigned the bridge to save the fort that he called "a fine example of the mason's art." During World War II Fort Point housed soldiers from the Sixth U.S. Coast Artillery, who guarded minefields and the antisubmarine net that spanned the Golden Gate.

The fort houses a visitor center and exhibits. Park personnel present historical demonstrations such as cannon loading and conduct half-hour guided tours of the fort throughout the day. Visitors may also take a self-guided tour. For guided tours and information, contact the information center in the fort (415–556–1693). Fort Point NHS is open Friday, Saturday, and Sunday, 10:00 A.M. to 5:00 P.M.

ENTRANCE FEE: No charge.

FACILITIES: A drinking fountain is located just outside the fort, and pit toilets are located approximately 150 yards from the fort. Modern toilet facilities are available 800 yards east of the fort, near the Administrative Office.

CAMPING: No camping is permitted at Fort Point National Historic Site. Campsites are at Marin Headlands (hike-in only) and China Camp in San Rafael.

FISHING: Fishing is permitted from the seawall surrounding Fort Point. Catches include perch, flounder, and an occasional bass. A California fishing license is required to fish from the seawall but not from the nearby pier.

GOLDEN GATE NATIONAL RECREATION AREA

Fort Mason, Building 201
San Francisco, CA 94123-1308
(415) 561–4700
goga_wr_information@nps.gov
www.nps.gov/goga

Golden Gate National Recreation Area was established in 1972 and comprises a beautiful and diverse area with 75,500 acres of beaches, redwood forests, lagoons, marshes, and historical places of interest. The park is located along the western and northern perimeters of the city of San Francisco, as well as south of the Golden Gate Bridge in San Mateo County and north of the bridge in Marin County.

Golden Gate National Recreation Area is a spectacularly beautiful park that comprises numerous individual areas. The park headquarters in Building 201 of Fort Mason in north San Francisco is a must stop for anyone intending to explore the park or sightsee in the city, and it is open from 9:30 A.M. to 4:30 P.M. on weekdays. Picnic tables and fishing piers are available here for relaxation. A wide variety of programs are scheduled on a regular basis throughout the national recreation area. A quarterly schedule of programs is available at the visitor centers.

Transportation around the San Francisco section is available on the Municipal Railway (MUNI) system (415–673–MUNI), and access to areas across the Golden Gate is provided by Golden Gate Transportation (415–332–6600). Ferries from San Francisco Pier 41 provide access to Alcatraz (415–705–5555) and Angel Island (415–435–5390).

Because of the great diversity within Golden Gate National Recreation Area, it is not possible to cover each area and every activity available to visitors. Two of the more popular areas of the park follow.

SAN FRANCISCO AREA

Alcatraz: A 1½-mile guided tour of this former prison takes approximately two hours. A Blue and Gold ferry leaves from Pier 41 at Fisherman's Wharf approximately every forty-five minutes beginning at 9:30 A.M. Call (415) 705–5555 for reservations. Call (415) 561–4926 for program information.

Baker Beach: A sandy shore area that is popular for fishing, picnicking, hiking, and sunbathing. Includes a 1904 battery with an operational disappearing gun (415–561–4323).

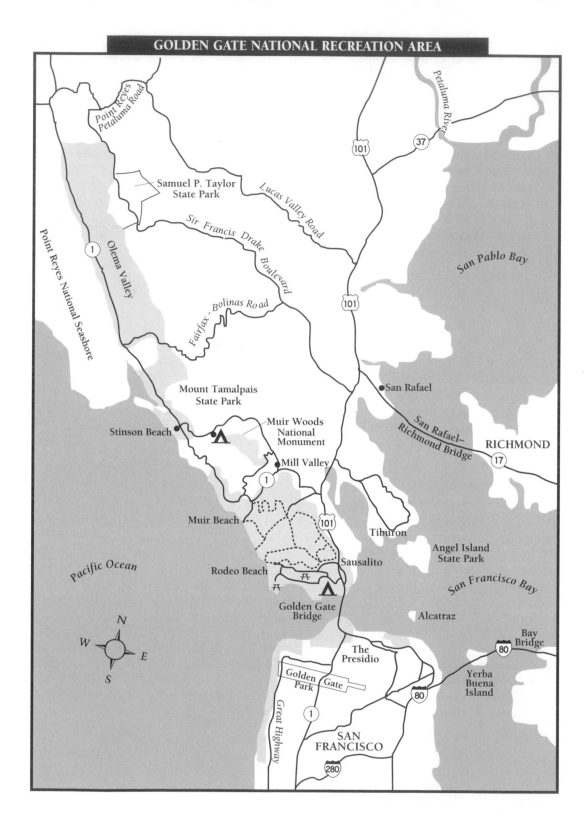

GOLDEN GATE NATIONAL RECREATION AREA

Point Reyes Petaluma Road

Petaluma River

101

37

Samuel P. Taylor State Park

Lucas Valley Road

Sir Francis Drake Boulevard

101

San Pablo Bay

Point Reyes National Seashore

1

Olema Valley

Fairfax - Bolinas Road

San Rafael

San Rafael–Richmond Bridge

RICHMOND

17

Mount Tamalpais State Park

Muir Woods National Monument

Stinson Beach

Mill Valley

1

Muir Beach

101

Pacific Ocean

Tiburon

Angel Island State Park

Rodeo Beach

Sausalito

San Francisco Bay

Golden Gate Bridge

Alcatraz

N
W   E
S

The Presidio

Bay Bridge

80

Golden Gate Park

Yerba Buena Island

80

Great Highway

1

SAN FRANCISCO

280

China Beach: A small beach nestled in a protective cove where late-nineteenth-century Chinese fishermen anchored their boats and camped on the shore. Includes a picnic area with grills (415–556–8642).

Cliff House: A popular Victorian-era resort complex that was constructed in 1909 to replace two earlier structures. Excellent viewpoints of the coast are available, with offshore Seal Rocks serving as home for sea lions and marine birds (415–556–8642).

Crissy Field: Part of the Presidio, it provides a quiet stretch of shoreline for hiking, fishing, or picnicking. A spectacular shoreline park includes restored wetlands, recreational facilities, and a historic military airfield (415–561–4323).

Fort Funston: A loop trail with picnic areas provides vistas of coastal scenery. Hang gliders often use the cliffs and strong winds (415–239–2366).

Fort Mason: A former U.S. Army post dating back to the Civil War that now houses Golden Gate National Recreation Area's headquarters and a visitor center. The Fort Mason Center includes galleries, performing arts spaces, exhibit areas, shops, and restaurants (415–561–2700).

Fort Point: See the separate listing for Fort Point National Historic Site.

Land's End: A part of the park famous for its great ocean views. Eagles Point overlook has excellent views of the entrance to the Golden Gate. Shipwrecks are visible during low tide (415–556–8642).

The Presidio: One of the country's best-known military establishments, transferred to the National Park Service in 1994. Visitors can experience more than 200 years of history by taking a 1-mile walk around the Presidio's main post. A map and guidebook are available in the temporary Presidio Visitor Center in the Officers' Club at 50 Moraga Avenue. The visitor center is open daily from 9:00 A.M. to 5:00 P.M. (415–561–4323).

NORTH OF THE GOLDEN GATE

Angel Island: A state park with picnicking, hiking, and beautiful scenery (415–435–1915).

Marin Headlands: Wind-swept ridges, beaches, and protected valleys that offer a major change from San Francisco's urban setting (415–331–1540).

Mount Tampalpais: A recreational area with hiking trails that lead through redwood forests, grasslands, and wildflower meadows in spring. Includes picnic areas, a campground, and seasonal lodging and food service. Administered by Mount Tampalais State Park (415–388–2070).

Muir Beach: A sheltered cove that offers opportunities for hiking and viewing the coastal scenery. Dangerous swimming conditions (415–388–2595).

Muir Woods: See the separate California listing for Muir Woods National Monument.

Stinson Beach: A 3-mile sandy beach that offers various types of water recreation (415–868–0942).

Tennessee Valley: A narrow, secluded valley that is popular with hikers, cyclists, and horseback riders. Includes a 1.7-mile trail that meanders through hills and past a quiet lagoon to a remote black-sand beach. Low tide provides a view of an 1853 shipwreck (415–331–1540).

ENTRANCE FEE: All areas are free with the exception of Muir Woods ($3.00 per person) and the ferry to Alcatraz Island.

FACILITIES: Lodging is available in San Francisco and surrounding communities. Food can be found at numerous locations near the park. Hostels are located at Fort Mason and Fort Barry.

CAMPING: Backcountry camping is available in the Marin Headlands (415–331–1540), and campgrounds are at Mount Tamalpais State Park (415–388–2070). There are private campgrounds located along State Route 1. For additional information, see the camping section under Point Reyes National Seashore.

FISHING: Surf fishing is possible at two piers and numerous locations along the beaches.

JOHN MUIR NATIONAL HISTORIC SITE

4202 Alhambra Avenue
Martinez, CA 94553-3883
(925) 228–8860
JOMU_Interpretation@nps.gov
www.nps.gov/jomu

John Muir National Historic Site was established in 1964 to preserve the home of John Muir and to commemorate his contributions to conservation and literature. The park is located in Martinez, California, approximately 25 miles northeast of Oakland.

John Muir immigrated to the United States from Scotland in 1849, when he was eleven years old. After living in Wisconsin and acquiring an interest in both mechanics and biology, he started on his now-famous walks in 1867. Over the years his treks took him through much of the American wilderness, as well as to Alaska, South America, Africa, India, the Orient, and Australia. His special place of interest was the Sierra Nevada.

Muir began writing in the 1870s and continued until his death in 1914. A great deal of the writing was undertaken at the house that is preserved at the site where Muir lived from 1890 until 1914. Muir had resolved to do what he could to make the wilderness better loved and preserved for future generations. He was an important influence in President Theodore Roosevelt's decisions to add 148 million acres of forests, twenty-three national monuments, and five national parks to our nation's forest and park system.

The National Park Service has restored the buildings and grounds to their appearance at the time John Muir lived here. The site is open Wednesday through Sunday, from 10:00 A.M. to 5:00 P.M., except on Thanksgiving, Christmas, and New Year's Day. Park Service personnel are available to provide information, and a movie dealing with Muir's life is presented six times daily in the visitor center. Guided tours of the house are offered daily at 2:00 P.M. Guided tours for groups are offered by reservation only. Tours at other times are self-guided, and a booklet is available in the visitor center.

ENTRANCE FEE: $3.00 per person; good for seven days. Children ages sixteen and under are free.

FACILITIES: No facilities other than a small picnic area and bookstore are available at the site, but food and lodging can be found nearby. Drinking water and rest rooms are provided in the visitor center. A picnic area is located at Nancy Boyd Park, south of the historic site on Pleasant Hill Road.

CAMPING: No camping is permitted at the site, and no campgrounds are in the immediate vicinity.

JOSHUA TREE NATIONAL PARK

74485 National Park Drive
Twentynine Palms, CA 92277-3597
(760) 367–5500
jotr_information@nps.gov
www.nps.gov/jotr

Joshua Tree is a 794,000-acre national park that was established to preserve a section of California desert containing a notable variety of rich vegetation. The park is 140 miles east of Los Angeles. From the west it is approached via Interstate 10 to a point 15 miles east of Banning, where Highway 62 to Joshua Tree and Twentynine Palms fronts the north entrances. The south entrance is 35 miles east of Indio via Interstate 10.

At Joshua Tree National Park, two desert ecosystems determined by different elevations converge. Desert plants in both systems have to be able to adapt to survive in a harsh environment. They must be able to go for prolonged periods without water, yet be able to absorb large amounts of moisture during brief rainstorms. Some plants spread roots close to the surface, while others have roots growing deep into the earth.

One of the park's features is the Joshua tree. It grows to heights of 40 feet and during March and April bears white blossoms in clusters 8 to 14 inches long. The tree is usually found at elevations above 3,000 feet in the central part of the park.

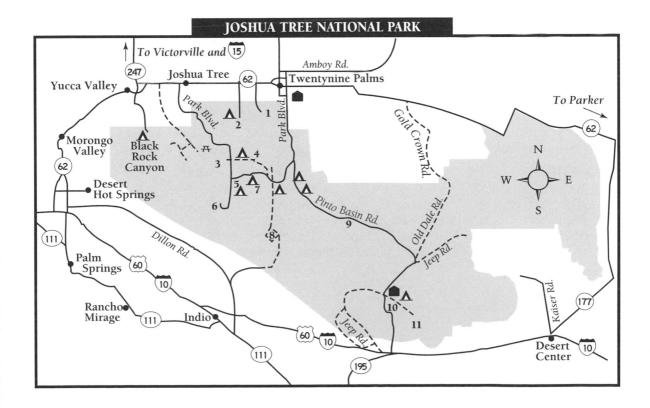

The visitor will find five oases of California fan palms within the park. The largest, in Lost Palms Canyon, contains more than one hundred palms. It is 4 miles by trail from the visitor center at Cottonwood Spring. The oasis at Fortynine Palms Canyon, just inside the northern boundary, is reached by a 1½-mile trail (one way).

The main visitor center is just outside the north entrance, near Twentynine Palms. Exhibits and a self-guided nature trail are located here. A visitor center is also located at Cottonwood Spring. Other points of interest (keyed with numbers corresponding to those found on the map) are:

1. A moderately strenuous trail (3 miles round-trip) to Fortynine Palms Oasis, where water-loving plants thrive.

2. A ½-mile loop Hidden Valley Nature Trail, accessible from Indian Cove Campground.

3. A trail system that winds between massive boulders and leads through a legendary cattle rustler's hideout.

4. Barker Dam, which forms a small reservoir. At one time the dam provided water for cattle and for mining use.

5. Lost Horse Mine, accessible via trail (4 miles round-trip).

6. Keys View, at 5,185 feet, which provides a panoramic view.

7. A moderately strenuous trail (3 miles round-trip) to the Ryan Mountain summit, which provides several outstanding viewpoints.

8. An 18-mile self-guided motor nature tour that winds through fascinating desert landscape. Four-wheel drive is required.

9. A self-guided nature trail, Cholla Cactus Garden, that contains some of the plants of the Colorado desert.

10. Cottonwood Spring, a palm oasis noted for its bird life.

11. A trail (7½ miles round-trip) that leads to the park's largest group of palms, Lost Palms Oasis.

ENTRANCE FEE: $10.00 per vehicle or $5.00 per person; good for seven days.

FACILITIES: Overnight accommodations and food service are available in nearby towns but not in the park. Water and flush toilets are available at the visitor center and at the campgrounds at Black Rock Canyon and Cottonwood Spring.

CAMPING: Nine campgrounds are available in the park. The only locations with water and flush toilets are Black Rock Canyon (100 spaces, reservations recommended) and Cottonwood Spring (62 spaces and 3 group sites), near the park's south entrance. Those with vault toilets and no water include Belle (20 spaces), Hidden Valley (39 spaces), Indian Cove (101 spaces and 13 group sites), Jumbo Rocks (125 spaces), Ryan (31 spaces), Sheep Pass (6 group sites), and White Tank (15 spaces). Reservations are required for all group sites. For reservations, call (800) 365–2267, or visit the Web site at reservations.nps.gov.

LASSEN VOLCANIC NATIONAL PARK

P.O. Box 100
Mineral, CA 96063-0100
(530) 595–4444
LAVO_Information@nps.gov
www.nps.gov/lavo

Lassen Volcanic National Park comprises 106,000 acres and was established in 1916 to protect boiling springs, fumaroles, mud pots, and sulfurous vents surrounding a volcano last active around 1921. The park is located in northeastern California, about 42 miles east of Redding off State Highway 44.

Lassen Volcanic National Park is a beautiful and relatively uncrowded mountainous area of peaceful pine and fir forests, sparkling lakes, cinder cones, and geothermal landscape surrounding the largest plugged-dome volcano in the world. The park and its dominant feature are named for Peter Lassen, who in the mid-1800s guided settlers near here and attempted to establish a town. Topping out at 10,457 feet, Lassen Peak is the southernmost volcano in the Cascade Range, which stretches from northern California to Canada. Until the eruption of Mount Saint Helens in 1980, this peak was best known as the last volcano to erupt in the lower forty-eight states. The volcano began as a vent on the northern flank of a much larger extinct volcano that collapsed hundreds of thousands of years ago. Lassen Peak began a seven-year period of eruptions in May 1914, with the largest taking place in 1915, when the peak blew a large cloud nearly 7 miles into the stratosphere.

The park's main access is via paved and winding Highway 89, which loops around Lassen Peak from southwest and northwest entrance points. This is an outstanding drive that offers access to campgrounds, hiking trails, picnic areas, a large geothermal area, mountain lakes, meadows, and snowbanks that linger through most of the summer. The road has a speed limit of 35 miles per hour and is typically open from June through October, depending on snowfall and weather. A road guide is available for sale at the entrance stations and information centers. Loomis Museum just inside the northwest entrance offers information, videos, and a display of photographs of the 1914–1915 eruption taken by B. F. Loomis. The museum is open daily from late June through early September and on weekends from late May to late June and during September. Lassen Chalet, just inside the southwest entrance, offers park information, gifts, and food service from mid-May to late August. The road provides access only to the western half of the park, which features huge mountains, jagged craters, and steaming sulfur vents. Other roads access Butt Lake in the park's northeast corner, Juniper Lake on the southeast corner, and Warner Valley on the southern border of the park.

Many of the park's 150 miles of trails begin from the roadside. A self-guided trail (3 miles round-trip) to Bumpass Hell begins 7 miles inside of the southwest boundary. This leads to the park's largest area in which to observe thermal activity. In addition to the trail to the Lassen Peak summit, there is the 4-mile (round-trip) Cinder Cone Trail, which climbs to the top of a 700-foot cinder cone. This latter trail begins at Butte Lake, at the northeast corner of the park. Daily ranger-led programs take place throughout the summer. Most of these begin from various points along the main road. The walk around Manzanita Lake is delightful and relatively easy.

ENTRANCE FEE: $10.00 per vehicle or $5.00 per person; good for seven days.

FACILITIES: Only minimal accommodations are present in the park. A camper store operating near the Manzanita Lake campground during summer months provides fast food, groceries, and gasoline. Limited food service is available at the Lassen Chalet, near the southwest entrance station, during the summer months. Overnight accommodations are available at Drakesbad Guest Ranch in Warner Valley, between June and September. Write California Guest Services, 2150 Main Street, Suite 5, Red Bluff, CA 96080 (530–529–1512, ext. 120 in season, 209–763–2850 off-season). Ranger stations are located at Manzanita Lake, Summit Lake, Butte Lake, Juniper Lake, and Warner Valley.

CAMPING: Improved campgrounds are located at Manzanita Lake (179 spaces, pay showers), Summit Lake North (46 spaces), and Southwest (21 spaces). The latter has campsites located approximately 100 yards from parking facilities, but the first can accommodate trailers and motor homes. All of these camps have fire rings, picnic tables, water, and flush toilets. Summit Lake usually fills earlier than the other two. Less-improved campsites (chemical toilets, tables, fire rings) are found at Summit Lake South (forty-eight spaces), Crags (forty-five spaces), Butte Lake (forty-two spaces), Warner Valley (eighteen spaces), and Juniper Lake (eighteen spaces). Juniper Lake and Warner Valley are not recommended for trailers.

FISHING: Fishing is permitted anywhere except Emerald Lake, Manzanita Creek, and within 150 feet of the inlet to Manzanita Lake. A California fishing license is required, and possibilities

Lassen Volcanic National Park

include brown, brook, and rainbow trout. Grassy Creek, connecting Horseshoe and Snag Lakes, is closed from October 1 to June 15. Manzanita Lake is catch and release only. Only artificial lures and single barbless hooks can be used.

LAVA BEDS NATIONAL MONUMENT

1 Indian Wells Headquarters
Tulelake, CA 96134
(530) 667–2282
labe_superintendent@nps.gov
www.nps.gov/labe

Lava Beds, which comprises 46,500 acres, was established as a national monument in 1925 to preserve a rugged landscape formed by volcanic activity and the historic battlefields of the Modoc War. The monument is located in extreme north-central California, 45 miles southeast of Klamath Falls, Oregon.

Centuries ago, a group of vents spewed great masses of molten basaltic lava over this region of the country. As the rivers of liquid rock cooled and hardened, the landscape of Lava Beds

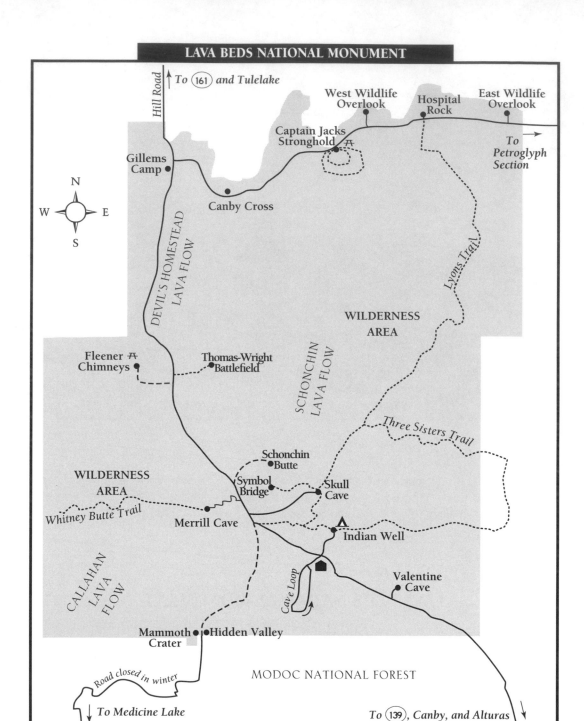

LAVA BEDS NATIONAL MONUMENT

To (161) and Tulelake

Hill Road

West Wildlife Overlook

Hospital Rock

East Wildlife Overlook

Captain Jacks Stronghold

To Petroglyph Section

Gillems Camp

N
W E
S

Canby Cross

DEVIL'S HOMESTEAD LAVA FLOW

WILDERNESS AREA

Lyons Trail

Fleener Chimneys

Thomas-Wright Battlefield

SCHONCHIN LAVA FLOW

Three Sisters Trail

Schonchin Butte

Symbol Bridge

Skull Cave

WILDERNESS AREA

Whitney Butte Trail

Merrill Cave

Indian Well

CALLAHAN LAVA FLOW

Cave Loop

Valentine Cave

Mammoth Crater

Hidden Valley

MODOC NATIONAL FOREST

Road closed in winter

To Medicine Lake

To (139), Canby, and Alturas

National Monument was born. Cinder cones are scattered throughout the area, and both smooth and rough (such as Devil's Homestead and Schonchin Flow) lava flows cover the monument. A number of these lava flows created lava-tube caves that are found throughout the area. Twenty-six caves, twenty-one of which are located on Cave Loop Road, are developed for visitors.

The only major Indian war to be fought in California took place in the lava beds. In November 1872 a group of 150 Modocs took refuge in the lava beds after skirmishes with settlers and the U.S. Army. Over the next four and a half months, fifty Modoc warriors used their knowledge of the local terrain to stand off a siege by nearly 600 troops. After peace negotiations stalled, some warriors convinced Captain Jack, the Modoc leader, to attack the peace commissioners during negotiations. Two members of the commission were killed. The Modocs were forced to abandon their stronghold a week later. After additional battles, the war ended with Captain Jack's capture on June 1, 1873. Jack and three other Modoc leaders were executed, while the survivors were sent to Oklahoma. Modoc War sites in the monument include Captain Jack's Stronghold (self-guided trail), Hospital Rock and Gillems Camp (army campsites), Canby Cross (the site of the attack on the peace commission), and the Thomas-Wright battlefield (site of a battle after the Modocs left the Stronghold).

A visitor center is located 3.6 miles inside the southeast entrance; a small museum explains the history and geology of the area. During summer months, park rangers give guided walks, cave tours, and campfire programs. A loop road south of headquarters provides access to many of the developed lava-tube caves. Numerous trails are located throughout the monument. Schonchin Butte, one of the largest cinder cones, can be climbed, and a trail leads to Black Crater.

Near the visitor center, Mushpot Cave is lighted for an easy self-guided tour that takes about twenty minutes. The tour is worthwhile and should be a visitor's first order of business after viewing the visitor-center exhibits. The remainder of the caves are without lighting, so flashlights must be used. These may be borrowed at the visitor center. For those with even a mild interest in caves, a trip through one or more of these is a must. It is a unique experience that by itself makes a trip to the monument memorable.

ENTRANCE FEE: $10.00 per vehicle or $3.00 per person; good for seven days.

FACILITIES: Food and lodging are not available within the monument, but both can be found in either Tulelake or Klamath Falls. Water and modern rest rooms are located at headquarters and at the campground. The picnic areas at Fleener Chimneys and Captain Jack's Stronghold have no water.

CAMPING: Indian Well Campground (forty-three spaces) is open all year; grills, tables, water, and flush toilets are provided. The campground is located a short distance from the visitor center, with sites interspersed among juniper trees that provide some shade for campers but not much for their vehicles.

FISHING: No fishing is available at Lava Beds National Monument. Fifteen miles south of the park on USDA Forest Service land, Medicine Lake provides excellent trout fishing. A California fishing license is required. An area map showing the location of the lake is available in the Lava Beds Visitor Center.

MANZANAR NATIONAL HISTORIC SITE

P.O. Box 426
Independence, CA 93526
(760) 878–2932
manz_superintendent@nps.gov
www.nps.gov/manz

Manzanar National Historic Site comprises 813 acres and was authorized in 1992 to preserve the Manzanar War Relocation Center and commemorate the World War II internment of Japanese Americans. The site also interprets the area's history with respect to American Indians and agricultural settlement. The historic site is located in southeastern California, 12 miles north of Lone Pine, just off U.S. Highway 395.

Less than three months after the December 7, 1941, Japanese attack on Pearl Harbor, President Franklin D. Roosevelt signed an executive order empowering the secretary of war to round up West Coast citizens of Japanese ancestry and Japanese resident aliens. The Manzanar Relocation Center became the first of ten internment camps that held a total of approximately 118,000 citizens. The center was located on the site of the former community of Manzanar that had been abandoned when the city of Los Angeles purchased the land in the late 1920s for its water rights. The first Japanese Americans arrived from Los Angeles on March 21, 1942. By July the camp had a population of nearly 10,000, most of whom came from the Los Angeles area. Manzanar grew into a small town with 36 blocks of wooden barracks within a 1-square-mile area. The camp eventually included eighteen residential buildings for staff personnel, an auditorium, laundry, automotive repair shops, a service station, a hospital, garages, a post office, mess halls, apartment buildings, and a garment factory. Substantial farming took place outside the fenced center area, and a chicken farm had been completed by the end of 1943. Following the war, the buildings and materials at Manzanar were sold for salvage, and by December 1946 only a few buildings remained. Many of the buildings removed from Manzanar remain in use in various Owens Valley communities.

The historic site's visitor center in the renovated camp auditorium has exhibits and park personnel to help interpret the history of Manzanar. Although the internment camp was dismantled following the war, the National Park Service is in the process of reconstructing a "demonstration block" that will provide visitors with an idea of what camp life was like. One of the original mess halls that had been moved from the camp to the town of Bishop, where it served as a hospital during the 1940s, has been returned to the national historic site, along with its original oil stove, refrigerator, and food serving counter. The National Park Service plans to acquire additional structures and items that were once at Manzanar. A 3.2-mile self-guided auto tour road leads past the historic entrance sign, concrete foundations, the mess hall, sentry posts, the camp auditorium, ruins of the administrative complex, portions of the water system, and the camp cemetery. A tour description and map are available at the camp entrance. A walking tour of the camp takes one to two hours. A self-guided tour booklet is available at the Interagency Visitor Center in Lone Pine and the Eastern California Museum in the town of Independence. Guided walks and talks are given during summer weekends when adequate personnel are available.

ENTRANCE FEE: No charge.

FACILITIES: Rest rooms and drinking water are in the visitor center. Food and lodging facilities are in the towns of Independence and Lone Pine.

CAMPING: Camping is not permitted at the historic site. Numerous public campgrounds operated by the National Forest Service and the county are in the Independence/Lone Pine area.

MOJAVE NATIONAL PRESERVE

222 East Main Street, Suite 202
Barstow, CA 92311
(760) 255–8800
MOJA_superintendent@nps.gov
www.nps.gov/moja

Mojave National Preserve was created in 1994 to protect 1.6 million acres of fragile desert that includes volcanic cinder cones, sand dunes, creosote bush and cactus, Joshua tree forests, and high-elevation piñon, juniper, and sagebrush. The preserve is located in southeastern California, bounded on the north by Interstate 15 and on the south by Interstate 40. It is accessible from either interstate.

Mojave National Preserve comprises a huge (twice the size of Yosemite National Park) tract of pristine desert that is rich in geology and wildlife. Mojave NP is the third largest National Park Service area in the contiguous forty-eight states. Three of North America's deserts, the Mojave, Great Basin, and Sonoran, meet in this preserve that serves as home to a variety of birds and nearly 300 species of animals, including bighorn sheep and desert tortoises. The preserve has rock art from the native desert people who once lived here and old mines and ranches from more recent inhabitants. Nearly half the preserve is designated as wilderness. Providence Mountain State Recreation Area, administered by the California Department of Parks and Recreation, offers ninety-minute guided cavern tours. Call (760) 928–2586 for information or group reservations. The recreation area is within Mojave NP boundaries.

The preserve provides a variety of activities including sight-seeing, camping, and hiking. Points of interest include 700-foot Kelso Dunes, the historic Kelso Depot, which is now a museum and information center, numerous volcanic cinder cones, and 7,929-foot Clark Mountain, the highest peak in the preserve. Hunting is permitted in designated areas. Summer temperatures can be extreme, with very hot days and cold nights, so it is important to come prepared with appropriate clothing. Water is available in the campgrounds. Maps and brochures with camping information, hiking trails, and points of interest are available by mail from monument headquarters in Barstow or at the Mojave Desert Information Center at the base of the World's Tallest Thermometer in Baker. Call (760) 733–4040 for current conditions. An information center is also located in the town of Needles at 707 West Broadway (760–928–2512).

ENTRANCE FFF· No charge.

FACILITIES: No overnight accommodations are available in the preserve. Limited food items can be purchased in Baker and Nipton. Gasoline, water, and telephones are in only a few locations outside the preserve. Lodging, groceries, and supplies are in surrounding towns.

CAMPING: Two developed campgrounds operated by the national preserve each have vault toilets, picnic tables, fire rings, and limited water. Mid Hills, at an elevation of 5,600 feet, is cooler and has twenty-six sites in a piñon-juniper woodlands, but requires traversing an 8-mile unpaved road that is not recommended for motor homes or trailers. The Hole-in-the-Wall Campground, at 4,400 feet and bordered by volcanic rock walls, has thirty-five sites and a dump station. Call (760) 326–6322 for reservations or information for a group campground near the Hole-in-the-Wall ranger station. Providence Mountains State Recreation Area offers six campsites with fire rings, tables, water, and flush toilets. Roadside camping is limited to areas that have been traditionally used for this purpose.

MUIR WOODS NATIONAL MONUMENT
Mill Valley, CA 94941-2696
(415) 388-2595
goga_muir_woods_nm@nps.gov
www.nps.gov/muwo

Muir Woods National Monument was established in 1908 to preserve 550 acres of old-growth redwood that was spared from logging. This popular national monument is part of Golden Gate National Recreation Area. It is 12 miles north of the Golden Gate Bridge and is reached via U.S. Highway 101 and California Highway 1. Vehicles over 35 feet long are prohibited on access roads that are steep and winding.

Millions of years ago at least forty species of giant trees related to today's redwood and sequoia grew throughout the Northern Hemisphere. Today, the coast redwood grows only in a 500-mile-long, 30-mile-wide belt along the Pacific Coast, from just south of Monterey to the southwestern corner of Oregon. This is where the Pacific Ocean produces fog and a cool damp climate in protected or sheltered areas such as Muir Woods. In this park some specimens have reached more than 250 feet in height, while farther north in the state, trees exceed 370 feet.

Redwoods resist fire, insects, and fungi, with their thick, asbestos-like bark filled with tannic acid. Although these trees have survived three to five fires per century, the last natural fire in the Muir Woods was in 1845. Recent controlled burns along the Ben Johnson Trail allow visitors and researchers to observe the benefits of low-intensity burns. The tree's root system is surprisingly shallow but may radiate for up to 100 feet.

The park is open from 8:00 A.M. to sunset. The visitor center, with exhibits and a bookstore, is located in the park's southeast corner. The monument is designed to be seen primarily by hiking. About 2 miles of the main walking trails are either boardwalks or are paved and therefore accessible to wheelchairs and strollers. Six miles of trails connect with those of Mount Tamalpais State Park to provide the visitor with many hours of exercise, enjoyment, and quiet. Bridges along Redwood Creek make short loops possible, and trailside exhibits, signs, and markers are placed throughout the monument. A self-guided portion of the trail (with booklet) lies between the second and third bridges. Park rangers, volunteers, and interns give daily programs.

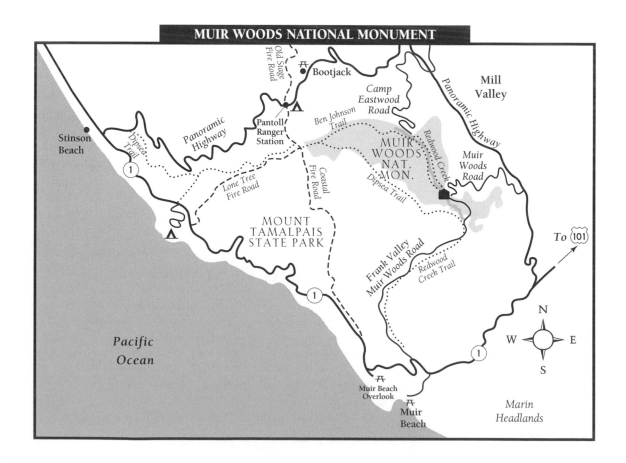

Be warned that the monument is quite crowded during summer months and on winter weekends when the weather is nice. During summer weekends the park is packed. As a result, parking is often difficult and solitude on the loop trails is elusive. It is best to visit early in the morning or later in the afternoon and get off the main walking path onto some of the trails. No bikes, horses, or dogs are permitted.

ENTRANCE FEE: $3.00 per person. Children ages sixteen and under are free.

FACILITIES: The park's only facility is a concession shop near the visitor center that sells snacks and souvenirs. Drinking water and rest rooms are located near the park entrance. The nearest picnic facility is at Muir Beach, about 3 miles southwest of the park.

CAMPING: No camping or picnicking facilities are in the monument. Mount Tamalpais State Park, surrounding Muir Woods, provides walk-in tent-style camping with tables, grills, water, and rest rooms. Automobile parking is about 100 yards from the camping sites. To reach this area at Pantoll, take the Panoramic Highway north after leaving Muir Woods. Another state park is located 26 miles northwest via Highway 1. See the camping section under Point Reyes National Seashore.

NATIONAL AIDS MEMORIAL GROVE

856 Stanyan Street
San Francisco, CA 94117
(415) 750-8340
aidsmemgrv@aol.com
www.aidsmemorial.org

National AIDS Memorial Grove is an affiliated area of the National Park Service that was authorized in 1996 to memorialize individuals who have died as a result of acquired immune deficiency syndrome (AIDS) and to support caregivers and those living with AIDS. The memorial is located in the eastern end of San Francisco's Golden Gate Park.

The National AIDS Memorial Grove is dedicated to the creation and long-term maintenance of the first living memorial to those lost to AIDS and in support of the individuals living with human immunodeficiency virus (HIV). This memorial is designed as a place for the living to mourn, remember, and begin the process of healing. The memorial grove is a seven-acre wooded area located in the eastern section of Golden Gate Park. The grove includes a woodland path, a valley floor of wildflowers and grasses, and a fern grotto. Monthly workdays for maintaining vegetation at the memorial grove have occurred since 1991.

ENTRANCE FEE: No charge.

FACILITIES: Food and lodging are available in the city of San Francisco. See the Facilities section of Golden Gate National Recreation Area for more information.

PINNACLES NATIONAL MONUMENT

5000 Highway 146
Paicines, CA 95043-9770
(831) 389–4485
PINN_visitor_information@nps.gov
www.nps.gov/pinn

Pinnacles National Monument was established in 1908 and contains the remains of an ancient volcano that has been eroded by wind, water, and freezing into spectacular pinnacles and spires. The park is located in west-central California, approximately 83 miles southeast of San Jose. The major part of the monument must be approached from the east via California Highways 25 and 146. The entrance to the west side of the monument, from U.S. 101 at Soledad, is not a through road and will not accommodate trailers or campers.

The jagged landscape of Pinnacles National Monument is the result of volcanic activity twenty-three million years ago. This activity was facilitated by a rift that developed when the Pacific Plate collided with and ripped off a portion of the North American Plate along the present-day San Andreas Rift Zone. As the Pacific Plate moved northwest, the cone which had built by the volcanic activity moved nearly 195 miles from its original location. Millions of years of erosion have taken their toll, and the rock formations of today are about one-third the height of the original volcano.

The rugged slopes of Pinnacles are covered by a brushy plant cover known as chaparral. The plants thrive in the hot, dry summers and sparse rainfall (15 inches) found in this area of California. This pygmy forest provides shelter for a variety of wildlife, including black-tailed deer, rabbits, raccoons, bobcats, and gray fox. Frequently seen birds include the acorn woodpecker, brown towhee, California quail, and turkey vulture.

The Bear Gulch Visitor Center, about 2 miles from the east entrance, has changing displays to help interpret the natural and cultural history of the area. The Chaparral Ranger Station at the west entrance has park information. Although the monument is open all year, its main seasons are spring and fall. Winter months bring the wet season, and summer months are quite hot, with daytime temperatures often exceeding 100 degrees Fahrenheit.

One of the park's main activities is hiking, and a number of trails are located throughout Pinnacles:

EAST SIDE

- Bear Gulch Trail (1.7 miles, one hour) is a self-guided trail connecting the visitor center with the Chalone Creek picnic area via the Bench Trail.

- Chalone Peak Trail (round-trip: 8 miles, five hours) wanders through stands of chaparral on an uphill trip from Bear Gulch Visitor Center to a fire lookout at the top of Chalone Peak.

- Condor Gulch Trail (1.7 miles, one and a half hours) connects the visitor center with the High Peaks Trail and provides good views of the pinnacle formations.

- High Peaks Trail (5.4 miles, three to five hours) begins at the Chalone Creek picnic area or at the parking area at the end of Bear Gulch picnic area. The 1,400-foot climb presents view points of the entire park.

- Moses Spring Trail (1¾ miles, one and a half hours) begins at the parking lot next to the picnic area and leads to the foot of the reservoir dam. The trail is self-guided, and leaflets are available at the visitor center. Return via the Rim Trail that overlooks Bear Gulch. Bear Gulch Cave is subject to seasonal closures. Check with the ranger before hiking.

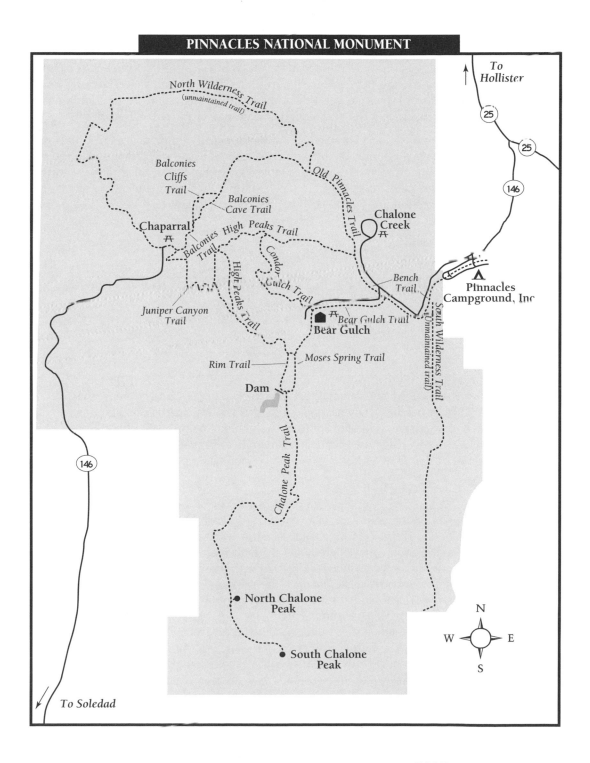

- Balconies Trail (one way: 1.2 miles, two hours) leads to Balconies Cave, which forces you to maneuver between and under boulders (take a flashlight). This trail connects to the Chalone Creek picnic area (east side) via the Old Pinnacles Trail. You can also return via the Balconies Cliffs Trail.

ENTRANCE FEE: $5.00 per vehicle or $2.00 per person; good for seven days. Children ages sixteen and under are free.

FACILITIES: No food services or accommodations are available in the monument. A camper store is located just outside the east entrance (short hours during summer weekdays). Drinking water and modern rest rooms are available at the visitor center, the Chaparral Ranger Station, and in the picnic areas. On the west side, the nearest services are in Soledad.

CAMPING: There are no National Park Service campgrounds, although a nice (125 sites) private campground is located just outside the park's east side. The sites offer some shade and are fairly widely spaced. The campground provides tables, grills, hot water, flush toilets, a swimming pool, showers (in poolhouse), and electric hookups. For information or reservations, write Pinnacles Campground, Inc., 2400 Highway 146, Paicines, CA 95043 (831–389–4462), or visit www.pinncamp.com.

POINT REYES NATIONAL SEASHORE
Point Reyes, CA 94956-9799
(415) 464–5137
pore_webmaster@nps.gov
www.nps.gov/pore/visit

Point Reyes was added as a National Park Service area in 1962 and has more than 70,000 acres of beaches, lagoons, and forested ridges backed by tall cliffs. The seashore's southern end is located approximately 22 miles northwest of San Francisco via California Highway 1. Park headquarters at Bear Valley is located near the town of Olema, 8 miles from the southern boundary.

Point Reyes National Seashore is a peninsula providing a habitat for more than 470 species of birds, seventy-two species of mammals, many types of other land and marine animals, and a great variety of plant life. The park is an "island" that has been separated from the mainland by the San Andreas Fault. Periodic movement along the fault has resulted in completely different types and ages of rocks on the peninsula as compared with those found on the mainland in the same area. During the 1906 earthquake, land on the west side of the fault moved as much as 21 feet northward. A short self-guided trail (thirty-five minutes) along the fault begins across the parking lot from the Bear Valley Visitor Center.

Park headquarters is located $1/4$ mile west of Olema on Bear Valley Road. Here the Bear Valley Visitor Center contains 250 natural history exhibits, an auditorium, 150 plant and animal specimens, and exhibits about the San Andreas Fault. Demonstrations, talks, and nature walks are conducted in the Bear Valley area on weekends year-round. From Bear Valley a paved road

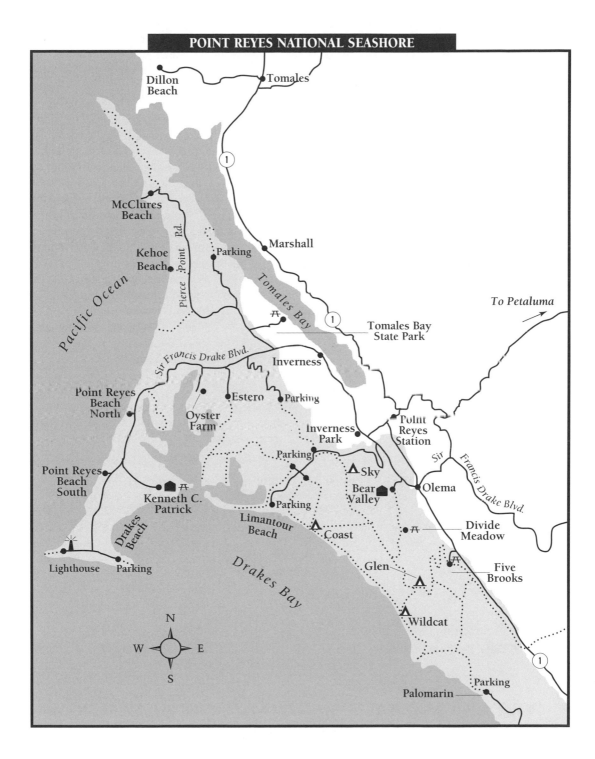

POINT REYES NATIONAL SEASHORE

Dillon Beach

Tomales

1

McClures Beach

Marshall

Kehoe Beach

Pierce Point Rd.

Parking

Tomales Bay

1

Tomales Bay State Park

Pacific Ocean

To Petaluma

Sir Francis Drake Blvd.

Inverness

Point Reyes Beach North

Estero

Parking

Oyster Farm

Inverness Park

Point Reyes Station

Sir

Parking

Sky

Francis Drake Blvd.

Point Reyes Beach South

Bear Valley

Olema

Parking

Kenneth C. Patrick

Drakes Beach

Limantour Beach

Parking

Coast

Divide Meadow

Lighthouse

Parking

Glen

Five Brooks

Drakes Bay

Wildcat

N
W   E
S

1

Palomarin

Parking

heads northwest through Inverness and then splits, with one road going north past Tomales Bay State Park and on to McClures Beach. The other branch leads to Drakes Beach (a good swimming beach and the point where Sir Francis Drake stopped in 1579 to make repairs to his ship) and Point Reyes. The historic Point Reyes Lighthouse is no longer operating but is open to the public. The lighthouse visitor center has exhibits of whales, wildflowers, birds, and maritime history. A deck on the back of the visitor center overlooks the historic lighthouse. The lighthouse, its stairs, and the lighthouse visitor center are open Thursday to Monday from 10:00 A.M. to 4:30 P.M. A visit here is worth the drive, but the 300-step stairway down to the lighthouse requires some effort. On weekends and holidays in good weather from late December to mid-April, the west end of Sir Francis Drake Boulevard is closed to vehicle traffic. Shuttle transportation to the lighthouse and Chimney Rock areas is available. A shuttle fee is charged for persons over 12 years old. Tickets are available at Drakes Beach. The road to Limantour Beach begins a short distance north of Bear Valley. Watching migrations of gray whales has become an increasingly popular activity. Peak migrations are in mid-January and mid-March. Whale watching requires a bus ride. Inquire at the Bear Valley Visitor Center.

Bear Valley Trailhead, near headquarters, is a gateway to more than 140 miles of trails. The most popular route is the 4 1/10-mile Bear Valley Trail, which winds through meadows and forests to the sea. Other trails branch from this main route and ascend into the high country of Inverness Ridge and the southern portion of the seashore. Bicycle use is restricted to designated trails, so riders should check at Bear Valley Visitor Center for specific information. Horses are permitted on most trails. Dogs are not permitted on the trails or in the campgrounds.

ENTRANCE FEE: No charge.

FACILITIES: No overnight accommodations or complete food service is available within the park, but both can be found nearby. Drinking water and modern rest rooms are located at park headquarters and at Drakes Beach. Limited food service is available at Drakes Beach.

CAMPING: Four hike-in campgrounds are open year-round. Coast, Sky, Glen Camp, and Wildcat Camp have water, rest rooms, tables, and grills. Sites may be reserved and are always full on weekends and holidays during the summer. Reservations can be made up to three months in advance by calling (415) 663–8054, Monday to Friday, 9:00 A.M. to 2:00 P.M. Users must register at Bear Valley Visitor Center and obtain a camping permit. No camping is permitted at Tomales Bay State Park, but a fairly large private campground (415–663–8001) is located on California Highway 1 in Olema. Six miles east of Olema on Sir Francis Drake Highway, Samuel P. Taylor State Park (415–488–9897) provides camping (sixty-eight spaces) with tables, grills, water, flush toilets, and hot showers. The park encompasses a large grove of redwoods.

FISHING: Surf fishing is permitted on all beaches, and a California fishing license is required. No freshwater fishing is available.

PORT CHICAGO NAVAL MAGAZINE NATIONAL MEMORIAL
c/o Eugene O'Neill National Historic Site
P.O. Box 280
Danville, CA 94526-0280
(925) 838–0249
EUON_interpretation@nps.gov
www.nps.gov/poch

Port Chicago Naval Magazine National Memorial was authorized in 1992 to recognize the role of the weapons facility during World War II and to commemorate the officers and sailors who lost their lives in 1944 in a mysterious explosion killing 320 men. The memorial is at the Concord Naval Weapons Station near Concord, California. Visits are by reservation only and include a guided tour.

Construction on Port Chicago commenced in 1942 when the U.S. Navy decided to expand its ability to supply ammunition to the Pacific Theater. By 1944 the facility was being utilized around the clock for loading munitions on ships. African-Americans under white officers were assigned to the dangerous duty at Port Chicago. Although the men were members of ordnance battalions, neither they nor their officers had received much training in cargo handling of explosives.

On July 17, 1944, two ships were docked at Port Chicago. The SS *Quinault Victory* was being prepared for loading on her maiden voyage. The SS *E.A. Bryan* was being loaded after returning from its first voyage. Three hundred twenty cargo handlers, crewmen, and sailors were working in the area, which was filled with nearly 5,000 tons of high explosives and incendiary bombs, depth charges, and ammunition. The 10:18 P.M. explosion killed all 320 men on duty, disintegrated one of the ships, destroyed structures around the pier, and damaged every building in Port Chicago. Another 390 people were wounded. Of the 320 men killed in the explosion, 202 were enlisted African-Americans.

Access to the site requires a reservation through the Eugene O'Neil National Historic Site. For information or reservations, call (925) 838–0249.

ENTRANCE FEE: No charge.

FACILITIES: The National Park Service has no facilities at the memorial.

REDWOOD NATIONAL AND STATE PARKS
1111 Second Street
Crescent City, CA 95531-4198
(707) 464–6101
REDW_information@nps.gov
www.nps.gov/redw

Redwood National and State Parks comprise nearly 106,000 acres of coastal redwood forests, with ancient groves of trees averaging 500 to 700 years of age and growing to more than 300 feet in height. The parks include 35 miles of rugged and beautiful Pacific shoreline. The park complex lies along U.S. 101 on the extreme northern coast of California. From the east the park complex is approached on U.S. 199 from Grants Pass, Oregon.

The redwoods of the Pacific Coast nearly overpower someone viewing them for the first time, especially a person from the East Coast who hasn't experienced the giant trees of the West. Redwoods are the world's tallest trees, and some live as long as 2,000 years. Coast redwoods grow in a narrow strip along the Pacific Coast of California and southwestern Oregon.

Unfortunately, only 4 percent of the original two million acres of redwoods remain. Redwood National and State Parks contain 45 percent of all old-growth redwood forests remaining in California. In addition to the featured redwoods, a visitor will find oak, cedar, and Douglas fir at the higher elevations; cedar, alder, maple, and hemlock along the streams and rivers; and Sitka spruce along the shoreline. Varied wildlife, including Roosevelt elk, fox, bobcat, cougar, black-tailed deer, and black bear, can be found in various locations within the park's boundaries. Birding is a popular activity as well, with both oceangoing and forest birds.

Redwood National and State Parks is a complex of parks operated through a cooperative agreement between the National Park Service and the California State Parks. The state parks were each established prior to Redwood National Park and include Jedediah Smith Redwoods, Del Norte Coast Redwoods, and Prairie Creek Redwoods. The complex of parks is approximately 45 miles long and only 7 miles wide at its widest point on the south end. U.S. Highway 101 traverses the entire length of the park, but this beautiful area is best seen by leaving Highway 101 and driving on side roads or, better yet, hiking some of the main trails. Bald Hills Road (steep grades and not recommended for trailers and motor homes), near the south entrance at Orick, leads to Lady Bird Johnson Grove, where a 1-mile self-guided loop trail winds through mature forest to the grove and site at which Lady Bird Johnson dedicated the national park in 1968. Be certain to exit off Highway 101 onto the Newton B. Drury Scenic Parkway that extends from 6 miles north of Orick to 4 miles south of Klamath. This drive threads through impressive old-growth redwood and provides access to Big Tree Wayside, where an easy walk passes by many huge trees. Eight-mile long Coastal Drive near Klamath offers magnificent views of the Pacific Ocean and Klamath River. During this drive you may see whales, sea lions, and pelicans from overlooks. Near the park's north entrance, Howland Hill Road (improved gravel with narrow spots) winds through a lush redwood forest and leads to the Stout Grove along the wild and scenic Smith River. Recreational vehicles and trailers are not permitted on either Coastal Drive or Howland Hill Road.

Nearly 200 miles of hiking trails are scattered throughout the parks, including the 35-mile-long Coastal Trail System between Crescent Beach in the north and Orick in the south. View points, exhibits, and beach access are provided as the trail winds along bluffs overlooking the Pacific Ocean. The Redwood Creek Trail, east of Orick, provides an 8$^{1}/_{2}$-mile path to the Tall Trees Grove. This grove contains some of the tallest known trees in the world. The grove is also reached via a 17-mile drive from the Redwood Information Center and a 3-mile round-trip hike. A free permit for the access road can be obtained at the information center. Park rangers present evening programs and guided walks in summer throughout the park. Information centers are located at Hiouchi (summer only), Crescent City, and Orick.

ENTRANCE FEE: No entrance fee is charged for driving through Redwood National Park. Use of the state parks may entail a $4.00 user fee that is applicable to all three state parks.

FACILITIES: A number of motels and food outlets are available along U.S. Highway 101. A hostel is located 17 miles south of Crescent City (707–482–8265). Most modern accommodations are in towns located near park boundaries, Crescent City to the north and Orick to the south. Eureka, a relatively large town, is approximately 45 miles south of the park's south entrance.

CAMPING: Redwood National and State Parks offer four developed campgrounds and several primitive walk-in campgrounds. Hiker/biker sites are at Miners Ridge and Ossagon Creek in Prairie Creek State Park. Developed campgrounds include Jedediah Smith (106 RV or tent sites, flush toilets, showers, dump station) in an old-growth forest, Mill Creek (145 RV or tent sites, flush toilets, showers, dump station) in a second-growth redwood forest, Elk Prairie (75 RV or tent sites, flush toilets, showers, dump station) in an old-growth forest, and Gold Bluffs Beach

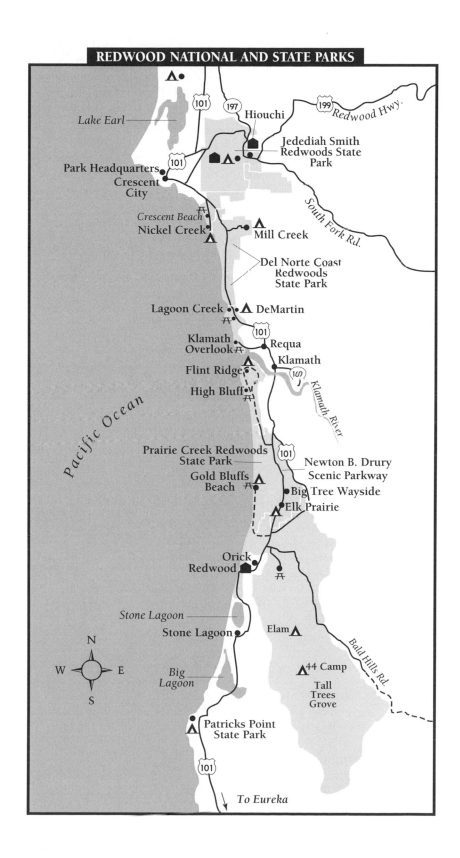

REDWOOD NATIONAL AND STATE PARKS

Lake Earl

101 197 **Hiouchi**

199 *Redwood Hwy.*

Jedediah Smith Redwoods State Park

101

Park Headquarters Crescent City

Crescent Beach
Nickel Creek

Mill Creek

South Fork Rd.

Del Norte Coast Redwoods State Park

Lagoon Creek · **DeMartin**

101

Klamath Overlook

Requa

Klamath

Flint Ridge

101

Klamath River

High Bluff

Pacific Ocean

Prairie Creek Redwoods State Park

101

Newton B. Drury Scenic Parkway

Gold Bluffs Beach

Big Tree Wayside

Elk Prairie

Orick Redwood

Stone Lagoon

Stone Lagoon

Elam

N
W · E
S

Big Lagoon

44 Camp Tall Trees Grove

Bald Hills Rd.

Patricks Point State Park

101

To Eureka

(29 tent sites and 27 RV sites, flush toilets, solar-heated showers) on the Pacific Ocean. Gold Bluffs Beach is accessed near the south end of the park via an unpaved road. The developed campgrounds are operated by the California State Parks System, not the National Park Service, so holders of Golden Age and Golden Access Passports are not granted discounts on camping fees. Reservations for any of these campgrounds can be made by calling (800) 444–7275. Online reservations can be made at www.CAescapes.com. A $7.50 nonrefundable reservation fee is charged.

Camping is available at a number of nearby state parks, county parks, and recreation areas. Tolowa Dunes State Park, north of Crescent City, and Humboldt Lagoons State Park and Patrick's Point State Park, south of Orick, each offer campsites. Six Rivers National Forest has four campgrounds with a total of eighty-seven sites for tents, campers, and small trailers. These are located about thirty minutes east of Highway 101 on U.S. 199. Other, more distant, campgrounds are located in Six Rivers, Klamath, and Trinity national forests. Camping is also available at private campgrounds and trailer parks along Highway 101.

FISHING: This is an excellent area for salmon and steelhead trout. Surfcasting for red-tail perch is also a popular activity. A California fishing license is mandatory for both ocean and freshwater fishing. California regulations apply throughout the area.

SAN FRANCISCO MARITIME NATIONAL HISTORICAL PARK

Fort Mason, Building E
San Francisco, CA 94123
(415) 561–7100
safr_interpretation@nps.gov
www.nps.gov/safr

This park of fifty acres was established in 1988 to preserve and celebrate the maritime history of the Pacific Coast. The historical park includes museum exhibits, historic ships, an aquatic park, research collections, and a maritime store. San Francisco Maritime National Historical Park is located just west of Fisherman's Wharf on San Francisco Bay in the city of San Francisco. The park is best reached via public transportation (municipal bus or the Powell and Hyde cable car), as parking is in short supply in this area of the city.

A visit to San Francisco Maritime National Historical Park is a trip to this historic city's rich maritime past. Settled by the Spanish in 1776, the city boomed following the 1849 discovery of gold in the Sierra Nevada foothills. The gold rush brought ships full of merchants, laborers, and fortune seekers from around the world. Many ships were left in the harbor after crews abandoned their vessels in a rush to the gold fields. Several decades later, sailing ships were lured here by the grain trade.

The heart of the national historical park is the Maritime Museum, with models of historic ships, an excellent exhibit on maritime communications, a video presentation, and exhibits on steam technology, whaling, and the California gold rush. The museum is located at 900 Beach Street at the foot of Polk Street. It is open daily from 10:00 A.M. to 5:00 P.M.

Nearby, Hyde Street Pier is home to a number of historic sailing vessels that are open to visitors. The pier was constructed in 1922 for automobile ferries between San Francisco and Sausalito. This served as part of a U.S. highway until the Golden Gate Bridge was opened in 1937. Among the vessels at the pier are a merchant ship that carried lumber from the Pacific Northwest, a sidewheel ferry, an oceangoing tug, a paddle tug, and the last San Francisco Bay scow schooner still afloat. The Maritime Store at the entrance of Hyde Street Pier has books, posters, cards, and gifts appropriate to maritime history. A short distance east, Pier 45 is home to the USS *Pampanito,* a 1943 World War II fleet submarine that sank six Japanese ships. Call (415) 775–1943 for information. For those with time, a 3½-mile walk along the shoreline from the museum to Fort Point provides both exercise and relaxation.

Fort Mason Center contains three research collections, which include an extensive maritime library, archives, manuscripts, logbooks, ship plans, and historic photographs. Park personnel schedule numerous activities including talks, guided walks, ship tours, and classes and workshops. Visitors should check at the museum for a current schedule.

ENTRANCE FEE: No charge for entrance to the Maritime Museum or to walk along Hyde Pier and view the vessels. A $5.00 admission is required to board the historic vessels. Children ages 16 and under are free. Any national park pass is valid for admission.

FACILITIES: Food and lodging are abundant in the wharf area. Although natives normally stay away from this area, many visitors enjoy trying seafood offered by the many outdoor vendors. An American Youth Hostel at Fort Mason provides low-cost lodging for recreational travelers of all ages. Visitors may picnic in Aquatic Park at the terminus of the Powell and Hyde cable car.

CAMPING: See the camping section under Golden Gate National Recreation Area (California).

FISHING: Fishing is permitted along the waterfront.

SANTA MONICA MOUNTAINS NATIONAL RECREATION AREA

401 West Hillcrest Drive
Thousand Oaks, CA 91360
(805) 370–2301
samo_interpretation@nps.gov
www.nps.gov/samo

Santa Monica Mountains National Recreation Area was established in 1978 and comprises 150,000 acres of rugged landscape and shoreline within easy reach of millions of nearby residents. The park is located between the cities of Beverly Hills and Oxnard in an east-west corridor bordered on the north by U.S. 101 and on the south by Highway 1 and the Pacific Ocean.

Santa Monica Mountains National Recreation Area is the culmination of years of effort toward the goal of establishing parklands and preserving open spaces in a heavily populated and rapidly growing area. The Santa Monica Mountains are a coastal range stretching 46 miles west of Los Angeles. The area contains mountains, grasslands, oak woodlands, freshwater and saltwater marshes, and plunging waterfalls. Wildlife includes mountain lions, deer, bobcats, red-tailed hawks, and golden eagles. The park visitor center, located at 401 West Hillcrest Drive in

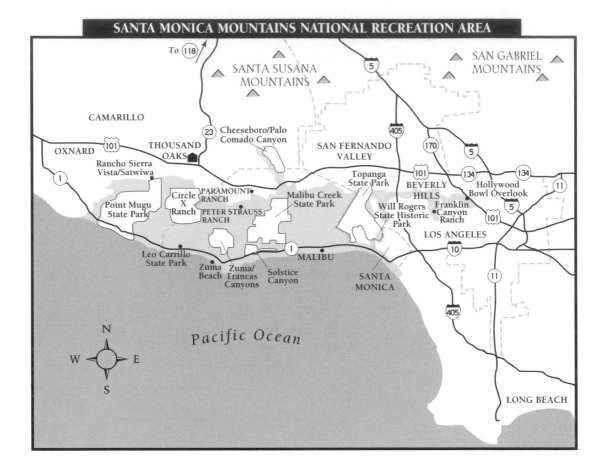

Thousand Oaks, offers information on recreation opportunities available in the mountains, including maps and guidebooks. Exhibits and film displays are also available. One excellent way of seeing much of the recreation area is to drive 54 winding miles through the park on scenic Mulholland Drive/Highway.

A wide assortment of activities, including hikes, guided walks, talks, astronomy programs, concerts, bird-watching, trail maintenance, and campfire programs are offered in the national recreation area. There is truly something for everyone, with the majority of activities scheduled on weekends. A quarterly calendar of events is available at the visitor center. Below is a short sketch of some of the popular locations in the national recreation area. Locations with an asterisk (*) are National Park Service facilities.

Cheeseboro/Palo Comado Canyon: Formerly home to the Chumash and ranchers, this area offers miles of trails that lead through oak savanna, rugged rocky canyons, and rolling grasslands. This is the home of numerous owls, hawks, and other birds of prey.

Circle X Ranch: A former Boy Scout camp, the ranch includes trails, a group campground (call 805–370–2300, ext. 1702, for reservations), and a ranch house that can serve as a meeting room for up to seventy-five people (call 805–370–2308 for reservations). From here you can hike to Sandstone Peak, the highest point in the Santa Monica Mountains, and on a clear day view several of the Channel Islands.

Franklin Canyon Site (310–858–7272): A Santa Monica Mountains Conservancy–operated natural refuge that is surrounded by the city. This site once served as a retreat for one of the area's wealthy families that built a Spanish-style home here around 1935. This area, a few miles south of Sunset Boulevard, offers trails, picnicking, and an opportunity to observe wildlife.

Hollywood Bowl Overlook: Located on Mulholland Highway above the Hollywood Bowl, this overlook offers striking views of the Bowl and the many concerts and events taking place there.

Leo Carrillo State Park (818–880–0350): More than a mile of ocean beach fronted by cave-riddled bluffs. Three campgrounds for tenters and RV owners.

Malibu Creek State Park (818–880–0350): An area of rugged cliffs and gorges, slopes of chaparral, grasslands, and live oak groves. Fifteen miles of hiking and riding trails wind through the park.

*Paramount Ranch: A 760-acre area that features a western town movie set, opportunities for watching filming, and places for walking, horseback riding, and picnicking.

*Peter Strauss Ranch: Acquired as a weekend retreat at the turn of the twentieth century, the ranch was converted into an amusement park that fell into disrepair after closing in 1960. Actor Peter Strauss purchased the property in 1976 and lived here until 1983. The ranch has a 0.6-mile trail, a swimming pool that could accommodate up to 3,000 people, and a terrazzo tile dance floor, where big band concerts were held in the 1940s and 1950s. Parking is east of the ranch on Mulholland Highway. Concerts are offered periodically during summer months.

Point Mugu State Park (818–880–0350): Beaches, cliffs, picnic areas, and campgrounds along 5 miles of ocean shoreline. This park provides 70 miles of hiking and riding trails through canyons and across rugged uplands.

*Rancho Sierra Vista/Satwiwa: A 1,151-acre site with hiking trails, a Native American culture center, and picnic areas.

*Solstice Canyon: A haven from city life that provides greenery even during the hot, dry summers. Five easy to strenuous hiking trails of 1.2 to 3.9 miles provide access to wildlife, ocean views, and historic structures.

Will Rogers State Historic Park (310–454–8212): Will Rogers' home for the seven years prior to his death in 1935, the park has a visitor center, nature center, and hiking trails in addition to the historic grounds and ranch house.

Zuma Beach County Park: One of Los Angeles' best-known beaches; offers swimming, surfing, and hiking.

*Zuma/Trancas Canyons: A 5,859-acre site offering critical wildlife habitat in the heart of the Santa Monica Mountains. Hiking trails lead through this undeveloped area.

ENTRANCE FEE: No charge.

FACILITIES: A variety of facilities, including food and lodging, are available along roads through and bordering the park.

CAMPING: Camping is available in Point Mugu State Park (140 spaces), Malibu Creek State Park (60 spaces), and Leo Carrillo State Park (135 spaces). All three parks can accept trailers and campers of up to 31 feet. From March through September, reservations are requested (800–444–7275). Group camping (ten to seventy-five people) is available at Circle X Ranch (vault toilets). Reservations are required (805–370–2300, ext. 1702).

FISHING: Limited fishing is available throughout the park with a California fishing license. The most popular areas are the beaches and the public pier in Santa Monica.

SEQUOIA NATIONAL PARK
KINGS CANYON NATIONAL PARK

47050 Generals Highway
Three Rivers, CA 93271
(559) 565–3341
SEKI_Interpretation@nps.gov
www.nps.gov/seki

General Grant and Sequoia National Parks were established in 1890. Kings Canyon National Park was established separately in 1940 and incorporated General Grant National Park. Today, the parks' combined 1,300 square miles are administered together. The parks are especially noted for groves of giant sequoias growing on plateaus surrounded by the High Sierra. Sequoia and Kings Canyon are located in central California, between Yosemite and Death Valley. Access is from the west, with State Highway 180 from Fresno leading into Kings Canyon and Route 198 from Visalia entering Sequoia. No road crosses the Sierra Nevada range in either park.

The Sierra Nevada is the result of an uplifting of the earth's crust millions of years ago. Later, during the Great Ice Age, glaciers quarried canyons and scooped basins, giving the mountains their present shape. Once the glaciers began melting, the basins turned into lakes and plant life returned to the region. The sequoias dominating the park were once widespread but now grow only on the western slope of the Sierra. Although not as tall as the related coastal redwoods, the sequoias are immense, with trunk sizes that are simply amazing.

The parks' three major developed areas are Lodgepole, Grant Grove, and Cedar Grove. Generals Highway connects Ash Mountain, Lodgepole, and Grant Grove. Entering at Ash Mountain, the road passes through Giant Forest, which contains some of the finest groups of giant sequoias, including the General Sherman tree—the world's largest living tree. The area is covered with trails, and short walks to Moro Rock, Beetle Rock, and Sunset Rock provide excellent viewpoints. Visitor centers are located at Ash Mountain and Lodgepole, and a new museum is in Giant Forest.

After leaving the park at Lost Grove, the road wanders in a northwesterly direction to Grant Grove, an isolated section of Kings Canyon. Here, the visitor can see the General Grant tree—the Nation's Christmas tree. Nearby are other large sequoias, and a visitor center with exhibits and a slide presentation is about a mile away. Be sure to visit this area of giant trees. Big Stump Basin, where large trees were cut during the logging era before the basin became part of Kings Canyon National Park, is reached via a self-guided trail near the south entrance. The Grant Grove area is convenient to both Cedar Grove and Giant Forest (about 30 miles to each), which makes it a good place to stay if you have only limited time. The road from Grant Grove to Cedar Grove (30 miles) is open from about mid-April to mid-November, and the view of the canyon is something not to be missed. Cedar Grove is one of the centers of activity in Kings Canyon. Visitors will find it considerably warmer than Grant Grove. Here peaks rise to a mile or more above the South Fork of the Kings River. The river is fair for fishing, but because of the swift current and very cold water, it is not suitable for swimming or rafting. The end of the road is the site of major trailheads to the high country (long-term parking is available). A self-guided nature trail is nearby. The trailhead to Mount Whitney, the highest mountain in the contiguous United States, is reached along a paved road from Lone Pine on the Sierras' east side.

SEQUOIA NATIONAL PARK; KINGS CANYON NATIONAL PARK

McClure
Meadow

INYO
NATIONAL
FOREST

Le Conte
Canyon

John Muir Trail and Pacific Crest Trail

Bench Lake

SIERRA NATIONAL
FOREST

KINGS CANYON
NATIONAL PARK

Kings Canyon Scenic Byway

Cedar Grove
Visitor Center
and Village

Mist
Falls

Rae
Lakes

Sequoia National Forest

Charlotte
Lake

Grant Grove Visitor
Center and Village

Big Stump
Entrance

Roaring
River

Stony Creek Village

Lost
Grove

Wuksachi
Village

Lodgepole
Visitor Center
and Village

Tyndall
Creek

Dorst Creek

Crystal
Cave

Wolverton

Mount
Whitney

Giant Forest

Bearpaw
Meadow

Crabtree

Pacific

Giant
Forest
Museum

SEQUOIA
NATIONAL
PARK

Rock
Creek

Crest Trail

Ash Mountain
Entrance

Foothills
Visitor
Center

Atwell
Mill

Mineral King
Ranger Station

Little
Five
Lakes

Lookout
Point
Entrance

Cold
Springs

198

Hockett
Meadows

Kern
Canyon

INYO
NATIONAL
FOREST

South Fork

SEQUOIA NATIONAL FOREST

Ranger-guided walks to areas of interest in both parks are provided throughout the year. Schedules are posted in lodges, campgrounds, and visitor centers. Campfire programs are presented at Lodgepole, Grant Grove, Dorst, Cedar Grove, and Mineral King. Saddle horses and pack animals may be rented at corrals near Wolverton, Mineral King, Grant Grove, Cedar Grove, and at various locations on the Sierras' east side. More than 700 miles of trails are open to horses. Limited tours (fee required) of Crystal Cave are scheduled Friday through Monday during May and September and daily during summer months. A steep $1/2$-mile trail leads to the cave entrance.

Winter season at Sequoia and Kings Canyon is from December through March. Cross-country ski tour centers are at Grant Grove and Lodgepole, where ski and snowshoe rentals are available. Many miles of marked trails are in the Grant Grove and Giant Forest areas. A 3-mile marked trail from Wolverton to Giant Forest is available for cross-country skiing. Sleds, tubes, and platters are permitted at Wolverton and Grant Grove.

LODGING: Lodging is available all year at Grant Grove Lodge, which offers hotel rooms and cabins. Stony Creek Lodge, located 15 miles north of Giant Forest Village in Sequoia National Forest, has rooms in a two-story building that is open from May through Labor Day, depending on weather. Cedar Grove Lodge, in the Cedar Grove area of Sequoia/Kings Canyon National Park, has eighteen rooms in a modern two-story wooden building that is open from mid-May to mid-October, depending on weather. For information on reservations in any of these facilities, write Kings Canyon Park Services, 5755 East Kings Canyon Road, Suite 101, Fresno, CA 93727. Call (866) 522–6966, or visit the Web site at www.sequoia-kingscanyon.com. A new lodging facility north of Lodgepole, Wuksachi Village and Lodge, with 102 rooms, was completed in 1999. For reservations, write Delaware North Park Services, 5410 East Home Avenue, Fresno, CA 93727. Call (888) 252–5757, or visit the Web site at www.visitsequoia.com.

ENTRANCE FEE: $10.00 per vehicle or $5.00 per person; good for seven days.

FACILITIES: Restaurants are open year-round at Grant Grove and Wuksachi Village. Food service is available at Stony Creek and Cedar Grove from late May to October. General supplies are available at Cedar Grove, Lodgepole, Grant Grove, and Stony Creek.

CAMPING: A variety of campgrounds are located within the two parks. Most offer tables, grills, water, and flush toilets. In Sequoia, the Giant Forest area has Lodgepole (214 spaces, dump station, pay showers, store) and Dorst (204 spaces, 7 group sites, dump station). Lodgepole fills first, and campground reservations are available by calling (800) 365–2267 or on the Web at reservations.nps.gov. In the Mineral King area, Atwell Mill (twenty-one spaces) and Cold Springs (forty spaces) have pit toilets. No trailers are permitted in either campground. At lower elevations are Buckeye Flat (twenty-eight spaces, no trailers or recreation vehicles), Potwisha (forty-two spaces, dump station, swimming), and South Fork (ten spaces, pit toilet, trailers not recommended).

In Kings Canyon, the Grant Grove area has Azalea (110 spaces), Crystal Springs (62 spaces), and Sunset (179 spaces, limited trailer space). A market and pay showers are located within walking distance of these campgrounds. In the Cedar Grove area are Canyon View (37 spaces, 4 group sites), Moraine (120 spaces), Sentinel (82 spaces), and Sheep Creek (111 spaces, dump station). Of these, Sentinel generally fills first and is the most crowded, while Moraine has somewhat less shade and is the least crowded. The amphitheater and ranger station are at Sentinel Campground.

FISHING: Many wilderness lakes and streams contain golden, rainbow, brook, and brown trout. The most popular fishing spots are along the Kings River and the forks of the Kaweah River. A California fishing license is required and may be purchased at the stores.

WHISKEYTOWN NATIONAL RECREATION AREA

P.O. Box 188
Whiskeytown, CA 96095-0188
Park Headquarters (530) 242–3400
Park Visitor Center (530) 246–1225
WHIS_Interpretation@nps.gov
www.nps.gov/whis

Whiskeytown National Recreation Area, established in 1965, comprises 42,500 acres of some of Northern California's most beautiful mountain landscapes and includes oak woodlands, mixed conifer forests, and the 3,000-acre Whiskeytown Lake. Whiskeytown is a part of the Whiskeytown-Shasta-Trinity National Recreation Area, which is operated by the National Park Service. The USDA Forest Service operates the Shasta and Trinity units. The national recreation area is located in north-central California, approximately 230 miles north of San Francisco and a short distance north of the town of Redding. From I–5, take the 299 west exit for approximately 8 miles to the visitor center.

Nestled within the Klamath Mountains watershed and steeped in the colorful history of the California gold rush, the clear blue waters of Whiskeytown Lake are often referred to as the jewel of the northstate. Man-made Whiskeytown Lake is part of the Central Valley Water Project that provides water and power to the Central Valley of California.

The recreation area offers visitors a wealth of lake-oriented and backcountry activities and is host to a variety of wildlife, including black bears, mountain lions, kokanee salmon, and bald eagles. With 36 miles of shoreline and numerous coves, the lake is an inviting place during the summer, when temperatures average 95 degrees Fahrenheit. Water activities include sailing, boating, kayaking, swimming, scuba diving, and fishing. Three boat-launching ramps and two designated swim areas with sandy beaches are open to visitors. The lake's shallow areas begin to warm by late May and offer relief from the hot summer temperatures.

Extensive mountains and canyons, ranging in elevation from 800 feet to over 6,200 feet at Shasta Bally, surround the lake to form the largest part of the recreation area. The recreation area includes eight year-round creeks with waterfalls and deep pools. Old-growth forest stands, extensive mountains, and canyons provide a chance for solitude, while roads and trails throughout the area allow opportunities for hiking, mountain biking, and horseback riding.

Whiskeytown NRA is a land rich in the cultural history of the Wintu Indians and the pioneers of the California gold rush. Visitors can learn about the history of this area by touring the Tower House Historic District. Historic buildings, mines, and water ditches dating to the 1850s allow visitors to step back in time. Ranger programs typically include hikes, kayak tours, and gold panning. Evening programs are offered seasonally.

ENTRANCE FEE: $5.00 per vehicle per day or $10.00 for seven days.

FACILITIES: Visitor center exhibits, three boat ramps, snack bars, and boat rentals are available during the summer at Oak Bottom and Brandy Creek. Restaurants and lodging are in Redding and French Gulch.

CAMPING: Oak Bottom offers tent sites, some of which are lakeside, and RV sites (separate parking lot sites) with access to flush toilets, pay showers, water, and dump stations. Reservations are available for the summer season by calling (800) 365–2267 or through the Website at reservations.nps.gov. Brandy Creek RV Campground offers paved parking spots on an access road. Two tent-only group sites that can each hold fifty persons are available by reservation only. Several drive-in primitive camping sites (vault toilets, fire grate, picnic table, and bear-proof locker) are available in the backcountry. Required permits are available at park headquarters.

FISHING: Fishing is good either from a boat or from shore. The lake is stocked with rainbow and brown trout. Largemouth, smallmouth, and spotted bass and kokanee salmon are also in the lake. A California fishing license is required.

YOSEMITE NATIONAL PARK

P.O. Box 577
Yosemite National Park, CA 95389-0577
(209) 372–0200
www.nps.gov/yose

Yosemite National Park was established in 1890 and comprises what may be the most beautiful 747,956 acres in the United States. Granite peaks and domes rise above green or snow-covered meadows in the heart of the Sierra Nevada. The park is located in east-central California, approximately 190 miles due east of San Francisco via California Highway 120 east and west, Highway 140 from Merced, and Highway 41 from Fresno. While in the Yosemite area, consider exploring California Highway 49 on the park's west side. Here you will wander through many areas made famous by gold-seekers in 1849. On the park's east side, the ghost town of Bodie, near Mono Lake, is super. Bodie is a state park managed by the California State Department of Parks and Recreation.

Yosemite represents all that is good and most that is bad about the National Park System. The scenery is quite possibly the best of any national park. Yosemite contains beautiful valleys, high-country meadows, sparkling lakes, and spectacular waterfalls. The park's elevations range from 2,000 feet to more than 13,000 feet above sea level, which produces an outstanding variety of both animal and plant life. The bad part is that because of the area's beauty, visitors and campers have loved parts of the park nearly to death. Yosemite Valley is especially heavily used during the summer months. Bears can be a problem, and visitors are advised to remove food, trash, and odorous items from vehicles. Food-storage lockers are available for campers.

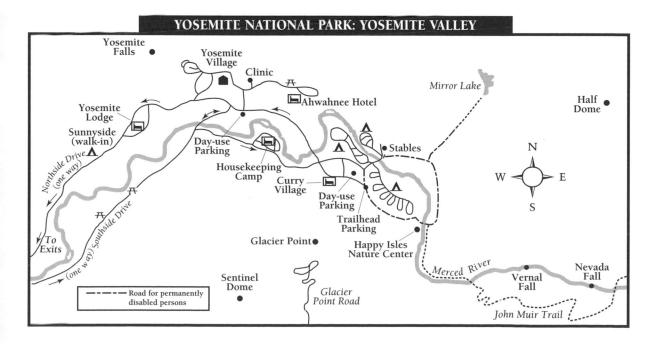

YOSEMITE NATIONAL PARK: YOSEMITE VALLEY

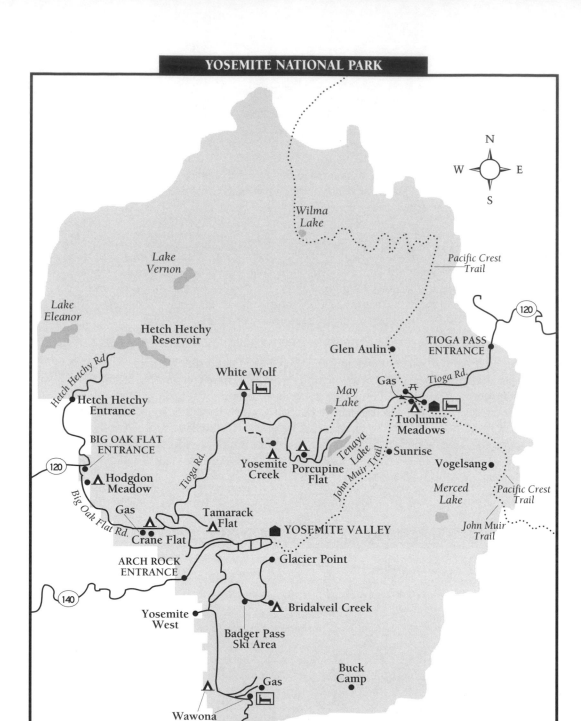

There are four major entrances into Yosemite National Park—two from the west, one from the south, and one from the east. Tioga Road is the only road that bisects the park in an east-west direction. To experience the high elevations, it is necessary to use Tioga Road because the high country is toward the east side and away from Yosemite Valley. The road is usually closed from mid-November through early June from Crane Flat to the Tioga Pass entrance.

Most organized activity at Yosemite is in Yosemite Valley. Yosemite Village contains a visitor center and most modern conveniences that can be found in any small town. The entrance road follows the Merced River to all the main buildings and valley campgrounds. A free shuttle-bus service in the east end of the valley greatly simplifies getting around the valley floor. This service was introduced to reduce auto emissions and traffic congestion. Parking is available at Curry Village and Yosemite Village for day-use visitors. The valley is open all year and contains often-photographed features such as El Capitan, Half Dome, Yosemite Falls, and Bridalveil Fall. The falls are most active in the early summer months.

Although most visitors spend the majority of time in the valley, Yosemite contains many other worthwhile features. A large grove of giant sequoias is located near the south entrance. Two smaller giant sequoia groves can be found near Crane Flat on the west side of the park. Near the south entrance at Wawona is the Pioneer Yosemite History Center—an exhibit of historic buildings where, during the summer, visitors will find living-history demonstrations and horse-drawn vehicles.

Fifty-five miles from the valley across Tioga Road is Tuolumne Meadows. At an elevation of 8,600 feet, this is the largest subalpine meadow in the High Sierra. It is also a center for high country pack trips and hikes.

Perhaps the best-known activity at Yosemite is rock climbing. A lesser-known but equally exciting activity is hang gliding. This sport is permitted under special regulations. If these are too dangerous, visitors can try some of the 800 miles of hiking trails. Guided horse rides are available at Wawona and Tuolumne Meadows during summer months. Swimming is available in the park's rivers or at lodge swimming pools. Nightly interpretive programs are available at campgrounds and at concessioner facilities.

Winter activities at Yosemite include downhill skiing at Badger Pass with four lifts, one rope tow, a rental shop, and ski school. Several trails are available for cross-country skiing, and a guide map is available. Other winter activities include snowshoeing, ice skating at Curry Village, and guided trips at Badger Pass. Glacier Park Road from Badger Pass to Glacier Point is closed to vehicles from late fall to late spring and is groomed for cross-country skiing.

ENTRANCE FEE: $20 per vehicle or $10 per person; good for seven days.

LODGING: Seven lodging facilities of varying quality and price are situated within Yosemite. Yosemite Lodge, Curry Village, the Ahwahnee, and Housekeeping Camp are in Yosemite Valley. The Ahwahnee is the most upscale of the four, while Housekeeping Camp offers canvas and cement structures for a relatively inexpensive camping-type experience. The grand Wawona Hotel is outside the valley, toward the park's south entrance. White Wolf Lodge and Tuolumne Meadows Lodge offer tent cabins and a few regular cabins on Tioga Pass. The High Sierra Camps offer overnight accommodations for hikers. For reservations at any of these facilities, write Yosemite Reservations, 5410 East Home Avenue, Fresno, CA 93727; call (559) 252–4848; or check out the Web site at www.yosemitepark.com. Yosemite's facilities, especially those in Yosemite Valley, are packed during summer months, so it is necessary to make reservations early. Only the Ahwahnee, Yosemite Lodge, and the Wawona are open year-round.

FACILITIES: Nearly anything can be found somewhere in Yosemite. Lodging, restaurants, and stores are located at Wawona, El Portal, Tuolumne Meadows, White Wolf, and in Yosemite Valley. Reservations are advised for all overnight accommodations. Medical facilities are provided in Yosemite Valley at Yosemite Medical Clinic. A self-service laundry is open year-round at Housekeeping Camp, and pay showers are available at Curry Village. Filling stations can be found summer only at Tuolumne Meadows and at Wawona and Crane Flat all year. The valley also includes a kennel. Tours are available.

CAMPING: Developed campgrounds are located throughout the park, with the four in the valley usually filling very early. There are nearly 418 spaces in Yosemite Valley, with the largest campgrounds at Upper Pines (238 spaces) and Lower Pines (60 spaces). Upper Pines is open all year. All of these have picnic tables, fire rings, and flush toilets, and each is near a shuttle-bus stop. Dump stations are located at the Upper Pines campground. The valley campgrounds are very crowded, sometimes resembling giant parking lots. The park's other improved campgrounds are at Bridalveil Creek (110 spaces), Crane Flat (166 spaces), Hodgdon Meadow (105 spaces), Tuolumne Meadows (304 spaces), Wawona (93 spaces, store, and dump station nearby), and White Wolf (87 spaces). Unimproved campgrounds are located at Porcupine Flat (fifty-two spaces), Tamarack Flat (fifty-two spaces), and Yosemite Creek (seventy-five spaces). Reservations for Valley campsites are advised. Call (800) 436–7275 or visit the Web site reservations.nps.gov. A limited number of campsites made available by cancellations are offered on a first-come, first-served basis at a small station in the day-use parking area near Curry Village.

FISHING: Five species of trout—brook, brown, cutthroat, golden, and rainbow—are found in Yosemite waters. Rainbow and brown are most abundant. A state fishing license is required, and the season is from the last Saturday in April to mid-November. Inquire at park visitor centers or information stations for park-specific fishing regulations.

COLORADO

STATE TOURIST INFORMATION
(800) 265–6723
www.colorado.com

BENT'S OLD FORT NATIONAL HISTORIC SITE

402 Santa Fe Avenue
La Junta, CO 81050
(719) 383–5010
www.nps.gov/beol

Bent's Old Fort National Historic Site comprises 800 acres and became part of the National Park Service in 1960 to commemorate how Bent's Old Fort opened up the West to the United States. The park is in southeastern Colorado, 8 miles east of La Junta and 13 miles west of Las Animas on Colorado Highway 194.

The early 1800s saw an influx of traders into the Santa Fe and Taos area of what is now New Mexico. Caravans from Independence, Missouri, the main staging point, traveled to Santa Fe by two routes. The main trail ran across the Kansas plains to the Cimarron Crossing of the Arkansas River. At this point the trail broke into two branches. The Cimarron Cutoff crossed the Comanche-inhabited Cimarron Desert and offered little water. The Mountain Branch continued along the Arkansas River and turned southwest near Timpas Creek. The second route was longer, but it offered greater safety and more trees and water.

The two Bent brothers and partner Ceran St. Vrain decided in the early 1830s to build a trading establishment. Because of the location they chose, the men knew that a strong fort would be required. The enclosed adobe structure took many men years to construct.

Over a period of years, the merchants became trusted friends of the Indians and built a booming business. Finished goods were brought to the fort from Missouri, where they were exchanged for buffalo robes and beaver pelts. The men opened additional stores in Santa Fe and Taos. The annexation of Texas in 1845 brought turmoil to the region because U.S. troops used the fort as a staging area for invasions of New Mexico. The influx of soldiers, settlers, and

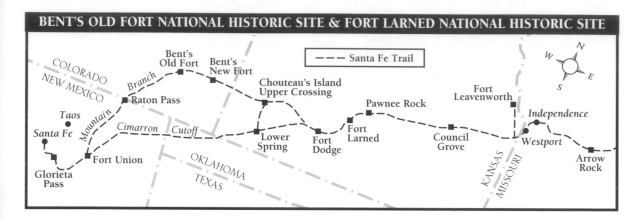

adventurers resulted in conflict with the once-peaceful Indians, and trade eventually came to a halt. It is thought that reduced trade and a cholera epidemic among the Indians caused William Bent to set fire to the fort and move 38 miles down the Arkansas River. There he built a structure that became known as Bent's New Fort (hence, the present name for the initial structure). Although the old fort was temporarily rehabilitated for use as a stage station, it was once again abandoned so that by the early 1900s, only parts of the old walls were still standing.

During 1975 and 1976, Bent's Old Fort was reconstructed on the original foundation to its 1845–1846 appearance. Interpretive Park Service and volunteer personnel are on duty daily inside the fort. Guided walks and a twenty-minute film are offered periodically throughout the day. The site is open from 8:00 A.M. to 5:30 P.M. from June 1 to August 31, and from 9:00 A.M. to 4:00 P.M. from September 1 through May 31.

ENTRANCE FEE: $3.00 per adult; $2.00 for ages six to twelve; children under age six are free.

FACILITIES: Water and rest rooms are located at the parking lot and at the reconstructed fort. Food services and lodging are found in La Junta and Las Animas.

CAMPING: No camping is permitted in the park. Private campgrounds are nearby in La Junta. For travelers on Highway 50, the Corps of Engineers' John Martin Reservoir provides pleasant camping (fifty-one mostly shaded sites, water, flush toilets, no showers, no hookups) 3 miles south of the town of Hasty. Hasty is approximately 27 miles east of Bent's Old Fort.

BLACK CANYON OF THE GUNNISON
NATIONAL PARK

102 Elk Creek
Gunnison, CO 81230
(970) 641–2337
cure_info@nps.gov
www.nps.gov/blca

Black Canyon of the Gunnison National Monument was added to the park system in 1933 to preserve 12 miles of a spectacular and unspoiled canyon that has been cut by the Gunnison River. The designation was changed to a national park in 1999, and the park now preserves 14 miles of the canyon. The park is located in west-central Colorado, with both rims accessible by automobile. The north rim is reached over a 14-mile road (6 miles of gravel) originating from Colorado Highway 92, east of Crawford. The south rim is 5 miles north of U.S. 50 via a paved road, County Highway 347, beginning 6 miles east of Montrose.

The Black Canyon was formed over a period of two million years by the continuous erosive forces of the Gunnison River. The river and its seasonal floods have produced a canyon with depths ranging from 1,750 to 2,660 feet and widths of as little as 1,100 feet (at Chasm View). The erosive Gunnison has cut faster than its tributaries, resulting in canyons hanging high over the main gorge. The walls are mostly Precambrian rock, from light to dark gray in color—hence, the name. In many places pinkish granite intrusions provide colorful highlights, as can be seen on the "Painted Wall."

The river established its course by cutting through soft volcanic rock. It then continued to carve into the hard crystalline rocks of the present canyon. Pinnacles in the eastern area of the park have been created with the assistance of the river, as its flow followed the layers of less resistant rock.

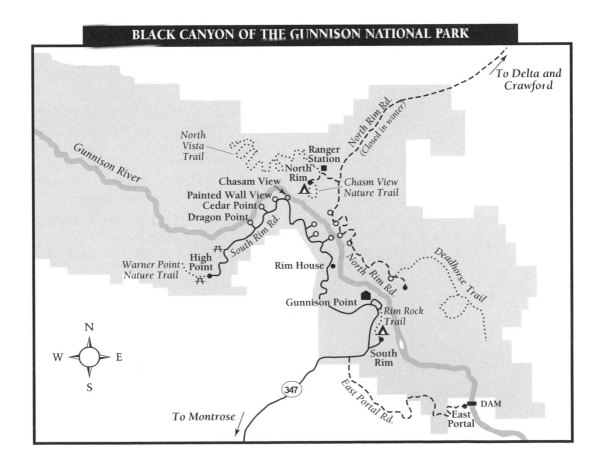

BLACK CANYON OF THE GUNNISON NATIONAL PARK

Visitors should first stop at the visitor center, where information and exhibits on the life and geology of the park are available. The paved road following the south rim is seldom more than 1/4 mile from the canyon. Spectacular views are available from numerous short foot trails, beginning from parking areas along the road's side. Interpretive signs are generally located at the end of each trail, and a self-guided trail is located at Cedar Point. Trail booklets are available for the Rim Rock Trail (starting at the South Rim Campground), the Warner Nature Trail (starting at High Point), and Chasm View Nature Trail (on the north rim). During summer months, conducted walks and evening programs take place in the park.

ENTRANCE FEE: $7.00 per vehicle or $4.00 per person; good for seven days. Children ages sixteen and under are free.

FACILITIES: No food or overnight accommodations are available at the park, but they can be found in nearby communities.

CAMPING: The park has two campgrounds. North Rim Campground (thirteen spaces) provides tables, grills, water (trucked in), and pit toilets and is open from May through October. South Rim Campground (eighty-nine spaces) has similar facilities but is open year-round. Commercial campgrounds are located in Montrose.

FISHING: Brown and rainbow trout inhabit the Gunnison River, although access is difficult. A Colorado fishing license is required.

COLORADO NATIONAL MONUMENT

Fruita, CO 81521-0001
(970) 858–3617
COLM_Superintendent@nps.gov
www.nps.gov/colm

Colorado National Monument was established as part of the National Park System in 1911. The park comprises 20,454 acres of steep-walled canyons and monoliths, in a beautiful sandstone region. The park is in west-central Colorado, just west of the city of Grand Junction via I–70 or U.S. Highways 6 and 50.

Many western movie scenes shot in Monument Valley, Arizona, could just as easily have been filmed in Colorado National Monument. Water, wind, and freezing have produced some spectacular red canyons. Even though the area's annual 11-inch rainfall is relatively sparse, it generally occurs in concentrated bursts of such intensity as to have a pronounced effect on the landscape. Monument Canyon, in the park's northern end, is one of Colorado National Monument's most impressive areas.

Rim Rock Drive is a 23-mile, narrow, winding paved road that connects the east and west entrances. The drive is one of the finest offered in any park in the country. Visitors will see many outstanding formations, and a number of parking overlooks are provided. A visitor center near the west entrance is open all year and offers a slide program and exhibits that explain the monument's history and geological formations. It is best to drive the park road from west to east so that the visitor center can be a first stop.

A number of hiking trails provide access to the park's interior. Trails include 2 1/4-mile Serpents Trail near Devils Kitchen Picnic Area and the longer Monument Canyon (6 miles), Black

COLORADO NATIONAL MONUMENT

Ridge (5½ miles), and Liberty Cap (7 miles) Trails. There are a number of short trails, including the self-guided Alcove Trail near the visitor center.

ENTRANCE FEE: $5.00 per vehicle or $3.00 per person; good for seven days.

FACILITIES: Picnic areas with tables, grills, water, and flush toilets are located near both the east and west entrances. No food, gasoline, or overnight accommodations are available at the monument, but all three are available at Fruita (3 miles north of the west entrance) or Grand Junction (4 miles east of the east entrance).

CAMPING: Saddlehorn Campground (eighty spaces) is adjacent to the visitor center, 4½ miles south of the west entrance. The campground is open all year and offers tables, charcoal grills, and flush toilets. Juniper and piñon trees provide some shade. Saddlehorn Campground provides campers with a spectacular view of the Grand Valley. Private campgrounds are in Grand Junction and Fruita.

CURECANTI NATIONAL RECREATION AREA

102 Elk Creek
Gunnison, CO 81230
(970) 641–2337
cure_info@nps.gov
www.nps.gov/cure

Curecanti National Recreation Area, administered under a cooperative agreement with the Bureau of Reclamation since 1965, comprises more than 40,000 acres. The recreation area consists of three reservoirs, known as the Wayne Aspinall Storage Unit. Two reservoirs are set in the deep canyon of the Gunnison River. The park is paralleled by U.S. 50 in west-central Colorado. The eastern border is approximately 6 miles west of the town of Gunnison.

The reservoirs of Curecanti National Recreation Area, part of the Upper Colorado River Storage Project, result from three dams constructed on the Gunnison River. These three reservoirs provide visitors with a wide variety of water sports and other outdoor activities amid the spectacular scenery of Colorado mesa and canyon country. The land in this region has been shaped by volcanic activity and the erosive forces of nature. Evidence of both is easily seen along the shores of the reservoirs and on the walls of the surrounding cliffs.

Because of the cold winters, the normal visitor season is from mid-May through mid-October. Evening naturalist programs are regularly scheduled during summer months, and activity schedules are posted in visitor-use areas. The park's main visitor center is at Elk Creek, where visitors can view exhibits. In Cimarron there is an information station with a narrow-gauge railroad exhibit. An 1895 trestle, a steam locomotive (Engine 278 is one of three of this type left in the United States), and several cars, including a caboose from the Denver and Rio Grande Western Railroad, can be seen.

A ninety-minute naturalist-staffed boat tour of the Upper Black Canyon, a dramatic, fjord-like canyon, begins just below Blue Mesa Dam on Morrow Point Reservoir. The early history of the region, including accounts of the Ute Indians and the Denver and Rio Grande Western Railroad's narrow gauge line, are some of the themes discussed. Reaching the point of departure requires going down 232 steps and walking for a half hour, but the views from the bottom of the 400 to 1,000-foot canyon are outstanding. Reservations are recommended for the boat tours (970–641–2237).

ENTRANCE FEE: No charge. There are boating permit fees.

FACILITIES: No overnight lodging is available in the park, but accommodations and most services are available in Montrose, Gunnison, and other nearby towns. A nice restaurant is adjacent to the marina at Elk Creek. Ranger stations and first aid are available at Cimarron, Lake Fork, and Elk Creek. Marinas at both Elk Creek and Lake Fork offer boat repairs and rentals, gasoline, guided fishing tours on Blue Mesa and Morrow Point, fishing tackle, and groceries.

CAMPING: The most developed campgrounds, with tables, grills, water, flush toilets, and dump stations, are at Cimarron (22 spaces), Elk Creek (179 spaces, pay showers), and Lake Fork (87 spaces, pay showers). Campgrounds at Dry Gulch (ten spaces), East Portal (fifteen spaces), Gateview (seven spaces), Ponderosa (twenty-nine spaces), Red Creek (two spaces), and Stevens Creek (fifty-four spaces) have pit toilets. Only Elk Creek is open all year.

FISHING: Federal and state fish hatcheries annually stock more than three million fish in the reservoirs. Anglers can enjoy year-round, high-country trout fishing at Curecanti. Ice fishing for rainbow and German brown trout is popular from December through March, and trolling and bank fishing become popular as soon as open water appears in the spring. Trolling fishermen find the rainbow, brown, and lake (mackinaw) trout fishing good throughout the season, with the best kokanee salmon fishing in late June and July. A Colorado fishing license is required and may be purchased at the Elk Creek Marina.

DINOSAUR NATIONAL MONUMENT

4545 E Highway 40
Dinosaur, CO 81610-9724
(970) 374–3000
DINO_Superintendent@nps.gov
www.nps.gov/dino

Dinosaur National Monument, established in 1915, contains fossil remains of dinosaurs and other ancient animals. The 210,000-acre park also includes spectacular canyons cut by the Green and Yampa Rivers. The park straddles the border of northeast Utah and northwest Colorado. Access from U.S. 40 is via State Highway 149 at Jensen, which goes north to the Dinosaur Quarry and the main fossil area of the park. Access to the canyons is via Harpers Corner Self-Guided Scenic Drive at monument headquarters, a few miles east of Dinosaur.

Dinosaur National Monument contains a deposit of fossil bones of crocodiles, turtles, and dinosaurs. Dinosaur Quarry, located 7 miles north of Jensen, Utah, in the southwestern portion of the monument, offers an exposed wall of the quarry. The center is open daily from 8:00 A.M. to 4:30 P.M. during winter and 8:00 A.M. to 7:00 P.M. during the busier summer season. A shuttle bus operates between the main parking area and the quarry daily during the summer because of limited parking space at the quarry. It closes on Thanksgiving, Christmas, and New Year's Day.

In addition to the quarry area, Dinosaur offers some spectacularly wild and scenic country. A part of the park is reached by automobile, but most of it is available only to those willing to walk or raft. The 31-mile Harpers Corner Self-Guided Scenic Drive winds north from monument headquarters, which is located 2 miles east of Dinosaur, Colorado. The road has interpretive signs at overlooks and three nature trails. This road is paved and is generally open from April through October. The road ends with a 1-mile self-guided nature trail to view numerous canyons cut by the Green and Yampa Rivers. Four accessible pit toilets are the only facilities on the road. Visitors should plan to spend from two to four hours for the round-trip.

Backcountry roads are available for the more adventurous motorists, but they are impassable when wet. These are generally rough and dusty and lead to more-remote areas. One of the most spectacular, Echo Park Road, begins just south of the park boundary on Harpers Corner Self-Guided Scenic Drive. This is a 13-mile dirt road that passes by Indian petroglyphs and Whispering Cave. No trailers, heavy vehicles, or low-clearance vehicles should be driven here because of steep grades and sharp turns. Generally accessible roads are available in the northern and eastern parts of the monument. Self-guided nature trails are found at Split Mountain Campground, Gates of Lodore, Monument Headquarters, and Harpers Corner Self-Guided Scenic Drive, and raft trips are available through private concessioners. Information on river running is available at the visitor center. Private river runners are required to have a river permit (fee charged) to navigate Dinosaur's rivers.

ENTRANCE FEE: $10.00 per vehicle or $5.00 per person; good for seven days. Fees are collected only at the Dinosaur Quarry area on the Utah side of the park.

FACILITIES: Motels and cafes are available at Dinosaur, Rangely, Craig, and Vernal. Food, gas, and ice are available at these towns and at Jensen. Medical facilities are offered in Craig, Rangely, and Vernal. Ranger stations are located at some public-use areas. Those at Deerlodge Park and Echo Park may be open in summer months.

DINOSAUR NATIONAL MONUMENT

CAMPING: The only two improved campgrounds are Split Mountain Gorge (group camping only during summer; reservations required) and Green River (ninety-nine spaces, summer only), both located on a paved road east of the Quarry Visitor Center. The campgrounds have picnic tables, fire grates, water, and flush toilets. Programs are available at Green River Campground some nights in summer. Green River Campground is shadier. Primitive campgrounds are located at Deerlodge Park (eight spaces, no water), Echo Park (seventeen spaces), Gates of Lodore (seventeen spaces), and Rainbow Park (four spaces, no water). These have pit toilets and picnic tables.

FISHING: The Green and Yampa Rivers are generally muddy, and fishing for catfish is fair at best. Trout fishing is occasionally good in Jones Creek. Either a Utah or a Colorado license must be obtained, depending on where you fish.

FLORISSANT FOSSIL BEDS NATIONAL MONUMENT

P.O. Box 185
Florissant, CO 80816-0185
(719) 748–3253
FLFO_Information@nps.gov
www.nps.gov/flfo

Florissant Fossil Beds, which comprises nearly 6,000 acres, was added to the National Park System in 1969 to preserve the fossil insects, seeds, and leaves that are found here in abundance. Standing petrified sequoia stumps are also on display. The park is located in central Colorado, approximately 36 miles west of Colorado Springs on U.S. 24. From the small town of Florissant, turn south on Teller County Road No. 1.

Fossils in this area have been preserved in sedimentary rock at the bottom of an ancient lake that existed here approximately thirty-four million years ago. Mudflows from a nearby volcanic field buried trees in the ancient forests and later dammed the stream to form the lake. Later, as the volcanic activity showered materials through the air, a large variety of plants and animals died and settled to the lake's bottom. Here they were buried in fine ash and other sediments that eventually compacted to form shale, and the plants and animals became fossilized. Over time Lake Florissant filled with volcanic materials until erosion later exposed the lake bed.

The monument is open from 8:00 A.M. to 7:00 P.M. (until 4:30 P.M. in winter) daily, except Thanksgiving, Christmas, and New Year's Day. The visitor center provides a display of many of the fossils that have been found here. Included are dragonflies, beetles, ants, spiders, fish, mammals, and birds. Also housed here are fossil leaves and blossoms from earlier relatives of birches, maples, willows, beeches, roses, and hickories. Giant petrified sequoia tree stumps have been excavated and can be seen along a ½-mile self-guided trail behind the visitor center and along a 1-mile trail just north of the center. In the summer, park rangers present interpretive talks and lead guided walks several times each day. A map with descriptions of the 14 miles of trails is available in the visitor center. The Hornbek Homestead, a short distance north of the visitor center, offers an excellent look at a homestead common in this region in the late 1800s and early 1900s. During winter months, visitors can cross-country ski and snowshoe on all the trails. Snowmobiling is prohibited. Dogs are not permitted on any of the trails.

ENTRANCE FEE: $3.00 per person; good for seven days. Children ages sixteen and under are free.

FACILITIES: Neither food services nor overnight accommodations are available in the park. Nearby towns of Woodland Park, Florissant, Lake George, Cripple Creek, and Divide have motels, food, and fuel. The visitor center provides water and modern rest rooms, and a picnic area is nearby. Two other picnic areas are available, one at Hornbek Homestead and another at an old farm site on Lower Twin Rock Road. Dogs are not permitted in either area.

CAMPING: No camping is permitted at the monument. Private campgrounds are located in Cripple Creek and along U.S. 24 toward Colorado Springs. The USDA Forest Service provides campgrounds near Lake George in Pike National Forest.

GREAT SAND DUNES NATIONAL MONUMENT AND PRESERVE

11500 Highway 150
Mosca, CO 81146-9798
(719) 378–6300
GRSA_Interpretation@nps.gov
www.nps.gov/grsa

Great Sand Dunes National Monument and Preserve comprises nearly 81,000 acres. The original national monument was established in 1932 to preserve North America's tallest sand dunes. The preserve was added in November 2000. The monument is located in south-central Colorado, 17 miles north of U.S. 160 via Colorado Highway 150. The park is approximately 38 miles from Alamosa.

The desert floor of the San Luis Valley is surrounded to the east and northeast by the Sangre de Cristo Mountains, to the west by the San Juan Mountains, and to the south by the San Luis

Great Sand Dunes National Monument and Preserve

Hills. This trap, combined with the prevailing southwesterly winds and the sand and silt that for centuries have been carried into the basin, has produced sand dunes piled to heights of up to 750 feet. The winds produce some changes in the details of the dunes, but the main mass has changed relatively little over the years. The eastern boundary of the dunes is formed by Medano Creek. The small dunes found east of the creek have been formed from sand blowing across the streambed when it is dry.

The visitor center has exhibits on the area. The center is closed all federal holidays in winter. Rangers conduct walks to the dunes and give evening campfire programs from Memorial Day to Labor Day. The Montville Nature Trail ($^{1}/_{2}$ mile) is located north of the visitor center; leaflets are provided for a nominal fee.

Medano Pass Primitive Road begins near the campground and provides access to the national preserve for four-wheel-drive, high-clearance vehicles. In addition, a concessioner operates four-wheel-drive tours over the road during summer months. For information, write Great Sand Dunes Oasis, 5400 Highway 150 North, Mosca, CO 81146 (719–378–2222).

The most popular activity in the park is hiking on the dunes. Routes are optional because there are no trails; however, most hikes begin from the dunes parking area. Campers may start at the campground. During summer months, hiking in the morning or late afternoon is most pleasant. The sand can be quite hot; wear appropriate shoes when hiking. Watch for lightning. Bring water, a hat, and sunscreen. Pets must be on a leash.

ENTRANCE FEE: $3.00 per person; good for seven days. Children ages sixteen and under are free.

FACILITIES: No lodging or food service is provided in the park, but food, snacks, and gasoline are available just outside the south entrance from May through October. Overnight accommodations can be found nearby and in Alamosa. Water, tables, and fire grates (charcoal only) are provided at the picnic area. Rest rooms with flush toilets are provided at the picnic area and the visitor center.

CAMPING: Piñon Flats Campground, with forty-four sites, is open year-round. An additional forty-four individual sites and three group sites (by reservation only) are open in summer. The campground provides tables, grills, water, flush toilets, and a dump station. Facilities are limited in the off-season. A private campground near the park has full hookups. Backcountry camping requires a free permit, available at the visitor center.

HOVENWEEP NATIONAL MONUMENT

McElmo Route
Cortez, CO 81321
(970) 562–4282
hoveinfo@nps.gov
www.nps.gov/hove

Hovenweep National Monument, which comprises 785 acres, was established in 1923 to preserve six clusters of ruins of pre-Columbian Pueblo Indians. The monument straddles the Utah–Colorado border and is 45 miles from Cortez, Colorado. Approaches range from paved to graded dirt and gravel roads.

The inhabitants of Hovenweep were prehistoric Pueblo Indians who occupied the Four Corners region until A.D. 1300. Their culture was similar to that of the inhabitants of Mesa Verde to the east. The Pueblos raised crops, gathered wild foods, and hunted. They also were excellent artists and craftworkers. For centuries they lived in small, scattered villages. During the early 1100s, however, they began moving into larger pueblos. By 1200 they had moved to the heads of the Hovenweep canyons and had built pueblos and towers, perhaps to protect the permanent springs. The long draws into the canyons could be terraced to hold back the soil and provide sheet-water irrigation for crops. By the late 1200s the Hovenweep area was deserted, partly because of a long period of drought.

Today's piles of masonry indicate the sizable population that once lived at Hovenweep. The monument consists of six groups of ruins: the Square Tower Ruins and Cajon Ruins in Utah, and the Holly, Hackberry, Cutthroat Castle, and Horseshoe ruins in Colorado. These ruins are

HOVENWEEP NATIONAL MONUMENT

all notable for their square, oval, circular, and D-shaped towers, many of which are built on boulders or rim edges.

Square Tower is the monument's best-preserved site. The 1½-mile Square Tower Loop Trail offers a close view of the structures in the group. A wheelchair-accessible trail leads to an overlook at Stronghold Point. The interior of the canyon has been closed to the public, but daily scheduled ranger-guided walks to the Square Tower and a petroglyph panel are available seasonally, generally April through October. The other sites are isolated and difficult to reach. A 4-mile trail from Square Tower leads to Holly Ruin. The Cajon Ruins consist of two large pueblos that have been ravaged by both time and relic hunters. Holly, Hackberry, and Cutthroat Castle sites consist of towers and pueblos. A high-clearance vehicle is required to reach these.

Temperatures at the monument tend to be moderate, although summer daytime temperatures can exceed 100 degrees Fahrenheit. June is generally a good month to avoid because of the presence of small biting gnats. Fall is probably the best time to visit.

ENTRANCE FEE: $6.00 per vehicle or $3.00 per person; good for seven days.

FACILITIES: No lodging or food service is available at the monument. Limited supplies can be purchased at Hatch Trading Post, 16 miles west, or at Ismay Trading Post, 14 miles southeast. The nearest overnight accommodations are at Blanding and Bluff in Utah and Cortez in Colorado. Water and rest rooms are provided at the visitor center and the campground. Gas is available in Aneth (20 miles to the south), Blanding, and Cortez.

CAMPING: A campground (thirty-one spaces) near the visitor center is open all year and has tables, grills, and flush toilets. The campground is rarely filled.

MESA VERDE NATIONAL PARK

P.O. Box 8
Mesa Verde National Park, CO 81330
(970) 529–4465
meve_general_information@nps.gov
www.nps.gov/meve

Mesa Verde National Park, which comprises more than 52,000 acres, was established in 1906 to protect the most notable and best-preserved pre-Columbian cliff dwellings in the United States. The park is located in the southwestern corner of Colorado, 10 miles east of Cortez and 35 miles west of Durango on U.S. 160.

The ancestral Puebloans of Mesa Verde went through three distinct stages. The earliest people, known as the Basketmakers, lived in clustered dwellings dug into the ground (pithouses) on mesa tops. Here they grew beans, squash, and corn in the rich soil. By the mid-700s A.D. descendants of the Basketmakers (Pueblos) began to construct surface dwellings with vertical walls and flat roofs. Over time, these square, stone structures were joined together in long-row villages (pueblos). By 1075 they had begun building thicker walls, which made the buildings strong enough to support more than one story. Sometime in the late 1100s, a small percentage of the people of Mesa Verde left their homes on mesa tops and constructed cliff dwellings, for which this park is best known. Exactly what prompted this move to the cliffs is uncertain, although possible reasons include protection from the elements and enemies. The dwellings may also have been constructed for religious or psychological reasons. Less than one hundred years later, the people left Mesa Verde and moved south to the pueblos of New Mexico and Arizona.

Far View Visitor Center, 16 miles from the park entrance, contains displays of contemporary Indian arts and crafts. Approximately halfway from the entrance to Far View is Park Point, which offers a viewpoint of the Four Corners region. The 12-mile drive from Far View to Wetherill Mesa (Memorial Day weekend through Labor Day only) offers some excellent views of the park. This mesa was heavily damaged by a fire in 2000, but the cliff dwellings were not harmed. An archaeological museum at Chapin Mesa contains artifacts and exhibits of life at Mesa Verde. Park personnel are available in each area to answer visitors' questions. During summer months, park rangers conduct trips through some of the sites (tickets are required) and present campfire programs each evening. Also during the summer local Indians offer craft demonstrations and other cultural presentations. Schedules are at the visitor center or museum. During winter months, walks are guided only to Spruce Tree House.

Hiking in Mesa Verde is restricted. In the Morefield Area, Prater Ridge Trail (7.8 miles), Knife Edge Trail (1.5 miles), and Point Lookout Trail (2.3 miles) require no permit. In the headquarters area, hikers must register at the trailhead for Petroglyph Point Trail (2.8 miles) or Spruce Canyon Trail (2.1 miles).

ENTRANCE FEE: $10.00 per vehicle or $5.00 per person; good for seven days. A $2.50 per person fee is charged for ranger-guided tours of Long House, Cliff Palace, and Balcony House.

FACILITIES: Far View Lodge, 15 miles inside the park, offers 150 motel-type rooms with private balconies that provide wonderful vistas. Dinner only is served in an attractive dining room at the lodge, while breakfast and lunch are available at Far View Terrace, 1/4-mile away. Reservations and information may be obtained by writing ARAMARK Mesa Verde, P.O. Box 277,

MESA VERDE NATIONAL PARK

Mancos, CO 81328 (800–449–2288). Food service is available at Morefield, Spruce Tree Terrace, and Wetherill Mesa, as well as at Far View. Rest rooms are provided at all four locations. Groceries and gasoline may be purchased at Morefield. All facilities, with the exception of Spruce Tree Terrace, are closed in winter.

CAMPING: Morefield Campground (477 spaces and 17 group camps) is 4 miles inside the park entrance. It provides tables, grills, water, a dump station, and flush toilets. Pay showers, a laundry, and a grocery are located within easy walking distance. The campground and the nearby facilities are open from early May until late October.

ROCKY MOUNTAIN NATIONAL PARK

1000 Highway 36
Estes Park, CO 80517-8397
(970) 586–1206
ROMO_Information@nps.gov
www.nps.gov/romo

Rocky Mountain National Park, established in 1915, comprises 265,769 acres of some of the most beautiful and easily accessible high-mountain country in North America. The park is located in north-central Colorado, with the main entrance near Estes Park, approximately 65 miles from Denver and 91 miles from Cheyenne. Rocky Mountain may also be approached from the town of Grand Lake on its southwestern boundary.

The area of the present-day Rocky Mountains was once covered by a great sea. More than a hundred million years ago, the sea began to recede, and the ancestral Rockies gradually rose above the old seabed. Over a period of millions of years, the mountains were eroded by the wind and water until only a high rolling plain was left. Approximately sixty million years ago, another gradual uplifting produced today's Rocky Mountains. The range began to erode almost immediately, and then about one million years ago, the ice age created giant glaciers that left U-shaped valleys, lakes, and moraines. Small glaciers are still in the park today.

The most accessible parts of the park lie along Trail Ridge Road, a 50-mile paved road (open in summer only) connecting Estes Park with Grand Lake, which reaches a height of more than 12,000 feet. Before driving the road, a stop at one of the visitor centers (Beaver Meadows near Estes Park or Kawuneeche near Grand Lake) will prove worthwhile. Trail Ridge Road stays above treeline for 11 miles and has numerous viewpoints, and the Alpine Visitor Center at Fall River Pass offers exhibits to help interpret this part of the park. Old Fall River Road is a section of the original road crossing the mountains and is open from West Horseshoe Park Junction to Fall River Pass. West of Endovalley, the gravel road is one-way uphill (westward).

The paved road to Bear Lake offers easy but congested access to a high-mountain basin. A shuttle-bus service is provided during the summer months. (Note: During the summer of 2004, access will be by shuttle bus only due to major construction.) Here a beautiful lake is combined with a number of the park's trailheads. The parking lots here and at Glacier Gorge Junction often fill early during summer. Two of the more popular trails beginning here are Dream Lake (2 miles round-trip) and Emerald Lake (3.6 miles round-trip). The park has more than 350 miles of trails, and horses are allowed on many of them. Cross-country skiing and snowshoeing are popular in winter. Hiking, technical climbing, wildlife watching, and horseback riding are popular in summer months. Ranger-led programs are offered throughout the year.

ENTRANCE FEE: $15.00 per vehicle or $5.00 per person; good for seven days. A $15.00 fee is charged for backcountry permits from May through October.

FACILITIES: No lodging is available inside the park, but accommodations are available in both Estes Park and Grand Lake. For information, write the Chamber Resort Association in

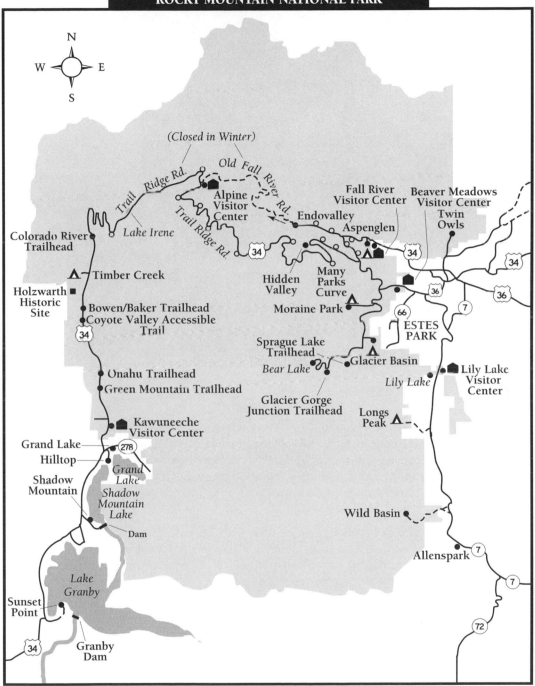

ROCKY MOUNTAIN NATIONAL PARK

N
W E
S

(Closed in Winter)

Trail Ridge Rd.

Old Fall River Rd.

Lake Irene

Trail Ridge Rd.

Alpine Visitor Center

Endovalley

Fall River Visitor Center

Beaver Meadows Visitor Center

Twin Owls

Aspenglen

34

34

34

Colorado River Trailhead

Timber Creek

Holzwarth Historic Site

Bowen/Baker Trailhead
Coyote Valley Accessible Trail

34

Hidden Valley

Many Parks Curve

Moraine Park

36

36

7

ESTES PARK

66

Onahu Trailhead

Green Mountain Trailhead

Sprague Lake Trailhead

Bear Lake

Glacier Basin

Lily Lake

Lily Lake Visitor Center

Kawuneeche Visitor Center

278

Glacier Gorge Junction Trailhead

Longs Peak

Grand Lake

Hilltop

Shadow Mountain

Grand Lake

Shadow Mountain Lake

Dam

Wild Basin

7

Allenspark

7

Lake Granby

Sunset Point

34

Granby Dam

72

Rocky Mountain National Park

Estes Park, CO 80517 (800–443–7837), or the Chamber of Commerce in Grand Lake, CO 80447 (800–531–1019). Food service is provided by a concessioner at the Fall River Pass store (summer only). Water and rest rooms are available at various locations, including the visitor centers and campgrounds. During summer, horses with guides can be hired at two locations inside the park on the east side or from a number of liveries outside both the east and west park boundaries.

CAMPING: Aspenglen (54 spaces), Glacier Basin (150 spaces, 12 group camps, dump station), Longs Peak (26 spaces, tents only), Moraine Park (247 spaces, dump station), and Timber Creek (100 spaces, dump station) all provide tables, grills, water, and flush toilets. Camping limit is seven days parkwide. At Long's Peak it is three days. Moraine Park, Longs Peak, and Timber Creek are open all year. Campsites at Glacier Basin and Moraine Park may be reserved. Call (800) 436–7275, or on the Web at reservations.nps.gov. Two hundred and sixty-seven backcountry campsites are available all year but may be in snow during winter. All overnight stays require permits that must be obtained from the Backcountry Office; call (970) 586–1242.

FISHING: German brown, brook, rainbow, and cutthroat trout are maintained by natural reproduction in the mountain streams and lakes. The fish are generally not large, and live bait is prohibited except under special circumstances. Fishing is not permitted in Bear Lake. A Colorado fishing license is required.

GUAM

TOURIST INFORMATION
(800) 873–4826
www.visitguam.org

WAR IN THE PACIFIC NATIONAL HISTORICAL PARK

115 Marine Drive, Haloda Building
Hagåtña, Guam 96922
(671) 472–7240
wapa_administration@nps.gov
www.nps.gov/wapa

War in the Pacific National Historical Park comprises nearly 2,000 acres. The park was authorized in 1978 to commemorate the bravery and sacrifices of those involved in the Pacific Theater of World War II. The park includes historic sites associated with the 1944 battle for Guam and consists of seven units on the western and southern shores of Guam.

On December 7, 1941, Pearl Harbor was attacked. A few hours later, Japanese dive-bombers attacked the island of Guam. The island remained under Japanese control for two and a half years, until American forces returned on July 21, 1944. After twenty days of bitter fighting, on August 10, 1944, the island was retaken. The recapture of Guam cost more than 7,000 American and 17,500 Japanese casualties.

War in the Pacific National Historical Park consists of seven separate units, all located on the west side of the island. The T. Stell Newman Visitor Center, open daily except Thanksgiving, Christmas, and New Year's Day, is located on Marine Drive (Highway 1) in the village of Asan. Here visitors will find audiovisual programs and exhibits depicting the events surrounding the Pacific war and the battle for Guam. A patio on the first floor provides a view of the beach where American troops landed while under attack from Japanese defense positions in the hills above Asan Beach. The park preserves these historic landing beaches, cliffs, and ridges that were significant battle sites in 1944. Park brochures are available at the visitor center, and park rangers can assist with information. Fishing, hiking, picnicking, and (for those with experience) snorkeling and diving are among the recreation opportunities available in the park. The park beaches and picnic areas are open to vehicular access from 7:30 A.M. to 6:30 P.M. daily.

ENTRANCE FEE: No charge.

FACILITIES: Food and lodging are available in nearby villages. Drinking water and rest rooms are available at the visitor center. There are also rest rooms at Asan Beach and Ga'an Point but no drinking water.

FISHING: Fishing is permitted in units fronting on the Philippine Sea.

HAWAII

STATE TOURIST INFORMATION
(808) 923–1811
www.visit.hawaii.org

HALEAKALĀ NATIONAL PARK

P.O. Box 369
Makawao, Maui, HI 96768-0369
(808) 572–4400
HALE_Interpretation@nps.gov
www.nps.gov/hale

Haleakalā National Park comprises 30,183 acres and was established in 1916 to preserve the outstanding features of Haleakalā Volcano and the unique plants and animals that can be found there. Haleakalā rises 10,023 feet above sea level, and its last volcanic activity occurred over 200 years ago, near sea level. The summit of Haleakalā is a ninety-minute drive from Kahului via Highways 37, 377, and 378. The eastern section of the park (Kīpahulu District) is a three-hour, 55-mile drive from Kahului via Highways 36, 360, and 31, which is a narrow, winding road.

The island of Maui was formed by two volcanoes spewing lava until they merged as one land mass. Haleakalā, the larger of the two, is believed to have once stood more than 13,000 feet above sea level, in addition to 20,000 feet above its base on the ocean floor. During a period of dormancy, rain cut streams down the mountain's slopes and created a large valley, commonly referred to as the crater, near the summit. Later volcanic activity filled the valley with lava and formed cinder cones.

Park Headquarters Visitor Center is located 1 mile inside the summit district, on Highway 378. Personnel are available to answer questions and provide permits and publications. Ten miles up the road, Haleakalā Visitor Center has exhibits and provides an excellent view of the crater, weather permitting. Interpretive talks are given daily at the summit building, 1 mile farther.

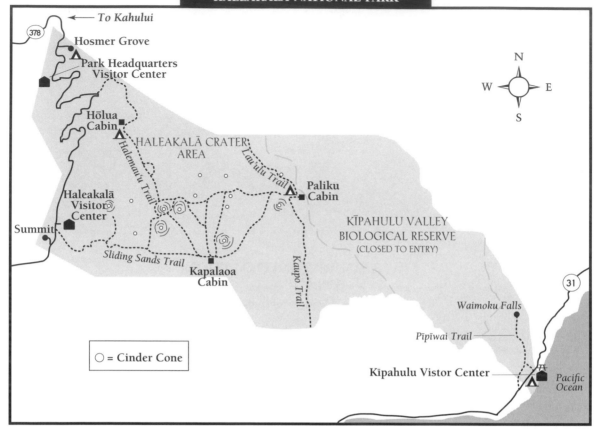

On the east side of the park, the abundant vegetation and tropical nature of the Kīpahulu area stand in vivid contrast to the flows and cinder cones of the summit area. Sparkling pools connected by waterfalls are fed by a rain forest receiving 400 inches of rain annually.

A variety of trails and guided walks are available in the park. Short, self-guided walks are located in the summit area. Halemau'u Trail views Ke'anae Valley and Ko'olau Gap on the 1-mile walk from the highway to the valley rim. At the northwest corner of the park, the $1/2$-mile Hosmer Grove Nature Trail displays the interplay between native and exotic plants. A $1/4$-mile trail to the Leleiwi Overlook provides identification of native plants and a spectacular view of the crater. Self-guided day and overnight hikes through the crater are also available along the Sliding Sands Trail that begins near the Haleakalā Visitor Center. In the Kīpahulu area, self-guided walks begin at the newly renovated Kīpahulu Visitor Center. The $1/2$-mile round-trip Kuloa Point Trail takes visitors over a coastal cliff to the lower pools of 'Ohe'o. Here visitors may swim at their own risk. (Note: Flash flooding can occur at any time; even if it is sunny, it may be raining in higher elevation areas.) The Pīpīwai Trail goes to 400-foot Waimoku Falls through native rainforest and an alien bamboo forest. Native Hawaiian cultural demonstrations and hikes are offered at Kīpahulu. Ranger-guided hikes are available in both areas of the park. Call for schedules. When hiking, dress in layers, as weather at the summit ranges from 35 degreees Fahrenheit in the winter to 60 degrees Fahrenheit in the summer, with weather changing rapidly.

ENTRANCE FEE: $10.00 per vehicle or $5.00 per person; good for seven days.

FACILITIES: No overnight motel accommodations, food services, stores, or service stations are located within the park. From Kīpahulu (Route 31 to Hāna), these services are located approximately 10 miles away in Hāna. No drinking water is available at Kīpahulu. From the summit of Haleakalā, a service station is approximately 28 miles away on Route 37, and restaurant and lodge facilities are located within 22 miles on Route 377. Both visitor centers in the summit area have rest room facilities and drinking water. All visitor centers are wheelchair accessible.

CAMPING: Hosmer Grove Campground (total capacity of fifty people, with a maximum of twelve per group) in the summit area of the park has tables, drinking water, chemical toilets, and a cooking shelter with barbecue grills. This is a drive-in campground. No permit is required, and space is on a first-come, first-served basis. Camping in the wilderness is permitted in two locations. Each of these is accessible by trail only. A permit is required and can be obtained at park headquarters between 8:00 A.M. and 3:00 P.M. on the day you hike in. Two campgrounds—one near Hōlua cabin (total capacity of twenty-five people) and one near Palikū cabin (twenty-five people)—offer primitive facilities including pit toilets and nonpotable water. Three wilderness cabins are available to winners of a lottery held three months prior to the month of the desired stay. Kīpahulu Campground near ʻOheʻo Gulch offers a few tables, grills, and pit toilets, but no drinking water. All campgrounds have a limit of three nights per month.

FISHING: The Kīpahulu Campground and a picnic area are located near the ocean. Fishing in Kīpahulu must be done according to state fishing regulations.

HAWAII VOLCANOES NATIONAL PARK

P.O. Box 52
Hawaii National Park, HI 96718
(808) 985–6000
HAVO_Interpretation@nps.gov
www.nps.gov/havo

Hawaii Volcanoes National Park comprises 217,000 acres and was added to the National Park System in 1916. Active volcanism continues in the park. The most recent eruption has been continuing since January 3, 1983, and has built the largest landform on the east rift zone—PuʻuʻOʻo, a cinder and spatter cone. Hawaii Volcanoes National Park is located in the southeastern corner of the island of Hawaii. The visitor center is approximately 29 miles southwest of Hilo on Hawaii Highway 11, which bisects the park.

Millions of years ago a hot spot in the earth's mantle in the middle of the Pacific caused lava and gases to spurt from cracks 18,000 feet beneath the ocean's surface. As additional layers of lava were added, the island of Hawaii emerged from the sea. The island is 90 miles across at its base and measures nearly 32,000 feet from ocean floor to summit.

Active volcanoes include 13,677-foot Mauna Loa and 4,000-foot Kīlauea. Mauna Loa has been intermittently active during recent times, with large eruptions occurring in 1926, 1942, 1950, and, most recently, in 1984. Kīlauea, one of the most-studied volcanoes in the world, has had its summit collapse to form a broad, shallow depression. Its eruptions have generally been characterized by mild and nonexplosive activity, except in 1790 and 1924.

Hawaii Volcanoes National Park

Two main roads in the park provide access to scenic viewing areas and trailheads. Crater Rim Drive is an 11-mile paved road passing lush rain forest, raw craters, and areas of devastation. Along the road are trails and overlooks such as Thurston Lava Tube, which has a trail through lush rain forest and part of a tube through which once rushed glowing lava (0.3 mile, fifteen minutes); the paved Devastation Trail (0.6 mile, thirty minutes); and overlooks at Kīlauea, Kīlauea Iki, Steaming Bluff, and the Jaggar Museum.

Chain of Craters Road is a scenic drive that descends 3,700 feet in 20 miles and ends where a 1995 lava flow crossed the road. There may be opportunities for viewing active lava flows from the end of the road. A more remote drive in the park is Mauna Loa. This 10-mile paved road from Kīpuka Puaulu to an overlook part way up Mauna Loa is quite narrow but can be worthwhile on a clear day. A loop trail in Kīpuka Puaulu (1.1 miles, one hour) leads into an older forest where many varieties of native trees grow. From a turnoff halfway down the Chain of Craters Road, visitors can drive to the top of Hilina Pali, a series of steep cliffs that provide a spectacular view of the southeast seacoast of the island.

A museum at park headquarters contains exhibits and paintings that help to tell the story of the island. Daily programs include talks by park personnel and a color film of recent volcanic activity.

ENTRANCE FEE: $10.00 per vehicle or $5.00 per person; good for seven days.

FACILITIES: Volcano House, on the rim of Kīlauea Caldera, is operated by a concessioner. Information and reservations are available by writing Volcano House, P.O. Box 53, Hawaii National Park, HI 96718 (808–967–7321). Food service is available at the hotel. Groceries, gasoline, and merchandise may be purchased in the town of Volcano, 1 mile outside the park on Highway 11. Automobile repair facilities are 21 miles outside the park at Kea'au.

CAMPING: Camping is limited to seven days a month and thirty days a year at the park's developed campground, Namakani Paio (ten spaces, two group camps). It offers camper cabins (rented through Volcano House), a pavilion, fireplaces, and flush toilets.

FISHING: Fishing is restricted to native Hawaiians and their guests within the park, except for backcountry areas west of Halape.

KALAUPAPA NATIONAL HISTORICAL PARK

P.O. Box 2222
Kalaupapa, HI 96742-2222
(808) 567–6802
KALA_Interpretation@nps.gov
www.nps.gov/kala

Kalaupapa National Historical Park comprises 10,779 acres and was authorized in 1980 to preserve and interpret the experiences and memories of the past, especially with regard to Hansen's disease (leprosy). The park is on the central northern coast of the island of Molokai. Access is very limited.

For many years individuals with Hansen's disease were banished to isolated locations, despite the fact that this is one of the least contagious of all communicable diseases. Kalaupapa was a settlement where people in Hawaii with Hansen's disease were sent for "treatment." The first group of patients arrived at the settlement in 1866, one year after King Kamehameha V's signing of an act setting apart land for isolating persons with Hansen's disease. From the fear and hopelessness that surrounded this disease when the settlement was established, medical advancements and changing attitudes have resulted in Hansen's disease being treated on an outpatient basis.

The park is composed of the Kalaupapa peninsula, adjacent cliffs and valleys, and submerged lands and waters out to ¼ mile from shore. Spectacular cliffs, valleys, a volcanic crater, rain forest, lava tubes and caves, and offshore islands are all in the park. Both geography and regulations make access to the park relatively difficult. All visitors other than guests of patients and staff must tour historic Kalaupapa and Kalawao on a commercial tour guided by Hansen's disease patients who have lived most of their lives at Kalaupapa. For information, write Father Damien Tours, c/o Kalaupapa Settlement, Kalaupapa, HI 96742, or call (808) 567–6171. For those without the time or energy to arrange a visit to the historical park, Pala'au State Park provides an excellent view of the Kalaupapa peninsula from the edge of steep cliffs. The state park is at the end of highway 470, about 10 miles northwest of Kaunakakai.

ENTRANCE FEE: No charge.

FACILITIES: There are no public facilities in the park. Overnight stays are limited to invited guests of residents.

CAMPING: No camping is available in the park. The nearest camping is at Pala'au State Park.

FISHING: Fishing is available for invited guests only.

KALOKO–HONOKŌHAU NATIONAL HISTORICAL PARK
73-4786 Kanalani Street, #14
Kailua-Kona, HI 96740
(808) 329–6881
KAHO_interpretation@nps.gov
www.nps.gov/kaho

Kaloko-Honokōhau National Historical Park was established in 1978 to protect 1,160 acres that served as the site of an important Hawaiian settlement before the arrival of European explorers. The park is located on the west (Kona) coast of the island of Hawaii, a short distance north of the town of Kailua-Kona.

The area forming Kaloko-Honokōhau National Historical Park was once a successful settlement whose inhabitants harvested sea life, cultivated vegetables, and raised chickens, dogs, and pigs. These people actively traded with others who lived farther inland on the island. Remaining evidence of the settlement includes house platforms, rock art, trails, canoe landings, and religious sites. The park also contains two fishponds that utilized the tides to trap fish. With its massive seawall, Koloko fishpond provides an example of the ancient people's engineering skills. The natural sand enclosure at 'Aimakapā fishpond demonstrates their capability to live in harmony with their environment.

The abundant tidal areas and wetlands in the park remain an important home for many waterbirds, including several species that are found in other areas within Hawaii, but nowhere else in the world. The fishponds also serve as a habitat for waterfowl.

The park headquarters (open weekdays, 7:30 A.M. to 4:00 P.M.) is located in the Kaloko Industrial Park, 2 miles south of the Ke-āhole Airport. Turn inland on Hinalani Street and take the first right onto Kanalani Street; then turn right into the fourth driveway. A visitor contact station is located at 'Ai'ōpio fish trap.

ENTRANCE FEE: No charge.

FACILITIES: Drinking water and concessions are not available in the park. Rest rooms are located at 'Ai'ōpio fish trap and at Kaloko fishpond. Food and lodging are available in Kailua-Kona.

FISHING: Fishing is permitted in Kaloko-Honokōhau National Historical Park, but there is no net fishing in the pond.

PUʻUHONUA O HŌNAUNAU
NATIONAL HISTORICAL PARK

P.O. Box 129
Hōnaunau, Kona, HI 96726-0129
(808) 328–2326
PUHO_Interpretation@nps.gov
www.nps.gov/puho

Puʻuhonua o Hōnaunau (Place of Refuge of Hōnaunau) comprises 182 acres where, until 1819, vanquished Hawaiian warriors, noncombatants, and taboo breakers could escape death by reaching its sacred grounds ahead of their pursuers. The park is located in the southwestern section of the island of Hawaii, 111 miles from Hilo and 20 miles south of the resort center of Kailua-Kona. From Highway 11, turn west on Route 160, which goes by the park entrance.

The object of war in old Hawaii was to exterminate the enemy, including noncombatant members of the opposing side. Vanquished warriors and noncombatants on both sides could receive sanctuary in Hawaii's places of refuge. Although there were at least six refuges on the island of Hawaii at any one time and a number on other inhabited islands of the Hawaiian chain, the one contained in Puʻuhonua o Hōnaunau National Historical Park is historically the most important and the one still nearly intact. The refuge accepted all who sought sanctuary, including those who broke ancient laws. These individuals were absolved by priests before returning home in peace.

The great wall surrounding the place of refuge was constructed around A.D. 1550 in order to provide physical protection to the refugees. Although the seaward end of the south wall has been battered by high surfs, it once probably extended almost to the sea. The wall was built without mortar. An ancient temple that at one time contained the bones of important chiefs and honored males (no females) has been restored by the National Park Service.

The park's visitor center is located beside the parking area. Cultural demonstrations on the grounds vary from day to day and may include canoe carving, thatching a grass hut, and fishing as the ancient Hawaiians did. Coves, cliffs, tidal pools, and associated marine life are easily visited along the shoreline.

ENTRANCE FEE: $5.00 per vehicle; good for seven days.

FACILITIES: No lodging or food service is available at the site. Both may be found on nearby Highway 11. Water and rest rooms are provided at the visitor center.

FISHING: Saltwater fishing from the shoreline is permitted.

PUʻUKOHOLĀ HEIAU NATIONAL HISTORIC SITE

P.O. Box 44340
62-3601 Kawaihae Road
Kawaihae, HI 96743-4340
(808) 882–7218
PUHE_Interpretation@nps.gov
www.nps.gov/puhe

Puʻukoholā Heiau comprises 85.3 acres and was added to the National Park System in 1972 to preserve the historically significant temple associated with Kamehameha the Great, who founded the Historic Kingdom of Hawaii, and the property of John Young, who fought for Kamehameha the Great during the period of his ascendancy to power. The site is located in the northwestern section of the island of Hawaii. It is reached via State Route 270 and is about 12 miles from Waimea.

In 1782 Kamehameha became ruler of the northwest half of the island of Hawaii and unsuccessfully attempted to gain control of the remaining part. After he conquered the islands of Maui, Lanai, and Molokai, Kamehameha's cousin attacked Kamehameha's territory on the Big Island. Before returning to the Big Island, Kamehameha sent his aunt to find the prophet Kāpoūkahi. Kamehameha returned to the Big Island and unsuccessfully fought his cousin. After returning to Kawaihae, Kamehameha received word from his aunt that he would control all the islands if he built a large temple to his family war god. The result was a temple atop Puʻukoholā started in 1790 and finished one year later. The prophecy was fulfilled in 1810 after years of war, when Kamehameha became ruler of all the Hawaiian Islands. After Kamehameha's death in 1819, his son abandoned past religious traditions and ordered all temples destroyed.

The temple platform was constructed without the use of mortar by setting lava rocks and boulders together. Three long, narrow steps cross the side that faces the sea so the interior could be viewed from canoes floating offshore. For purposes of preservation and safety, the temples are currently closed to the public.

In addition to Puʻukoholā Heiau, the park includes a number of other interesting features. On the hillside between Puʻukoholā Heiau and the sea is the ruin of Mailekini Heiau, a temple used by Kamehameha's ancestors. Just offshore is the site of another temple, submerged and probably covered by silt, Hale-ō Ka-puni Heiau, which was dedicated to the shark gods. This temple was last seen in the 1950s, when the rock platform was visible at low tide. The stone leaning post is a rock used by a high chief to lean against as he watched sharks circle about Hale-ō Ka-puni Heiau before devouring the offerings he had placed there. Below Mailekini Heiau is Pelekāne, the site of the king's residence at Kawaihae. In 1790, British sailor John Young was stranded on Hawaii and became a close friend and military adviser of Kamehameha. The site of Young's home is north of Puʻukoholā Heiau across State Road 270.

A small visitor center just off Highway 270 provides information and exhibits on Kamehameha and the park's history. A relatively rugged, steep trail leads from this point to major features of the park.

ENTRANCE FEE: No charge. Guided tours are $1.00 per person.

FACILITIES: No food service or lodging is available at the site. Gasoline and oil and a convenience store for supplies are located 1 mile away. Water and rest rooms are provided at the park's visitor center.

CAMPING: No camping is permitted at the site, but camping and swimming are available nearby at Samuel Spencer County Park. Water and flush toilets are provided.

FISHING: The park's shoreline is a poor location for surf fishing. Better access is available at Samuel Spencer County Park.

USS *ARIZONA* MEMORIAL

1 Arizona Memorial Place
Honolulu, HI 96818-3145
(808) 422–2771
USAR_Administration@nps.gov
www.nps.gov/usar

The USS *Arizona* Memorial was established in 1962 as a memorial marking the spot where the Japanese sank the battleship USS *Arizona* during the December 7, 1941, attack on Pearl Harbor. The National Park Service took over the memorial, visitor center, and tour operations in October 1980. The park is located on the island of Oahu, about twenty minutes west of downtown Honolulu on Kamehameha Highway (Highway 99).

On November 26, 1941, a Japanese task force of thirty-one ships plus a Special Attack Force of twenty-seven submarines set out from Japan to the Hawaiian Islands. The purpose of the mission was to destroy America's Pacific Fleet. The first wave of Japanese aircraft arrived over their targets at 7:48 A.M. on December 7, 1941, and, meeting little opposition, strafed and bombed at will. In addition to the strike at Pearl Harbor, the Japanese attacked other installations such as Wheeler Air Field, Kanehoe Naval Air Station, Hickam Airfield, Ewa Marine Corps Air Station, Ford Island Naval Air Station, and Bellows Airfield. The USS *Arizona* sank with a loss of 1,177 crew members only nine minutes after being hit by a 1,760-pound armor-piercing aerial bomb shortly after the attack commenced.

The park's visitor center is directly off Kamehameha Highway (Highway 99), near Aloha Stadium. Visitors should stop at the information desk and obtain free numbered tour tickets that are issued on a first-come, first-served basis. Prior to boarding a shuttle boat that provides access to the memorial, visitors are shown a 23-minute documentary film about the Pearl Harbor attack. The visitor center also has a museum with photographs, personal memorabilia, and other exhibits. The 184-foot memorial spans the mid-portion of the sunken battleship. Ironically, Alfred Preis, an Austrian immigrant who was sent to a local internment camp from December 1941 to March 1942, designed the memorial that was dedicated on Memorial Day

1962. The concave silhouette symbolizes America's turning the initial tragedy at Pearl Harbor into an ultimate victory.

The memorial is often crowded, and long waits can occur. Visitors awaiting their number being called to begin the tour can browse through exhibits inside the visitor center. Exhibit panels along the water's edge have descriptive images of Pearl Harbor as it was in 1941 compared with the port as it is today. Visitors may also tour the nearby World War II submarine USS *Bowfin* ($8.00 adults, $3.00 children ages four to twelve) and the battleship *Missouri* ($16.00 adults, $8.00 children ages four to twelve). Special guided tours of both boats are available at extra charge. The USS *Arizona* Memorial is open from 7:30 A.M. to 5:00 P.M. with the exception of Thanksgiving, Christmas, and New Year's days. Tours begin at 8:00 A.M., and the last tour leaves at 3:00 P.M. Tickets for the day may be gone by 1:00 P.M. during the summer and holiday seasons.

ENTRANCE FEE: No charge.

FACILITIES: A snack bar is available. A bookstore with military books and related interpretive material is operated by the nonprofit *Arizona* Memorial Museum Association. Drinking water and rest rooms are available at the visitor center.

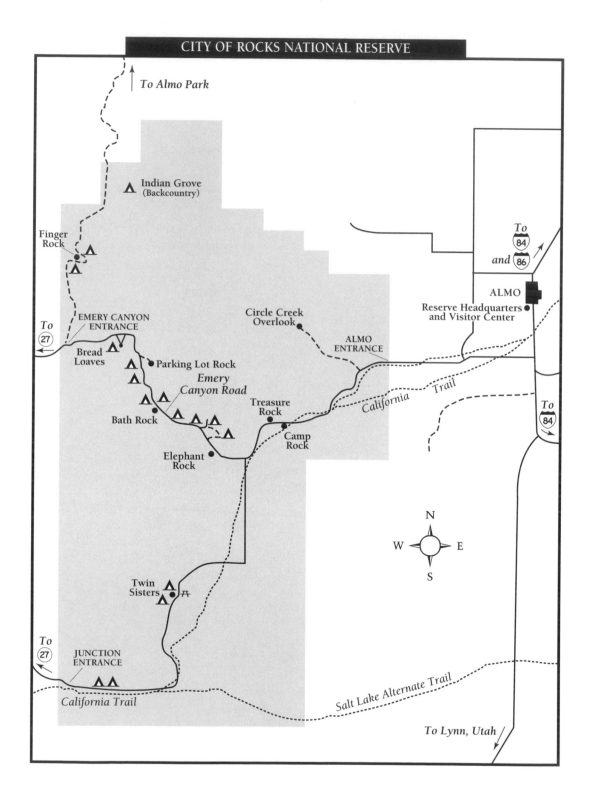

CITY OF ROCKS NATIONAL RESERVE

To Almo Park

Indian Grove
(Backcountry)

Finger
Rock

To
27

EMERY CANYON
ENTRANCE

Bread
Loaves

Parking Lot Rock

Emery
Canyon Road

Bath Rock

Circle Creek
Overlook

ALMO
ENTRANCE

Treasure
Rock

Camp
Rock

Elephant
Rock

California Trail

To
84
and 86

ALMO

Reserve Headquarters
and Visitor Center

To
84

Twin
Sisters

N
W E
S

To
27

JUNCTION
ENTRANCE

California Trail

Salt Lake Alternate Trail

To Lynn, Utah

IDAHO

STATE TOURIST INFORMATION
(800) 635–7820
www.visitid.org

CITY OF ROCKS NATIONAL RESERVE

P.O. Box 169
Almo, ID 83312-0169
(208) 824–5519
CIRO_Ranger_Activities@nps.gov
www.nps.gov/ciro

City of Rocks National Reserve comprises slightly more than 14,000 acres (one-half private, one-half public) and was established in 1988 to preserve significant cultural and natural resources, including scenic granite spires, sculptured rock formations, and visible remnants of the California Trail. The reserve is located in south-central Idaho, 50 miles south of the town of Burley via Highway 27 from the west and Highway 77 from the east. Reserve headquarters, with a visitor center, is in the town of Almo.

The monoliths, spires, and domes found in City of Rocks National Reserve are the result of millions of years of erosion from wind and water. As overlying rocks and granite cracked and fractured, underlying granite was eroded to form the shapes that can be seen today by visitors. Exposed formations range in age from relatively recent to more than two billion years. The varied rock formations located in the reserve have made this one of the prime areas for climbers from around the world.

This area was once traversed by Shoshone and Bannock Indians. By 1843, settlers traveled through City of Rocks via the California Trail, which linked Sacramento, California, with St. Joseph, Missouri, and the Salt Lake Alternate Trail. It is estimated that 50,000 people passed through in 1852 on their way to the California gold fields. Remnants of the California Trail are still visible.

City of Rocks is in the high desert, 5,000 to 8,000 feet above sea level, where the summer temperature can range from freezing to more than 100 degrees Fahrenheit. This environment supports aspen, Douglas fir, and lodgepole pine and, at lower elevations, sagebrush, pinōn pine, and juniper. A variety of wildflowers can be seen in spring and summer. Wildlife includes mule deer, mountain lions, bobcats, porcupines, coyotes, fox, skunk, and a variety of birds.

Thirty miles of hiking trails are in the reserve. An easy, 300-foot trail leads around Camp Rock, where California-bound pioneers left their signatures. Other trails range from an easy 1/2 mile to one requiring a strenuous 5-mile hike to scenic areas of the reserve. Mountain biking is permitted on over 5 miles of trails and 12 miles of gravel roads. Camping with stock is welcome within the reserve, which includes 12 miles of equestrian trails. Call (208) 824–5519 for details. The City of Rocks contains a great number and variety of difficult climbs and is a favorite site for North American technical rock climbers.

The Reserve Headquarters/Visitor Center in a historic building in Almo is open daily from 8:00 A.M. to 4:30 P.M., April 15 through October 31, and on weekdays during the rest of the year, except holidays. Reserve personnel are available for information on weather, road conditions, camping, climbing, and to answer other questions. Field guides, climbing guides, books, maps, and other items may be purchased at the visitor center.

ENTRANCE FEE: No charge.

FACILITIES: Potable water is available only at a hand pump at the Emery Canyon Road summit, 3/4 mile above Bath Rock. All other water should be boiled or purified. Telephones, gasoline, and food supplies are available at Almo and Oakley, while the nearest full services are in Burley.

CAMPING: Seventy-eight primitive camping sites are scattered along the main road. Each site has a table and a grill. Vault toilets are located throughout the reserve. Two vehicles and eight people are allowed at each site. Campsites may be reserved. A permit is required for overnight backcountry use. Permits may be obtained at the visitor center.

CRATERS OF THE MOON NATIONAL MONUMENT AND PRESERVE

P.O. Box 29
Arco, ID 83213-0029
(208) 527–3257
crmo_information@nps.gov
www.nps.gov/crmo

Craters of the Moon National Monument and Preserve was established in 1924 and substantially expanded in 2000 to protect 754,000 acres of rugged and remote landscape, including three major lava fields. The area within the monument and preserve is cooperatively managed by the National Park Service and the Bureau of Land Management. The park is in south-central Idaho with the visitor center approximately 18 miles southwest of the gateway town of Arco, on U.S. 20/26/93.

One thing is certain, Craters of the Moon is one of the most unique places you will ever visit. The fact that in 1969 the astronauts of Apollo 14 came here to learn about surface features they could expect to encounter on the moon provides a good indication of the environment you will experience. Volcanic activity in this region, called the Snake River Plain, occurred over millions of years, although the lava fields at Craters of the Moon are much younger and were formed by eruptions that ended only 2,000 years ago. The park is comprised of three separate lava fields and 250,000 acres of sagebrush grasslands. The lava fields lie along the Great Rift, a 62-mile-long zone of cracks in the earth through which mild eruptions produced small cinder cones and extensive lava flows. The monument and preserve include over twenty-five volcanic cones, with outstanding examples of splatter cones. There are excellent examples of pahoehoe and lava, as well as rafted blocks, tree molds, and lava tub caves.

Although desolate looking, the park thrives with wildlife and plants. Flowers bloom, birds sing, and mammals scurry about the strange geologic formations. More than 375 species of plants are found in the monument. The flowers are usually at their peak in mid-June. The monument also provides a home for nearly 2,000 insect species, 10 amphibians and reptiles, 169 types of birds, and 48 mammals.

Many interesting points in the park can be reached by means of a 7-mile paved loop drive. Seven trailheads lead from the road or one of its nearby side roads. Two of the longer trails lead into Craters of the Moon Wilderness Area, which contains the largest portion of the monument. The hike to the Tree Molds area will take about two hours, and the trail to Echo Crater will consume considerably more time. The Devils Orchard Nature Trail begins at the end of a spur road near the start of the loop. This 1/2-mile self-guided trail takes the hiker through a display of cinder fields and crater-wall fragments and requires approximately twenty minutes to complete. Self-guided and easy-to-walk North Crater Flow Trail begins at a turnout just south of the campground. Two different parking lots provide access to the beginning of a trail to North Crater and Big Craters. Although longer (1 3/4 miles) and quite rigorous, the views into the crater vents are spectacular.

One fascinating feature of the park is the cave area. These caves are lava tubes and can be reached by hiking a short trail at the end of one of the side roads of the loop drive. The caves were formed when the surface of lava flows cooled and hardened. This crust formed an insulating barrier so that the still-molten material in the interior continued to flow. Later, when the eruption stopped, lava drained out of the tubes. The largest cave is Indian Tunnel (800 feet). Beauty, Dewdrop, and Boy Scout caves are smaller and more difficult to enter. The Boy Scout Cave contains a floor of ice that can be quite slippery.

The park is open twenty-four hours daily, year-round. The visitor center has a museum with exhibits that explain the natural and cultural history of the area. It is open daily from 8:00 A.M. to 6:00 P.M. from June to Labor Day, and until 4:30 P.M. the remainder of the year except winter holidays. During summer months, ranger-guided hikes are conducted each day, and campfire programs are presented most evenings. December, January, and February are usually the best months for skiing and snowshoeing. (Check at the visitor center for where to go.) In winter, the 7-mile loop drive is closed and groomed for cross-country skiing.

ENTRANCE FEE: $5.00 per vehicle or $3.00 per person; good for seven days.

FACILITIES: Accommodations, food service, and gasoline are not available within the park but can be found in the town of Arco. Modern rest rooms and drinking water are at the visitor center and the campground.

CAMPING: A unique campground (fifty-one spaces) located near the visitor center just off the main highway is set in the volcanic field amid cinders and volcanic rocks. Charcoal grills, tables, drinking water, and flush toilets (summer only) are provided. Little shade is available. No wood fires are permitted. Campsites are not plowed of snow in winter.

HAGERMAN FOSSIL BEDS NATIONAL MONUMENT

221 North State Street
P.O. Box 570
Hagerman, ID 83332-0570
(208) 837–4793
hafo_ranger_activities@nps.gov
www.nps.gov/hafo

Hagerman Fossil Beds National Monument comprises 4,280 acres and was authorized in 1988 to preserve an area containing extraordinary and abundant fossils. The monument is located in south-central Idaho, on the west bank of the Snake River near the small town of Hagerman. From Hagerman, drive 4.7 miles south on U.S. 30 over the bridge crossing the Snake River. Turn right on the first road and drive approximately 2.5 miles to the first parking lot for the boardwalk overlook, which has several wayside exhibits and the Emigrant Trail trailhead across the road. Another overlook is at the top of the grade.

Three and a half million years ago, the area that is now the Hagerman Valley was part of a flood plain near a huge lake. Twice the annual rainfall of today produced open grassland and streams. The environment supported vegetation, including pine woodland and hardwood trees, and a variety of wildlife, including camels, llamas, antelope, ducks, egrets, zebralike horses, mastodons, pelicans, storks, and swans. Seasonal flooding buried the skeletons and bones of the plants, birds, and animals under layers of sediment and preserved the fossils that are found in this area today.

The steep bluffs overlooking the Snake River west of Hagerman contain fossils that went largely unnoticed until 1928, when a local rancher showed fossil bones to an employee of the

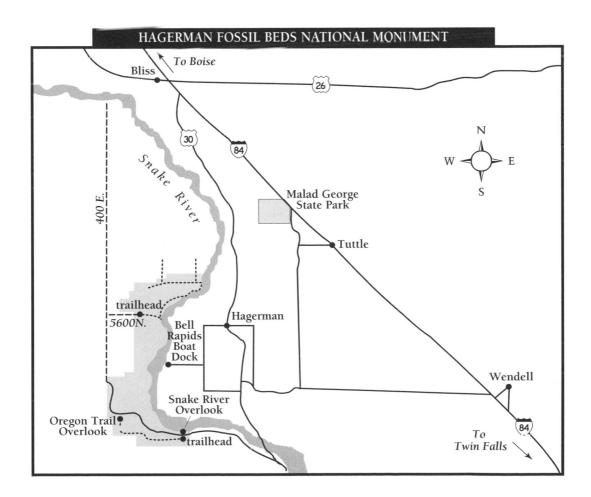

U.S. Geological Survey, who passed them to the Smithsonian Institute. Subsequent excavation unearthed the remains of beaver, birds, fish, frog, mastodon, rabbit, turtle, and the largest single deposit ever found of an extinct species of zebralike horse. No fossil collection is permitted.

Hagerman National Monument is a relatively new addition to the National Park Service and has limited facilities and personnel. A temporary visitor center with exhibits and audiovisual programs is located along Highway 30 in the town of Hagerman. The center is open daily from 9:00 A.M. to 5:00 P.M. from Memorial Day to Labor Day, and 10:00 A.M. to 4:00 P.M. Thursday through Sunday the remainder of the year. Rangers are available to answer questions about the monument and fossils. A trailhead across the road from the first overlook provides access to the Emigrant Trail. Parking for horse trailers is at the top of the grade. A second overlook on this road provides a view of the wagon ruts made by travelers on the Oregon Trail. A more extensive trail system on the north end of the monument is open to hiking, mountain bikes, and horseback riding. Information on the monument's trail system is available at the visitor center or at trailheads. The trails extend downriver to BLM land. Access to the trails is limited. Because of landslides, rattlesnakes, and scorpions, entering the park can be dangerous. Stop at the visitor center, or call (208) 837–4793 for information.

ENTRANCE FEE: No charge.

FACILITIES: The only visitor facilities in the monument are trails. Food and lodging are available in the town of Hagerman and in other nearby towns. Rest rooms and water are available in the visitor center in Hagerman.

CAMPING: Three Island Crossing State Park, approximately 25 miles northwest of Hagerman, near the town of Glenns Ferry, has fifty campsites, water, tables, and flush toilets. There is a dump station at the state park and in Hagerman. Several commercial RV parks are located south of Hagerman along Highway 30, and there are two north of town.

FISHING: Anglers may fish in the Snake River or nearby lakes and creeks. An Idaho fishing license is required.

NEZ PERCE NATIONAL HISTORICAL PARK
39063 U.S. Highway 95
Spalding, ID 83540
(208) 843–2261
NEPE_Administration@nps.gov
www.nps.gov/nepe

Nez Perce National Historical Park was authorized in 1965. It comprises thirty-eight historical sites scattered over a large area of eastern Washington, northeast Oregon, western Montana, and northern Idaho that illustrate a chapter in the history and culture of the American Northwest.

For thousands of years the valleys, prairies, and plateaus of north-central Idaho and adjacent Oregon and Washington have been home to the Nez Perce people. In 1965 Nez Perce National Historical Park was established to commemorate the legends and history of the Nez Perce and their interaction with explorers, fur traders, missionaries, soldiers, settlers, gold miners, loggers, and farmers who moved through or into the area. Originally the park comprised twenty-four

NEZ PERCE NATIONAL HISTORICAL PARK

sites scattered across north-central Idaho. In 1992 new legislation added fourteen sites in Washington, Oregon, Montana, and Idaho. The park headquarters is located at Spalding, Idaho, 11 miles east of Lewiston. Visitor centers are currently located at Spalding and Big Hole National Battlefield near Wisdom, Montana.

In 1805 Meriwether Lewis and William Clark led a small group across the Bitterroot Mountains into Nez Perce country. The Nez Perce received them graciously, gave them supplies, and told them about the river route to the Pacific. Soon fur trappers and traders, both British and American, followed in their wake. By 1855, so many settlers came demanding land that the government was forced to define a reservation for the Nez Perce. Most of their traditional land was inside the new boundaries, but greed for land and gold within the reservation led to the "Steal Treaty" of 1863, in which 90 percent of the original land was taken for white settlement. When Nez Perce bands outside the 1863 treaty area were forced to move, trouble began, resulting in the War of 1877, which lasted four months and covered 1,500 miles, from Wallowa, Oregon, to Bear Paw, Montana, just 40 miles short of the Canadian border.

ENTRANCE FEE: There is an entrance fee at Big Hole National Battlefield: $5.00 per vehicle or $3.00 per person.

FACILITIES: Gas, food, and lodging are available in the towns adjacent to the park.

CAMPING: Although no camping is provided by the Park Service, the area offers a diversity of camping opportunities. Clearwater, Nez Perce, and Wallowa-Whitman national forests have campgrounds, as does the Corps of Engineers' Dworshak Reservoir. Winchester, Hellsgate, and Timothy State Parks are all within thirty minutes' driving time of Spalding.

FISHING: Major rivers flow throughout the park areas, offering some of the finest sport fishing in the country. Each state requires a fishing license, with an additional steelhead permit required on the Clearwater River in Idaho.

IOWA

STATE TOURIST INFORMATION
(800) 345–4692
www.traveliowa.com

EFFIGY MOUNDS NATIONAL MONUMENT
151 Highway 76
Harpers Ferry, IA 52146-7519
(563) 873–3491
EFMO_superintendent@nps.gov
www.nps.gov/efmo

Effigy Mounds comprises 2,526 acres. It was established in 1949 to preserve outstanding examples of prehistoric Indian mounds, some of which are in the shapes of birds and bears. The park is located in northeastern Iowa, 3 miles north of Marquette on Iowa Highway 76.

Effigy Mounds National Monument has 206 known prehistoric mounds, of which 31 are in the form of bear and bird effigies and the remainder are conical, compound, or linear shaped. The oldest mound excavated in the park, belonging to the Red Ocher Culture, has been dated to be about 2,500 years old. Burial offerings included large chipped blades, dart points, and spherical copper beads. Other mounds, from a culture dating from 100 B.C. to A.D. 600, have been excavated, revealing pottery and projectile points.

The Effigy Mounds people occupied this land beginning approximately A.D. 600. They differed from the earlier mound builders not only in constructing mounds in effigy forms but also in using copper for tools instead of ornaments and in burying their dead with few lasting offerings. By about 1400, the Effigy Mounds people were replaced by Indians of the Oneota Culture.

The park's visitor center contains museum exhibits and an audiovisual presentation on the history of Effigy Mounds. It is open daily (except winter federal holidays) from 8:00 A.M. to 4:30 P.M., with extended hours in the summer. The North Unit contains the self-guided Fire Point

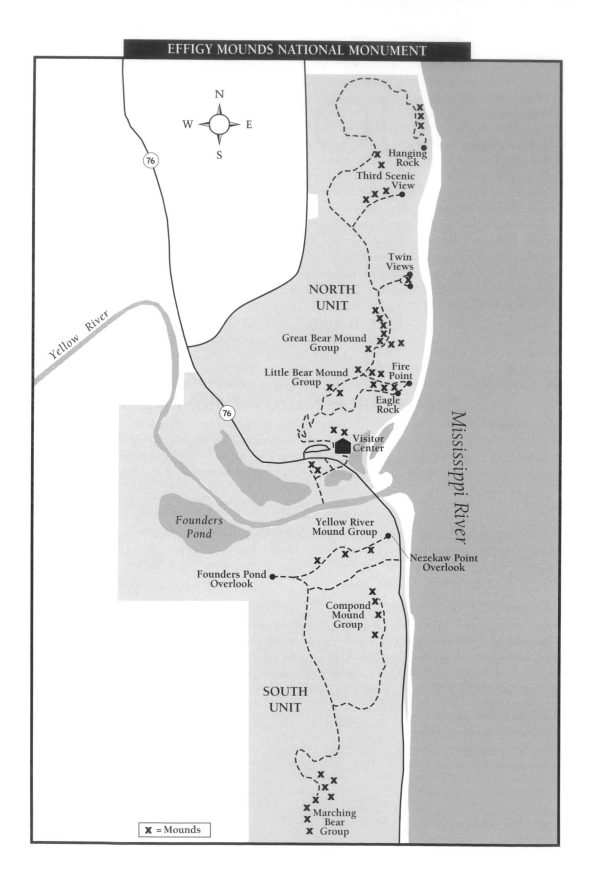

EFFIGY MOUNDS NATIONAL MONUMENT

N
W ◉ E
S

76

Yellow River

76

NORTH UNIT

Hanging Rock

Third Scenic View

Twin Views

Great Bear Mound Group

Little Bear Mound Group

Fire Point

Eagle Rock

Visitor Center

Mississippi River

Founders Pond

Yellow River Mound Group

Nezekaw Point Overlook

Founders Pond Overlook

Compond Mound Group

SOUTH UNIT

Marching Bear Group

X = Mounds

Trail, which provides access to some of the park's major points of interest, including twenty-five mounds and viewpoints on 300-foot bluffs along the Mississippi River. Trail markers and exhibits help interpret the walk. Ranger-guided walks are given frequently during summer months. A longer walk along the Hanging Rock Trail takes visitors to other points of interest. The South Unit contains the Marching Bears Mound Group, a spectacular collection of effigy mounds (ten bears, three birds, and two linear mounds). The trail is self-guided and approximately 2 miles one-way.

ENTRANCE FEE: $5.00 per vehicle or $3.00 per person; good for seven days. Children ages sixteen and under are free.

FACILITIES: No lodging or food service is available in the park. Rest rooms and drinking water are provided in the visitor center.

CAMPING: No camping is permitted at Effigy Mounds National Monument. Seven miles south, on top of a bluff, Pikes Peak State Park offers eighty sites, most of which have electrical and water hookups. Eight miles northwest, Yellow River State Forest offers 126 sites but no showers.

FISHING: No fishing is available at the park. There is a trout stream in Yellow River State Forest, 8 miles northwest of Effigy Mounds.

HERBERT HOOVER NATIONAL HISTORIC SITE

110 Parkside Drive
West Branch, IA 52358-0607
(319) 643–2541
heho_interpretation@nps.gov
www.nps.gov/heho

Herbert Hoover National Historic Site comprises 187 acres and was established in 1965. The site includes the cottage where Hoover was born, several buildings related to the former president's childhood, the gravesites of Hoover and his wife, Lou Henry Hoover, and the Herbert Hoover Presidential Library–Museum. The historic site is located in eastern Iowa, 10 miles east of Iowa City, in the town of West Branch. Take Exit 254 from I–80.

Herbert Hoover—humanitarian, mining engineer, statesman, and thirty-first president of the United States—was born August 10, 1874, in the small town of West Branch, Iowa. His father, a blacksmith, died when Herbert (called Bert or Bertie as a child) was only six years old, and his mother died three years later. Herbert lived with relatives in West Branch until age eleven, when he took the train to Oregon to live with an uncle and his family. The values he learned as a child from his family, the Quaker Church, and his friends in West Branch helped shape Herbert Hoover's life and affected the lives of all those he was to assist during his career as a public servant.

Hoover earned a degree in geology in 1893 as a member of Stanford University's first graduating class. He subsequently worked in the California gold mines and accumulated substantial wealth while engaged in mining engineering projects in Australia, China, and England. In

Herbert Hoover Birthplace Cottage, Herbert Hoover National Historic Site

London when World War I commenced, Hoover was asked to organize a relief effort that eventually helped feed millions of people in thirty-three nations. Following the war, he continued his public service by serving for eight years as secretary of commerce. In 1928 Herbert Hoover was nominated as the Republican candidate and elected president in a landslide victory over New York's Alfred Smith. The stock market crash nine months after his inauguration doomed any chance for reelection, as much of the American public held him responsible for the country's economic woes. Following a major election defeat in 1932 by Democratic candidate Franklin Roosevelt, Hoover returned to California, where he devoted much of his time to the Hoover Institute at Stanford University. He also served on presidential commissions in the 1940s and 1950s to study both famine relief and the reorganization of the executive branch of the federal government. Hoover died on October 20, 1964, and was buried on a hillside overlooking his birthplace. His wife's remains were later moved here from California.

Stop first at the visitor center to view a twelve-minute film and pick up a brochure that includes a map illustrating the historic site's layout. From here it is a short walk to the birthplace cottage built in 1871 by Hoover's father and grandfather, a blacksmith shop similar to that operated by his father, a schoolhouse built in 1853, and the Friends (Quaker) Meetinghouse completed in 1857, all of which are open to visitors. You will also want to walk through downtown West Branch, which has fine examples of early-twentieth-century architecture, many of which are included in the National Register of Historic Places. The impressive Herbert Hoover Presidential Library–Museum includes interesting exhibits plus a twenty-two-minute film. The museum also houses a collection of Hoover's presidential papers. The museum was dedicated in 1962 by former presidents Hoover and Harry Truman. Buildings in the national historic site are open from 9:00 A.M. to 5:00 P.M. daily except Thanksgiving, Christmas, and New Year's Day.

ENTRANCE FEE: $3.00 per person, including entrance to the national historic site buildings plus the presidential library, the latter of which is operated by a private foundation. Visitors with any of the national park passes are required to pay $1.00 to enter the presidential library.

FACILITIES: Rest rooms and drinking water are at the visitor center and the presidential library. Restaurants and a food store are in downtown West Branch. Lodging is in West Branch and nearby Iowa City.

CAMPING: The nearest public camping is at Lake Macbride, approximately 9 miles north of Iowa City via Highway 1. This state facility has 121 sites, approximately half with hookups.

KANSAS

STATE TOURIST INFORMATION
(800) 252–6727
www.travelks.com

BROWN V. BOARD OF EDUCATION NATIONAL HISTORIC SITE

424 South Kansas Avenue, Suite 220
Topeka, KS 66603-3441
(785) 354–4273
BRVB_interp_ranger@nps.gov
www.nps.gov/brvb

Brown v. Board of Education National Historic Site was established in 1992 to commemorate the 1954 Supreme Court decision that ended legal racial segregation in America's public schools. The historic site is located at the former Monroe Elementary School in the city of Topeka in northeast Kansas.

Before the famous 1954 U.S. Supreme Court decision in *Brown v. Board of Education of Topeka,* racial segregation was justified in parts of the United States on the basis that separate but equal educational facilities were legally permissible. An 1896 U.S. Supreme Court decision had held that "separate but equal" facilities were permissible in public transportation, a ruling that was subsequently applied to other activities, including education. In 1952, there were several other desegregation cases pending before the Supreme Court that were consolidated and argued under the name of *Brown v. Board of Education.* Local attorneys from Topeka, Kansas, Delaware, Virginia, the District of Columbia, and South Carolina collectively worked with lawyers for the Legal Defense Fund of the National Association for the Advancement of Colored People (NAACP), headed by Thurgood Marshall, in preparing the groundwork. This legal engagement clarified the right of all citizens not to be subjected to arbitrary restrictions designed to oppress a group of people in transportation, housing, and education. The Court, led by Chief Justice

Earl Warren, delivered the unanimous opinion that "separate but equal educational facilities are inherently unequal."

The site's National Park Service headquarters is housed in the Main Post Office Building at 424 South Kansas Avenue. It is open weekdays from 8:00 A.M. to 4:00 P.M. except federal holidays. Offsite interpretive programs are available by calling park headquarters. Monroe Elementary School, one of four segregated elementary schools for African-American children in Topeka, is in the process of major renovation. When completed, the site will serve as an interpretive and resource center for information about the impact on the civil rights movement of *Brown v. Board of Education.* The school is not currently open to the public except with tours arranged in advance through site headquarters.

ENTRANCE FEE: No charge.

FACILITIES: The National Park Service provides no facilities. Food service and lodging are in and around Topeka.

CAMPING: County-operated Lake Shawnee Campground (913–267–1156), 2 miles south of Topeka off I–70 at East Kansas, offers 179 sites with tables, grills, flush toilets, and a dump station. Electrical and water hookups are available at mo00st sites. Perry State Park (785–246–3449), 16 miles northeast of Topeka via state roads 24 and 237, offers 120 sites with tables, grills, flush toilets, and a dump station.

FORT LARNED NATIONAL HISTORIC SITE

Route 3, Box 69
Larned, KS 67550-9321
(620) 285–6911
FOLS_superintendent@nps.gov
www.nps.gov/fols

Fort Larned National Historic Site, which comprises 718 acres, was incorporated into the National Park Service in 1966 to protect the remains of a key military base along the Santa Fe Trail. The fort is located in southwestern Kansas, 6 miles west of the town of Larned on Kansas Highway 156. Also see the map under Bent's Old Fort National Historic Site (Colorado).

From 1821 to 1880 the Santa Fe Trail served as an important route for commercial traffic between Missouri and Mexico. Plains Indians, concerned about the increasing number of people and wagons moving across their lands, initiated attacks that disrupted commerce, mail shipments, and immigrant travel. The resulting demand for protection caused the U.S. government to build a series of army posts for security and escort duty along the Santa Fe Trail. Fort Larned, named for U.S. Army Paymaster-General Colonel Benjamin Larned, was constructed in 1860 as one of these posts. Beginning in 1861, the fort served as a distribution point for the payment of goods to Indian tribes who stayed on their reservations and maintained the peace. By 1868 the organized Indian threat had dissipated, and tribes were moved to new reservations in Indian Territory. During the early 1870s, the fort housed soldiers who were charged with protecting construction workers on the Santa Fe Railroad. The railroad replaced the Santa Fe Trail when it was completed in July 1878. Fort Larned was then abandoned, except for a small number of soldiers who remained to protect the property.

The initial fort on this site consisted of poorly built adobe structures that by 1868 had been replaced with nine stone-and-timber buildings constructed around a quadrangular parade ground. These are the buildings still standing at the national historic site. The original blockhouse was dismantled around 1900 and later reconstructed by the National Park Service. Most of the buildings, including barracks, a commissary, and officers' quarters have been restored to their original appearance. The visitor center, housed in the barracks building next to the parking lot for the handicapped, has a museum with exhibits of clothing, weapons, and equipment used by Fort Larned soldiers and Plains Indians. It also has a ten-minute audiovisual presentation and a bookstore. Brochures for a self-guided walk of the fort are available here. Ranger-led walks and living history programs are presented seasonally. The Santa Fe Trail Ruts Area is a separate section of the historic site located on an unpaved county road about 4 miles south and 1 mile west of the fort. The historic site is open daily late May to early September from 8:00 A.M. to 6:00 P.M. It is open from 8:30 A.M. to 5:00 P.M. the remainder of the year. The historic site is closed Thanksgiving, Christmas, and New Year's Day.

ENTRANCE FEE: $5.00 per family or $3.00 per person; good for seven days.

FACILITIES: Drinking water and rest rooms are in the visitor center. A shaded picnic area is located at the entrance to the site. Food and lodging are in the town of Larned.

CAMPING: No camping is permitted at the site, but there is a private campground in the town of Larned.

FORT SCOTT NATIONAL HISTORIC SITE
Old Fort Boulevard
P.O. Box 918
Fort Scott, KS 66701-0918
(620) 223–0310
fosc_interpretation@nps.gov
www.nps.gov/fosc

Fort Scott National Historic Site comprises seventeen acres. It was established as an area of the National Park Service in 1979, although federal planning and financial assistance were authorized in 1965 to help preserve and restore this important fort of the mid-1800s. Fort Scott is located in southeastern Kansas, 90 miles south of Kansas City and 60 miles north of Joplin, Missouri. In the town of Fort Scott, the site is located on Old Fort Boulevard.

Built on a shoestring budget by soldiers and a few skilled craftsmen between 1842 and 1848, Fort Scott was part of a chain of military posts designed to maintain peace between white settlers to the east and Plains Indians and relocated eastern tribes to the west. The fort was constructed of local timber from the bottomlands and stone from the surrounding hills. Named for General Winfield Scott, the fort is perhaps best known as the home of dragoons—elite troops of the frontier army who were trained to fight either on foot or on horseback. With little trouble

Fort Scott National Historic Site

from Indians, troops stationed at the fort were directed to patrol the territory and escort caravans on the Santa Fe Trail. During the Mexican War dragoons from Fort Scott fought in two important battles. By 1853 the frontier had moved farther west, and there seemed to be no further military need for the fort, whose troops were transferred north to Fort Leavenworth. Within a couple of years the fort's buildings were sold at auction.

This area became a magnet for radicals and troublemakers in the 1850s, when Kansas was opened to white settlers who were permitted to vote whether the state would allow slavery. In 1857 and again in 1858 federal troops returned to the town of Fort Scott in order to quell civilian unrest. Kansas entered the Union as a free state in 1861. The fort's military importance was resurrected during the Civil War, when it became a major complex that included a supply depot, training ground, army hospital, and military prison. Fort Scott served as home for the first African-American troops from a northern state. The final military hurrah occurred during 1869–1873, when the fort became headquarters for the Post of Southeast Kansas, with soldiers stationed to protect the construction of railroads in southeast Kansas.

The historic site is open daily from 8:00 A.M. to 6:00 P.M. from April through October. It opens an hour later the remainder of the year and is closed Thanksgiving, Christmas, and New Year's Day. The visitor center, with information, a twelve-minute video program, and book sales, is located in the former post hospital directly across from the visitor parking lot. A museum is in the reconstructed infantry barracks next door to the visitor center. The site includes eleven significant buildings, with thirty-three historically furnished rooms that are open to the public through self-guided tours. The restored and reconstructed buildings include barracks, stables, post headquarters, officers' quarters, powder magazine, post hospital, guardhouse, quartermaster storehouse, and the post bakery. The site also includes a walking trail through a portion of five acres of restored tallgrass prairie. Guided tours and interpretive programs are offered on weekends during summer months. Call the historic site about special programs such as a Civil War reenactment in April, American Indian Heritage Weekend in September, and Living History Programs on Memorial Day and Labor Day weekends.

ENTRANCE FEE: $3.00 per person. Children ages sixteen and under are free.

FACILITIES: Rest rooms and drinking water are in the visitor center and one of the barracks buildings. Food and lodging are available in the town of Fort Scott, which surrounds the historic site.

CAMPING: No camping is permitted in the park. A city-operated campground is approximately 2 miles from the historic site. Two state parks within 25 miles of the site offer camping facilities.

NICODEMUS NATIONAL HISTORIC SITE

304 Washington Avenue
Bogue, KS 67625
(785) 839–4233
nico_Ranger_Activities@nps.gov
www.nps.gov/nico

Nicodemus National Historic Site was authorized in 1996 to interpret and help preserve the oldest remaining western town established by African Americans during the reconstruction period following the Civil War. The national historic site is located in the unincorporated town of Nicodemus in north-central Kansas on U.S. Highway 24 and approximately 37 miles northeast of I–70 at Wakeeney.

Between 1860 and 1880 the black population of Kansas increased from 627 to 43,107 as African Americans migrated from the South to the Midwest following the Civil War. The town of Nicodemus is one of several all-black Kansas towns that were settled during this period. Named for a legendary slave, the town was officially founded on September 17, 1877. From a few early arrivals in the summer of 1877, within a decade, the town had a bank, two newspapers, a post office, a livery stable, a literary society, and even an ice cream parlor. The county's black population grew until it reached a peak of 595 in 1910, but by 1950, only a small number of residents remained.

Nicodemus National Historic Site is a relatively new addition to the National Park system, and the National Park Service is currently working on a management plan for the site. The site includes an African Methodist Episcopalian church, a limestone and stucco building erected in 1907 and in active use until the 1940s, and four privately owned buildings, including the First Baptist Church, which was built in 1907 and continued in use until 1977; the St. Francis Hotel, a two-story limestone structure erected in 1880; Nicodemus School, built in 1918 on the site of an earlier schoolhouse; and Township Hall, built in 1939 by the Works Progress Administration. The Township Hall is now leased from the Nicodemus Township Board by the National Park Service as a visitor center that is open daily from 8:30 A.M. to 5:00 P.M. The staff will provide an orientation, and visitors can view exhibits about the history of Nicodemus and blacks in the West. During summer months, walking tours are available with prior arrangements (call 785–839–4233). A "Homecoming Celebration" is observed on the last weekend of July each year. For information about the Homecoming, call (785) 421–5639.

ENTRANCE FEE: No charge.

FACILITIES: Rest rooms are provided in the Nicodemus Township Hall. North of the hall the National Park Service maintains a roadside park, with a picnic area with tables, water, and a portable toilet. Food and lodging are located along Highway 24.

CAMPING: Ten miles east of Nicodemus on U.S. Highway 24, Webster State Park offers one hundred camping sites with water, grills, tables, flush toilets, and a dump station. Thirty-six of the sites have electrical and water hookups. Camping is also available in the cities of Stockton (19 miles east) and Hill City (13 miles west) along U.S. Highway 24.

FISHING: Fishing is available in Webster Reservoir at Webster State Park. A Kansas fishing license is required.

TALLGRASS PRAIRIE NATIONAL PRESERVE

P.O. Box 585
226 Broadway Street
Cottonwood Falls, KS 66845
(620) 273–6034
tapr_interpretation@nps.gov
www.nps.gov/tapr

Tallgrass Prairie National Preserve was established in 1996 to preserve, protect, and interpret nearly 11,000 acres of nationally significant tallgrass prairie ecosystem. The preserve also includes the historic buildings and cultural resources of the former Spring Hill Ranch. The national preserve is located in the Flint Hills of east-central Kansas, just north of Strong City, on Highway 177.

This 10,894-acre remnant of tallgrass prairie was purchased in 1994 by the National Park Trust, a private, nonprofit land conservancy dedicated to protecting America's national parks. The former Spring Hill Ranch is home to nearly 400 species of plants and 150 types of birds. Nearly all this land will continue to be owned by the National Park Trust, with no more than 180 acres owned by the federal government. The entire preserve is managed by the National Park Service through a cooperative agreement with the National Park Trust.

The preserve is currently under development, but programs are expanding. The site is open from 9:00 A.M. to 4:00 P.M. daily, with the exception of Thanksgiving, Christmas, and New Year's Day, and during inclement weather. The focal point of the preserve is 470 acres of the remaining tallgrass prairie. Buildings include the main ranch house, constructed in 1881, a massive three-story limestone barn, carriage house, chicken house, curing/spring house, outhouse, and icehouse. An information station offers a ten-minute video presentation, exhibits, and brochures. A bookstore provides visitors with educational materials about the prairie, American Indians, and the rich ranching legacy of the Flint Hills. Visitors can tour the ranch headquarters area on their own with the help of a brochure and wayside exhibits. House tours are available every

TALLGRASS PRAIRIE NATIONAL PRESERVE

hour on the half hour beginning at 9:30 A.M. and ending at 3:30 P.M. Living history programs are offered on weekends from Memorial Day through Labor Day. The one-room schoolhouse is open May through October on weekends from noon to 4:00 p.m., and a ranger-led bus tour (fee charged) is offered daily at 11:00 A.M. and 1:00 and 3:00 P.M. Bus tours for groups of fifteen or more are available on a reservation basis. The 1¾-mile loop Southwind Nature Trail offers an opportunity for a leisurely stroll through the prairie grassland and by the Lower Fox Creek Schoolhouse.

ENTRANCE FEE: No charge. The bus tour is $5.00 per adult; $3.00 for children ages five to eighteen; and free for children ages four and under.

FACILITIES: Food and lodging are available in Strong City, Cottonwood Falls, Emporia, and Council Grove. At the preserve, drinking water is available only at the information station. Portable toilets are across from the barn.

CAMPING: No camping is permitted in the preserve at this time. Two miles west of Cottonwood Falls, Chase State Fishing Lake offers ten campsites with pit toilets. Several U.S. Army Corps of Engineers campgrounds, some with flush toilets, are approximately 20 miles north of the preserve at Council Grove Lake.

LOUISIANA

CANE RIVER CREOLE NATIONAL HISTORICAL PARK

400 Rapids Avenue
Natchitoches, LA 71457
(318) 352–0383
CARI_Superintendent@nps.gov
www.nps.gov/cari

Cane River Creole National Historical Park comprises 207 acres and was authorized in 1994 to preserve significant landscapes, sites, and structures associated with the development of the Creole culture. The national historical park, situated within a 40,000-acre heritage area, includes two plantations and the historic district of the town of Natchitoches. The park is located in west-central Louisiana, southeast of Natchitoches, off Highway 1. Headquarters is at Oakland Plantation on Highway 494. Take I–49 to Exit 127, the Flora/Cypress exit. Drive east 1 1/2 miles on Highway 120. Cross Louisiana Highway 1 to Louisiana Highway 494. Drive 4 miles on Highway 494 to Oakland Plantation.

The separate units of Cane River Creole National Historical Park are situated within Cane River National Heritage Area, a 40,000-acre tract of public and private land that extends 1 mile on either side of the Cane River from the southern boundary of Natchitoches to Monette's Ferry. The National Heritage Area is designed to preserve and interpret the historical and cultural heritage of the region. The Visitor Contact Center, located at Oakland Plantation, 4836 Louisiana Highway 494 in Bermuda, Louisiana, is open daily from 8:30 A.M. to 4:30 P.M. Visitation to Cane River Creole National Historical Park is by guided tour only.

Two major units of the historical park are the Oakland and Magnolia plantations. Oakland Plantation, which dates from the first half of the nineteenth century, was founded by Jean Pierre

Emmanuel Prud'homme, a second-generation native of French descent. The plantation includes the main house, carriage house, stable, carpenter's shop, cabins, and about twenty additional buildings, all of which survived the Civil War. Prud'homme's descendants occupied and farmed the plantation until the late 1900s, when it was acquired by the National Park Service. Guided tours of Oakland Plantation are offered daily at 9:00 and 11:00 A.M. and 1:00 and 3:00 P.M.

Magnolia Plantation was established in 1835 by Ambrose Lecomte and his wife, who were to become the largest slaveholders in the parish. Surviving buildings include the blacksmith shop, eight brick slave cabins, and a gin barn. The main house was burned during the Civil War by retreating Union troops and has been reconstructed on its original site, which is outside the park boundaries. Magnolia Plantation is open for guided tours by reservation only. Requests are welcome, and park personnel are usually able to honor most requests. Call (318) 356–8411.

ENTRANCE FEE: No charge.

FACILITIES: No facilities are provided by the National Park Service. Food and lodging are available in Natchitoches.

CAMPING: A National Forest Service campground with ten sites is 3 miles north of Natchitoches on State Road 117. Several private campgrounds are near Natchitoches.

JEAN LAFITTE NATIONAL HISTORICAL PARK AND PRESERVE

365 Canal Street, Suite 2400
New Orleans, LA 70130-1142
(504) 589–3882 (recorded message)
(504) 589–2133 (visitor information)
JELA_Interpretation@nps.gov
www.nps.gov/jela

Jean Lafitte National Historical Park and Preserve was established in 1978 and includes the former Chalmette National Historical Park. The park contains seven separate sites in southern Louisiana that preserve significant examples of historical, cultural, and natural resources of the Mississippi Delta region. The Acadian sites are 60 to 150 miles west of New Orleans. The other sites are located in and around the city of New Orleans.

The Mississippi Delta region is rich in cultural and natural history. The river brought a stream of people and products from all parts of the globe to its point of drainage into the Gulf of Mexico. Jean Lafitte National Historical Park and Preserve is named for Jean Lafitte, the self-styled privateer whose men and munitions helped Andrew Jackson win the Battle of New Orleans in 1815 against a much larger British force. The park preserves six sites showing the diversity of this history.

Acadian Cultural Center: Located at 501 Fisher Road, Lafayette. The center interprets cultural resources of the Acadian people who were relocated to the Mississippi Delta region from

Nova Scotia, Canada, over a twenty-year period beginning in 1765. Exhibits allow visitors to interact with and understand traditional and contemporary Acadian culture. The Cultural Center is open daily from 8:00 A.M. to 5:00 P.M., except Christmas and Mardi Gras. A forty-minute film is shown hourly from 9:00 A.M. to 4:00 P.M. Call (337) 232–0789 for information.

Barataria Preserve: Located on State Highway 45, about 12 miles south of New Orleans, this area of rich coastal wetlands includes bayous, live oak, and alligators. There are about 9 miles of self-guided trails that provide access to the wetlands. Twelve miles of waterways are available for nonmotorized craft such as canoes. Ranger-guided canoe tours are available on weekends and evenings of a full moon. The visitor center (504–589–2330) offers audiovisual programs and exhibits on the area. It is open from 9:00 A.M. to 5:00 P.M. daily, except Christmas and Mardi Gras.

Chalmette Battlefield: Located 6 miles east of New Orleans off State Highway 46, this site preserves the battlefield where Andrew Jackson's militia, with the help of Lafitte, halted a British force of approximately 10,000 soldiers sent to attack New Orleans in 1815. The visitor center (504–281–0510), open daily from 9:00 A.M. to 5:00 P.M., except Christmas and Mardi Gras, houses a small museum with uniforms and information about the military units that participated in the battle. There is a movie detailing the Battle of New Orleans. Programs about the battle are presented twice daily.

French Quarter Visitor Center: The visitor center, at 419 Decatur Street in downtown New Orleans (504–589–2636), provides exhibits, audiovisual programs, and demonstrations on the cultural diversity of the Mississippi Delta region. From the visitor center, rangers lead a variety of programs. The center is open daily from 9:00 A.M. to 5:00 P.M., except Christmas and Mardi Gras.

Prairie Acadian Cultural Center: Located at 250 West Park Avenue in Eunice, northwest of Lafayette, the center depicts the heritage of the Prairie Acadians. It includes artifacts, exhibits, and demonstrations that portray this unique culture. In cooperation with the city of Eunice, the National Park Service sponsors a live radio program in Cajun French every Saturday evening from 6:00 to 8:00 P.M. at the Liberty Theater. The Cultural Center is open Tuesday through Friday from 8:00 A.M. to 5:00 P.M., and on Saturday until 6:00 P.M. It is closed Sundays, Mondays, and Christmas. Call (337) 262–6862 for information.

Trails and Rails: Park rangers and volunteers, in partnership with Amtrak, provide weekly educational/interpretive programs during the summer on Amtrak's "Sunset Limited" between New Orleans and Lafayette, Louisiana; "City of New Orleans" between New Orleans and Jackson, Mississippi; and "Crescent" between New Orleans and Atlanta, Georgia.

Wetlands Acadian Cultural Center: Located at 313 St. Mary Street, Thibodaux, southwest of New Orleans, the center explores the water-based life of the Wetlands Acadians. Artifacts and exhibits depict a heritage of fishing, hunting, and trapping in the swamps, marshes, and coastal waters. Various films are shown on request, and music programs are offered on Monday evenings. The center is open Monday from 9:00 A.M. to 8:00 P.M.; Tuesday through Thursday from 9:00 A.M. to 6:00 P.M.; and Friday, Saturday, and Sunday from 9:00 A.M. to 5:00 P.M. It is closed for Christmas and Mardi Gras. Call (985) 448–1375 for information.

ENTRANCE FEE: No charge.

FACILITIES: No food or lodging is provided by the National Park Service, but both are available near the sites.

CAMPING: No camping is permitted in the park. Public and private campgrounds are available nearby.

FISHING: Fishing is available in the Barataria Preserve with a valid Louisiana fishing license.

POVERTY POINT NATIONAL MONUMENT

c/o Poverty Point State Commemorative Area
P.O. Box 248
Epps, LA 71237
(888) 926–5492
PovertyPoint@crt.state.la.us
www.crt.state.la.us (click on "State Parks")

Poverty Point National Monument was authorized in 1988 to commemorate a culture that thrived twelve centuries before Christ and to help preserve some of the largest prehistoric earthworks in North America. The monument is located in northeastern Louisiana, east of the city of Monroe via LA 134 and LA 577. From I–20, take the Delhi exit north on LA 17 to the town of Epps.

Between 1350 and 500 B.C., the inhabitants of Poverty Point built a complex of earthen mounds and ridges that overlook the Mississippi River floodplain. Materials and supplies used in the construction were acquired in trade from various points in the present-day United States. The ridges at Poverty Point form six semicircles, with the outer sections having a diameter of 3/4 mile. Evidence from excavations causes scientists to believe the ridges were constructed as foundations for dwellings. Earthen mounds at the site include Poverty Point Mound, a large bird-shaped mound that rises 70 feet from its 700-by-640-foot base. Another 20-foot-high conical mound was constructed over a bed of ash.

The historic site that forms the national monument is managed by the Louisiana State Park System. The area is open daily from 9:00 A.M. to 5:00 P.M. except Thanksgiving, Christmas, and New Year's Day. A museum provides visitors with an audiovisual presentation and displays artifacts found at the site. The park also includes an archaeological laboratory, observation tower, and self-guided hiking trails. A guided tram tour operates from March 1 through October 31.

ENTRANCE FEE: $2.00 per adult; children under fourteen and seniors over sixty-one are free.

FACILITIES: Rest rooms, drinking water, and soft drinks are available at the museum. Picnic areas are at the site. The nearest lodging is in Delhi, 16 miles south of the commemorative area.

CAMPING: No camping is permitted on the historic site. Private campgrounds adjoin the historic site and Chemin-A-Haut State Park, approximately 40 miles northwest, has twenty-six campsites with tables, grills, flush toilets, showers, and a dump station.

MINNESOTA

STATE TOURIST INFORMATION
(800) 657–3700
www.exploreminnesota.com

GRAND PORTAGE NATIONAL MONUMENT

Box 668
Grand Marais, MN 55604-0668
(218) 387–2788
grpo_superintendent@nps.gov
www.nps.gov/grpo

Grand Portage was designated a national historic site in 1951 and was changed to a national monument in 1958. It comprises 710 acres that were used as part of a principal route into the Northwest by Indians, explorers, missionaries, and fur traders. An old fur-trading depot is partially reconstructed here. The park is located in the northeastern tip of Minnesota, 151 miles northeast of Duluth on State Highway 61, a beautiful drive.

From approximately 1779 to 1802, Grand Portage served as headquarters for the North West Company, a highly profitable fur-trading enterprise that employed a large number of French-Canadian voyageurs. The North West Company supplied furs to vast European and American markets and also supplied trade goods to American Indians, who acquired a predilection for the trimmings of European society. The North West Company built its posts along the banks of the Pigeon River and at the Lake Superior end of the Grand Portage (the "Great Carrying Place"), an 8½-mile portage that wound its way through the woods, bypassing rapids on the lower end of the Pigeon River and becoming the acknowledged route to Canada's prime fur country.

The Grand Portage post became a convenient meeting place for the voyageurs, who had evolved into two groups based on geography: the north men, or "winterers," and the Montreal men, or "pork eaters." The north men would make their way to Fort Charlotte from the trading

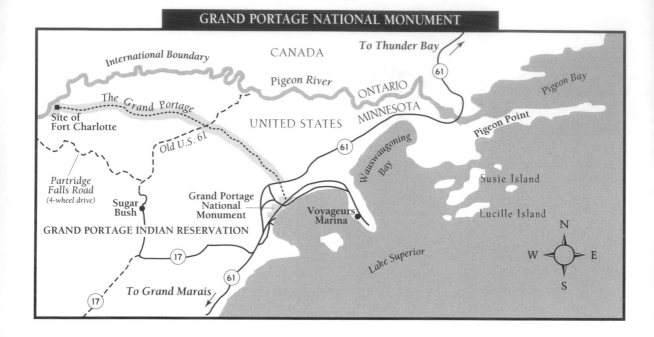

posts in the Canadian north each spring, while the pork eaters would journey to Grand Portage Bay via the French and Ottawa Rivers, then north and west across the Great Lakes. Hundreds of voyageurs, company partners, agents, clerks, and American Indians would then gather at Grand Portage in the middle of July for an annual Rendezvous. During this time the company partners held their annual meeting, while the pork-eater voyageurs would portage the canoe cargoes of furs and trade goods across the Grand Portage to Fort Charlotte or to the post at Grand Portage Bay, depending on whether the cargo was trade goods or furs. When the day's work was done, Rendezvous celebrations would commence, with plentiful food and free-flowing liquor—at least for those willing to part with the wages they had just received for the past year's work. On the final night of Rendezvous, the partners and their guests feasted and danced in the Great Hall, while the voyageurs and American Indians staged a celebration of their own outside the palisade walls. Soon after, the voyageurs took up their paddles and headed out for another season of travel and trade. Following Jay's Treaty in 1796, the newly formed United States decreed that it would levy duties on all merchandise and furs passing over the portage. In 1803, the North West Company packed up the buildings, lock, stock, and barrel, and built a new fur-trading post at the mouth of the Kaministiquia River in Ontario, Canada.

Monument lands are open year-round for hiking, cross-country skiing, and snowshoeing. The reconstructed stockade, great hall, kitchen, and canoe warehouse are open 9:00 A.M. to 5:00 P.M. from the end of May to mid-October, with guided tours, exhibits, and historical demonstrations available. A passenger ferry leaves the monument daily (summer only) for Isle Royale National Park, 22 miles offshore (fee charged).

Two hiking trails are available to visitors. The Mount Rose is a 1/2-mile trail that climbs 300 feet for a spectacular view overlooking the reconstructed fur-trade depot and Lake Superior. An interpretive brochure is available at the trailhead. The Grand Portage (8 1/2 miles) winds through the woods to the site of Fort Charlotte, a way station used for furs en route to Grand Portage.

ENTRANCE FEE: $6.00 per family or $3.00 per person.

FACILITIES: Grand Portage Lodge and Casino has full food service and overnight accommodations, as does Ryden's Border Store. Other limited services are located nearby. Grand Marais (36 miles southwest) provides a greater variety of alternatives. Drinking water and rest rooms are available at the monument. There are picnic facilities located on-site as well as 6½ miles north at Grand Portage State Park.

CAMPING: Camping is permitted only at two backcountry campsites located at Fort Charlotte. Campers must obtain a free camping permit from one of the rangers stationed at the monument or register at one of three self-registration boxes located along the Portage at Highway 61, old Highway 61, or at Fort Charlotte. Judge Magney State Park, located 20 miles southwest on Highway 61, has camping facilities, as do a few private campgrounds in the Grand Portage area.

MISSISSIPPI NATIONAL RIVER AND RECREATION AREA

111 East Kellogg Boulevard
St. Paul, MN 55101-1256
(651) 290–4160
MISS_info@nps.gov
www.nps.gov/miss

Mississippi NRRA was established in 1988 to preserve and enhance nearly 54,000 acres along a 72-mile corridor of the upper Mississippi River. The Mississippi River through the Minneapolis/St. Paul metropolitan area features diverse recreational opportunities and is highlighted by many nationally significant natural, cultural, historic, and economic resources. The north boundary is at the town of Dayton, and the south boundary is just south of the town of Hastings.

If any one river in America captures the spirit of the entire nation, it's the Mississippi. A mention of the name carries us back to another time of bustling river towns, paddleboats, Mark Twain, and the opening of the West. This great river helped shape a young nation, and its legends are known throughout the world. The power of the Mississippi River is alive today, exciting and ready for discovery.

The character of the Mississippi River changes more dramatically as it flows through the Minneapolis/St. Paul metropolitan area than anywhere else on its nearly 2,350-mile length. Emerging from the forests of the north, the river passes through one of America's largest urban areas and the heart of the Upper Midwest's cultural and commercial center before entering the open agricultural lands to the south.

Wild and shallow at the upper end, the river narrows as it creates a deep gorge beginning near downtown Minneapolis and St. Anthony Falls, the only true waterfall on the entire length of the river. The gorge extends several miles downstream to a point near downtown St. Paul, and by the time the Mississippi reaches its confluence with the St. Croix River, the river has widened to become a vast and powerful part of the largest inland navigation system on earth.

Parks and trails for biking, walking, in-line skating, and cross-country skiing are found along the river. The Great River Road follows the Mississippi River and provides many opportunities for motorists to stop at points of interests and overlooks. Canoeing, kayaking, fishing,

MISSISSIPPI NATIONAL RIVER AND RECREATION AREA

CITY OF DAYTON

Peninsula Point
Two Rivers
Historical Park

Coon Rapids Dam
Regional Park

Islands
of Peace

Anoka County
Riverfront
Regional Park

North
Mississippi
Regional Park

St. Anthony Falls

CITY OF
MINNEAPOLIS

Minnehaha
Regional
Park

CITY OF
SAINT PAUL

Hidden Falls–
Crosby Farm
Regional Park

Mississippi
Gorge

Battle Creek
Regional
Park

Minnesota

River

Lilydale-Harriet
Island-Cherokee
Regional Park

Historic
Fort Snelling

Spring Lake
Park Reserve

CITY OF
HASTINGS

St. Croix River

WISCONSIN

■ = Lock and Dam

and boating are popular at sites throughout the river corridor. A new visitor center for the Mississippi National River and Recreation Area is at 120 West Kellogg Boulevard, St. Paul, in the lobby of the Science Museum of Minnesota. The visitor center has exhibits and sells books, maps, and other merchandise. Park rangers are available to offer in-depth information about the river and recreation area and to assist in trip planning. Programs are offered by National Park Service rangers and staff from Minnesota State Parks, county and city parks, and other organizations that work along the river. A calendar of events is available at the visitor center or by visiting the Web site at www.mississippirivervisitorcenter.org.

ENTRANCE FEE: No fees are associated with the Mississippi River and Recreation Area, but some visitor centers and parks operated by other organizations do charge entry fees.

FACILITIES: The Mississippi National River and Recreation Area is made up of numerous parks operated by state, county, and municipal agencies, as well as private land. Visitors may explore and visit interpretive centers and educational facilities operated by these partner parks and other organizations within the river corridor. Food, lodging, and rest rooms are readily available throughout the corridor and the metropolitan area.

CAMPING: No National Park Service campgrounds are located within the corridor's boundaries. Private campgrounds can be found throughout the metropolitan area, as well as the adjoining St. Croix National Scenic Riverway.

FISHING: Fishing is permitted with a Minnesota state fishing license.

PIPESTONE NATIONAL MONUMENT

36 Reservation Avenue
Pipestone, MN 56164-1269
(507) 825–5464
PIPE_Interpretation@nps.gov
www.nps.gov/pipe

Pipestone National Monument comprises 283 acres of mostly tallgrass prairie and was established in 1937 to preserve the pipestone quarries where Indians for centuries obtained materials used in making ceremonial and personal pipes. The right to quarry pipestone is expressly reserved to Indians of all tribes by permit and continues to this day. The monument is located in southwestern Minnesota, adjacent to the north side of the town of Pipestone. It may be reached via State Highways 30 and 23 or U.S. 75.

More than a billion years ago, a thin clay layer was sandwiched between layers of sand deposited at the bottom of a sea. Later, additional sediment layers buried these deposits deep beneath the earth's surface, and pressure, heat, and chemical action changed the sand into quartzite and the red clay into stone. As the area was uplifted and eroded, a dense red mineral that today is called pipestone was exposed.

For centuries many Indian tribes traveled thousands of miles to mine the pipestone. Although difficult to quarry, the red stone, once extracted, is easily carved. The rare material was traded over a wide area and was particularly used for ceremonial objects such as sacred pipes. Today, only Indians are allowed to excavate the material.

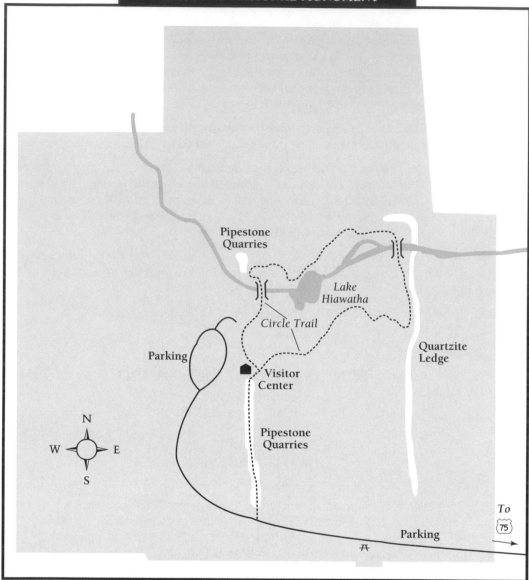

The park's visitor center is open from 8:00 A.M. to 5:00 P.M. (until 8:00 P.M. on summer weekends) and contains exhibits, an audiovisual program, and the Upper Midwest Indian Cultural Center. The Circle Trail, a 3/4-mile surfaced, self-guided trail, takes visitors past the quarries and through sections of remant tallgrass prairie. Markers are placed along the trail, and guide booklets are available in the visitor center. The monument is closed Christmas and New Year's Day.

ENTRANCE FEE: $5.00 per family or $3.00 per person; good for seven days.

FACILITIES: Food and lodging are available in the town of Pipestone. Drinking water and rest rooms are provided in the visitor center. Rest rooms are also at the picnic grounds on the south end of the monument.

CAMPING: No camping is permitted in the park. Split Rock Creek State Park (seventeen sites, pit toilets) is 8 miles south on Highway 23, and Blue Mounds State Park (seventy-six sites, flush toilets, showers, electricity, swimming beach) is 18 miles south on U.S. 75. A private campground is located just outside the park entrance.

ST. CROIX NATIONAL SCENIC RIVERWAY

P.O. Box 708
St. Croix Falls, WI 54024-0708
(715) 483–3284
SCAN_Interpretation@nps.gov
www.nps.gov/sacn

The St. Croix National Scenic Riverway was established in 1968 and enlarged in 1972 to preserve approximately 250 miles of rivers that show little evidence of disturbance. The park begins near the sources of the St. Croix and Namekagon Rivers in northern Wisconsin and follows the border between Wisconsin and Minnesota.

Thousands of years ago, this region of the United States was leveled by glacial ice flowing down from the north. As the climate warmed and the glacier melted, much of the resulting water used the St. Croix basin as an escape. The scraping of the advancing ice sheet combined with the later water runoff exposed ancient rocks and volcanic formations that are visible along the rivers.

The French were the first Europeans to venture into this region. Here they found the Dakota and Ojibwa tribes living in an area rich in both plant and wildlife. The St. Croix valley became an abundant source of beaver pelts for Europe until the early 1800s. After that, logging was to be the main industry until the 1920s. After beaver hats went out of fashion, the tremendous stands of virgin white pine along the St. Croix and Namekagon Rivers drew the attention of eastern lumber barons. Today, only scattered strands of white pine remain.

As one of the eight original wild and scenic rivers designated by Congress, the St. Croix Riverway protects stunning scenery, several endangered species, and numerous recreation opportunities near a large metropolitan area. The main visitor center at St. Croix Falls, Wisconsin, is open from May to mid-October, Friday to Monday from 9:30 A.M. to 4:30 P.M. (closed Tuesday to Thursday). The Namekagon Visitor Center is open Memorial Day to Labor Day, Thursday to Monday, from 9:00 A.M. to 4:30 P.M. During September it is open only on Saturday and Sunday.

Canoeing the riverway is one of the park's most popular activities. During late summer and fall, the water level is generally low, and the lower sections of the river provide the best trips. Most visitors find that 10 to 20 miles of paddling downstream is a full day. A listing of the numerous canoe outfitters located along the riverway may be obtained by writing the park superintendent. Park rangers are available at all the visitor centers to assist visitors planning trips. The Lower St. Croix is popular for powerboating, sailing, and houseboating. State parks along the riverway provide additional camping, picnicking, hiking, and interpretive exhibits.

ENTRANCE FEE: No charge.

ST. CROIX NATIONAL SCENIC RIVERWAY: UPPER SECTION

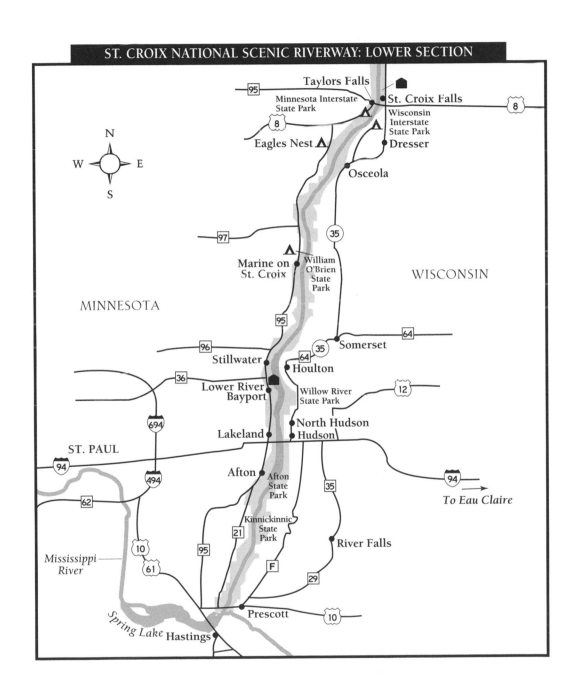

ST. CROIX NATIONAL SCENIC RIVERWAY: LOWER SECTION

N · W · E · S

Taylors Falls
95
St. Croix Falls
8
Minnesota Interstate State Park
8
Wisconsin Interstate State Park
Eagles Nest
Dresser
Osceola
97
35
Marine on St. Croix
William O'Brien State Park
WISCONSIN
95
96
35
64
Somerset
Stillwater
64
Houlton
Lower River Bayport
36
Willow River State Park
12
694
North Hudson
Lakeland
Hudson
ST. PAUL
94
494
Afton
Afton State Park
94
To Eau Claire
62
35
Kinnickinnic State Park
21
River Falls
10
95
F
61
Mississippi River
29
Spring Lake
Prescott
10
Hastings

MINNESOTA

FACILITIES: No food service or lodging is provided by the Park Service. Overnight accommodations and supplies are available in nearby communities.

CAMPING: A number of primitive campsites are located along the riverway. Walk-in campgrounds with vault toilets and water are located at some landings. Several state parks and state forests along the riverway maintain developed campgrounds.

FISHING: Bass, muskellunge, walleye pike, and sturgeon are found in the rivers, and the Namekagon is noted for brown trout. A state fishing license is required. Where the river forms a boundary between the two states, a license from either is valid.

VOYAGEURS NATIONAL PARK

3131 Highway 53
International Falls, MN 56649-8904
(218) 283–9821
voya_superintendent@nps.gov
www.nps.gov/voya

Voyageurs National Park was authorized in 1971 and established in 1975 to preserve 218,000 acres of beautiful forested lake country that was once inhabited by French-Canadian fur traders. The park is located in northern Minnesota and stretches for 55 miles along the U.S.–Canadian border east of International Falls. Four roads along U.S. 53 provide access, although most summer travel within the park depends on watercraft.

Most of this land, which has been shaped by glaciers into a system of countless waterways, remains as undeveloped and wild as it was when French-Canadian voyageurs made their way through here from Montreal to the Northwest. The pine and hardwood forests are broken only by lakes and occasional bogs, sand beaches, and cliffs. The south side of the Kabetogama Peninsula is dotted with numerous islands, while the north shore is broken with many coves and small bays. One former fur company trading post was located west of the park, in Fort Frances, north of International Falls.

One of the park's visitor centers is at Kabetogama, approximately 3 miles north of U.S. 53 on County Roads 122 and 123. Here visitors will find exhibits and information on the area. The Ash River Visitor Center is 11 miles east of Highway 53 on County Road 129. Both the Kabetogama and Ash River centers are open seasonally. The Rainy Lake Visitor Center is located 11 miles east of International Falls on Minnesota Highway 11. A variety of interpretive and children's programs are offered on Rainy and Kabetogama Lakes, including guided boat tours, Voyageur North Canoe trips, nature walks, and cross-country ski excursions.

ENTRANCE FEE: No charge.

FACILITIES: Lodging, food, and boating services are available at Kettle Falls, inside the park. This lodging complex consists of a historic two-story hotel plus three newer nearby wooden housekeeping villas. Kettle Falls is accessible only by boat or floatplane. For information, write Kettle Falls Hotel, 10502 Gamma Road, Ray, MN 56669, or call (888) 534–6835. Four resort communities adjacent to the park at Ash River, Crane Lake, Kabetogama, and Rainy Lake provide lodging, food, outfitting services, restaurants, motorboat and canoe rentals, gas, and guide

VOYAGEURS NATIONAL PARK

ONTARIO

N W S E

Sand Point Lake

Crane Lake

To Orr

53

Namakan Lake

Grassy Portage

Superior National Forest

Kettle Falls

Bleak Bay

Rainy Lake

Hiking Trail

Chain of Lakes Scenic Snowmobile Trail

Saginaw Bay

Kabetogama Peninsula

Ash River

Kabetogama State Forest

To Crane Lake

Kabetogama Narrows Information Station

Ash River Trail

129

CANADA

UNITED STATES

Cross-country Ski Trail

Woodenfrog

Kabetogama Lake

Rainy Lake

Black Bay

53

122

Kabetogama

MINNESOTA

Rat Root River

11

Rainy Lake

To International Falls

53

RAY

217

To Little Fork and 71

71

services. Groceries are available in Orr, Kabetogama, and Ray, and complete facilities can be found at International Falls.

CAMPING: More than 200 tent campsites and houseboat sites, accessible only by boat, are located throughout the park. Public camping facilities are available nearby in Kabetogama State Forest, and private camping with hookups is available at the four resort communities.

FISHING: Northern Minnesota is noted for sportfishing, especially walleye, northern pike, smallmouth bass, and crappie. A Minnesota license is required.

Voyageurs National Park (opposite page)

MISSOURI

STATE TOURIST INFORMATION
(800) 877–1234
www.missouritourism.org

GEORGE WASHINGTON CARVER
NATIONAL MONUMENT

5646 Carver Road
Diamond, MO 64840
(417) 325–4151
GWCA_Superintendent@nps.gov
www.nps.gov/gwca

George Washington Carver National Monument, which comprises 210 acres, was established in 1943 to memorialize the birthplace and childhood home of this famous educator, artist, scientist, and humanitarian. The monument is located in southwestern Missouri, approximately 10 miles southeast of Joplin. From either Neosho, Carthage, or when traveling west on I–44 from Springfield, Missouri, take U.S. 71 Alternate (Exit 18A) to the town of Diamond. From there, drive 2 miles west on County Highway V, then south ½ mile on Carver Road. When traveling east on I–44 from Tulsa, Oklahoma, take U.S. 71 (Exit 11A) to County Highway V, go 4½ miles east, then south ½ mile on Carver Road.

In the mid-1850s, Moses Carver and his wife, Susan, purchased a slave named Mary to help with their 240-acre farm in southwestern Missouri. Some time later, probably in 1864 or 1865, Mary gave birth to her second son, whom she named George. During this time, the Civil War was inflicting a period of suffering on the people of Missouri. Mary and George were carried off by a group of raiders, and, although George was eventually recovered by an acquaintance of Moses Carver, his mother was never heard from again. Upon his return to the farm, George and his brother, Jim, were taken in and raised by Moses and Susan Carver. George worked and learned alongside the Carvers before adopting their name and leaving for a black school in Neosho just prior to reaching his teens.

The remainder of George Washington Carver's life was a testimony to his initiative. After receiving honorable mention for a painting entered in the World's Columbian Exposition in Chicago in 1893, he earned bachelor's and master's degrees in botany from Iowa State University. In 1896 he accepted a position at Tuskegee Normal and Industrial Institute in Alabama, where he served for forty-seven years. During this period, Carver made significant contributions to Southern agriculture and received numerous awards. He is probably most notably remembered for transforming peanuts into products such as ink, soap, glues, dyes, milk, and cosmetics.

The monument is open from 9:00 A.M. to 5:00 P.M. daily except Thanksgiving, Christmas, and New Year's Day. A self-guided, ¾-mile trail begins near the visitor center parking lot. The trail is partially wheelchair accessible and winds through the natural setting that influenced Carver during his boyhood. It passes the Carver Birthplace site, the Carver Boyhood Statue, Williams Pond, the relocated 1881 Moses Carver house, and the Carver Family Cemetery. The visitor center houses a museum with exhibits that trace Carver's life from his birth into slavery on the Carver farm to his triumph as an artist, musician, educator, humanitarian, and world-renowned scientist. Two films documenting his life are shown continuously in the visitor center. The Carver Discovery Center for children is located in a separate building on the property and has interactive exhibits related to the life of George Washington Carver.

ENTRANCE FEE: No charge.

FACILITIES: No food or lodging is available in the park. Food can be found in the town of Diamond. Lodging is nearby in Joplin, Carthage, and Neosho. Water and rest rooms are at the visitor center. Picnic tables are available.

CAMPING: No camping is permitted at the monument. Private campgrounds are within approximately 15 miles of the park. Roaring River State Park provides camping approximately 50 miles southeast, near Cassville.

HARRY S TRUMAN NATIONAL HISTORIC SITE

223 North Main Street
Independence, MO 64050-2804
(816) 254–9929
hstr_superintendent@nps.gov
www.nps.gov/hstr

Harry S Truman National Historic Site was established in 1982 to preserve the home and memorialize the life of the thirty-third president of the United States. Truman's home is located in western Missouri in the town of Independence, near Kansas City. A visitor center with parking is located at Main Street and Truman Road. Truman Farm, a separate area that is part of the site, is in Grandview, 20 miles south of Independence.

Harry Truman was born in Lamar, Missouri, in 1884 and moved to Independence as a six-year-old boy. It was in Independence that he met Bess Wallace, his future wife, and graduated from high school. After working on the family farm, serving in the United States Army during World War I, and attempting a number of business ventures, Truman was elected Jackson County administrative judge in the early 1920s. By 1935, Harry Truman had been elected to the U.S. Senate and had moved to Washington. He was reelected once before successfully running as Franklin Roosevelt's vice president in 1944. Following Roosevelt's death in 1945, Truman assumed the presidency, to which he was elected in 1948. Deciding not to run again in 1952, Truman returned to Independence in 1953, where he purchased the house at 219 North Delaware Street from his mother-in-law's estate. Truman had lived in the house from his marriage in 1919 and returned to live there until his death in 1972 at the age of eighty-eight. Truman's wife, Bess, continued to live at the residence until her death ten years later.

The Truman Home Visitor Center, located at the intersection of Truman Road and Main Street, offers a twelve-minute audiovisual presentation about the home. The center operates daily from 8:30 A.M. to 5:00 P.M., except Thanksgiving, Christmas, and New Year's Day. Guided tours of the Truman home do not take place on Mondays between Labor Day and Memorial Day. Guided-tour tickets are sold at the visitor center on a first-come, first-served basis, so arrive early in the day. From the visitor center, the Truman home is 5 blocks west on Truman Road to Delaware Street. Parking in the Truman home neighborhood is extremely limited. Ask at the visitor center about RV and trailer parking.

The family farm where Harry Truman lived and worked from 1906 to 1917, when he left to serve in World War I, is a separate area of the historic site. The farm is 20 miles south of Independence in Grandview, Missouri. This site is open Friday, Saturday, and Sunday from Memorial Day through Labor Day. Tours are offered from 9:30 A.M. to 4:00 P.M. Tour tickets are free and available at the site. A map showing directions to the farm is available at the visitor center in Independence.

Other Truman-related sites in Independence include the Harry S Truman Presidential Museum and Library and the Jackson County Courthouse, where Truman's political career began. The courthouse features a thirty-minute audiovisual program about the president's life and his office and courtroom.

ENTRANCE FEE: $3.00 per adult; children ages sixteen and under are free.

FACILITIES: Rest rooms and drinking water are available at the visitor center and the library. Food is available nearby on the historic Independence Square, adjacent to the visitor center; lodging is available at the intersection of I–70 and Noland Road and Little Blue Parkway. Bed-and-breakfast establishments are available throughout the Harry S Truman National Historic Landmark District. Neither is offered by the National Park Service.

JEFFERSON NATIONAL EXPANSION MEMORIAL

11 North Fourth Street
St. Louis, MO 63102-1882
(314) 655–1700
jeff_superintendent@nps.gov
www.nps.gov/jeff/

Jefferson National Expansion Memorial comprises ninety-one acres and was designated part of the National Park system in 1935 to memorialize Thomas Jefferson and other American leaders who directed the territorial expansion of the United States, as well as the pioneers who explored and settled the West. This park, highlighted by the famous 630-foot Gateway Arch, is located on the St. Louis riverfront, within easy walking distance of downtown. Parking is available along the riverfront, just east of the memorial, or in a parking garage to the north on Washington Street.

As the people of the United States began moving westward following the Louisiana Purchase in 1803, St. Louis—with a strategic location on a bluff convenient to the Mississippi, Missouri, and other river approaches—became an important center of commerce, transportation, and culture. Along with being the headquarters of the western fur trade, the city was a congregating point for pioneers starting across the plains. Although most of this activity occurred along the riverfront, an 1849 fire destroyed much of the downtown area where the present park is located. Future growth moved uptown, and only two historical structures—the Old Courthouse and the Old Cathedral—still stand within the park boundaries.

The central feature of the park is Eero Saarinen's 630-foot stainless-steel arch, which was built to commemorate the city's historic role as a gateway for the westward pioneers. A passenger tram (fee charged), with eight five-passenger cars built on the order of baskets on a Ferris wheel, climbs each leg of the arch to an observation deck at the top. Beneath the arch, the Museum of Westward Expansion has exhibits interpreting the westward migration. Films about westward expansion and the building of the arch are shown periodically throughout the day. Waits of an hour or more to take the tram are common, but visitors can make a tram reservation (do this immediately upon your arrival) and spend the waiting time viewing the exhibits and movies. The grounds of the memorial are open daily from 6:00 A.M. to 11:00 P.M. The Gateway Arch and the museum are open daily from 8:00 A.M. to 10:00 P.M. from Memorial Day through Labor Day, and from 9:00 A.M. to 6:00 P.M. the remainder of the year. They are closed Thanksgiving, Christmas, and New Year's Day. The Old Courthouse, where Dred Scott sued for his freedom, has numerous exhibits on St. Louis history and is open daily from 8:00 A.M. to 4:30 P.M. but is closed Thanksgiving, Christmas, and New Year's Day.

ENTRANCE FEE: No charge. A fee is charged to ride the tram to the top of the arch and to view the films.

FACILITIES: Fast-food restaurants are located a short walk from the arch. Some food items are available at the Levee Mercantile Store in the visitor center. Drinking water, soft-drink machines, and rest rooms are provided in the visitation area beneath the arch and on surrounding city streets. Food and lodging are available a few blocks away in downtown St. Louis.

FISHING: Fishing is permitted in the Mississippi River across the road from the arch. Fishing access also is available 1/2 mile south and 1/2 mile north of the memorial.

OZARK NATIONAL SCENIC RIVERWAYS

404 Watercress Drive
P.O. Box 490
Van Buren, MO 63965-0490
(573) 323–4236
OZAR_Superintendent@nps.gov
www.nps.gov/ozar

Ozark National Scenic Riverways was established in 1964 to protect 134 miles of the beautiful Current and Jacks Fork Rivers and more than 80,000 acres of the land paralleling the rivers. This scenic area of wooded, rolling hills offers a variety of recreational activities, including camping, hiking, hunting, fishing, horseback riding, swimming, canoeing, and, best of all, tubing. The national scenic riverways is in southeastern Missouri, 150 miles south of St. Louis. State Highway 19 and U.S. Highway 60 provide primary road access into the area.

Ozark National Scenic Riverways

The Ozark Mountains of this region are remnants of a large range that has been eroded by wind and water. In addition to surface erosion, underlying limestone has developed large pockets as a consequence of water dissolving the rock. This has produced sinkholes, caves, and springs for which this area is well known. The park has over 300 recorded caves, including several that serve as critical habitat for two endangered species of bats. Most visitors come here for the beautiful Jacks Fork and Current Rivers that flow through oak-pine forests and beside limestone bluffs. The majority of the rivers' flow originates from seven major and hundreds of small springs within the park.

The riverways is spread over a wide region and includes several major activity areas. Alley Spring, on the site of what was once a small hamlet, has two nature trails, horse trails, a one-room schoolhouse that was moved here in 1971, and a three-story roller mill constructed in 1894 to provide local farmers with ground wheat flour. The mill serves as an interpretive center and is open daily from Memorial Day to Labor Day. Rest rooms are near each of the two picnic shelters. Big Spring, 4 miles south of Van Buren, has a historic district with a lodge and cabins built in the late 1930s by the Civilian Conservation Corps (CCC). Exhibits about the CCC are near Big Spring Lodge. This area is named for a spring that is one of the largest in the United States, with an average flow of 276 million gallons of water per day. Big Spring also has a craft demonstration area that is open on weekends from May through September. Round Spring, 13 miles north of Eminence on Highway 19, features a tranquil spring pool and an ancient cave. Cave tours are offered (fee charged) from May until September. The schedule for cave tours is available by calling (314) 323–4236.

The most popular activity in the park is floating the rivers. Canoes and tubes are available for rent from numerous concessionaires that provide drop-off and pickup service at various points along the rivers. Most have small stores with camping supplies, snacks, and sunscreen. For a list of NPS-approved concessionaires and their phone numbers, write the park superintendent, or visit the Internet at www.nps.gov/ozar and click on "canoeing." The upper stretches of the Jacks Fork River generally are easier to float during late winter and spring because of low water levels during summer. Maps and guides to both rivers are sold in the park. Canoes rent for approximately $40.00 per day and tubes for $5.00 to $10.00 per day, including drop-off and pickup.

ENTRANCE FEE: No charge. There is a $5.00 fee for the Round Spring Cave tour. Children ages twelve and younger are free.

FACILITIES: Lodging and food are available in the towns of Salem, Van Buren, Eminence, and Mountain View. Big Spring Lodge, the only lodging facility within the riverways' boundary, is located 4 miles south of Van Buren and is closed during the winter months. The lodge offers fourteen wood-and-stone cabins constructed by the CCC in the late 1930s. Most cabins have a full kitchen. A dining room in the main lodge building serves three meals a day. Call (573) 323–4332, or write Big Spring Lodge, P.O. Box 697, Van Buren, MO 63965. Canoe rentals are available at Akers Ferry, Pulltite, Round Spring, Two Rivers, Alley Spring, and nearby towns.

CAMPING: Campgrounds with tables, grills, water, and flush toilets include Pulltite (55 spaces, 3 group sites), Round Spring (60 spaces, 3 group sites, dump station, showers, laundry), Two Rivers (12 spaces, 2 group sites), Alley Spring (162 spaces, 3 group sites, dump station, showers), and Big Spring (123 spaces, 3 group sites, dump station, showers). Floaters may use gravel bars on both the Current and Jacks Fork Rivers for camping.

FISHING: Rock bass and smallmouth bass are the most abundant fish caught. Largemouth bass, walleye, and chain pickerel are also fairly common. Trophy trout are found in the Current River from the Montauk State Park boundary to Cedar Grove. A Missouri license is required. Fishing for trout requires a special stamp.

ULYSSES S. GRANT NATIONAL HISTORIC SITE

7400 Grant Road
St. Louis, MO 63123-1801
(314) 842–1867
ulsg_Interpretation@nps.gov
www.nps.gov/ulsg

Ulysses S. Grant National Historic Site, authorized in 1989, preserves the ten-acre core of the property known as White Haven, where Grant and his wife, Julia, made their home from 1854–1859. The site is located in south St. Louis County, adjacent to Grant's Farm off Highway 30 (Gravois Road).

Following his graduation from West Point in 1843, Lieutenant Ulysses S. Grant was assigned to army duty near St. Louis at Jefferson Barracks, at the time the nation's largest military base. At the suggestion of Fred Dent, his friend and former roommate, Grant became a frequent visitor to White Haven, the Dents' country estate. Here he met and fell in love with Fred's sister, Julia, who became his wife in 1848. Grant's military career sent them to various places around the country, and it was not until 1854, following his resignation from the army, that he and Julia were able to live together at White Haven. They struggled to farm the land for several years, lived in various places on the property, and raised their children, but ultimately the combination of poor weather and a bad economy forced the Grants out of farming. Soon the onset of the Civil War, Grant's resultant fame, and his two-term presidency changed their lives forever. Though the Grants intended to retire to White Haven and over time had purchased the land and made preparations accordingly, they never returned to live there.

The site has five historic structures, including the two-story main house, an adjacent summer kitchen, an icehouse, a chicken house, and a barn. The latter structure houses a museum. The visitor center has exhibits, an introductory video, a classroom, and a sales area. The park is open from 9:00 A.M. to 5:00 P.M. seven days a week, except Thanksgiving, Christmas, and New Year's Day. Ranger programs and self-guided walking tours are available daily, and special interpretive activities are held each month. Call the site for more information.

ENTRANCE FEE: No charge.

FACILITIES: No food or lodging is available at the site, although both can be found nearby. Rest rooms and a drinking fountain are located in the visitor center, which is also wheelchair accessible.

WILSON'S CREEK NATIONAL BATTLEFIELD

6424 West Farm Road 182
Republic, MO 65738-9514
(417) 732–2662
wicr_superintendent@nps.gov
www.nps.gov/wicr

Wilson's Creek, which comprises 1,750 acres, was authorized in 1960 to commemorate the site of an 1861 Civil War battle for control of Missouri. The park is located in southwestern Missouri, 10 miles southwest of Springfield and 3 miles east of Republic. It is reached from Interstate 44 by going south at Exit 70 on Missouri MM, east on Missouri M to Missouri ZZ, and south on Missouri ZZ to the park.

Missouri's strategic location and resources made its allegiance an important concern following the outbreak of the Civil War. The state was divided in its loyalties, with the governor an active Secessionist and Congressman Francis Blair a Unionist.

Hostilities came to a head on August 10, 1861, when 5,400 Union troops attacked a Confederate force of approximately 12,000 camped near Wilson's Creek. The attackers surprised the Confederates and quickly occupied a ridge subsequently named Bloody Hill. The battle raged for six hours before the Union forces retreated to Springfield. The Union commander, General Nathaniel Lyon, died during the battle, becoming the first Union general to die in battle in the Civil War.

Losses on both sides were heavy, with the North losing 1,317 men and the South losing 1,222. Although the Confederates held the field—and therefore won the battle—the Federals had helped their cause in Missouri. Because of the battle at Wilson's Creek and the Union victory at Pea Ridge seven months later, Missouri remained a Union state.

A visitor center features a thirteen-minute film, a spectacular battle-map display, a museum, and a sales area. A 5-mile self-guided driving tour features the restored 1852 Ray House and a ³/4-mile walking trail at Bloody Hill. Weekend and holiday living-history programs are featured during the summer months.

ENTRANCE FEE: $5.00 per vehicle or $3.00 per person; good for seven days.

FACILITIES: No facilities are located in the park, but food and lodging are available in the towns of Republic and Springfield. Drinking water and rest rooms are provided in the visitor center.

CAMPING: No camping is permitted in the park. A variety of public campgrounds are available within a thirty- to sixty-minute range. Private camping is available approximately 5 miles from the park, near I–44.

MONTANA

STATE TOURIST INFORMATION
(800) 541–1447
visitmt.com

BIG HOLE NATIONAL BATTLEFIELD

P.O. Box 237
Wisdom, MT 59761-0237
(406) 689–3155
biho_visitor_information@nps.gov
www.nps.gov/biho

Big Hole National Battlefield comprises 656 acres. It was authorized in 1910 to preserve the site of an 1877 battle between the U.S. Army and the Nez Perce Indians. The park is located in southwestern Montana, 89 miles southwest of Butte via Interstate 90, Interstate 15, and Montana 43. From Wisdom, drive 10 miles west on State Highway 43.

During the summer of 1877, a group of about 800 Nez Perce Indians began a journey from eastern Oregon and western Idaho, over the Bitterroot Mountains, and into Montana Territory. The reason for the trip was the influx of settlers, miners, and stockmen into the area that had been reserved for the Nez Perce under two separate treaties. Because the U.S. Army was charged with returning the Indians to the reservation, the two groups faced each other in battle a number of times during the chase. One such conflict occurred in the Big Hole Valley. Although the Nez Perce were able to hold off the attacking troops and escape, their losses were large and their spirit was broken. Two months later, after failing to obtain help from the Shoshone and Crow, the Nez Perce surrendered in the Bear Paw Mountains in northern Montana.

A visitor center with exhibits and an audiovisual program is open daily from 9:00 A.M. to 5:00 P.M. and with extended hours from Memorial Day to Labor Day. The battlefield is closed Thanksgiving, Christmas, and New Year's Day. Ranger programs on the Nez Perce and on 1870s military life are presented at the visitor center. A short drive to the lower parking area provides

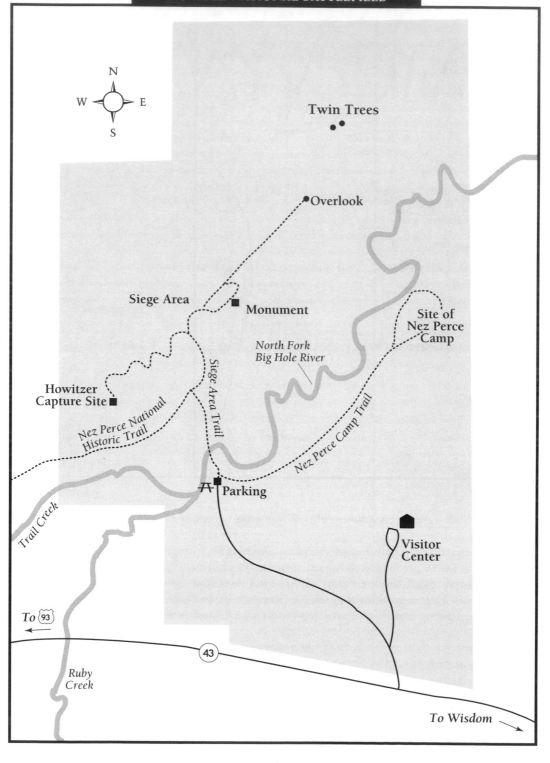

access to two foot trails that lead to the battle area. Each trail takes about forty-five minutes to walk. Another trail to the spot where a group of Indians captured an army howitzer takes about thirty minutes. During winter months the battlefield is accessible by snowshoes and cross-country skis. The lower parking area is not plowed, adding ½ mile each way. Allow a minimum of three hours to snowshoe or ski the trails.

ENTRANCE FEE: $5.00 per vehicle or $3.00 per person.

FACILITIES: No food or lodging is available in the park. A gasoline station, grocery store, restaurants, and lodging are located in Wisdom. Drinking water and rest rooms are provided in the visitor center.

CAMPING: No camping is permitted in the park. The very nice May Creek U.S. National Forest Service campground is located 7 ¼ miles west on Highway 43. It has twenty-one mostly level sites with grills, fire pits, tables, water, and pit toilets.

FISHING: Trout fishing is permitted in the North Fork of the Big Hole River with a Montana fishing license. Fishing is also available a short walk across the road from the May Creek campground.

BIGHORN CANYON NATIONAL RECREATION AREA

5 Avenue B, P.O. Box 7458
Fort Smith, MT 59035-7458
(406) 666–2412
20 Hwy 14A East
Lovell, WY 82431
(307) 548–2251
bica_superintendent@nps.gov
www.nps.gov/bica

Bighorn Canyon National Recreation Area was established in 1966. The recreation area comprises 68,490 acres, including the 71 miles of Bighorn Lake, which lies within a rugged, steep-walled canyon 2,000 feet deep. Bighorn Canyon is located in southeastern Montana and north-central Wyoming. The southern part of the recreation area is reached via U.S. 14A and 37 from Sheridan and Lovell, Wyoming, and via U.S. 310 from Billings, Montana. The northern portion and Yellowtail Dam are reached via Montana Highway 313 from Hardin, Montana.

Bighorn Canyon was cut over a period of millions of years. Yellowtail Dam was completed in 1966 to form 71-mile-long Bighorn Lake. The result is the creation of all types of water-related activities on one of the country's most scenic artificial lakes. In addition to recreation, the reservoir is used for power generation, irrigation, water supply, and flood control.

The canyon cuts across the north end of the Bighorn Mountains in a region where the middle Rocky Mountains border the Great Plains. Upstream from the dam are ½-mile-high limestone cliffs containing fossils that began forming when this region was covered by a shallow sea. Nearby, in the Pryor Mountains, the Bureau of Land Management administers 38,000 acres that have been set aside as a wild-horse range. Visitors may catch a glimpse of some of the wild horses near Sykes or Britton Springs, or from the Sykes Ridge Road or Tillet/Burnt Timber Ridge Road.

Yellowtail Visitor Center, located at the dam in the north end of the park, includes information on Crow Indian history and Yellowtail Dam. About 3 miles below the dam site, traces of the Bozeman Trail may be seen on the right bank of the river. This trail was used for transporting supplies from 1864 to 1868 between Fort Laramie, Wyoming, and Virginia City, Montana, after the discovery of gold in Montana.

At the park's south end, Bighorn Canyon Visitor Center offers an audiovisual presentation and exhibits. This was the first National Park Service building to be solar-heated. The Mason-Lovell Ranch Site and three other ranch sites can be visited. For those with boats, Barry's Landing and Ok-A-Beh have launching ramps. Gas is available only at the marina at Ok-A-Beh. The boat ramp at Horseshoe Bend has been dry for a number of years. Call ahead for boating conditions (307–548–5403).

ENTRANCE FEE: $5.00 per vehicle.

FACILITIES: Motels, restaurants, service stations, groceries, and sporting goods are available in Lovell, Wyoming, and Hardin, Montana. Motels, restaurant, grocery, gasoline, and guide service are available in or near Fort Smith, Montana.

CAMPING: Afterbay Campground (twenty-nine spaces) with a nearby twelve-space overflow area offers tables, grills, water, vault toilets, and a dump station. Horseshoe Bend (fifty-eight spaces) provides tables (some with shade shelters), grills, water, flush toilets, and a dump station. Trail Creek Campground at Barry's Landing (twelve spaces, with five spaces allocated for tent only) has no drinking water and more primitive facilities, tables, grills, and vault toilets. Black Canyon (twenty spaces) has a floating comfort station, no drinking water, and is accessible only by boat. Self-contained RVs are allowed to camp at Ok-A-Beh in the upper parking lot and in the parking lot at Barry's Landing.

FISHING: Bighorn Lake offers fishing for walleye (about 60 percent of all fish caught), rainbow and brown trout, perch, and black crappie. Bighorn River has rainbow and brown trout and is a world-class fishing area. A Montana or Wyoming fishing license is required, depending on where your fishing spot is located.

GLACIER NATIONAL PARK

West Glacier, MT 59936-0128
(406) 888–7800
glac_information@nps.gov
www.nps.gov/glac

Glacier National Park was established in 1910 and comprises more than one million acres of beautiful wilderness area, including lakes, mountains, and more than thirty glaciers. Some travelers who have seen much of the United States and many of the areas of the National Park system consider this to be the most outstanding park in the country. Glacier is located in northwestern Montana, with the west entrance 32 miles from Kalispell via U.S. 2 and the east entrance 62 miles west of Cut Bank via U.S. 2 and U.S. 89.

The landscape of Glacier tells a story that began millions of years ago. Over a long period of time, compacted limestone was covered with sediments, which in turn were covered with new layers of limestone. Approximately seventy million years ago, pressures within the earth caused the rock to warp and break, until the western section was pushed over the eastern part. This overthrust lasted for millions of years, until a 300-mile section of the earth's crust had been moved more than 37 miles to the east. Much later, the park's surface was shaped by glaciers that formed numerous U-shaped valleys.

GLACIER NATIONAL PARK

Glacier's three visitor centers at St. Mary (mid-May to October), Apgar (late April to late October, weekends other months), and Logan Pass (mid-June to mid-October) provide exhibits and information on the park. Glacier is crossed by the 52-mile Going-to-the-Sun Road. This road, mostly closed in winter, crosses through the heart of the Rockies at the treeline and provides one of America's most spectacular and scenic drives. Vehicles longer than 21 feet or wider than 8 feet are prohibited on Going-to-the-Sun Road between Avalanche Campground and the

Sun Point parking area. Rock overhangs may cause difficulty for vehicles over 10 feet high driving west from Logan Pass. Another outstanding drive is along Many Glacier Road, which leaves U.S. 89 at Babb, 9 miles north of St. Mary. Concessioner Glacier Park, Inc. operates thirty-two of the park's famous red "Jammer" buses, named for the days when drivers jammed the gears of the standard transmission. These 1930s sedans originally built by White Motor Company have been modernized to offer Glacier visitors a variety of park tours with stops at all the park lodges.

Numerous outdoor activities are available in Glacier. Guided walks, slide-illustrated presentations, and campfire programs are offered on a daily basis from mid-June through Labor Day. Schedules are posted at ranger stations, visitor centers, and campgrounds. Horseback trips ranging from two hours to all day are operated out of Many Glacier and the Lake McDonald Lodge area. Information on guided backpacking trips and equipment rental may be obtained by writing Glacier Wilderness Guides, Box 330, West Glacier, MT 59936. Call (800) 521–7238 or (406) 387–5555.

Boating on the many lakes found in the park is a popular activity. Motorboats are permitted only on Bowman, Two Medicine, McDonald, Waterton, Sherburne (only hand-carried craft permitted), and St. Mary Lakes. Motors have a limit of 10 h.p. on the first two. Personal watercraft (jet skis) are not permitted. Boats may be rented at Many Glacier, Apgar, Rising Sun, Two Medicine, and Lake McDonald Lodge. Excursion boat cruises, many with a ranger-naturalist on board, are offered at Many Glacier, Rising Sun, Waterton Lake, Two Medicine, and Lake McDonald Lodge.

During winter months, cross country skiing and snowshoeing have become increasingly popular. There is no downhill ski facility, and snowmobiling is not permitted. Going to the-Sun Road from West Glacier to the Lake McDonald Lodge (10 miles) is the only road open to automobile traffic in winter.

LODGING: Six lodging facilities with accommodations that range from rustic cabins to a beautiful mountain lodge are within the boundaries of Glacier National Park. Two lodges are on the west side of the park in the small village of Apgar. Lake McDonald Lodge is 10 miles from Apgar along Going-to-the-Sun Road. Rising Sun offers duplex cabins toward the east side of Going-to-the-Sun Road, and two facilities are at Many Glacier on the park's east side. Two lodges outside but near the park should also be considered. Glacier Park Lodge is just outside the east boundary in the town of East Glacier. The beautiful Prince of Wales Hotel is in Waterton National Park, Glacier's sister park north of the border. For information or reservations for the lodges noted here, except Apgar Village Lodge, write Glacier Park, Inc., P.O. Box 2025, Columbia Falls, MT 59912. Call (406) 892–1375. To reach Apgar Village Lodge, call (406) 888–5484, or write to P.O. Box 410, West Glacier, MT 59936. A wide range of accommodations are in the towns of West Glacier, Kalispell, Whitefish, and Columbia Falls on the park's west side.

Two backcountry chalets are available to hikers and horseback riders. Sperry Chalet is open from early July to mid-September with traditional overnight accommodations and food service. For reservations, call (888) 345–2649, or on the Web at www.sperrychalet.com. Granite Park Chalet is operated as a hiker shelter with rooms and beds provided. Guests bring and prepare their own meals. For additional information or reservations, call (800) 521–7238.

ENTRANCE FEE: $20.00 per vehicle or $5.00 per person; good for seven days.

FACILITIES: Restaurants are located in or near each of the lodges. The village of Apgar offers an ice cream shop, restaurant, gift shops, and National Park Service visitor center. There are restaurants and a small general store in the Many Glacier area. Full services are in West Glacier, Kalispell, Whitefish, Columbia Falls, East Glacier, St. Mary, and neighboring communities.

CAMPING: Developed campgrounds with tables, grills, water, flush toilets, and dump stations are located at Apgar (192 spaces, 10 group camps), Avalanche (87 spaces), Fish Creek (180 spaces), Many Glacier (110 spaces), Rising Sun (83 spaces), Sprague Creek (25 spaces, no dump station, no towed trailers or units longer than 21 feet), St. Mary Lake (148 spaces), and Two Medicine (99 spaces). Less-developed campgrounds with pit toilets are at Bowman Lake (forty-eight spaces, no large trailers), Kintla Lake (thirteen spaces, no large trailers), Cutbank (nineteen spaces, RVs not recommended), Logging Creek (eight spaces, RVs not recommended), and Quartz Creek (seven spaces, RVs not recommended). The camping limit at all these sites is seven days. Most campgrounds are available on a first-come, first-served basis. Fish Creek and St. Mary campgrounds may be reserved through the National Park Service Reservation System by calling (800) 365–CAMP or on the Web at reservations.nps.gov. Campsites are limited to eight people and two vehicles per site. Utility hookups are not available at any of the campsites.

Sixty-five backcountry camps are accessible by trail only. Visitors planning to camp overnight in Glacier's backcountry must stop at a visitor center or ranger station and obtain a Backcountry Use Permit. Backcountry permits may be reserved in advance, in person, or by mail. Permits are valid only for the dates, locations, and party size specified. Certain campgrounds have a one-night stay limit. Separate fees are charged for advance reservations and backcountry camping. For information on backcountry camping, contact Glacier National Park, West Glacier, MT 59936, or call (406) 888–7800.

FISHING: Glacier has some good fishing lakes and many miles of streams. Rainbow, brook, and cutthroat trout are found in Swiftcurrent, Josephine, and Grinnell Lakes, as well as in the lakes of Upper Swiftcurrent Valley in the Many Glacier area and the Middle and North Forks of the Flathead River on the park's south and west boundaries. Grayling live in a few waters in the Belly River country. Some catch-and-release regulations apply in the park. A Montana fishing license is not needed to fish in Glacier National Park, but a copy of the regulations should be obtained at visitor centers and ranger stations.

GRANT–KOHRS RANCH NATIONAL HISTORIC SITE

P.O. Box 790
Deer Lodge, MT 59722-0790
(406) 846-2070
www.nps.gov/grko/home.htm

Grant–Kohrs Ranch comprises 1,500 acres and was added to the National Park Service in 1972 to preserve the headquarters of one of the country's largest and best-known nineteenth-century open range cattle-ranching empires. The site is located in western Montana, adjacent to the town of Deer Lodge. Exit off I–90 on U.S. 10 until reaching the fairgrounds. For travelers with an interest in the history of the Old West, this stop is a must.

Grant–Kohrs Ranch saw its beginnings in the 1850s, when Canadian trader Johnny Grant settled in the Deer Lodge Valley to become one of the area's early ranchers. Within a decade he

Glacier National Park (opposite page)

was running more than 2,000 head of cattle, and in 1862, he constructed one of the largest homes in Montana Territory. In 1866 Grant sold his ranch to Conrad Kohrs, a German-born miner and butcher, for $19,200. From the unfenced ranges of the 1860s and 1870s, Kohrs and his partner and half-brother, John Bielenberg, witnessed the transformation of the range cattle industry to an era of fencing, feed raising, and planted pastures. With a 28,000-acre home ranch in western Montana and cattle grazing on millions of acres of public land in eastern Montana, Kohrs and Bielenberg shipped as many as 10,000 head of cattle to Chicago annually.

Following the deaths of Kohrs and Bielenberg in the early 1920s, the ranch was operated by Kohrs's grandson, who preserved the house, its furnishings and outbuildings, and papers documenting its rich history. Today the site remains a working ranch, with Texas longhorn, shorthorn, and Hereford cattle, Belgian draft horses, and poultry.

The site is open daily except Thanksgiving, Christmas, and New Year's Day. A small visitor center with exhibits relating the ranch's heritage is located across U.S. 10 from the fairgrounds. From here, a self-guided trail takes visitors to the bunkhouse, blacksmith shop, and many other outbuildings. In addition, park rangers conduct free tours of the Kohrs ranch house with its outstanding original furnishings. Reservations for the house tours are made at the visitor center on a first-come, first-served basis. A living history program from May through September depicts traditional cowboy and ranch life.

ENTRANCE FEE: No charge.

FACILITIES: No food or lodging is available in the park, but restaurants, motels, grocery stores, and gasoline stations are available within 1 mile, in Deer Lodge. Water and rest rooms are provided near the visitor center and at the ranch.

CAMPING: No camping is permitted at the site. Lost Creek State Park is approximately 25 miles away (northwest of Anaconda) and offers primitive camping facilities. Two private campgrounds are in the town of Deer Lodge. For those traveling on I–90, a nice campground (sixteen spaces, flush toilets, grills, water, and tables) in Montana's Beavertail Hill Recreation Area is 53 miles west of Deer Lodge.

FISHING: There is good fishing at the Clark Fork River. The river is a 1/2-mile walk, and a Montana fishing license is required.

LITTLE BIGHORN BATTLEFIELD
NATIONAL MONUMENT

P.O. Box 39
Crow Agency, MT 59022-0039
(406) 638–3204
libi_superintendent@nps.gov
www.nps.gov/libi

Little Bighorn Battlefield National Monument (formerly Custer Battlefield) comprises 765 acres and was established as a national cemetery in 1879 (changed to a national monument in 1946) to commemorate the site of the famous Battle of the Little Bighorn. The park is in southeastern Montana, approximately 1 mile from Exit 510 off I–90 and U.S. 212.

LITTLE BIGHORN BATTLEFIELD NATIONAL MONUMENT

87
112
90

*To Crow Agency
and Hardin*

212

N
W E
S

CROW

INDIAN

To Busby

RESERVATION

Indian Memorial

National
Cemetery

Last
Stand
Hill

**LITTLE
BIGHORN
BATTLEFIELD**

Calhoun
Hill

Little Bighorn River

Battlefield Road

Indian
Village
Site

LITTLE BIGHORN

87
90

Weir Point

Garryowen
Post Office

VALLEY

Reno-Benteen
Battlefield

*To Lodge Grass
and Sheridan*

Two years after the discovery of gold in the Black Hills in 1874, the areas reserved for the Cheyenne and Lakota were swarming with goldseekers. When the Indians left the reservation, the army was called upon to force their return. Lieutenant Colonel George Custer was part of one of three separate expeditions sent to converge on the main body of Indians in southeastern Montana. He and the Seventh Cavalry were ordered to approach the Indian concentration on the Little Bighorn. Custer divided his regiment into three battalions and attacked. When the battle ended, Custer and the 209 men of his battalion were dead. An additional fifty-three men from the other two battalions were also killed. Indians removed most of their dead from the battlefield, but their casualties are estimated at fewer than one hundred.

The monument's visitor center, which opens at 8:00 A.M. daily, contains historical exhibits and literature to help interpret the area. The visitor center closes at 7:30 P.M. from Memorial Day to Labor Day, 6:00 P.M. in spring and fall, and 4:30 P.M. during the winter. Veterans from Indian battles and more recent wars are buried in a national cemetery just west of the visitor center. (Custer is buried at West Point.) At Custer Hill, where a monument has been erected over the mass grave of soldiers killed in the battle, visitors have a view of most of the battlefield. The national monument also includes a memorial to Native American participation in the battle. Five miles beyond the main part of the monument is a detached section where two other battalions fought the Indians. Guided walks, bus tours, lectures, and audiovisual presentations are given daily during summer months. Self-guided tours are available.

ENTRANCE FEE: $10.00 per vehicle or $5.00 per person; good for seven days. There is no charge for visiting the National Cemetery.

FACILITIES: No lodging or food service is available in the monument. Rest rooms and drinking water are provided at the visitor center. A motel, restaurant, and gas station are located a short distance from the park entrance at Exit 510 off I–90 and U.S. Highway 212.

CAMPING: No camping is permitted in the monument. A small private campground is located at the intersection of I–90 and 212, about a mile from the park entrance. Larger private campgrounds are located in Hardin, 15 miles north. Public camping facilities are available at Bighorn Canyon National Recreation Area, approximately 40 miles away.

FISHING: Non-Indians are not permitted to fish in the Little Bighorn River, which is no longer stocked and supports only catfish. Nearby, the Bighorn River (also on the Crow Reservation) offers some of the finest trout fishing in the Northwest. Outfitters are available in the Fort Smith area of Bighorn Canyon National Recreation Area.

NEBRASKA

STATE TOURIST INFORMATION
(800) 228–4307
visitnebraska.org

AGATE FOSSIL BEDS NATIONAL MONUMENT

301 River Road
Harrison, NE 69346
(308) 668–2211
agfo_ranger_activities@nps.gov
www.nps.gov/agfo

Agate Fossil Beds National Monument, which comprises approximately 2,700 acres, was established in 1965 to preserve three renowned quarries that contain numerous well-preserved mammal fossils. The park is located in extreme western Nebraska on State Highway 29, approximately 23 miles south of the town of Harrison.

During an age when dinosaurs roamed the land, the area where Agate Fossil Beds National Monument is located was once part of a huge, shallow sea. The sea eventually receded and was replaced by tropical lowlands in the region that is now the Great Plains. Over a long period of time the climate became cooler and drier, and the land was able to support grasses, while small trees and bushes grew beside shallow streams. The vegetation and moderate climate allowed this land to serve as a habitat for large numbers of plant-eating mammals and their predators. As the Rocky Mountains rose to the west, less rain fell over the land, which became drier and unable to support either vegetation or animal life. Animals congregated at withering waterholes but had to venture farther and farther out to locate vegetation. Eventually, many of the animals died near the waterholes, and their remains were buried by sand, ash, and sediment. These remains are the fossils for which the national monument was established.

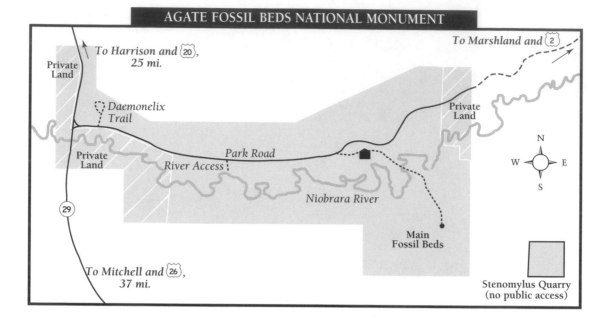

AGATE FOSSIL BEDS NATIONAL MONUMENT

To Marshland and (2)

To Harrison and (20), 25 mi.

Private Land

Daemonelix Trail

Private Land

Private Land

Park Road

River Access

Niobrara River

N

W · E

S

29

To Mitchell and (26), 37 mi.

Main Fossil Beds

Stenomylus Quarry (no public access)

Owners of the ranch that once included most of the monument first discovered fossils here in the late 1800s. Initial excavations at Agate Fossil Beds took place in 1904 when two scientists from the Carnegie Museum in Pittsburgh, Pennsylvania, worked here. One year later, a professor and four students from the University of Nebraska opened a quarry at University Hill. Subsequent excavations have occurred periodically since that time. Excavations at Agate Fossil Beds have resulted in outstanding collections in museums around the world.

The monument is open daily from 8:00 A.M. to 5:00 P.M., with extended hours during the summer. It is closed Thanksgiving, Christmas, and New Year's Day. The visitor center houses three rooms of exhibits, a theater, and a gallery of gifts given by Indian visitors to the Cook family, owners of the Agate Springs Ranch. Items on display include a whetstone used by Chief Crazy Horse and a pipestone pipe used prior to negotiations of the Fort Laramie Treaty of 1868. Visitors can view a video program and displays of fossils and artifacts. Ranger-led programs are offered from Memorial Day to Labor Day. Fossil Hills Trail from the visitor center leads to University and Carnegie Hills, where most of the fossil digs were conducted. The hike takes approximately one hour. Near the entrance to the monument, the 1-mile Daemonelix Trail leads to the fossilized corkscrew burrows of the small prehistoric beaver.

ENTRANCE FEE: $5.00 per vehicle or $3 per person; good for seven days.

FACILITIES: Drinking water and rest rooms are in the visitor center. A picnic area is near the visitor center. Restaurants, lodging, gasoline, and groceries are in Mitchell, 37 miles south, and Harrison, 25 miles north.

CAMPING: No camping facilities are available within the monument. A nice campground is located at Fort Robinson State Park, 23 miles east of Harrison on U.S. 20. Camping is also available in the town of Harrison. For those heading south, city parks in Scottsbluff and Gering provide campsites.

FISHING: The Niobrara River flows through the monument, and trout may be taken with a Nebraska fishing license.

CHIMNEY ROCK NATIONAL HISTORIC SITE

P.O. Box 27
Gering, NE 69341-0027
(308) 436–4340
www.nps.gov/chro

Chimney Rock National Historic Site, which comprises eighty-three acres, was designated an affiliated area of the National Park Service in 1956 to preserve the most famous landmark for pioneers traveling along the Oregon Trail. The entire site is managed by the Nebraska State Historical Society. The site is located in western Nebraska, 3½ miles south of the town of Bayard. From near the intersection of U.S. 26 and State Highway 92, a 1½-mile gravel road leads to within ½ mile of the site.

Chimney Rock is one of the best-known natural landmarks in the United States. Located a little more than a mile south of the North Platte River, the 500-foot-high rock formation was used by settlers as a point of reference as far back as the early 1800s. It is most famous, however, as a landmark for westward travelers along the Oregon Trail. The plains to the east of

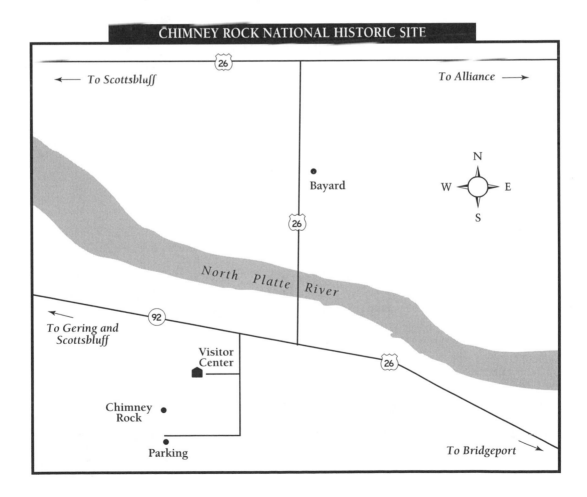

CHIMNEY ROCK NATIONAL HISTORIC SITE

Chimney Rock made it visible to the pioneers for many miles, and it warned them of the mountains ahead.

A small visitor center, operated by the Nebraska State Historical Society, is located on State Road 92, near the site. The center is open from Memorial Day to Labor Day and contains exhibits on the history of Chimney Rock. Other exhibits on this park and on the passage along the Oregon Trail are presented in the visitor center at Scotts Bluff National Monument, 23 miles to the west. Visitors wishing to hike to the spire are advised to wear hiking boots and to watch for rattlesnakes. Information on possible routes may be obtained at the visitor center.

ENTRANCE FEE: $2.00 per person; children are free with adult admission.

FACILITIES: There are no facilities at the site. Lodging and food are available along U.S. 26 and State Highway 92.

CAMPING: No camping is permitted at the site. Camping is available approximately 10 miles southeast in Bridgeport State Recreation Area.

HOMESTEAD NATIONAL MONUMENT OF AMERICA

8523 West State Highway 4
Beatrice, NE 68310-9146
(402) 223–3514
HOME_Interpretation@nps.gov
www.nps.gov/home

Homestead National Monument of America was authorized in 1936 to commemorate the homesteading movement and the impact the movement had on the people and the land. It covers close to 200 acres of prairie and woodland on the site of one of the first claims filed under the Homestead Act of 1862. The park is located in southeastern Nebraska, 40 miles southwest of Lincoln via U.S. 77 to Beatrice and 4½ miles west on Nebraska Highway 4.

After decades of pressure to donate public land to settlers, on May 20, 1862, President Abraham Lincoln signed into law the Homestead Act of 1862, which permitted citizens who came West to stake a claim to 160 acres of unappropriated government land. To receive full title, the claimants were required to pay a small filing fee, live on the land, build and live in a house, cultivate ten acres of crops, and make improvements over a five-year period. Subsequent land acts increased the amount of land that homesteaders could claim as settlers moved westward to more arid land. These later acts also changed the time and other requirements to obtain title to government lands. By the 1930s most of the land in the lower forty-eight states had been claimed, although a few places could still be homesteaded until 1976, when the act was repealed for the lower forty-eight states. Alaska was given a ten-year extension so that land could be homesteaded there until 1986.

Although it is impossible to prove who the nation's first homesteader was, the claim to Daniel Freeman's homestead, on which the monument is located, was filed early during the first day (January 1, 1863) on which claims were permitted. Freeman and his wife are buried near the monument's eastern boundary. A trail to the grave site provides a panoramic view of the quarter-section homestead.

A visitor center near the monument entrance offers an eighteen-minute video presentation along with displays of historic objects and pictures showing life during the homesteading years. The park buildings are open Monday through Friday from 8:30 A.M. to 5:00 P.M., Saturday and Sunday (Labor Day to Memorial Day) 9:00 A.M. to 5:00 P.M., and Saturday and Sunday (Memorial Day to Labor Day) 8:30 A.M. to 5:00 P.M. The monument is closed on Thanksgiving, Christmas, and New Year's Day. An 1867 homestead cabin from a neighboring township was moved near the visitor center to show how typical homesteaders lived. A 2½-mile trail system winds from the visitor center through the second-oldest tallgrass prairie restoration in the United States to the original Freeman cabin site, other Freeman building sites, the Freeman graves, and the squatters cabin site near Cub Creek. The trail is a worthwhile walk.

The Freeman School, a furnished one-room schoolhouse that served students from 1872 to 1967, is located on Highway 4, ¼ mile west of the visitor center. At the time it closed, the school was the oldest continuously used one-room school in the state of Nebraska. It is also the site of teaching that was the basis for the first court battle over the use of religion in the classroom. The Freeman School is open to visitors upon request, depending on staff availability.

ENTRANCE FEE: No charge.

FACILITIES: Water and rest rooms are provided in the visitor center. A small picnic area is available. Restaurants, motels, and supermarkets are located in Beatrice, 4 miles to the east.

CAMPING: No camping is permitted at the monument. The city of Beatrice (4 miles east) has two city parks with camping facilities. Chatauqua Park—on the south side of town, 3½ blocks east off Highway 77 on Grable Street—has tables, water, electrical hookups, a dump station, and hot showers. Riverside Park—on the west side of Beatrice, 4 blocks north off Court on Sumner—has tables, water, electrical hookups, and a swimming pool.

FISHING: Although permitted in Cub Creek, which flows through the monument, fishing is pretty much a losing proposition. Your luck will be better in the Big Blue River. A Nebraska fishing license is required.

MISSOURI NATIONAL RECREATIONAL RIVER

P.O. Box 591
O'Neill, NE 68763
(402) 336–3970
interpretation_mnrr@nps.gov
www.nps.gov/mnrr

Missouri National Recreational River was authorized in 1978 to protect a 59-mile stretch of the Missouri River. A second 39-mile nearby upper stretch and two tributaries were added in 1991. The two sections of the river are located in northeastern Nebraska on the South Dakota border.

The original segment of the recreational river begins at the Gavins Point Dam near Yankton, South Dakota, and ends 59 miles downriver at the southern end of Ponca State Park. This section is prized for the islands, bars, and chutes formed by the river. The second stretch, flowing through landscape from presettlement days, was added over a decade later. It includes 39 miles of the Missouri, 20 miles of the lower Niobrara River, and 8 miles of Verdigre Creek. This upper

MISSOURI NATIONAL RECREATIONAL RIVER

Missouri River segment begins at the Fort Randall Dam near Pickstown, South Dakota, and ends near Running Water, South Dakota.

Wayside exhibits interpreting the river's features are at most access sites, overlooks, and parks. The National Park Service and the U.S. Army Corps of Engineers operate the Lewis and Clark Visitor Center at the Gavins Point Dam. Information is also available at Niobrara and Ponca state parks. A variety of outdoor activities are available including camping, fishing, canoeing, boating, swimming, and bird-watching. Canoeing is best on the upper reach of the Missouri. During the summer, Niobrara State Park offers guided boat rides to the vicinity of the Niobrara–Missouri River confluence.

ENTRANCE FEE: No charge for the Missouri National Recreational River. The state parks do charge entry fees.

FACILITIES: Rest rooms and water are provided in the Lewis and Clark Visitor Center. Food and lodging are in nearby towns. Rental cabins are in Niobrara and Ponca state parks.

CAMPING: Niobrara State Park (402–857–3373), 1 mile west of the town of Niobrara, offers 119 sites with tables, grills, flush toilets, showers, and a dump station. Some sites have electrical hookups. Ponca State Park (402–755–2987), 2 miles north of the town of Ponca, has 164 sites with similar facilities. Corps of Engineers facilities are at the Fort Randall Dam and Gavins Point Dam.

FISHING: Fishing is popular on both stretches of the Missouri. A Nebraska or South Dakota license is required.

NIOBRARA NATIONAL SCENIC RIVER

P.O. Box 591
O'Neill, NE 68763
(402) 336–3970
stuart_schneider@nps.gov
www.nps.gov/niob

Niobrara National Scenic River comprises 21,074 acres and was authorized in 1991 to protect a 76-mile stretch of an extraordinary Great Plains river and preserve an ecological crossroads between eastern woodlands, western grasslands, and mountain timber. The river is located in north-central Nebraska, with the upper portion beginning at Borman Bridge, southeast of the town of Valentine, and the lower portion ending at Nebraska Highway 137, north of the town of Newport.

The Niobrara is a 300-mile river that begins in the eastern Wyoming plains and disappears when it merges with the Missouri River in northeastern Nebraska. Over its course, it has cut into the plains as much as 300 feet, allowing water from the Ogallala aquifer to seep out of the valley walls and add to the river's flow. The western half of the Scenic River includes more than ninety waterfalls, the highest of which drops nearly 70 feet.

This area of Nebraska serves as the meeting ground of humid eastern and dry western air masses that cause many species of plant and animal life to reach the limits of their range. Eastern forest species such as American elm and black walnut reach their western limits here.

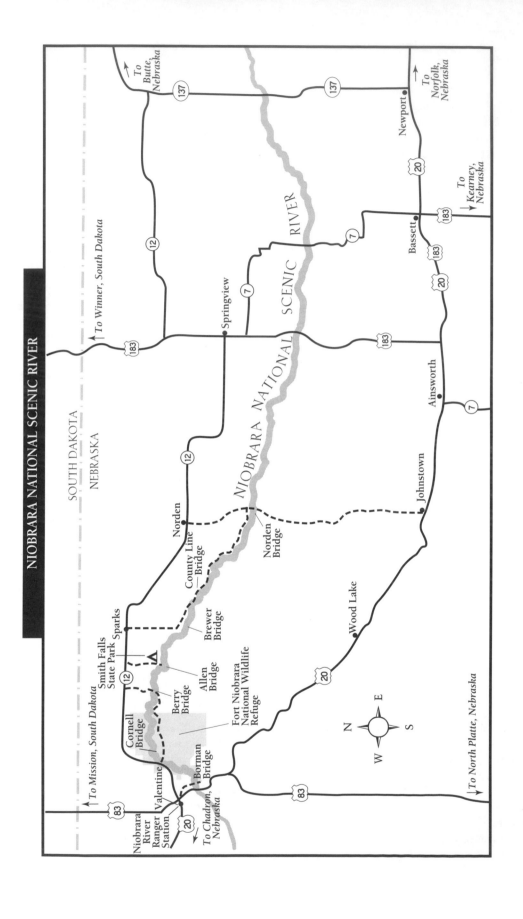

Likewise, western species such as ponderosa pine and horizontal juniper terminate in this area. Even northern forest species including paper birch and quaking aspen reach their southern-most limits in the Niobrara Valley.

One of the river's major activities is canoeing and tubing along the western section. The Fort Niobrara launch area near the Cornell Bridge on Highway 12 east of Valentine is a popular location to begin a trip. A number of firms in Valentine supply canoes and tubes. A list of outfitters is available from the National Park Service or the Valentine Chamber of Commerce. Call (402) 336–3970 for information. Hiking and sight-seeing are also popular, especially at Smith Falls State Park through which the river flows. Nature trails are at the park and Fort Niobrara National Wildlife Refuge, which offers a driving tour through elk and bison pastures.

ENTRANCE FEE: No charge.

FACILITIES: Visitor centers are at the wildlife refuge (operated by the U.S. Fish and Wildlife Service) and at Smith Falls State Park (operated by the Nebraska Game and Parks Commission). The National Park Service maintains a ranger station in Valentine. Lodging and food service are available in the towns of Valentine and Ainsworth.

CAMPING: Public camping with tables, fire rings, flush toilets, and showers is available at Smith Falls State Park. Reservations are available (402–376–1306). The park may be reached via a 4-mile gravel road from Highway 12. A number of private campgrounds are along the first 30 miles of the river between the wildlife refuge and Norden Bridge. Two commercial campgrounds are near the town of Valentine.

FISHING: Fishing in the river is likely to produce marginal results. A Nebraska fishing license is required.

SCOTTS BLUFF NATIONAL MONUMENT

P.O. Box 27
Gering, NE 69341-0027
(308) 436–4340
scbl_webmaster@nps.gov
www.nps.gov/scbl

Scotts Bluff National Monument, which comprises more than 3,000 acres, was proclaimed a national monument in 1919 to preserve two of a series of massive sandstone and clay bluffs rising 800 feet above the North Platte River. These bluffs became prominent landmarks for travelers bound for Utah, Oregon, and California. The monument is located in western Nebraska, 3 miles west of Gering via Nebraska Highway 92. From Interstate 80, take the Kimball exit and drive north on Nebraska 71 for 42 miles.

Scotts Bluff is a remnant of an ancient high plain that was gradually eroded by wind and water over several million years. Hundreds of feet higher than today's surrounding Great Plains, Scotts Bluff is protected by a durable cap rock above layers of volcanic ash, sandstone, and siltstone that have eroded away around it. This dry, windy land is home to hardy inhabitants including prairie dogs, squirrels, foxes, badgers, coyotes, and rabbits. Other animals, including buffalo, bighorn sheep, and pronghorn antelopes, were once prevalent but have disappeared.

Scotts Bluff National Monument

Scotts Bluff has served for several hundred years as a prominent landmark for trappers, traders, emigrants, the Pony Express, and present-day travelers. It was well known to Native Americans for many years before white settlers returning east from the Pacific Coast in 1812 happened on the North Platte route. Within the next decade the bluff became a familiar sight to traders in wagon caravans heading west toward the Rocky Mountains. Their caravan route beside the bluff and through the Rocky Mountains became famous as the 2,000-mile Oregon Trail. The original route took emigrants far to the south of the bluff, but by the gold rush days of the early 1850s most travelers chose the improved trail through Mitchell Pass, just south of Scotts Bluff. Named for Hiram Scott, a clerk who died near here in 1828, it is estimated that at least 350,000 people going west passed by Scotts Bluff between 1841 and 1869. The Pony Express went out of business after only eighteen months when the coast-to-coast telegraph began operation. In 1869 the Union Pacific and Central Pacific railroads linked in Utah, and the Oregon Trail fell into disuse.

The monument is open daily from 8:00 A.M. to 7:00 P.M. Memorial Day through Labor Day. Reduced hours are observed the remainder of the year, and the monument is closed Christmas and New Year's Day. The visitor center offers three rooms of historic and geological artifacts and the paintings of photographer and artist Will Henry Jackson. Guided ranger walks and living history presentations take place during summer months. A short trail leads to the location where Jackson camped in 1866. Ruts along the Oregon Trail carved by settlers' wagons are plainly visible in several locations within the monument. Visitors may drive a paved road or hike the Saddle Rock Trail to the top of the bluff. Both routes are 1.6 miles long, and a guide booklet for the trail is available at the visitor center. An overlook at the top of the bluff offers a view of the Oregon Trail approach to Mitchell Pass. Be certain to visit nearby Chimney Rock National Historic Site (in this chapter) and Fort Laramie National Historic Site (in the Wyoming section) while you are in the vicinity. Information is available at the visitor center.

ENTRANCE FEE: $5.00 per vehicle.

FACILITIES: Food and lodging are not available at the monument, but both are in either Gering or Scottsbluff. Drinking water and modern rest rooms are at the visitor center.

CAMPING: No camping is permitted at the monument. The town of Gering operates an RV campground along Highway 71, while the town of Scottsbluff maintains the Riverside Park campground southwest of the city. Both sites offer tables, grills, hookups, showers, and a dump station.

Great Basin National Park

NEVADA

STATE TOURIST INFORMATION
(800) 237–0774
travelnevada.com

GREAT BASIN NATIONAL PARK

100 Great Basin National Park
Baker, NV 89311-9700
(775) 234–7331
grba_interpretation@nps.gov
www.nps.gov/grba

Great Basin National Park was established in 1986 to protect 77,082 acres of wild and rugged high desert country that includes spectacular mountains and an extensive cave system. The park is located near the Nevada–Utah border. Park headquarters is 10 miles south of U.S. Highways 6 and 50 and 5 miles west of the small town of Baker, Nevada.

The West's Great Basin incorporates western Utah and nearly all of Nevada in a giant panorama of parallel north-south mountain ranges and sagebrush-covered valleys. Great Basin National Park, formerly Lehman Caves National Monument (established 1922) and Wheeler Peak Scenic Area, sits in the middle of this huge desert. The park's three main attractions are Wheeler Peak, which at 13,063 feet is one of the highest mountains in the Great Basin; Lehman Caves, an extensive cavern system of limestone and marble decorated with stalactites and stalagmites; and the ancient bristlecone pines that grow beneath Wheeler Peak.

The park's range of natural environments results from the great variations in elevation. Numerous types of plants and animals may be observed by visitors. Mule deer feed in the higher meadows, and coyotes and cougars are occasionally seen. Plant life depends on the season. Wildflowers begin blooming in the lower country during spring and gradually appear higher on the mountain as the summer progresses. In the fall, slopes are streaked with golden aspen

To Ely

Wheeler Peak Scenic Drive

Lower Lehman Creek

Lehman Caves

Wheeler Peak

Upper Lehman Creek

488

Baker

Baker Creek

487

159

(for high-clearance vehicles only)

NEVADA | UTAH

21

Lexington Arch

To Las Vegas

To 15

93

6 50

N
W E
S

leaves. During years of normal precipitation, the higher peaks are covered with snow for more than six months.

Bristlecone pines live longer than any other earth organism and are one of the outstanding attractions at Great Basin National Park. These ancient trees, which can live for nearly 5,000 years, are found throughout the Great Basin, generally at elevations between 9,000 and 11,000 feet. In the park, a grove of bristlecones on the northeast flank of Wheeler Peak can be reached via a 3-mile round-trip hike, which also passes through an Engelmann spruce and limber pine forest.

The formation of Lehman Caves began millions of years ago, when the water table was higher and the climate was more humid than it is today. Water charged with carbon dioxide dissolved the more-soluble rocks, and as the water table gradually fell, the process of cave decoration began. Stalactites, stalagmites, columns, and shields (round disks of calcite) are all found in abundance throughout the caves. The caves take their name from rancher Absalom Lehman, who was probably the first white man to explore them. Lehman guided parties through the underground rooms from 1885 until his death in 1891.

The visitor center is open daily except Thanksgiving, Christmas, and New Year's Day. Visitors with sufficient time should stop at the visitor center, take the cave tour, and drive the scenic paved road to the base of Wheeler Peak. Conducted tours of the cave (fee charged) require about ninety minutes and cover approximately 1/2 mile via a paved trail. Tours depart from the visitor center, and warm clothing is suggested because of the cave's 50 degree Fahrenheit temperature. Photography (no tripods) is permitted in the cave.

The paved road to Wheeler Peak climbs approximately 3,000 feet from the visitor center. Large motor homes and trailers are not recommended beyond Upper Lehman Creek. At the terminus of the road, visitors will find a number of trails to lakes and to a bristlecone pine grove. The Wheeler Peak road is closed in winter.

ENTRANCE FEE: No charge. A fee is charged for cave tours.

FACILITIES: Refreshments, meals, and souvenirs are available at the visitor center from April through October. Modern rest rooms and picnic tables are also located here. No overnight accommodations are provided within the park, but restaurants, a small grocery, credit card gas pumps, and limited accommodations are available in the town of Baker. Gasoline is available at the Border Inn on the Utah–Nevada border on U.S. Route 50-6. Ely, Nevada, 70 miles west, is the nearest major town.

CAMPING: Three campgrounds are located along Wheeler Peak Scenic Drive. Lower Lehman Creek (eleven sites) and Upper Lehman Creek (twenty-four sites) are closest to the visitor center and generally fill first. Wheeler Peak (thirty-seven sites), at an elevation of 9,886 feet, is at the end of the scenic road. Baker Creek (thirty-four sites) is 4 miles south of the visitor center via a gravel road. All the campgrounds offer vault toilets, tables, grills, and water.

FISHING: The park offers good fishing opportunities in three creeks and two of the five lakes. Lahonton cutthroat trout are found in Baker Lake, while Johnson Lake has brook trout. Snake, Lehman, and Baker Creeks each support rainbow trout. Baker Creek also has brown trout. A Nevada fishing license with a trout stamp is required. Use of live bait is prohibited.

LAKE MEAD NATIONAL RECREATION AREA

601 Nevada Highway
Boulder City, NV 89005
(702) 293–8920
lame_interpretation@nps.gov
www.nps.gov/lame

Lake Mead National Recreation Area was established in 1936 and comprises almost 1 1/2 million acres of clear water and desert landscape, making it an attractive area for water-related activities. The park is located in southern Nevada and northwestern Arizona. Main access is via U.S. 93, which connects Las Vegas to Kingman, Arizona. When approaching on I–15 from the west, take the Highway 146 exit to Henderson, Nevada, and turn south on U.S. 93/95 and Interstate 515 to Boulder City. Tour buses from Las Vegas make regular trips to the recreation area and Hoover Dam.

Lake Mead and Lake Mohave combine to stretch for more than 180 miles. Both lakes have been formed from the construction of hydroelectric dams on the Colorado River. The most famous of these, Hoover Dam, was completed in 1935.

The park lies astride the Grand Wash Cliffs, which form a transition between two major geographical provinces in North America. To the east, the Colorado has carved a series of canyons (including the Grand Canyon) through high country known as the Colorado Plateau. After leaving the western portal of the Grand Canyon at Grand Wash Cliffs, north-south mountains of the Basin and Range province divert the river southward toward the Gulf of California. Broad enclosed valleys draining toward the river separate the mountain ranges of this region. In the Lake Mead section, the Colorado breached the mountains and provided the local basins with drainage to the south.

The park is open year-round, although daytime temperatures during summer months may rise above 110 degrees Fahrenheit. The main visitor center is a few miles northeast of Boulder City on U.S. 93. Daily tours of Hoover Dam are discontinued until further notice. Call for current status of tours. Park personnel present ranger programs and hikes at various locations; schedules are posted at campgrounds and ranger stations, and on the park's Web site. Much of the park's summer activity is water-related. Swimming is allowed anywhere on the lake, except where signs indicate NO SWIMMING. Keep in mind there are no lifeguards. Concessioners offer boat trips to various locations, and docking facilities for private boats are located at six marinas on Lake Mead and two marinas on Lake Mohave.

ENTRANCE FEE: $5.00 per vehicle or $3.00 per person; good for five days. There is also a lake-use fee for boats.

FACILITIES: Most modern facilities, including lodging and food services, are available in Boulder City, Henderson, Las Vegas, North Las Vegas, Searchlight, Overton, Bullhead City, and Kingman. Developed areas in the park are:

Boulder Beach: Ranger station, picnic areas, launching ramp, campground, marina, boat rentals, store, lodging, marine supplies, and restaurant. Write Lake Mead Resort, 322 Lakeshore Road, Boulder City, NV 89005 (702–293–3484; 800–752–9669). Motel only (702–293–2074); trailer village only (702–293–2540).

Callville Bay: Ranger station, launching ramp, small boat and houseboat rentals (800–255–5561), marina, picnic area, campground, store, trailer village, marine supplies, and restaurant. Write Callville Bay Resort, HCR 30 Box 100, Las Vegas, NV 89124 (702–565–4813; www.callvillebay.com).

Cottonwood Cove: Ranger station, picnic shelter, launching ramp, small boat and houseboat rentals (800–255–5561), campground, marina, store, lodging, marine supplies, trailer village, and restaurant. Write Cottonwood Cove Resort, P.O. Box 1000, Cottonwood Cove, NV 89046 (702–297–1464; www.cottonwoodcoveresort.com).

Echo Bay: Ranger station, launching ramp, campground, marina, boat rentals, gasoline, store, lodging, marine supplies, trailer village, and restaurant. Write Echo Bay Resort, HC 30 Box 30, Overton, NV 89040 (702–394–4000 or 800–752–9669).

Katherine: Ranger station, lodging, trailer village, marina, campground, picnic area, launch ramp, restaurant, grocery, gasoline, laundry, houseboat rentals. Write Lake Mohave Resort, Katherine Landing, Bullhead City, AZ 86430 (520–754–3245 or 800–752–9669).

Las Vegas Bay: Ranger station, marina, campground, launch ramp, restaurant, grocery, gasoline, and laundry. Write Las Vegas Bay, P.O. Box 91150, Henderson, NV 89009 (702–565–9111).

Overton Beach: Ranger station, marina, trailer village, snack bar, grocery, marine fuel, and laundry. Write Overton Beach Marina, Overton Beach, NV 89040 (702–394–4040).

LAKE MEAD NATIONAL RECREATION AREA

Temple Bar: Ranger station, lodging, trailer village, marina, campground, picnic area, launch ramp, restaurant, and marine fuel. Write Temple Bar Resort, Temple Bar, AZ 86443 (520–767–3211 or 800–752–9669).

Willow Beach: Ranger station, restaurant, grocery, marine supplies, gasoline. Write Willow Beach Harbor, HC 37 Box 12, Willow Beach, AZ 86445 (520–767–4747 or 800–696–7238).

CAMPING: The park includes seven campgrounds. All have flush toilets and dump stations. All trailer villages listed below have hookups and are operated by private concessioners. Showers are also concessioner-operated. Stores are located near most campgrounds. Campgrounds in the park are Boulder Beach (154 spaces, 5 group camps, 80 trailer sites, showers, laundry), Callville Bay (80 spaces, 20 trailer sites), Cottonwood Cove (149 spaces, 75 trailer sites, laundry), Echo Bay (166 spaces, 58 trailer sites, laundry), Katherine (173 spaces, 27 trailer sites, laundry), Las Vegas Bay (89 spaces), Overton Beach (50 trailer sites, laundry), and Temple Bar (153 spaces, 14 trailer sites, laundry).

FISHING: Lake Mead is especially noted for its largemouth bass, striped bass, and channel catfish. Lake Mohave is stocked with rainbow trout in the upper end and largemouth and striped bass farther down the lake. Sunfish and crappie are also taken in these lakes. A Nevada or Arizona fishing license is required, and a stamp from the other state must be affixed to the license when you're fishing from a boat.

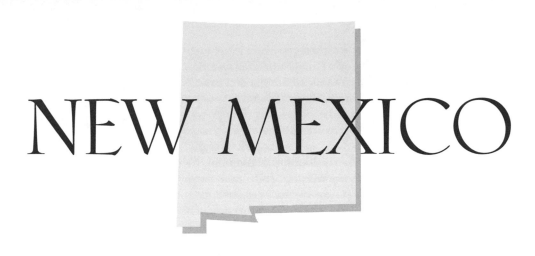

NEW MEXICO

STATE TOURIST INFORMATION
(800) 545–2040

www.newmexico.org

AZTEC RUINS NATIONAL MONUMENT

84 County Road 2900

Aztec, NM 87410

(505) 334–6174

www.nps.gov/AZRU

Aztec Ruins, which comprises 319 acres, was established in 1923 to preserve a large Ancestral Pueblo Indian community. The park is located in northwestern New Mexico, north of the town of Aztec, just west of the junction of U.S. 550 and New Mexico Highway 516.

After the people of the Colorado Plateau region developed farming and a more sedentary lifestyle, the ancestral Pueblo cultural system, now referred to as the Chaco Phenomenon, began to grow. The West Ruin at Aztec, open to the public, is a Chaco-style greathouse of more than 400 rooms and kivas built in the early 1100s. Visitors may tour the West Ruin, which is actually only a portion of a larger community consisting of several other unexcavated greathouses, plazas, great kivas, tri-wall kivas, and smaller residential buildings. Prehistoric roadways, now barely visible, link the structures within this community. Short, well-defined road segments suggest a connection to hundreds of smaller residential sites along the Animas River valley and point toward other Chacoan communities in the Four Corners area. Aztec may have served as a major ceremonial, administrative, and trade center for the surrounding population. By the 1150s the Chaco system waned, and a different cultural style emerged that had its roots in the Mesa Verde area to the north. Some remodeling of the pueblo occurred, and the pueblo flourished in Mesa Verde style until the 1300s, when the people left the buildings uninhabited.

The park is open daily from 8:00 A.M. to 5:00 P.M. (until 6:00 P.M. from Memorial Day to Labor Day), except Thanksgiving, Christmas, and New Year's Day. The visitor center has an interesting video and exhibits such as pottery, baskets, and other items made by the Pueblo people who lived here. Rangers give interpretive talks during the summer months. A paved self-guided trail leads through the West Ruin, which has rooms with their original roofs, and to a reconstructed kiva, a semi-subterranean room that was used for community activities. Visitors are cautioned to stay on the trails, because the walls crumble easily.

ENTRANCE FEE: $4.00 per adult; children ages sixteen and under are free; good for seven days.

FACILITIES: Food and lodging are not available at the monument, but both may be found in Aztec. Drinking water and modern rest rooms accessible to wheelchairs are located in the visitor center. A shaded picnic area is also available.

BANDELIER NATIONAL MONUMENT

HCR 1 Box 1, Suite 15
Los Alamos, NM 87544-9701
(505) 672–3861, extension 517
www.nps.gov/band

Bandelier National Monument comprises 32,737 acres, including 23,267 acres of wilderness area, and was established in 1916 to preserve thousands of archaeological sites related to the ancestral Pueblo Indians. The monument is located in north-central New Mexico, 46 miles northwest of Santa Fe. From Santa Fe, drive north on U.S. 285 to Pojoaque, and turn west on New Mexico Highway 502 to New Mexico Highway 4. Visitors to Bandelier National Monument will find it worthwhile to spend at least a half day at the science and historical museums in the nearby town of Los Alamos.

Bandalier National Monument, named for a nineteenth-century anthropologist, is located on the slopes of a gigantic volcano that erupted over a million years ago. The eruption covered the surrounding area with ash flows hundreds of feet thick. As the massive eruptions emptied the volcano's interior, the mountain collapsed and formed a saucer-shaped depression more than 16 miles in diameter. This caldera is now the Jemez Caldera National Preserve. The plateau formed by the ash flows was subsequently eroded by water from rain and snow, forming the picturesque mesas and sheer canyons that are so characteristic of the area today.

For thousands of years, Indians have lived in this area. By the 1100s, groups had begun settling in small farming villages. By the 1400s, these people, ancestors of the present Pueblo Indians, were building large villages on canyon bottoms, mesa tops, and along the bases of cliffs. By the mid-1500s, the people had left these villages behind, moving downslope to locations along the Rio Grande.

The park features most accessible to visitors are in Frijoles Canyon. Here, along a stream at the bottom of a deep gorge, lie nearly 2 miles of ancestral Pueblo settlements. The people built masonry houses of one to three stories; houses along the base of the cliffs included cave rooms carved into the volcanic ash. For centuries the Indians farmed, made pottery, wove cotton cloth, gathered wild plants, and developed complex social and religious customs. It is uncertain why they moved to their present homes along the Rio Grande, but by the time the Spanish arrived in the area, the villages on the plateau were unoccupied.

= Archaelogical Site

The monument's visitor center has museum exhibits, an audiovisual presentation, and a bookstore. Personnel are on duty to provide an orientation and answer questions. Visitor center hours vary, depending on the season and staffing. Guided walks, interpretive talks, and evening campfire programs are available during summer months. A popular silent walk in the darkness among the archaeological sites near the visitor center is offered weekly from Memorial Day to Labor Day. Trails of varying distance and difficulty start in the area of the visitor center. The main self-guided loop trail to excavated sites near the visitor center is an easy one-hour walk. Seventy miles of backcountry trails are also available for hikers. Trails are open during daylight hours. Pets are not permitted on the trails. Free wilderness permits, which are available at the visitor center, are required for overnight hikes.

A detached section of the park, Tsankawi, is located 13 miles north of Frijoles Canyon on Highway 4. Here a large unexcavated village is reached via a 1½-mile self-guided trail (one and a half hours) beginning at the highway. The trail provides access to a number of interesting features, including petroglyphs and cave structures.

ENTRANCE FEE: $10.00 per vehicle or $5.00 per person; good for seven days.

FACILITIES: No lodging is available in the park, but motels and B&Bs are located in White Rock and Los Alamos. Drinking water and rest rooms are available at the visitor center and the campground. A curio store with a snack bar is near the visitor center, and an exceptionally lovely picnic area along Frijoles Creek is next to the visitor center.

CAMPING: Juniper Campground (ninety-four sites) provides tables, fire grills, water, flush toilets, and a dump station. The campground may be closed from December to March, depending on the weather. Ponderosa Group Campground (two sites, groups only) is located 6 miles west of the entrance and has tables, grills, water, and pit toilets. Ponderosa is usually open from April 15 to November 1, depending on the weather. Reservations are required (505–672–3861, ext. 534) for groups of ten to fifty. For backpackers with a free wilderness permit, a number of camping zones are available in the backcountry (no fires, pets, or weapons permitted). Wilderness permits must be picked up in person at the visitor center.

CAPULIN VOLCANO NATIONAL MONUMENT

P.O. Box 40
Capulin, NM 88414-0040
(505) 278–2201
capo_administration@nps.gov
www.nps.gov/cavo

Capulin Volcano National Monument, which is comprised of 793 acres, was established in 1916 to protect a symmetrical cinder cone rising high above the surrounding plain. The sighting of this prominent cinder cone by travelers some distance away makes it an important landmark today, as it undoubtedly was for the early pioneers. The park is located in northeastern New Mexico, 3 miles north of the town of Capulin, just east off State Road 325.

Capulin Volcano (pronounced cah-poo-LEEN) is the cone of an extinct volcano that rises more than 1,000 feet above its relatively flat surroundings. The volcano was active between 56,000 and 62,000 years ago, and the mountain is composed primarily of cinders, ash, and rock debris from these explosions, which lasted only a few years. From the highest part of the rim, where the crater drops approximately 415 feet, the visitor can see parts of New Mexico, Colorado, and Oklahoma.

A visitor center with exhibits explaining volcanoes and the geographical area surrounding Capulin Mountain is located approximately ½ mile inside the park entrance. From here a 2-mile paved road circles and climbs the mountain to a parking area at the rim. At this point, a 1-mile self-guided hiking trail follows the rim of the crater. The walk is fairly strenuous and takes approximately thirty-five minutes, but the time is well spent. It is probably less strenuous to walk the trail counterclockwise. There is also a 0.2-mile trail from the parking area to the crater's bottom and a short (ten-minute) nature trail by the visitor center. You may want to call ahead to determine hours of operation, which vary seasonally.

The monument contains a surprising variety of plants and wildlife. Porcupines, squirrels, and deer are relatively abundant, and golden eagles are seen on occasion. Extensive plant life is located both at the mountain's base and on Crater Rim Trail.

ENTRANCE FEE: $5.00 per vehicle or $3.00 per person; good for seven days.

FACILITIES: Food and lodging are not available in the park. Both are available in nearby Capulin, Des Moines, Clayton, and Raton. Both the visitor center and picnic area have water and rest rooms with flush toilets. Pit toilets are available at the rim parking area.

CAMPING: No camping is permitted at the monument. Camping is available in the towns of Capulin and at Clayton Lake State Park (thirty-three sites, flush toilets, showers), 12 miles northwest of Clayton on Highway 370. Camping is also available at Sugarite State Park (forty-five sites, flush toilets, showers), 6 miles north of Raton and 33 miles west of Capulin.

CARLSBAD CAVERNS NATIONAL PARK

3225 National Parks Highway
Carlsbad, NM 88220-5354
(505) 785–2232
cave_park_information@nps.gov
www.nps.gov/cave

Carlsbad Caverns National Park, which comprises 46,775 acres, was established as a national monument in 1923 (changed to a national park in 1930). This series of caverns—one of the largest underground chambers yet discovered—features many spectacular and strange formations. The park is located in southeastern New Mexico on U.S. 62/180, 20 miles southwest of the town of Carlsbad and 150 miles east of El Paso.

Carlsbad Caverns National Park lies in the Guadalupe Mountains of southeastern New Mexico. These mountains are the exposed remains of a limestone reef that was formed during the Permian Age—about 250 million years ago. Rainwater that became carbonic acid dripped through cracks and dissolved rock, but the main force in creating the caves was hydrogen sulfide from the oil and gas deposits to the east. It mixed with the water in the caves and created a weak sulfuric acid that easily dissolves limestone. This is the process by which Carlsbad Caverns' famous large chambers came to exist. These chambers are also highly decorated with stalactites, stalagmites, helicites, and cave popcorn.

In addition to the ninety-four caves in the park, the rugged landscape of the Chihuahuan Desert offers many interesting features. The range in elevation in the park results in a variety of plants and animals. A total of 740 species of plants, 64 species of mammals, 44 species of reptiles and amphibians, and 331 species of birds have been identified here.

The park's visitor center sits 7 miles inside the park entrance on a high bluff near the cavern entrance. The view from the top is impressive, and roadside exhibits and panoramic views along the paved road add enjoyment to the drive. No fee is charged to drive to the visitor center and view its excellent exhibits. The visitor center is open year-round except Christmas Day. Tickets

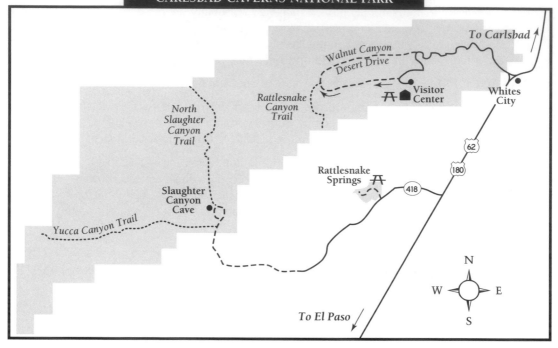

for all cavern tours are sold here. Two tours are self-guided and require a general entrance fee of $6.00. (This fee is covered by any of the national park passes.) One of the self-guided tours is a 1-mile paved trail using the traditional explorer's route that descends 750 feet on a steep, winding path. This is the most rigorous of the tours. An elevator is available for a return to the visitor center. The second self-guided tour descends on an elevator for a tour of the Big Room. Each tour requires an hour to an hour and a half, depending on the speed at which you walk. Audio handsets to help interpret your tour are available for rental in the visitor center. Various ranger-led tours (separate charge) depart throughout the day. Reservations for ranger-led tours can be arranged at the visitor center or by calling (800) 967–2283. Advance reservations can be helpful on busy days. First-time visitors are likely to enjoy the self-guided tour of the Big Room. If sufficient time is available, you may want to choose the natural entrance and also tour the Big Room before ascending back to the visitor center. This combination generally requires about two-and-a-half hours. Cave entry begins at 8:30 A.M., with the last entry using the natural entrance at 3:30 P.M. and 5:00 P.M. for the Big Room self-guided tour. A jacket (56 degrees Fahrenheit inside temperature) and shoes with rubber soles are strongly recommended.

Nature trails are near the visitor center. Ranger-guided walks into the desert are scheduled during summer months. Permits to hike into the backcountry are free and may be obtained at the visitor center information desk. One of the park's most popular activities in the summer is watching the bats fly from the cavern entrance each evening just before sunset. These bats, which winter in Mexico, feed at night on flying insects. A large seating area just outside the natural cave entrance is available for watching the bats. This is worth the effort.

ENTRANCE FEE: No fee is required to enter the park or visitor center, but a fee is charged for entrance to the cavern. Self-guided cave tours are $6.00 per person ($3.00 for children ages six through fifteen), and ranger-guided tours are subject to an additional charge depending on the tour. National Park, Golden Age, and Golden Access passes are accepted for self-guided tours. Golden Age and Golden Access passes receive a 50 percent reduction in ranger-led tours.

FACILITIES: A restaurant and a gift shop are attached to the visitor center. Food service is also provided in the cavern near the elevator. A kennel is available for pets. No lodging is available in the national park, but a large Best Western motel is in Whites City just outside the park entrance. Full facilities are 20 miles northeast in the town of Carlsbad. The Carlsbad Chamber of Commerce can be reached at (505) 785–2486. Drinking water and rest rooms are in the visitor center. Picnic facilities are at the visitor center and at Rattlesnake Springs, 8 miles southwest of the park entrance on Slaughter Canyon Road.

CAMPING: No camping is permitted in the park, but private campgrounds are located in nearby communities. Brantley Lake State Park, 15 miles north of Carlsbad via U.S. 285, has fifty-one sites with water, tables, grills, and electrical hookups. Call (505) 457–2384 for information.

CHACO CULTURE NATIONAL HISTORICAL PARK
Box 220
Nageezi, NM 87037
(505) 786–7014
CHCU_Interpretation@nps.gov
www.nps.gov/chcu

Chaco Culture National Historical Park comprises nearly 34,000 acres and was established in 1907 to preserve numerous ancestral Pueblo structures, including dozens of monumental buildings called greathouses. In architecture, complexity of community life, social organization, and regional integration, the people of Chaco Canyon attained a unique cultural expression that was not duplicated before or since. The park, located in northwestern New Mexico, is open all year except Thanksgiving, Christmas, and New Year's Day. The preferred and recommended access route to the park is from the north, via U.S. 550 and County Roads 7900 and 7950. From the north, turn off U.S. 550 at County Road 7900, 3 miles southeast of Nageezi and approximately 50 miles west of Cuba (at mile 112.5). This route is clearly signed from U.S. 550 to the park boundary (21 miles). The route includes 5 miles of paved road and 16 miles of dirt road. **Note: Many maps do not show the current road access from the north.** Two roads access Chaco from the south. These roads can vary in condition from very rough to impassable. If you are traveling from the south, call ahead for directions and the latest road conditions.

From A.D. 850 to 1150, Chaco Canyon was the center of Chaco culture and the ceremonial and economic core of the San Juan Basin. The Chacoan ancestral Pueblo people designed and planned the imposing greathouses and constructed them over decades and even centuries. These impressive buildings may have been used only periodically during times of ceremony, commerce, and trading, when temporary populations arrived in the canyon for these events. The dozens of great houses in Chaco Canyon were connected by "roads" to more than 150 greathouses built thoughout the region.

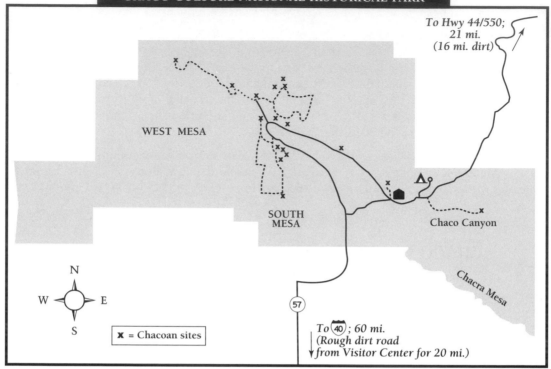

These structures were often oriented to solar, lunar, and cardinal directions. Lines of sight between the greathouses allowed for communication. Sophisticated astronomical markers, communication features, water control devices, and formal earthen mounds surrounded the greathouses. The buildings were placed within a landscape surrounded by sacred mountains, mesas, and shrines that still have deep spiritual meaning for modern Native American descendants.

The Chacoans developed an extensive trading network for turquoise. Raw turquoise was imported from distant mines and transformed with exquisite craftsmanship into beads, necklaces, and pendants. Extraordinary quantities were found throughout Chaco Canyon in the form of finished ornaments, worksite debris, and offerings. Great amounts of such jewelry may have been traded to the regional center of Paquimé (Casas Grandes) in northern Mexico and throughout the Southwest.

After prevailing for 300 years, Chaco Canyon declined as a regional center during the mid-1100s, when new construction ceased. Chacoan influence continued on at Aztec Ruins (see earlier entry in this chapter) and other centers to the north, south, and west into the late 1100s and 1200s. In time the people shifted away from Chacoan ways, migrated to new areas, reorganized their world, and interacted with foreign cultures. Their descendants are the modern Southwest Indians.

At the park visitor center, museum displays, exhibits, a bookstore, and films help explain the history of the Chacoan people. Rangers are available to assist with trip planning, issue backcountry hiking permits, and provide schedules of guided hikes and evening programs.

Chaco Culture National Historical Park (opposite page)

Una Vida, a mostly unexcavated great house, is a short walk from the visitor center parking area. Beyond the visitor center, a paved one-way loop road about 9 miles in length passes near six of the largest greathouses, where self-guided trails begin. Parking areas along the drive allow visitors to access the sites of Pueblo Bonito, Chetro Ketl, Hungo Pavi, Pueblo del Arroyo, Kin Kletso, and Casa Rinconada. Each trail takes forty-five minutes to one hour to complete. All trails and the loop drive close between sunset and sunrise. Apart from the self-guided loop tour, you can hike four backcountry trails to see the remote sites or to view the greathouses from overlooks on the cliffs above. Free backcountry hiking permits are available at the visitor center.

ENTRANCE FEE: $8.00 per vehicle or $4.00 per person; good for seven days.

FACILITIES: No food, lodging, gasoline, repair services, or firewood are available at the park. Limited supplies can be purchased at convenience stores on U.S. 550. The nearest lodging is at the Inn at the Post (bed-and-breakfast) at Nageezi Trading Post (505–632–3646). Kitchen privileges are available (no restaurant).

CAMPING: The Gallo Campground, 1 mile from the visitor center, is open year-round on a first-come, first-served basis. The forty-nine spaces and two group sites can fill by noon in the summer. Picnic tables, fireplaces, flush toilets, and a dump station are provided. Water is available at the visitor center parking lot only. Bring your own wood or charcoal. Trailers over 35 feet cannot easily be accommodated. There are no hookups. No overnight camping is permitted in the backcountry.

EL MALPAIS NATIONAL MONUMENT

123 East Roosevelt Avenue
Grants, NM 87020
(505) 285–4641 or (505) 783–4774
www.nps.gov/ELMA

El Malpais National Monument comprises 114,848 acres and was established in 1987 to preserve the geological and archaeological resources of a volcanic area that features ice caves and a 17-mile lava-tube system. This area was also a home for Pueblo Indians. The monument is located in west-central New Mexico and is accessible via State Highways 53 and 117.

El Malpais (which means "the badlands" in Spanish) National Monument is a lava-filled valley formed by centuries of volcanic activity. Major features of the monument can be accessed via State Highways 53 and 117 and County Road 42. High-clearance, four-wheel-drive vehicles are advised for all roads other than State Highways 53 and 117. The Information Center is 23 miles south of Grants on State Highway 53. Information is also available at the ranger station/visitor center on Highway 117, near the turnoff to Sandstone Bluffs Overlook. Some activities require permits that should be obtained before your trip. The impressive Northwest New Mexico Visitor Center on the north side of I–40 at Exit 85 has a wealth of information about all the public lands in this region, including El Malpais National Monument, El Morro National Monument (see separate entry), El Malpais National Conservation Area, and Cibola National Forest. Here you will find brochures, books for sale, and dozens of audiovisual presentations, including a great forty-five-minute film on traveling Route 66. Personnel are available to answer your questions and provide suggestions for getting the most from a visit to this part of the state.

EL MALPAIS NATIONAL MONUMENT

Along State Highways 53 or 117, visitors can hike the Zuni-Acoma Trail, an ancient Indian trade route connecting two pueblos. The rugged 7½-mile hike (one-way) crosses four major lava flows, and a brochure is available. Nearby, El Calderon is a forested area that includes a lava flow, a lava-tube cave, a cinder cone, and a bat cave. Near the monument's west boundary, a privately operated and privately owned area has a large cinder cone and a lava tube with ice year-round.

Along State Highway 117 visitors will drive up to a ridge of sandstone that offers a view of the lava flows and surrounding countryside. Seven miles south of the bluffs, in El Malpais National Conservation Area, is the largest accessible arch in New Mexico. Just south of the arch, this scenic drive passes through a narrow corridor formed by lava that flowed near the base of 500-foot sandstone cliffs.

Off County Road 42 (which may be impassable during inclement weather, even with four-wheel drive), which loops between the two state highways, visitors will find a trail that leads to several lava-tube caves. Farther south are wilderness areas that present spectacular views, including numerous cinder cones.

ENTRANCE FEE: No charge.

FACILITIES: Along Highway 117 picnic areas are located at The Narrows and Sandstone Bluffs. Along Highway 53 picnic areas are located at the Zuni-Acoma trailhead, the El Calderon area, and the El Malpais Information Center. Full services are available in Grants.

CAMPING: There are no campgrounds in the monument, but primitive camping is permitted. Sixteen miles west of Bandera Crater, nearby El Morro National Monument offers a small but pleasant campground. For more information, see the camping section under El Morro National Monument. For those traveling on I–40, Bluewater Lake State Park offers water, electrical hookups, showers, fishing, boating, and swimming.

EL MORRO NATIONAL MONUMENT
HC 61, Box 43
Ramah, NM 87321-9603
(505) 783–4226
ELMO_Superintendent@nps.gov
www.nps.gov/elmo

El Morro National Monument, established in 1906, comprises nearly 1,300 acres, highlighted by Inscription Rock, a soft sandstone monolith on which thousands of inscriptions have been carved by explorers and settlers. The park is located in western New Mexico, 58 miles southeast of Gallup via State Highways 602 and 53, and 43 miles southwest of Grants via State Highway 53.

El Morro ("The Bluff") rises nearly 200 feet above the valley floor. It was named by the Spanish conquistadors who used this site and its natural water basin, filled by rain and melted snow, as a resting spot from the late sixteenth century through the eighteenth century. Before the Spanish came, the ancestral Pueblo Indians had abandoned pueblos on the mesa. From the first Spanish inscription in 1605, the sandstone monolith has served as a register for people and cultures in this area of the Southwest. The first Anglo-Americans to inscribe their names at El

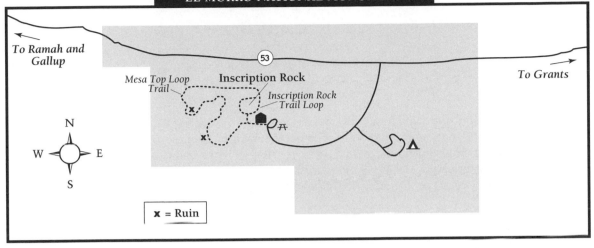

Morro were Lieutenant J. H. Simpson and artist R. H. Kern. Their inscriptions may still be seen. After their visit in 1849, numerous other individuals—including traders, Indian agents, soldiers, surveyors, and settlers—added their names to the rock. On the top of El Morro are the ruins (mostly unexcavated) of ancestral Pueblo Indian pueblos.

A small but nice visitor center is open daily from 9:00 A.M. to 5:00 P.M. (until 7:00 P.M. in summer), except Christmas and New Year's Day. Here you will find exhibits and an audiovisual presentation to help interpret the history of the people who inhabited and traveled through this area. The visitor center also has a nice selection of books for purchase. Rangers and volunteers are on duty to help answer questions and provide advice that will allow you to get the most out of your visit. A self-guided trail begins behind the visitor center and leads past inscriptions at the base of the cliff. This hike may be extended to the top of the bluff, where pueblo ruins are located. Do not walk the trail without first picking up a guide booklet available for loan in the visitor center. Information in the booklet is keyed to numbered stops along the trail. The first portion of the trail along the inscriptions involves a walk of about 1/2 mile and takes approximately forty-five minutes. If you climb to the top, you will have a total walk of 2 miles and spend about ninety minutes. The walk to the top requires a 200-foot climb, and the trail on the mesa is of moderate difficulty. The mesa-top trail may be closed during heavy snowfalls as well as periods of heavy lightning.

ENTRANCE FEE: $3.00 per person; good for seven days. Children ages sixteen and under are free.

FACILITIES: No food service or lodging is available in the park, but both can be obtained at Grants and Gallup. A small cafe is just outside the park. Food service and very limited camping supplies are available at Ramah, 13 miles west of the monument. Picnic tables are located in front of the visitor center, where water and rest rooms (with hot water) are provided.

CAMPING: A small, attractive campground (nine spaces) is open year-round, except for temporary closings forced by snowstorms, and offers tables, grills, water, and vault toilets. The campground is about 0.8 mile from the visitor center. A commercial RV park is near the monument entrance.

FORT UNION NATIONAL MONUMENT

P.O. Box 127
Watrous, NM 87753-0127
(505) 425–8025
foun_administration@nps.gov
www.nps.gov/foun

Fort Union National Monument, which comprises 720 acres, was added to the National Park Service in 1954 to preserve the ruins of an important fort on the Santa Fe Trail during the period 1851 to 1891. The monument is located in northeastern New Mexico, 8 miles north of I–25 (Exit 366), at the end of State Highway 161. Fort Union is 28 miles northeast of Las Vegas, New Mexico.

Fort Union was established when the U.S. Army decided in 1851 to move its headquarters and depot out of Santa Fe. The log buildings of the first fort served as an army base of operations on the Santa Fe Trail and as the principal quartermaster depot of the Southwest. From 1851 until the beginning of the Civil War in 1861, soldiers from Fort Union battled Apaches, Utes,

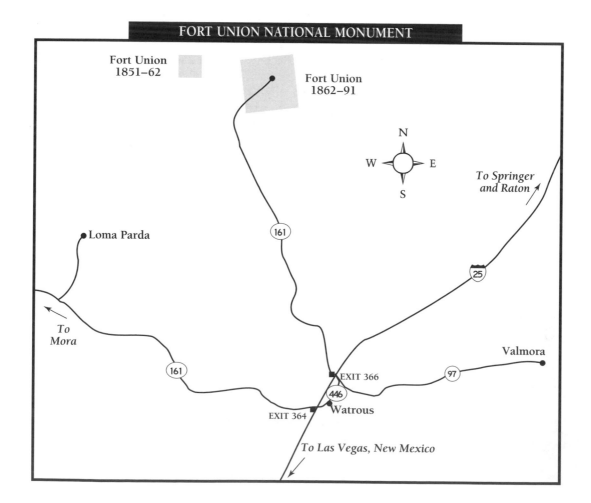

Kiowas, and Comanches. Concern about a Confederate invasion of New Mexico resulted in the construction of an earthwork fortification in 1861. Although the fort was never attacked, soldiers from the fort were involved in major clashes that secured New Mexico for the Union.

Following the war, Fort Union was again rebuilt, this time with adobe, and continued to serve as the supply depot for the forts throughout the territory. The fort remained as a key outpost in the Southwest until it was abandoned by the military in 1891.

The park is open from 8:00 A.M. to 5:00 P.M. during the winter, except Thanksgiving, Christmas, and New Year's Day, and from 8:00 A.M. to 6:00 P.M. during the summer. While walking among the ruins, keep in mind that the fort consisted of three parts. Military activities were conducted in the post, and the depot was concerned with transportation and supply of other Southwestern forts. The third part of Fort Union, the arsenal, stored and distributed arms and ammunition. As was typical with forts in the Southwest, no stockade or wall surrounded Fort Union. The National Park Service is currently attempting to halt deterioration of the adobe walls of the fort's buildings. A visitor center has exhibits and artifacts to assist in understanding the fort's history. Recorded messages and pictures are located along foot trails. Ruts of the Santa Fe Trail are visible in numerous places at the fort and its surrounding area. Visitors are welcome to walk the remains of this famous trail that connected Santa Fe with Independence, Missouri.

ENTRANCE FEE: $3.00 per adult; children ages sixteen and under are free.

FACILITIES: Food and lodging are not available in the park. Las Vegas, New Mexico, has overnight accommodations. Water and rest rooms are provided in the visitor center, and picnic tables are available

CAMPING: No camping is permitted at Fort Union. Storrie Lake State Park, on State Road 518 (33 miles from Fort Union), offers thirty-seven campsites with sheltered tables, flush toilets, and showers

GILA CLIFF DWELLINGS NATIONAL MONUMENT
HC 68 Box 100
Silver City, NM 88061-0100
(505) 536–9461
GICL_Information@nps.gov
www.nps.gov/gicl

Gila Cliff Dwellings National Monument, which comprises 533 acres, was established in 1907 to preserve some excellent Mogollon cliff dwellings in natural cavities on the face of a sandstone cliff. The monument is located in southwestern New Mexico, 44 miles north of Silver City via paved State Highway 15. The road is unsafe for trailers more than 20 feet long.

Ruins in the Gila Cliff Dwellings area date back to the second century A.D. At that time, people constructed circular dwellings with floors below ground level. Archaeologists refer to the people of this period as the Mogollon. The monument also has remains of later structures that are variations of these pithouses and were built in this area until around 1000, when square stone adobe structures began to be built above ground. During this same period, the Pueblo people began constructing cliff dwellings in natural caves. But the Pueblo people also built in the open. Both examples of Pueblo settlements are found here. These people farmed the mesa tops and floodplains and were skilled weavers and potters. By the early 1300s, they abandoned this area, and why they left or where they went is unknown.

Seven natural caves are located high on the southeast side of one cliff, and five of these contain cliff-dwelling ruins. About forty rooms are in these structures, which probably housed eight to ten families at a time. Walls were made from stone and timbers, the latter dating from the 1270s. By the early 1300s, for unknown reasons, the Mogollon had abandoned these dwellings.

A visitor center with exhibits and information to help interpret this historic area is open from 8:00 A.M. until 5:00 P.M. in summer and 8:00 A.M. to 4:30 P.M. in winter. The park is closed on Christmas and New Year's Day. From the visitor center, a short drive to a parking area at the end of the road provides access to the monument's main area. Guide leaflets with numbers keyed to trail markers are available at the trailhead. The 1-mile loop trail is steep in places and takes about one hour to walk (round-trip). The dwellings are accessible 8:00 A.M. to 6:00 P.M. in summer, 9:00 A.M. to 4:00 P.M. the rest of the year.

ENTRANCE FEE: $10.00 per vehicle or $3.00 per person. Children ages twelve and under are free.

FACILITIES: Food services and accommodations are not available at the monument, but a store at Gila Hot Springs offers groceries, snacks, soft drinks, gasoline, and ice. Drinking water and rest rooms are located in the visitor center.

CAMPING: The USDA Forest Service operates Lower Scorpion Campground (seven spaces) and Upper Scorpion Campground (thirteen spaces) between the visitor center and the cliff dwellings. Both are open all year and have tables, grills, water (May–October), and flush toilets. Two less-developed campgrounds with pit toilets and no water are located 5 miles east of the visitor center. A commercial campground is at Gila Hot Springs.

FISHING: Fishing is available in the Gila River with a New Mexico fishing license.

PECOS NATIONAL HISTORICAL PARK

P.O. Box 418
Pecos, NM 87552-0418
(505) 757–6414, extension 1
PECO_Visitor_Inormation@nps.gov
www.nps.gov/peco

Pecos National Historical Park, a National Park Service unit since 1965, was expanded and redefined in 1990 to preserve what remains of six diverse cultural themes and educate the public about these resources. The park is located off I–25 in north-central New Mexico, 25 miles southeast of Santa Fe. Exit I–25 at the Rowe or Pecos interchanges, and follow the signs. The park is located 2 miles south of the Village of Pecos on Highway 63.

Native Americans began using the Pecos Valley to make a livelihood by hunting large animals some 12,000 years ago. The Native American lifestyle changed during the years preceding the arrival of the Spaniards. Distinct cultures emerged, sedentary tribes replaced the previously mobile hunters, and new technologies, social organizations, and allegiances were formed to sustain the population.

When the Spanish explorers arrived at the gates of Pecos Pueblo in 1540, they found 2,000 Native Americans living there and conducting a prosperous trading economy that brought many Pueblo communities from the Rio Grande Valley together with many Plains tribes to the east. Spanish colonization proceeded, imposing a new government and religion on the entire region, including Pecos Pueblo, where the largest seventeenth-century mission in all of New Spain was built. The church was destroyed in the Pueblo Revolt of 1680. Another was rebuilt over the rubble of the former church. Both the mission and ruins of the great Pueblo of Pecos are the main attraction for visitors today.

The park's other resources reflect the several Hispanic families who built homesteads along the Pecos River during the Mexican era, the trade and stage stops along the Santa Fe Trail that spurred on the economic growth of the area and ushered in the U.S. government, the Civil War Battle of Glorieta Pass, and twentieth-century ranching.

The park's visitor center addresses the complex history of the area. A ten-minute film provides an overview and prelude to the 1¼-mile self-guided trail that leads through the main ruins. Ranger-guided tours to the Austin/Fogelson ranch house, Glorieta Battlefield, and Santa Fe Trail are available by reservation. The visitor center is open daily from 8:00 A.M. to 5:00 P.M. (until 6:00 P.M. during the summer), except Christmas and New Year's Day.

ENTRANCE FEE: $3.00 per person; good for seven days.

FACILITIES: The park's main complex has visitor rest rooms and a picnic area. Food and lodging are not available in the park. Restaurants, drive-ins, a deli, and some small grocery stores operate in Pecos, 2 miles north of the park's visitor center. Lodging is available in Santa Fe.

CAMPING: No camping is permitted at the park, however, there are seven USDA Forest Service campgrounds and four commercial campgrounds ranging from 5 to 20 miles from the park. For information on Forest Service campgrounds, write Santa Fe National Forest, P.O. Box 1689, Santa Fe, NM 87501, or call (505) 757–6121.

PETROGLYPH NATIONAL MONUMENT

6001 Unser Boulevard NW
Albuquerque, NM 87120-2033
(505) 899–0205
PETR_Interpretation@nps.gov
www.nps.gov/petr

Petroglyph National Monument was established in 1990 to protect an area of 7,200 acres that contains more than 20,000 prehistoric and historic Native American and Hispanic images pecked or carved in rock. The monument is cooperatively managed by the National Park Service and the City of Albuquerque. The monument is located on the west side of Albuquerque. Drive west on I–40 and exit north on Unser Boulevard. The visitor center is 3 miles north of I–40.

The varied petroglyphs of masks, animal figures, geometric shapes, spirals, and stars found in Petroglyph National Monument were mostly created between A.D. 1300 and 1700, although some may be as much as 3,000 years old. The symbols, most of which reflect the society and religion of the Native peoples, are not well understood. The monument has more than 300 archaeological sites to help interpret 12,000 years of human use of this area.

The park is accessible at several locations including the visitor center at 4735 Unser Boulevard NW. The visitor center, with information about the park's features, is open daily from 8:00 A.M. to 5:00 P.M. except Thanksgiving, Christmas, and New Year's Day. One mile south of the visitor center on Unser Boulevard, Rinconada Canyon offers a 2½-mile unpaved trail along the base of the escarpment. This location contains a high concentration of petroglyphs. The Boca Negra Unit at the north end of the monument is open from 8:00 A.M. to 5:00 P.M. and offers a picnic area and rest rooms. A series of five volcanic cones in the Volcanoes Day Use Area of the park's west side is accessed via an unpaved road off Paseo del Volcan (exit 149 off I–40).

ENTRANCE FEE: No charge, with the exception of Boca Negra Canyon, which charges $2.00 on weekends and $1.00 during the week.

FACILITIES: Rest rooms, drinking water, and picnic tables are available at the visitor center and Boca Negra Canyon. Food and lodging are available nearby.

CAMPING: No camping is permitted in the monument. Camping facilities are available in the Albuquerque area.

SALINAS PUEBLO MISSIONS NATIONAL MONUMENT

Box 517
Mountainair, NM 87036
(505) 847–2585
sapu_superintendent@nps.gov
www.nps.gov/sapu

Salinas Pueblo Missions National Monument (formerly Gran Quivira National Monument) was established in 1980. It consists of 1,071 acres, including the ruins of four seventeenth-century Franciscan stone churches and three large Indian villages from an earlier Pueblo culture. The monument is located in central New Mexico in three separate units near the town of Mountainair, at U.S. 60 and New Mexico 55.

In the stones of Salinas Pueblo Missions National Monument are faint echoes of communities that existed there centuries ago. The first Indians began living in this area during the ninth century. As time passed and different cultures were introduced into the area, the inhabitants adapted a successful way of life in this marginal and frequently hostile environment. By the seventeenth century, Salinas had become an important trading center, with Gran Quivira being one of the larger villages in the region.

Although the first Spanish expedition into what is now the southwestern United States occurred in 1540, the first known visit to the Salinas area by any European was in 1598. Even though the Spanish did not find the expected mineral riches and crops were difficult to grow, they nevertheless attempted to settle the land and convert the Indians to Christianity. By the early 1670s, the area was vacated by both the Spanish and the Indians. Two of the primary factors that led to the abandonment were severe drought and raids by Apaches.

The monument's headquarters and visitor center are in the town of Mountainair. Here, 1 block west of the intersection of U.S. 60 and State Highway 55, visitors will find exhibits, an audiovisual program, and information on the history of this area. The three areas of ruins are:

Abo Ruins (9 miles west on U.S. 60, 3/4 mile north on New Mexico 513). This site features sophisticated church architecture and a large unexcavated pueblo. A 1/2-mile wheelchair accessible trail winds through unexcavated mounds and visible pueblo walls. Trail guides are provided. Call (505) 847–2400.

SALINAS PUEBLO MISSIONS NATIONAL MONUMENT

x = Sites of Salinas Pueblo Missions N.M.

Gran Quivira Ruins (26 miles south on New Mexico 55). This site has two churches and significant excavated pueblo ruins with excavated kivas. A visitor center has exhibits. A guidebook is available to interpret the trail through the ruins. Call (505) 847–2770.

Quarai Ruins (8 miles north on New Mexico 55 and 1 mile west). This area includes the most complete Salinas church and has artifacts on display in a small museum. Trails lead past unexcavated mounds and excavated mission ruins. Trail guides are provided. Telephone (505) 847–2290.

ENTRANCE FEE: No charge.

FACILITIES: Food and lodging are available in Mountainair. Drinking water is available at all sites. Rest rooms are available at the visitor center and at all three sites. A picnic area with tables is provided at each of the three sites.

CAMPING: No camping is permitted in any of the areas of the monument. Manzano Mountains State Park (eighteen spaces), with tables (some sheltered), grills, flush toilets, and hot water (no showers), is located 15 miles north of Mountainair off Highway 55. Turn west at the south end of the town of Manzano, and go 3 miles on a paved road. Open only in the spring and summer. Call (505) 847–2820.

FISHING: Fishing is available in Manzano Lake, a small body of water located in the village of Manzano.

WHITE SANDS NATIONAL MONUMENT

P.O. Box 1086
Holloman AFB, NM 88330-1086
(505) 679–2599
whsa_interpretation@nps.gov
www.nps.gov/whsa

White Sands National Monument, which comprises 145,000 acres, was established in 1933 to preserve dunes of glistening white gypsum sand standing 10 to 60 feet high. The park is located in south-central New Mexico, approximately 54 miles northeast of Las Cruces and 15 miles southwest of Alamogordo via U.S. 70/82.

The features of this area were created millions of years ago (although the current dune field is only about several thousand years old), when a downfaulting of a portion of the earth's crust left surrounding mountains and highlands containing layers of gypsum rock. As rain and melting snow eroded the deposits, the dissolved gypsum washed into Lake Lucero and dried in the wind and sunshine of the basin. The encrusted lake bed is constantly scoured by a southwest

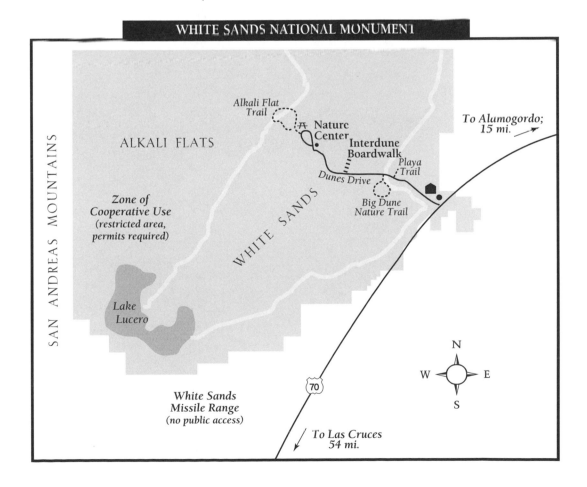

wind, and sand-sized gypsum crystals are swept toward the white dunes. As each dune grows and moves farther from the lake, new ones form. Because of the harsh environment in the dunes area, plants and animals have developed unique features that permit their survival.

A visitor center at the park entrance has a seventeen-minute orientation video and exhibits to help visitors interpret this unique area. A paved road leading into the main part of the dunes (16 miles round-trip) has wayside exhibits at pull-out spaces along the right-hand side. The best dunes for climbing are near the end of the Dunes Drive. The monument has a 1-mile self-guided nature trail and a $4\frac{1}{2}$-mile (round-trip) backcountry trail through the heart of the dunes. A $\frac{1}{4}$-mile wheelchair accessible boardwalk is available. During summer, ranger-guided walks and evening programs are offered every night. Auto caravans to Lake Lucero are offered every month.

ENTRANCE FEE: $3.00 per person; good for seven days. An additional fee is charged for the Lake Lucero tour and the Moonlight Bicycle tour.

FACILITIES: No lodging or food is offered at the park. The nearest motels and dining are 15 miles east in Alamogordo. Water and modern rest rooms are at the visitor center. Additional rest rooms (no water) are located in the picnic area.

CAMPING: No campground is located at the park. The nearest public camping facilities are in Lincoln National Forest, 35 miles east, and at Aquire Springs, 30 miles west. Oliver Lee Memorial State Park offers camping 10 miles south of Alamogordo on U.S. 54.

NORTH DAKOTA

STATE TOURIST INFORMATION
(800) 435–5663
www.ndtourism.com

FORT UNION TRADING POST NATIONAL HISTORIC SITE
15550 Highway 1804
Williston, ND 58801-8680
(701) 572–9083
FOUS_Superintendent@nps.gov
www.nps.gov/fous

Fort Union Trading Post encompasses 442 acres and was authorized for inclusion into the National Park System in 1966 to preserve the site of the principal fur-trading post in the Upper Missouri River region from 1828 until 1867. The fort is located in western North Dakota, 25 miles southwest of Williston via U.S. 2 and North Dakota 1804.

John Jacob Aster's American Fur Company constructed Fort Union in 1828. The site, near the junction of the Yellowstone and Missouri Rivers, was well chosen, and the fort became the major fur trading post for the upper Missouri River. Fort Union commenced operation only a couple of years before clothing styles changed and men began choosing silk rather than beaver hats, with a resulting decline in the need for beaver pelts. However, an increased demand for buffalo hides combined with improved boat transportation on the Missouri River allowed the fort to continue prospering under several astute managers. The lucrative trade resulted in Indian bands camping a week or two on the grassy plain beside Fort Union Trading Post. Coming to the fort was not only a business event, but also a social occasion as Indians, trappers, and traders caught up on the latest news and gossip.

The fort's walls were constructed of cottonwood logs 18 feet high, grounded on stone foundations. The walls were 220 feet wide on the north and south sides and 240 feet long on the east and west sides. The imposing post commanded the upper Missouri fur trade and was a mecca for artists and scientists. By the 1860s conflict overtook the homelands of the Plains Indians. In 1867 Fort Union was sold to the U.S. Army and dismantled for use in expanding Fort Buford, a military post built in 1866, located 2 miles down the Missouri.

The site of Fort Union was covered with grass when the National Park Service acquired the property in 1966. The NPS was able to determine the line of the palisades and the locations of the stone bastions, powder magazines, and the Bourgeois (manager's) House. Between 1985 and 1991 the National Park Service reconstructed much of the trading post, including the Bourgeois House, log walls, Indian trade house, and stone bastions. Fir rather than the original cottonwood was used in the reconstruction to improve its durability.

The historic site's visitor center, inside the Bourgeois House, has exhibits, a bookstore, and a short slide program. It is open from 8:00 A.M. to 8:00 P.M. daily in summer and from 9:00 A.M. to 5:30 P.M. the remainder of the year. Park rangers offer guided tours and living history programs during summer months. You may find it interesting that the historic site's parking lot is in the state of Montana, while the fort is a short walk away in neighboring North Dakota. Park your car and walk into the neighboring state. A four-day fur-trade rendezvous is held annually during the third weekend in June. Located near Fort Union Trading Post is Fort Buford, a military outpost established in 1866 and abandoned in 1895. Fort Buford was expanded with materials taken from the dismantled Fort Union Trading Post. Another nearby attraction is the new visitor center at the confluence of the Yellowstone and Missouri Rivers that opened in August 2003 as part of the Lewis and Clark bicentennial celebration.

ENTRANCE FEE: No charge.

FACILITIES: The visitor center has drinking water, snack and pop machines, and rest rooms. Rest rooms and a nice picnic area with shelters are at Confluence Park. Food and lodging are in Williston and Sidney, Montana.

CAMPING: Camping is not permitted at the site but is available at Fort Buford State Historic Site, a short distance to the east.

FISHING: The park is located on the Missouri River, and fishing is permitted with a North Dakota or Montana fishing license.

INTERNATIONAL PEACE GARDEN
Route 1, Box 116
Dunseith, ND 58329
(701) 263-4390, (888) 432-6733
comments@peacegarden.com
www.peacegarden.com

International Peace Garden, an affiliated area of the National Park Service, comprises approximately 2,330 acres. It was dedicated in 1932 to commemorate the peaceful relations between the United States and Canada. The garden is located in north-central North Dakota on U.S. 281 and State Route 3, 15 miles north of Dunseith, North Dakota, and 15 miles south of Boissevain, Manitoba.

The International Peace Garden has a variety of plant life on its beautifully landscaped grounds, which cross the international border. Wooded areas, floral gardens, and two lakes provide visitors with a peaceful background for leisurely strolls that sometimes include glimpses of white-tailed deer, moose, and other wildlife. The garden includes an 18-foot working floral clock, a sunken garden, and more than 150,000 annual flowers planted each year. The Peace Chapel is non-denominational and features quotations from "people of peace" etched in the fossil-embellished limestone walls. The 120-foot Peace Towers welcome people from around the world. The four towers symbolize people from the four corners of the earth coming together to form two similar but distinct nations with a common base of democracy and beliefs. The newest addition to the Peace Garden is the New York World Trade Center Memorial Site. Additional features include 10 miles of bike paths and playgrounds.

The Interpretive Center, open daily from 9:00 A.M. to 5:00 P.M., features the history of the park, a tribute to Civilian Conservation Corps work at the park in the 1930s, and a "mini-greenhouse" that gives visitors an idea of how the plants are grown for the garden. Fun and educational interpretive programs are held daily for visitors of all ages. The Game Warden Museum and Educational Center also offers programs for children and their families. The

INTERNATIONAL PEACE GARDEN

To Boissevain, Manitoba

10

North Drive

Lakeview
Hiking Trail

Lake Stormon

Willis
Pavilion

Parking

Peace
Chapel

Bell Tower

Cafe/Gift
Shop

CANADA

Peace Towers

Parking

Interpretive
Center

Parking

Canadian
Customs

Entrance
Gate

Floral
Clock

UNITED STATES

Lake Udall

New York World Trade
Center Memorial Site

United
States
Customs

Administrative
Office

Greenhouse

Game Warden
Museum

hiking trail

N
W   E
S

Lodge

Masonic
Auditorium

South Drive

281

3

Athletic
Camp

Music Camp

Track

To Dunseith, North Dakota

museum has displays and exhibits about conserving and protecting the natural resources. Adjacent to the museum is a learning site that includes an aspen forest, a waterfall, lake, and wildflower beds. The Peace Garden is also the home of two youth camps, the International Music Camp and the Royal Canadian Legion Athletic Camp, where hundreds of youth spend their summers. The 2,000-seat Masonic Auditorium was build to provide a venue for the youth orchestras with the music camp. Free musical concerts are held here on Friday evenings and Saturday afternoons in June and July.

Driving tours of both units of the park and a walking tour of the formal gardens, chapel, and Interpretive Center take a total of about three hours. The Coach Riding Garden Tour (fee charged) is a guided tour through the formal gardens with stops at various points of interest, including the Peace Tower, Peace Chapel, and New York World Trade Center Memorial Site. Call (888) 432–6733 for information and reservations.

ENTRANCE FEE: $10.00 per vehicle; $5.00 per person.

FACILITIES: Food service and gifts are available in the formal area June to mid-September. An airport with a 3,000-foot paved runway is within walking distance of the park entrance. Rest rooms and picnic areas are in several locations. Overnight accommodations are available in nearby towns.

CAMPING: Approximately fifty camping sites offer tables, grills, rest rooms, and shower facilities. Half have concrete pads, electricity, water, and disposal facilities.

KNIFE RIVER INDIAN VILLAGES
NATIONAL HISTORIC SITE

P.O. Box 9
Stanton, ND 58571-0009
(701) 745–3300
knri_information@nps.gov
www.nps.gov/knri

Knife River Indian Villages National Historic Site, which comprises 1,758 acres, was authorized as part of the National Park Service in 1974 to preserve remnants of historic and prehistoric Indian villages containing an array of artifacts of Plains Indian culture. The park is located in central North Dakota, 1/2 mile north of the town of Stanton.

The Indians living along the Knife River were hunters and successful farmers. The Hidatsa, who lived here with their neighbors, the Mandan, built small villages of circular earth lodges. By the early 1800s, the prosperity of this area on the Missouri River was enhanced by Knife River's being at the center of a trade network among various tribes and Euro-Americans. The Lewis and Clark Expedition spent the winter of 1804–1805 at Fort Mandan, a few miles downstream of the Knife River villages. During the winter they met a young Shoshone woman named Sacagawea (Sakakawea) and her husband, Toussaint Charbonneau, and hired them to accompany the expedition as interpreters. Sacagawea and Charbonneau lived with the Hidatsa in Awatixa Village at the time.

Unfortunately, Europeans brought diseases that decimated the tribes around Knife River, and various smallpox epidemics broke out between the late 1700s and mid-1800s. In 1845 the

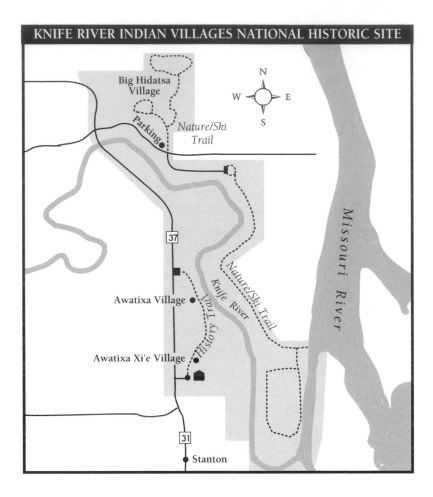

KNIFE RIVER INDIAN VILLAGES NATIONAL HISTORIC SITE

Mandan and Hidatsa banded together and moved 40 miles up the Missouri River and established Like-a-Fishhook Village. They were joined by the Arikara in 1862 and later became the Three Affiliated Tribes.

The park's visitor center is on County Road 37. Here visitors will find exhibits, a theater, and a full-scale furnished earthlodge that show the day-to-day life and customs of the Northern Plains Indians. Crafts made by descendants of these Village Indians are sold here. There is hiking access, by trail, to each of the three major village sites. Awatixa Village and Awatixa Xi'e Village are near the visitor center. Big Hidatsa Village is reached via a short trail that begins at a parking area in the north end of the park. Earthlodge tours are offered Memorial Day through Labor Day. The Northern Plains Indian Culture Fest is held the last full weekend of July.

ENTRANCE FEE: No charge.

FACILITIES: Limited meals are available in Stanton. Lodging can be found in nearby communities. Drinking water and rest rooms are provided at the park's visitor center.

CAMPING: No camping is available at the site. Approximately 15 miles north of Knife River Indian Villages, Sakakawea State Park provides a large camping area with tables, grills, drinking water, flush toilets, and showers. The state park is 1 mile east of Pick City, off Highway 200. A U.S. Army Corps of Engineers' campground is located 3 miles south of the town of Riverdale, downstream of the Garrison Dam.

FISHING: Fishing is permitted along the Knife and Missouri Rivers with a North Dakota fishing license. Both camping areas noted provide opportunities for fishing.

THEODORE ROOSEVELT NATIONAL PARK

P.O. Box 7
Medora, ND 58645-0007
(701) 623–4466
Thro_Interpretation@nps.gov
www.nps.gov/thro

Theodore Roosevelt National Park, established in 1947, comprises more than 70,000 acres, including scenic badlands along the Little Missouri River and part of Theodore Roosevelt's Elkhorn Ranch. The three separate units of the park are located in western North Dakota. The South Unit is along I–94, west of Belfield, near Medora. The Elkhorn Ranch site is reached via a gravel and dirt road; fording the Little Missouri River is necessary when accessing the site from the east. The North Unit is intersected by U.S. 85, 53 miles north of I–94.

The North Dakota Badlands are the result of erosion through ancient plains where waters had deposited materials from the Rocky Mountains. At one time the area's lowlands were covered by lakes, swamps, and a jungle. Some vegetation decomposed under layers of sediment and eventually turned to coal. Later, volcanoes to the west spewed ash that drifted eastward and either landed in this region or was carried in by ancient streams. Streams cut through the soft land areas and created the Badlands.

The park is named for Theodore Roosevelt, who lived and ranched in this area prior to being elected president of the United States. Roosevelt owned an open-range cattle ranch, the Elkhorn, and was a partner in another ranch, the Maltese Cross. The strenuous pioneer life and the rugged beauty of the Badlands had a profound effect upon Roosevelt. Although the time he spent here was short, it had a strong influence on his later decisions concerning the nation's natural and cultural resources.

At the South Unit the visitor center near the park's entrance includes a museum, with the restored Maltese Cross Cabin located in the rear. From here a 36-mile paved loop road provides access to some of this unit's highlights. Scoria Point allows the visitor to see where beds of burning lignite coal baked the surrounding sand and clay to red brick. Farther down the road is a lignite seam that burned until 1977 and is thought to have been ignited by a lightning-caused prairie fire in 1951. Visitors may walk to Buck Hill, which at 2,855 feet is one of the highest points in the park. The nature trail at Wind Canyon provides an overlook of the Little Missouri River. Trail rides are provided at Peaceful Valley Ranch. Seven miles east of Medora, off I–94, Painted Canyon Overlook provides a view of the badlands.

The park's North Unit is less crowded and more spectacular. It features a 14-mile scenic paved road to the vicinity of Sperati Point, the narrowest gateway in the Badlands. The river once flowed north from here but was blocked during the ice age. Little Mo Nature Trail, a 1.1-mile self-guided trail, begins at the southeast corner of Juniper Campground. About 1.5 miles west of here is the 1.4-mile (round-trip) Caprock Coulee Self-Guided Nature Trail, which is part of a 4-mile-loop hiking trail.

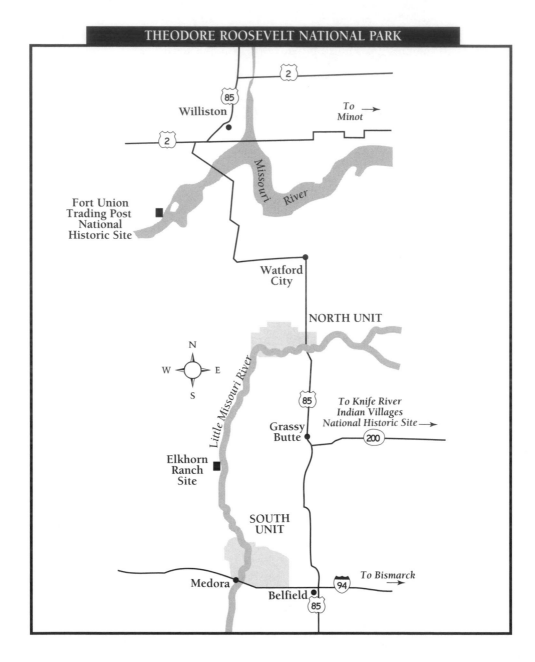

ENTRANCE FEE: $5.00 per person with a $10.00 maximum; good for both units of the park and for seven days.

FACILITIES: Lodging and food are not available within the park. Near the South Unit, Medora has restaurants, motels, service stations, and supplies. Painted Canyon Overlook provides rest rooms, picnic shelters, tables, and water. Fifteen miles north of the North Unit, Watford City has motels, restaurants, food stores, and service stations. Water and rest rooms are available at various locations in both units.

CAMPING: Located in cottonwood groves near the Little Missouri River, campgrounds in both units are exceptional. In the South Unit, Cottonwood (seventy-eight spaces) is open all year and has tables, grills, water, and flush toilets (pit toilets, October–May). A group site is available with reservation. Roundup Horse Camp (reservation-only group camp) is open from May through September and has tables, grills, water, and pit toilets. In the North Unit, Juniper (fifty spaces) is open all year and has tables, grills, water, and flush toilets (pit toilets October–May). A group site requires a reservation. No firewood is provided, and the gathering of firewood is prohibited in the park.

FISHING: The Little Missouri River flows through both the North and South units and provides catches of catfish and carp. Fishing requires a North Dakota fishing license.

OKLAHOMA

STATE TOURIST INFORMATION
(800) 652–6552
www.travelok.com

CHICKASAW NATIONAL RECREATION AREA

P.O. Box 201
Sulphur, OK 73086-0201
(580) 622–3165
chic_web_coordinator@nps.gov
www.nps.gov/chic

Chickasaw National Recreation Area, which comprises approximately 10,000 acres, was established in 1976 by consolidating Platt National Park, Arbuckle National Recreation Area, and additional lands. The recreation area provides access to numerous outdoor activities. It is located in south-central Oklahoma, just east of I–35, which connects Oklahoma City and Dallas.

Chickasaw National Recreation Area comprises two districts offering very different outdoor experiences. The historic Platt District (the former Platt National Park) is noted for its freshwater and mineral springs. The entire 900 acres of this area is also known for its historic landscape, which includes hundreds of stone structures constructed by the Civilian Conservation Corps of the 1930s and 1940s. On the east side, freshwater Buffalo and Antelope Springs are the source of Travertine Creek. A number of cold mineral-water springs are located in the central and western areas of this section. Travertine Nature Center offers exhibits, an orientation film of the area, a bookstore, and an environmental study area. During the summer, a daily children's nature program, nature films, and naturalist-conducted nature walks are offered. Various nature trails lead from this area.

The 9,000-acre Arbuckle District (the former Arbuckle National Recreation Area) is located 8 miles southwest of the historic Platt District. Here, Arbuckle Dam, at the confluence of three creeks, has resulted in the formation of a 2,350-acre lake that provides opportunities for fishing, boating, swimming, waterskiing, and scuba diving (with permit). Boat-launching ramps are located at Guy Sandy, The Point, and Buckhorn. Evening educational programs are held at the Buckhorn and The Point amphitheaters during the summer months.

More than 25 miles of flat to hilly trails provide a range of opportunities throughout both districts. A 2-mile-long accessible concrete trail winds along the south shore of Veterans Lake. A 9-mile multiuse trail allows hiking, mountain biking, and horseback riding between Veterans Lake and the Lake of the Arbuckles. Trail maps are available at the Travertine Nature Center bookstore.

ENTRANCE FEE: No charge.

FACILITIES: Food and lodging are not available in either district. Both are provided in nearby towns. Drinking water, rest rooms, and picnic areas are located throughout both districts.

CAMPING: In the Platt District, tables, grills, water, and flush toilets are provided at Central (10 group sites only), Cold Springs (63 sites), and Rock Creek (106 sites, dump station). In the Arbuckle District, Buckhorn (137 sites) and The Point (39 sites) include dump station, electrical and water hookups, and showers. Guy Sandy Campground (forty sites) offers tables, grills, drinking water, and chemical toilets. Rock Creek and Buckhorn are open year-round; the other campgrounds are open from mid-May to mid-September.

FISHING: Streams and Veterans Lake in the Platt District have sunfish, crappie, largemouth bass, and white bass. In the Arbuckle District, there is fishing for channel catfish, largemouth bass, sunfish, and crappie. An Oklahoma fishing license is required to fish at the park.

OKLAHOMA CITY NATIONAL MEMORIAL

P.O. Box 676
Oklahoma City, OK 73010-0676
(405) 235–3313
OKLI_Superintendent@nps.gov
www.nps.gov/okci

The Oklahoma City National Memorial comprises slightly over six acres and was established in 1997 to honor the victims, survivors, rescuers, and others who were impacted by the 1995 bombing of Oklahoma City's Alfred P. Murrah Federal Building. The memorial is in downtown Oklahoma City. From I–235 north, exit on Harrison Avenue, which merges into Sixth Street. On Sixth Street, the site is located between Robinson and Harvey Streets. Parking meters, pay lots, and garages are near the memorial.

On April 19, 1995, at 9:02 A.M., a bomb ripped through Oklahoma City's nine-story Alfred P. Murrah Federal Building. The explosion, from a truck bomb with 4,800 pounds of ammonium nitrate and fuel oil, could be felt 30 miles away. It killed 168 and injured another 500 men, women, and children. Ninety minutes later, one of two men later convicted of the bombing was picked up on a gun charge.

The memorial includes a three-acre symbolic memorial consisting of a reflecting pool, a children's area, 168 empty chairs as a reminder of the lives that were lost, an orchard, the 70-year-old American Elm Survivors' Tree, a memorial fence, and twin gates that frame the moment of destruction and mark the entrances to the memorial. The outside section of the memorial is accessible 24 hours a day, 365 days a year. Rangers are on duty daily, except Thanksgiving, Christmas, and New Year's Day, from 10:00 A.M. to 10:00 P.M. in spring and summer, and from 8:00 A.M. to 8:00 P.M. in fall and winter.

The National Memorial Center and the Institute for the Prevention of Terrorism are two enclosed units of the memorial. The Memorial Center is open Monday to Saturday from 9:00 A.M. to 6:00 P.M., and Sunday from 1:00 P.M. to 6:00 P.M. An entrance fee is charged for the Memorial Center, which is closed Thanksgiving, Christmas, and New Year's Day.

ENTRANCE FEE: Admission to the Memorial Center Museum is $9.00 adult, $6.00 senior, and $5.00 students. Children ages five years and younger are free. Tickets are sold until one hour before closing. National Park Service passes are not accepted for discounted or free entrance. No fee is charged for visiting the outdoor symbolic memorial.

FACILITIES: Rest rooms and drinking water are available for visitors. Restaurants and hotels are nearby.

WASHITA BATTLEFIELD NATIONAL HISTORIC SITE

P.O. Box 890
Cheyenne, OK 73628
(580) 497–2742
waba_ranger_activities@nps.gov
www.nps.gov/waba

Washita Battlefield National Historic Site comprises approximately 300 acres and was authorized in 1996 to commemorate an 1868 U.S. Cavalry attack on the southern Cheyenne village of Chief Black Kettle. The controversial attack has been described by some as a battle and others as a massacre. The historic site is located in western Oklahoma, approximately 140 miles west of Oklahoma City, near the small town of Cheyenne. It is approximately 25 miles north of I–40.

The Plains served as the scene for many famous and some infamous battles between the U.S. Cavalry and Native Americans. The 1868 battle that took place at Washita was actually precipitated four years earlier by a surprise cavalry attack at Sand Creek that destroyed the camp of Chief Black Kettle and Chief White Antelope. A subsequent peace treaty assigned the Arapahos, Cheyennes, Comanches, and Kiowas to reservations in Indian Territory. Restlessness among the Indians caused the U.S. Army to mount a winter campaign that resulted in four chiefs, including Black Kettle and Arapaho Chief Big Mouth, traveling to Fort Cobb to seek protection for their bands. Turned away by the fort's commander, the chiefs returned to their village in Washita Valley, where, in November 1868, they were attacked by troopers under the command of Lieutenant Colonel George A. Custer. The attack resulted in the deaths of from forty to fifty Indians, including Chief Black Kettle and his wife. The army captured fifty-three Cheyennes and suffered the loss of twenty-two of its own soldiers.

The historic site is new and relatively undeveloped. An overlook of the battlefield is open daily from dawn to dusk. A self-guided trail goes around the site, and a trail guide is available for sale at the Black Kettle Museum or at park headquarters. The Black Kettle Museum (donation requested) in the town of Cheyenne interprets the story of the Cheyenne and the Battle of the Washita. The museum is open from 9:00 A.M. to 5:00 P.M. every day in the summer. The rest of the year it is open Tuesday to Sunday and closed on Monday. It is closed on state holidays in winter only.

ENTRANCE FEE: No charge.

FACILITIES: There is a vault toilet and an accessible water fountain at the site.

CAMPING: No camping is permitted at the historic site. Foss State Park, on Highway 44, approximately 25 miles southeast of Washita Battlefield National Historic Site, has a campground (ninety-two spaces, tables, grills, dump station) with flush toilets, a swimming beach, and fishing. There are several private campgrounds in the town of Cheyenne.

OREGON

STATE TOURIST INFORMATION
(800) 547–7842
www.traveloregon.com

CRATER LAKE NATIONAL PARK

P.O. Box 7
Crater Lake, OR 97604-0007
(541) 594–3100
crla_information_requests@nps.gov
www.nps.gov/crla

Crater Lake National Park was established in 1902 to preserve a deep blue lake located in the caldera that resulted from the collapse of an ancient volcano. The lake is surrounded by lava walls 500 to 2,000 feet high. The park comprises 183,224 acres and is located in southern Oregon, 57 miles north of Klamath Falls. The major road into the park is Oregon Highway 62, which runs through the southwest corner. Only the south and west entrance roads to Rim Village are open from October through mid-June.

Crater Lake is located within the remains of the 12,000-foot volcano, Mount Mazama, which collapsed nearly 7,700 years ago after a series of eruptions drained its magma chamber. Additional volcanic activity after the collapse produced a cinder cone now known as Wizard Island. Over a period of centuries, the huge hole accumulated water from rain and snow. Only six lakes in the world are deeper than Crater Lake, which has been measured to a depth of 1,947 feet. Narrated boat tours are offered from July to mid-September by a concessioner. The one-and-three-quarter-hour trip circles the inside of the caldera and stops at Wizard Island.

A variety of plant life can be found in the park, including mountain hemlock; Shasta, red, and Douglas fir; and lodgepole, whitebark, and ponderosa pine. Wildflowers are abundant in July. Animals inhabiting the area include bears, deer, porcupines, bobcats, elk, coyotes, and many varieties of birds.

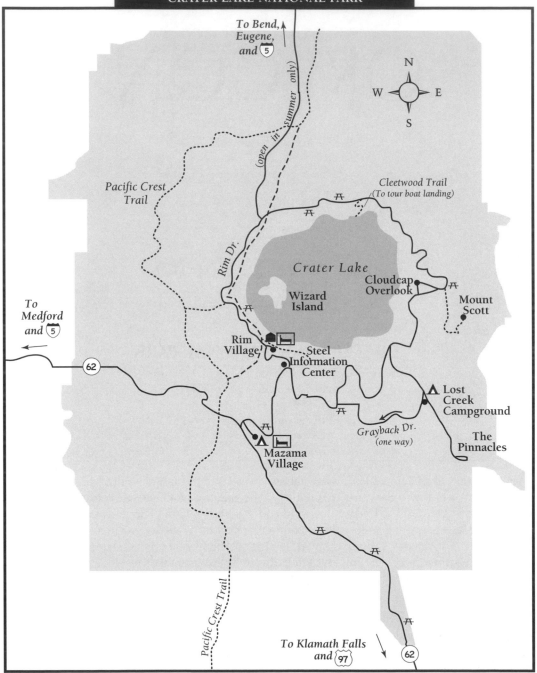

*To Bend,
Eugene,
and* (5)

N
W · E
S

*Pacific Crest
Trail*

(*open in summer only*)

Cleetwood Trail
(*To tour boat landing*)

Rim Dr.

Crater Lake

Wizard
Island

Cloudcap
Overlook

Mount
Scott

*To
Medford
and* (5)

Rim
Village

Steel
Information
Center

Lost
Creek
Campground

(62)

Grayback Dr.
(*one way*)

The
Pinnacles

Mazama
Village

Pacific Crest Trail

*To Klamath Falls
and* (97)

(62)

Crater Lake National Park receives an average of 533 inches of snow each year, which typically does not melt off until July. Visitors to the park in spring should be prepared for winter conditions. Many high-elevation trails are snow-covered until late July. During summer a variety of activities are available. A 33-mile paved road circles the lake and offers numerous scenic viewpoints. The visitor center at Rim Village provides information. A park ranger is on duty to answer questions. Talks on the origins of Crater Lake are presented throughout the day during summer months. Two nearby trails provide scenic views. Garfield Peak Trail (1.7 miles) begins behind the lodge and ends at a peak 1,900 feet above the lake. Discovery Point Trail (1½ miles) begins at the opposite end of Rim Village and leads to a point where the lake was discovered in 1853 by European-Americans. A number of other trails are located at various points around Rim Drive. Along the lake's north side, Cleetwood Trail (1.1 miles) descends steeply to Cleetwood Cove, the only access to the water. Launch trips around the lake and to Wizard Island originate here. A 6-mile paved road off Rim Drive leads to the Pinnacles. Here spires of pumice and welded tuff rise 200 feet out of Wheeler Creek Canyon.

Winter activities include cross-country ski trips around Crater Lake and snowshoeing. Snowmobiling on a designated road is permitted when the snow depth is 3 feet or more. No downhill ski facilities are available.

ENTRANCE FEE: $10.00 per vehicle or $5.00 per person; good for seven days.

FACILITIES: Lodging is available in the park from mid-May through mid-October. Crater Lake Lodge offers seventy-one rooms at a completely renovated hotel on the caldera edge. Mazama Village has motel-type units. Information and reservations can be obtained from Crater Lake Lodge, Inc., Crater Lake, OR 97604 (541–830–8700). A variety of food services are available from late May to early October. During winter, only light meals are served. During the summer months, some groceries may be purchased at Mazama Campground, and a gasoline station is open. Rest rooms are available at Rim Village, Park Headquarters, and the campground.

CAMPING: The park's major campground, Mazama (198 sites), 7 miles south of Rim Village, is one of the nicest in any of the major national park areas. It provides tables, grills, flush toilets, and a dump station. Sites are generally not squeezed together, and a few front on a canyon. G Loop offers the most secluded sites. A 1.7-mile trail behind the campground leads to the bottom of Annie Creek Canyon. Lost Creek Campground (sixteen spaces, tent camping only) is on the road to the Pinnacles and has water and toilets.

FISHING: The lake originally contained no fish but has been stocked. Rainbow trout and kokanee salmon still survive in the lake. No fishing license is required for Crater Lake, but one is required when fishing in the park streams.

FORT CLATSOP NATIONAL MEMORIAL

92343 Fort Clatsop Road
Astoria, OR 97103
(503) 861–2471, ext. 214
focl_superintendent@nps.gov
www.nps.gov/focl

Fort Clatsop National Memorial was incorporated into the National Park System in 1958 to memorialize the site where the Lewis and Clark expedition wintered in 1805–1806 following their historic journey from near St. Louis to the Pacific Ocean. A replica of the fort has been constructed on the site of the original. The memorial is in northwestern Oregon, 5 miles southwest of Astoria off U.S. Highway 101. Free shuttle service is provided from a new parking area 1 mile south of the fort and visitor center.

Daily life at Fort Clatsop

On May 14, 1804, forty-five men commenced what was to become the best-known expedition in American history. President Thomas Jefferson commissioned the expedition to explore the Missouri River to its source and find a route to the Pacific Ocean. Jefferson selected his personal secretary, Meriwether Lewis, as the group's leader. Lewis, in turn, invited his friend, William Clark, to join the group and share the command. The Corps of Discovery started its journey in three boats, departing from the mouth of the Missouri River near St. Louis. After spending the first winter 1,600 miles up the Missouri River at Fort Mandan in what is now North Dakota, the group departed April 7, 1805, with their new guide, Toussaint Charbonneau, his Shoshone wife, Sacagawea (her name is spelled and pronounced several ways), and their infant son.

The group sighted the Pacific Ocean in November 1805 after traveling down the Clearwater, Snake, and Columbia Rivers. Following ten days on the north shore of the Columbia River, the group decided to scout across the river, where elk were reported to be plentiful. Locating a suitable site for the winter, they cleared the land and on December 9, 1805, commenced building Fort Clatsop 3 miles up the Netul River (now the Lewis and Clark River). The fort, named for a friendly local Indian tribe, served as their home for three and a half months. Fort Clatsop is where they hunted, trapped, traded with local Indians, made buckskin clothing, and, most importantly, updated their journals and maps. About 15 miles southwest of the fort near the current town of Seaside, some of the men in the expedition boiled seawater to produce salt that was used to flavor food and preserve meat.

The visitor center at Fort Clatsop has exhibits, audiovisual programs, and a bookstore to enhance understanding of the expedition and the conditions faced by its members. An excellent thirty-two-minute film about the journey is shown each hour. The reconstruction of the fort is nearby, and trails to the spring and the historic canoe landing begin here. National Park Service rangers generally present costumed demonstrations during summer months; these often include flintlock demonstrations, and demonstrations on making candles, making buckskin clothes, and dressing skins. Hours are 9:00 A.M. to 6:00 P.M. in summer, 9:00 A.M. to 5:00 P.M. the rest of the year. Closed Christmas Day. Persons planning to visit the memorial are advised to call for information about program schedules.

ENTRANCE FEE: $5.00 per vehicle or $3.00 per person.

FACILITIES: No food or lodging is available in the park. Both may be found nearby. Rest rooms, drinking water, and a pay telephone are in the visitor center. A day-use picnic area with several shelters is nearby.

CAMPING: No camping is available in Fort Clatsop National Memorial. Eight miles northwest, Fort Stevens State Park provides camping for both tents (200 spaces) and trailers (300 spaces) with water, grills, tables, and 126 full hookups available. The state park offers fishing, hiking, bike trails, and ocean beaches. For information, call (503) 861–1671. Two private campgrounds, a KOA (503–861–2606) and Kampers West (503–861–1814), are also within 7 to 8 miles of the memorial.

FISHING: Although very few people fish in the memorial, fishing is permitted in season by boat in the Lewis and Clark River with an Oregon fishing license. The memorial does not have a boat launch. Fishing conditions are better in nearby streams outside Fort Clatsop National Memorial.

JOHN DAY FOSSIL BEDS NATIONAL MONUMENT

32651 Highway 19
Kimberly, OR 97848
(541) 987–2333
joda_Interpretation@nps.gov
www.nps.gov/joda

John Day Fossil Beds National Monument was incorporated into the National Park system in 1975 and comprises 14,000 acres. The monument preserves a fossil record where scientists unearth evidence of land plants and animals extending back six million to fifty-four million years. The park consists of three widely separated units in north-central Oregon. U.S. 26 runs in an east-west direction through the region, while U.S. 395 runs in a north-south direction. The Sheep Rock Unit is 5 miles west of the city of Dayville via U.S. 26. To reach the Painted Hills Unit, leave U.S. 26 near Mitchell and follow a marked country road for 6 miles. The Clarno Unit is on Oregon 218, 20 miles west of Fossil and 15 miles east of Antelope.

The fossil record of John Day was recognized early by the state of Oregon, which began to purchase land in this area during the 1930s. Although a few nearby land forms date from more than 250 million years ago, the record discovered in the monument covers most of the age of mammals. Various geologic epochs are marked by distinctive earth deposits containing outstanding fossil records. Fossil animals found here include species of ancient horse, oreodonts, tapirs, titanotheres, camels, mastodons, rodents, cats, rhinoceroses, and dogs.

Animals inhabiting the park include bobcats, coyotes, badgers, elk, mule deer, jackrabbits, and cottontail rabbits. Birds frequenting the river area and surrounding mountain slopes include Canada geese, ducks, greater blue heron, bluebirds, black-billed magpies, green-tailed towhees, California quail, red-tailed hawks, and bald and golden eagles. Visitors should watch for rattlesnakes in the park's sagebrush and juniper environment.

The park's headquarters is in the Sheep Rock Unit, along with the new Thomas Condon Paleontology Center, which houses the fossil museum and the visitor center. This unit includes outstanding examples of geological formations represented in the monument. The historic Cant Ranch includes a cultural museum containing exhibits on local ranching history. This location is a nice resting place; a short trail to Sheep Rock Overlook begins here. North of Cant Ranch at Blue Basin, two trails offer spectacular views of the basin and adjacent river valley. Farther north are a colorful rock formation at Cathedral Rock and an area of eroded lava flows and impressive outcrops of the John Day Group, with short self-guided trails, at the Foree area.

The Painted Hills Unit consists of an eroded landscape of volcanic ash deposits set within a vast picturesque valley. A ½-mile trail near the overlook, a short ¼-mile loop trail at Painted Cove, and the 1½-mile Carroll Rim Trail provide opportunities to see the colorful formations at close range.

Clarno includes ancient mudslides with two ¼-mile trails to the base of the brown-and-black palisades that offer views of plant fossils preserved in mudstone.

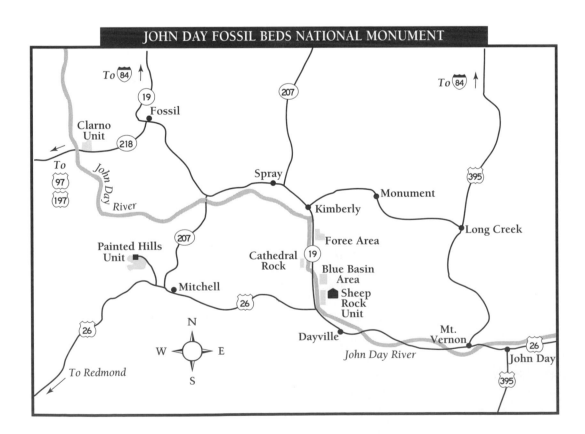

Scheduled ranger-conducted programs such as guided walks, museum talks, and off-site presentations are offered throughout the year. Wayside exhibits at overlooks along roads interpret outstanding features of each area of the park. In addition, the John Day River offers recreational opportunities. Fossil collecting is prohibited in the monument.

ENTRANCE FEE: No charge.

FACILITIES: Lodging, fuel, and food are available in nearby communities but not within the park. Hospitals are located in John Day, Madras, and Prineville. Drinking water and rest rooms can be found at the Sheep Rock, Painted Hills, and Clarno units.

CAMPING: No camping is available within any of the three units of the park, but nearby facilities are abundant.

FISIIING: The John Day River offers steelhead, smallmouth bass, and chinook fishing with an Oregon fishing license.

McLOUGHLIN HOUSE NATIONAL HISTORIC SITE

713 Center Street
Oregon City, OR 97045
(503) 656–5146
www.McLoughlinHouse.org

McLoughlin House was designated a national historic site in 1941 to preserve the home of Dr. John McLoughlin, often called the "Father of Oregon." The house is one of the few remaining pioneer dwellings in the region once known as Oregon Country. McLoughlin House, an affiliated area of the National Park system, is located in Oregon City, 13 miles southeast of Portland on I-205. The site is in McLoughlin Park between Seventh and Eighth Streets, about 4 blocks east of Pacific Highway (U.S. 99).

John McLoughlin was born in Quebec, Canada, in 1784. When he came to the Oregon Country in 1824, McLoughlin was already in charge of the Columbia District of Hudson's Bay Company. From Fort Vancouver, McLoughlin ruled an empire stretching from the Rocky Mountains to the Pacific Ocean and from Alaska to California. Although his primary responsibility was to facilitate activities associated with the fur-trading industry, he also helped develop other economic pursuits of the Northwest and provided assistance to the increasing numbers of immigrants moving into the region.

In 1829 McLoughlin and Governor George Simpson chose the falls of the Willamette River as a site for development. This eventually evolved into Oregon City, capital of the provisional and eventually territorial, government and chief town of Oregon Country. In 1845 Dr. McLoughlin resigned from the Hudson's Bay Company. In 1846 he moved to Oregon City and into the house where he lived until his death in 1857.

In 1909 a movement to preserve the house was successful, and the McLoughlin Memorial Association had the house moved from its original site at Third and Main Streets to its present site in McLoughlin Park. Since 1935 the house has been restored as nearly as possible to its original appearance. It contains period furniture, including some pieces that were at Fort Vancouver and many items that were owned by McLoughlin. In 1970 the remains of Dr. and Mrs. Marguerite McLoughlin were moved next to the house.

The site was established by cooperative agreement among the McLoughlin Memorial Association, the municipality of Oregon City, and the National Park Service. The house sits in a small city park, on a piece of land Dr. McLoughlin set aside for public use. Hours of operation are Tuesday through Saturday (fee charged) from 10:00 A.M. to 4:00 P.M. and Sunday from 1:00 to 4:00 P.M. McLoughlin House is closed on Monday and holidays and during the month of January. Visitors may take either a self-guided or a conducted tour. National Park Service passes are not accepted. Tickets for admission to the McLoughlin House are sold at the Barclay House, which is next door, in the park. A tourist information center operated by the local chamber of commerce is located on Washington Street on the north edge of town.

ENTRANCE FEE: $4.00 for adults, $3.00 for seniors, and $2.00 for children ages six to seventeen. Children ages five and under are free.

FACILITIES: Rest rooms are available at the site. Food and lodging can be found nearby in Oregon City.

CAMPING: No camping is permitted at the site. For those traveling south, Champoeg State Park (forty-eight spaces), approximately 24 miles southwest, provides full hookups, grills, and tables. From Oregon City take I–205, I–5 (south), and exit west on the Champoeg Park exit. For those traveling north, see the camping section under Fort Vancouver National Historic Site (Washington).

OREGON CAVES NATIONAL MONUMENT

19000 Caves Highway
Cave Junction, OR 97523-9716
(541) 592–2100
roger_brandt@nps.gov
www.nps.gov/orca/index.html

Oregon Caves National Monument was established in 1909 to protect eleven small caves and a 3-mile cave that has rare bats, endemic insects, and the earth's six main rock types. Transferred to the National Park Service in 1934, the monument has 480 acres of old growth, including part of the most diverse conifer forest in the world. The monument is located in southwestern Oregon, 20 miles east of Cave Junction via Oregon Highway 46. The last 8 miles are very winding and are not recommended for trailers.

The collision of North America and the Pacific Ocean destroyed an ocean basin and metamorphosed limestone into marble 153 million years ago. Uplift formed faults, joints, and other cracks. Underwater and stream enlargement of cracks dissolved the marble and formed the caves about 350 thousand years ago. Extensive formations include rimstone, stalagmites, stalactites, coralloids, flowstones, moonmilk, vermiculations, bell canopies, columns, cave "ghosts," scallops, domepits, pendants, and natural bridges.

After a hunter discovered the main cave in 1874, commercialization damaged the fragile cave. Restoration of the cave to its original state started in 1985, an effort that took a decade to complete and now constitutes the largest restoration effort of any national park cave in the nation. Annual precipitation, mostly snow during winter, is about 55 inches, and the average surface temperature is in the mid-40s. Many plants are at their range limit or are endemic to the Siskiyou/Klamath Mountains.

Most visitors take a ninety-minute, ranger-guided tour (fee charged) that covers ½ mile of the caves. There are about 500 stair steps in the cave (up and down) that must be negotiated. The tour can be strenuous for those with heart, walking, or breathing problems. Rubber- or vibram-soled shoes and warm clothing should be worn. Children under 42 inches in height cannot go on the tour, but ask about the special tours for families. Waits for a summer tour can exceed ninety minutes. Cave tours are closed on Thanksgiving and from December through February. Annual visitation is about 100,000, with 75 percent visiting in the summer. The national monument also has 5 miles of outdoor trails, with scenic views and meadows. These trails are maintained only in the summer, but are suitable for snowshoeing in the winter. Dogs are not permitted on the trails.

ENTRANCE FEE: No charge. The fee for cave tours is $8.00 for adults and $5.50 for children (those under 42 inches in height not permitted on tours).

FACILITIES: There is handicap access to rest rooms and to the first room in the caves. A restaurant and hotel in a historic district are open from mid-May to early September. A snack bar is open seasonally. For rates or reservations, write Oregon Cave Outfitters, P.O. Box 1824, Cave Junction, OR 97523 (541–592–3400 or 877–245–9022).

CAMPING: There is no camping or fire building in the monument. A concessionaire operates two campgrounds in the adjoining Siskiyou National Forest from about the end of May to early September. Cave Creek Campground is 4 miles from the park on Oregon 46. It has tables, grills, water, and pit toilets. Trailers are permitted only in Grayback Campground, located 8 miles down Oregon 46 from the park. Grayback has grills, water, a picnic area, flush toilets, and a phone. Campsites in both areas are secluded, and many are alongside a stream.

SAIPAN

AMERICAN MEMORIAL PARK

P.O. Box 5189-CHRB
Saipan, MP 96950
(670) 234–7207
amme_administration@nps.gov
www.nps.gov/amme

American Memorial Park is an affiliated area of the National Park Service that was authorized in 1978 as a living memorial to honor the sacrifices of the American and Marianas people in the Marianas Campaign of World War II. American Memorial Park is on the island of Saipan in the western Pacific, approximately 6,000 miles from the United States. On Saipan, the park is located immediately north of the town of Garapan.

More than 4,000 U.S. military personnel and islanders died during the Marianas Campaign in June 1944. This battle was considered by many as the most decisive of the Pacific theater because, once Saipan was secured, the Japanese supply and communication lines were severed and American bombers were able to move within range of Japan. The war with Japan ended fourteen months later. This park is a memorial and recreational park to honor the sacrifice of U.S. forces and islanders. The park's 133 acres (all nonfederal) are primarily a day-use area for local residents. The park contains several historical structures, including the remains of Japanese bunkers and gun emplacements. At the center of the park is the Court of Honor and Flag Circle, in which an American flag is flanked by flags of the U.S. Army, Navy, Marine Corps, and Air Force. A memorial inscribed with over 5,000 names of those who died surrounds the flags. The memorial was dedicated on June 15, 1994, the fiftieth anniversary of the invasion. A carillon bell tower tolls every half hour. Taps are played each evening to honor those who died.

Recreational facilities include a 1,200-seat amphitheater, four tennis courts, picnic areas, marina, and open fields for track, soccer, and football. A bike and jogging path connects some of the important sites as it winds throughout the park. A public marina, which is operated by the local government, is integrated within the park.

American Memorial Park also includes a thirty-acre wetland and mangrove forest that is home to numerous species of plants and birds. The adjacent mudflat is an important migratory bird site. Wetland and bird-watching tours are available with advance reservations.

ENTRANCE FEE: No charge.

FACILITIES: Complete food and lodging facilities are available nearby.

SOUTH DAKOTA

STATE TOURIST INFORMATION
(800) 732–5682
www.travelsd.com

BADLANDS NATIONAL PARK

P.O. Box 6
Interior, SD 57750 0006
(605) 433–5361
badl_information@nps.gov
www.nps.gov/badl

Badlands National Park, established as a national monument in 1939 (changed to a national park in 1978), comprises 244,000 acres of prairie grassland and a scenic eroded landscape, with mammal fossils that are between twenty-three million and thirty-eight million years old. The park is located in southwestern South Dakota. The Pinnacles entrance is 50 miles east of Rapid City, off I–90 (Exit 110), and the entrance at Cactus Flats is off I–90 (Exit 131), 71 miles east of Rapid City. Don't miss Wall Drug in the town of Wall. It is unique.

Today's Badlands were once covered by a large inland sea. Millions of years later the land was uplifted and exposed to a humid and warm climate. On this land roamed such animals as a saber-toothed cat and a camel the size of a dog. After dying, they were sometimes buried in mud from rivers, then under additional layers of sediment. Periodically, volcanic activity to the west produced layers of ash, which today appear as gray or white layers in the Badlands formations. Today, wind and water erode the soft sedimentary layers and leave the strange formations that give the park its name.

Badlands National Park has two visitor centers. Ben Reifel Visitor Center, located 8 miles south of I–90 via the northeast entrance, has exhibits and a movie to help interpret the Badlands. White River Visitor Center (open June–August only), in the south end of the park, has Indian cultural

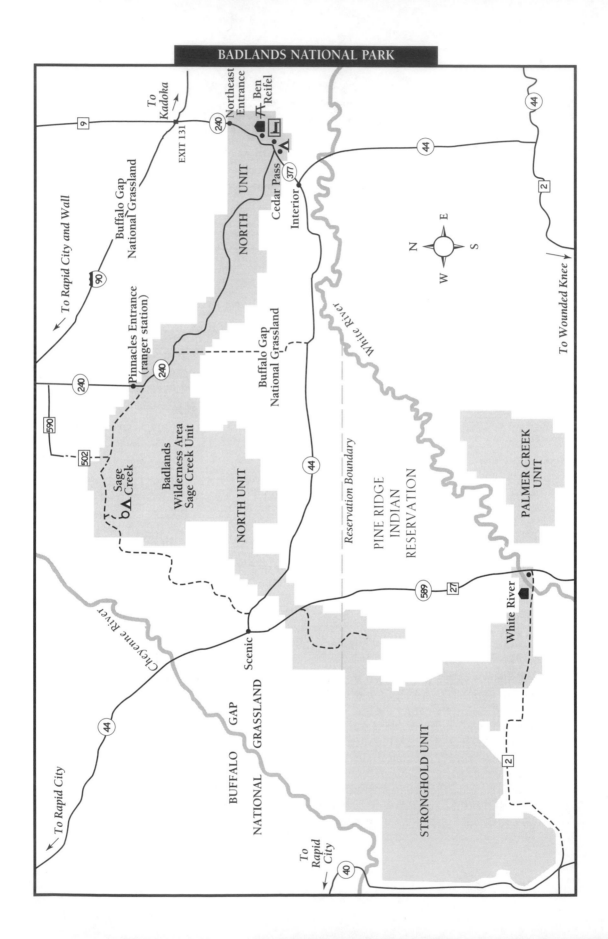

BADLANDS NATIONAL PARK

exhibits and a videotape program on the history of the Oglala Sioux. Wayside exhibits are located along the main park road, and self-guided nature trails are located near the Ben Reifel Visitor Center and along the park road. Ranger-conducted hikes and evening slide programs are available during summer.

ENTRANCE FEE: $10.00 per vehicle or $5.00 per person; good for seven days.

FACILITIES: Cedar Pass Lodge offers twenty-one air-conditioned cabins, as well as full-menu dining from April 15 through October 31. For information and reservations, write Cedar Pass Lodge, P.O. Box 5, Interior, SD 57750 (605–433–5460). Drinking water and rest rooms are located in the visitor center and the lodge.

CAMPING: Cedar Pass Campground (ninety-six spaces, four group sites) provides sheltered tables, water, flush toilets, and a dump station. Sage Creek Campground (no designated spaces) is free and has vault toilets but no water. Both campgrounds are open year-round.

JEWEL CAVE NATIONAL MONUMENT

R.R. 1, Box 60AA
Custer, SD 57730-9608
(605) 673-2288
jeca_interpretation@nps.gov
www.nps.gov/jeca

Jewel Cave National Monument, which comprises 1,275 acres, was established in 1908 to preserve a series of underground chambers connected by narrow passageways, with many side galleries and fine calcite crystal encrustations in the second-longest cave in the United States. The monument is located in southwestern South Dakota, 13 miles west of Custer via U.S. 16. For a map of the Black Hills region, see the map under Mount Rushmore National Memorial.

The caves in this region lie in a limestone layer that was deposited about 350 million years ago in a shallow, ancient sea. Later, after it was covered with layers of sediment, an uplift associated with the formation of the Rocky Mountains formed the Black Hills, and erosion exposed the interior of the Hills. As acidic water seeped into cracks in the limestone, the rock dissolved and caves were formed. The cave was named after the many jewel-like calcite crystals that form when calcite crystallizes out of standing water.

Jewel Cave was discovered in 1900 by two prospectors who recorded it as a mining claim. After failing to find valuable minerals, they attempted to turn it into a tourist attraction. In 1908 President Theodore Roosevelt proclaimed the cave a national monument.

The monument's visitor center contains exhibits and an information counter. Naturalist-guided tours (fee charged) are conducted through portions of the cave daily, except Thanksgiving, Christmas, and New Year's Day. Three types of tours are available. The Scenic Tour enters and leaves the cave by elevator in the visitor center; the Candlelight Tour (summer only) uses the historic entrance created by the cave's discoverers. This latter trip is quite strenuous and uses an unimproved trail. For those desiring an even more demanding trip, the Spelunking Tour (reservations required, summer only) is made to order. Individuals planning to visit the monument are advised to call ahead for tour times and availability. Reservations may be made two hours or more in advance for cave tours through the National Park Reservation Service (800–967–2283) or on the Internet at reservations.nps.gov.

ENTRANCE FEE: No charge. There is an $8.00 fee for regular cave tours and a $23.00 fee for the Spelunking Tour.

FACILITIES: Lodging is not available in the park. Snacks and soft-drink vending machines are available. Motels, restaurants, and service stations are available in Custer, South Dakota, and Newcastle, Wyoming. Drinking water and rest rooms are located in the visitor center.

CAMPING: No camping is permitted in the park. Public camping facilities are available nearby in Wind Cave National Park, Custer State Park, and Black Hills National Forest.

MOUNT RUSHMORE NATIONAL MEMORIAL

P.O. Box 268
Keystone, SD 57751-0268
(605) 574–2523
jim_popovich@nps.gov
www.nps.gov/moru

Mount Rushmore National Memorial, which comprises 1,278 acres, was dedicated on August 10, 1927, the same day work commenced on sculpting the heads of George Washington, Abraham Lincoln, Thomas Jefferson, and Theodore Roosevelt on the face of this granite mountain. The memorial is located in southwestern South Dakota, 25 miles southwest of Rapid City and 2 miles from the town of Keystone.

The idea of a large sculpture in the Black Hills region was first conceived in 1923. Although the project initially received little public support, opinion gradually changed, and authorization and funding eventually were obtained. In the fall of 1924, Gutzon Borglum, a sculptor then at work on Stone Mountain in Georgia, was invited to study the proposal. Borglum suggested that U.S. presidents be used as subjects and that the sculpture be on the smooth granite of Mount Rushmore. The original proposal had called for the figures of famous western heroes on another granite formation known as the Needles.

Borglum worked on the project from 1927 until his death in 1941. His son continued the work until funds were exhausted later that year. Although private donations supported the project in its early years, the federal government contributed most of the nearly $1 million the project consumed between 1927 and 1941.

The 60-foot-tall faces are best viewed under morning light. During summer evenings floodlights illuminate the faces at the end of the Evening Lighting Ceremony in the amphitheater. The Lincoln Borglum Museum orients visitors to the memorial and the Black Hills area. The museum has two theaters and the Mount Rushmore History Association bookstore, which provides educational materials. The Presidential Trail leads to the base of the mountain, where visitors can view the presidents' faces close-up. The studio of sculptor Gutzon Borglum is open during summer months. The memorial, information center, and museum are open year-round.

ENTRANCE FEE: No entrance fee is charged, but an $8.00 parking fee applies.

JEWEL CAVE NATIONAL MONUMENT, MOUNT RUSHMORE NATIONAL MEMORIAL, AND WIND CAVE NATIONAL PARK

N
W E
S

385

90

44

RAPID CITY

Pactola
Reservoir

79

16

Sheridan Lake

Rockerville

Hill City

Keystone

244

Mount Rushmore
National Memorial

16
385

Sylvan Lake

87

40

ALT 16

89

36

Custer

16

ALT 16

Jewel Cave
National
Monument

87

Custer
State Park

87

385

Wind Cave
National
Park

87

Pringle

79

89

385

101

Mount Rushmore National Memorial

FACILITIES: Meals, souvenirs, and handicrafts are available at the concession. Overnight accommodations are located in nearby communities.

CAMPING: No camping is permitted in the park. Public camping facilities are provided in a number of campgrounds in Black Hills National Forest and in Custer State Park and Wind Cave National Park.

WIND CAVE NATIONAL PARK

R.R. 1, Box 190
Hot Springs, SD 57747-9430
(605) 745–4600
wica_interpretation@nps.gov
www.nps.gov/wica

Wind Cave National Park, which comprises more than 28,000 acres, was established in 1903 to preserve a part of the mixed grass prairie ecosystem and a unique type of limestone cavern that is one of the longest caves in the United States. The park is located in southwestern South Dakota, approximately 60 miles south of Rapid City via U.S. Highways 16 and 385.

The 300- to 630-foot-thick limestone bed containing Wind Cave was deposited at the bottom of a great sea about 300 million years ago. Later, the region was covered with many layers of sediment before being uplifted approximately sixty million years ago. During the uplift, the limestone was fractured, allowing ground water to dissolve the limestone and deposit the calcite that now decorates the cave.

The cave is most noted for its "boxwork" formation, but other interesting decorations can also be seen. Unlike many other caverns, stalactites and stalagmites are uncommon in Wind Cave. The strong winds that blow in and out of the cave (hence, its name) are apparently caused by changes in atmospheric pressure on the outside. Although more than 108 miles of passages have been explored, the regular tours (fee charged) cover only 1½ miles of hard-surfaced trails with stairways and electric lighting. Rubber-soled shoes (low-heeled) and a light jacket (53 degrees Fahrenheit inside) are recommended for visitors desiring to tour the cave.

One of the park's most popular attractions is the bison herd that roams this wildlife sanctuary. A number of prairie-dog towns are located in the park, as are herds of elk, pronghorn, mule deer, and white-tailed deer. During summer months, park personnel conduct outdoor activities throughout the day. Schedules are posted at the visitor center, which also houses exhibits on prairie and forest resources, the area's history, and cave features.

ENTRANCE FEE: No charge. Fees for cave tours range in price from $6.00 to $20.00.

Bison Herd, Wind Cave National Park

FACILITIES: No overnight accommodations are available in the park, but motels, hotels, trailer courts, camping supplies, and service stations are located in Custer and Hot Springs. In the visitor center a vending area for snacks and a bookstore are open year-round.

CAMPING: Elk Mountain Campground (seventy-five sites), located 1 mile north of the visitor center, is open May 15 through September 15. Tables, grills, water, and flush toilets are provided. During the off-season (April 1–May 15 and September 15–October 30), pit toilets are available, but water is available only at the visitor center. Camping is also available in Custer State Park and Black Hills National Forest to the north and near Hot Springs to the south.

FISHING: Fishing for brown, brook, and rainbow trout is available in the general area.

TEXAS

STATE TOURIST INFORMATION
(800) 452–9292
www.traveltex.com

ALIBATES FLINT QUARRIES NATIONAL MONUMENT
Box 1460
Fritch, TX 79036-1460
(806) 857–3151
LAMR_Interpretation@nps.gov
www.nps.gov/alfl

Alibates Flint Quarries was authorized as a national monument in 1965. It comprises 1,333 acres in an area where, for nearly 12,000 years, pre-Columbian Indians dug agatized dolomite from quarries to make knives, projectile points, scrapers, and other tools. The monument is in northern Texas, 22 miles northeast of Amarillo. From Texas Highway 136, take the Cas Johnson Road, 6 miles south of Fritch, and drive 5 miles to the ranger station.

Tools made from flint dug in the Lake Meredith area of the Texas Panhandle have been found in many places in the Great Plains and the American Southwest. Evidence from archaeological excavations indicates almost continuous use of the flint quarries at Alibates from 10,000 B.C. to the late 1800s. Alibates flint is a hard, sharp-edged rock that, unlike most other flint, has a multitude of bright colors.

Although much of the mining at Alibates was done by nomads, some Indians did settle this area briefly from about A.D. 1200 to 1450. These Indians farmed in addition to mining and bartering flint.

A small ranger station at Bates Canyon has a few exhibits, and park personnel are on duty before and after tours to answer questions. Free guided walking tours of the quarry pits are available with advance reservation. Contact park headquarters for more information on tours (806–857–3151).

ENTRANCE FEE: No charge.

FACILITIES: The monument is undeveloped, and no visitor facilities other than the ranger station and comfort station are available. Meals and lodging are available in Fritch and Borger.

CAMPING: No camping is permitted at the monument. Campsites are available in McBride Canyon at nearby Lake Meredith National Recreation Area.

FISHING: No fishing is available in Alibates, but there is quite a lot of good fishing in nearby Lake Meredith.

AMISTAD NATIONAL RECREATION AREA

HCR-3, Box 5-J
Del Rio, TX 78840-9350
(830) 775-7491
Amis_Interpretation@nps.gov
www.nps.gov/amis

Amistad (the name means "friendship") National Recreation Area, designated on November 28, 1990, comprises 58,500 acres that provide numerous outdoor recreation opportunities, including boating, fishing, swimming, waterskiing, and hunting. The park is located along the Rio Grande in southwest Texas, near the town of Del Rio. Primary access is via U.S. 90.

Lake Amistad, the main attraction at Amistad National Recreation Area, is a result of the 1968 completion of Amistad Dam, 12 miles upstream from Del Rio. The dam, a cooperative undertaking between the United States and Mexico, was developed for flood control, water conservation, hydroelectric power, and recreation. It is constructed of a 254-foot-high concrete section in the Rio Grande channel connecting flanking earth embankments. Near the center of the dam is a U.S. Customs Station, an international monument, and the National Park Service Exhibit Center.

Rock art in the Lower Pecos River region is considered to be world class and comparable to that found in Europe and Australia. This region also contains some of the oldest dated and best-preserved archaeological deposits in North America. This region can only be reached by boat. Guided walking tours of rock art near the Pecos area are provided at Seminole State Historical Park.

Amistad Dam was constructed primarily for flood control, but visitors are attracted by the resulting reservoir's water-related activities, including boating, fishing, and swimming. Information about facilities and activities is available at park headquarters (west of Del Rio on U.S. 90) and at the Governors Landing ranger station. Major boat ramps are at Pecos River, Diablo East, and Rough Canyon. Boat rentals, rental slips, bait, and gasoline are available at the latter two locations. Boats on Lake Amistad must have a daily or annual permit (fee required). From spring to fall, water in the coves is pleasantly warm for swimming and waterskiing. The beaches are not protected by lifeguards. Swimming is not permitted in the harbor areas. Certain areas of the park are designated for hunting dove, duck, and quail with shotgun; deer, wild turkey, and javelina may be hunted with bow and arrow only. Interested individuals should inquire at the National Park Service headquarters.

ENTRANCE FEE: No charge for entrance. A lake fee is charged.

FACILITIES: Concessioner-operated stores are located at Diablo East and Rough Canyon. No lodging is available at the park, but motels, travel trailer parks, restaurants, and service stations are available in Del Rio and along U.S. 90 West, near the lake. Contact the Del Rio Chamber of Commerce at (830) 775–3551 or www.drchamber.com. Small boats and houseboats can be rented at Lake Amistad Resort & Marina (830–744–4157; www.lakeamistadresort.com).

CAMPING: The National Park Service operates developed campgrounds at Governors Landing, 277 North, Spur 406, and San Pedro. Each campground has vault toilets, covered picnic tables, and grills. Only Governors Landing has potable water. Drinking water is also available at park headquarters and at the Del Rio Civic Center. Dump stations are at both of the latter two locations. Several group campgrounds are available by reservation only (call 830–775–7491). Camping is permitted outside the developed area at Spur 406, but only within the posted campground boundaries. Commercial campgrounds with hookups are near the Diablo East, Rough Canyon, and Pecos River facilities.

FISHING: Principal sport fishing is for several species of bass, sunfish, and catfish. Catches of 8- to 10-pound bass and 40-pound catfish are not uncommon. Fishing in U.S. waters requires a Texas license and adherence to Texas fish limits and size specifications. Fishing in Amistad's Mexican waters (the border is indicated by numbered buoys along the main channel) requires a Mexican fishing license and adherence to Mexican regulations. Mexican licenses are available for purchase only in Mexico. Fishing is legal from shore anywhere away from harbors or designated swim beaches. Fishing docks are at Rough Canyon, Spur 454, and Governors Landing. Fish cleaning stations are at Diablo East, Rough Canyon, and Pecos.

BIG BEND NATIONAL PARK

P.O. Box 129
Big Bend National Park, TX 79834-0129
(432) 477–2251
bibe_info@nps.gov
www.nps.gov/bibe

Big Bend National Park, established in 1944, comprises more than 801,000 acres of desert, mountain ranges, steep-walled canyons, and ribbons of green plant life along the Rio Grande. The park is located in southwestern Texas on the Mexican border. Access from the north is via U.S. 385 from Marathon or State Highway 118 from Alpine. Enter from the west on Texas Ranch Road 170 from Presidio.

The land of Big Bend is one of vastness, adventure, and beautiful scenery. Its remoteness results in this park being less heavily used than better known and more convenient parks, even though Big Bend offers a variety of outdoor activities and a diversity of wildlife. People come here to hike, camp, raft the Rio Grande, and just relax and enjoy the spectacular landscape. Big Bend is a favorite place for many birdwatchers, who have observed 450 species in this area that is a migration route between South, Central, and North America. Big Bend is also home to many species of mammals, plants, insects, and bats. It is especially pleasant to visit during the long spring and fall seasons, when the weather is mild.

Visitor centers are located at Panther Junction (park headquarters), Persimmon Gap, Chisos Basin, and Rio Grande Village. These centers provide information and sell publications concerning the park. Entrance fees for private (including motorcycles and bicycles) and commercial vehicles are paid at the entrance stations or at Panther Junction. Park ranger interpreters present evening programs at Chisos Basin amphitheater all year and at Rio Grande Village during fall, winter, and spring. Ranger-conducted hikes and occasionally special programs are available; schedules are posted at various locations and on the park's Web site. Self-guided nature trails are at Rio Grande Village, Santa Elena Canyon, Panther Junction, Dagger Flat Road, and the Lost Mine Trail and Window View Trail in the Basin.

The 43-mile drive from Panther Junction to Santa Elena Canyon ends at a shaded picnic area, where high cliffs overhang the Rio Grande. A foot trail to the base of the 1,500-foot-high cliff leads upward to a panoramic viewpoint. From there the trail wanders 3/4 mile along the river. On the other side of the park, Boquillas Canyon is the longest (25 miles) of Big Bend's famous gorges. The path into the canyon descends gently after a short, steep climb.

Primitive roads offer access to scenery not available elsewhere in the park. These roads are patrolled infrequently, so those planning such trips should be well prepared and obtain current road information at park headquarters.

River trips on the Rio Grande are offered by outfitters outside the park. A permit is required to run the river, but no equipment rentals are available inside the park. The visitor centers offer a river brochure and can supply a list of outfitters.

ENTRANCE FEE: $15.00 per vehicle or $5.00 per person; good for seven days.

FACILITIES: Chisos Mountains Lodge in the Basin has a total of seventy-two rooms in motel-type units, stone cottages, and frame cottages, with reservations available from Big Bend Resorts, Chisos Mountains Lodge, Basin Rural Station, Big Bend National Park, TX 79834 (915–477–2291 or www.chisosmountainslodge.com). The lodge has a full service restaurant. Groceries and camping supplies are available at the Basin, Rio Grande Village, and Castolon. Minor auto repair and gas are available at Panther Junction. Gasoline is also available at Rio Grande Village. Diesel fuel is available at Panther Junction.

CAMPING: Campgrounds with tables, grills, water, and flush toilets are located at the Basin (65 spaces, 8 group sites, dump station), Cottonwood (31 spaces, 1 group site, pit toilets only), and Rio Grande Village (100 spaces, 4 group sites, dump station). A concessioner-operated trailer village with hookups is located at Rio Grande Village (twenty-five sites, pay showers). The road into the Basin is steep and winding. Trailers longer than 20 feet are not recommended, and recreational vehicles longer than 24 feet are advised to avoid the road.

FISHING: The Rio Grande provides catches of catfish. A free fishing permit is required and can be obtained at a visitor center.

BIG THICKET NATIONAL PRESERVE

3785 Milam Street
Beaumont, TX 77701-4724
(409) 839–2689
BITH_administration@nps.gov
www.nps.gov/bith

Big Thicket National Preserve comprises 86,068 acres and was authorized in 1974 to preserve a unique ecosystem of great diversity. Plants and animals from southwestern deserts, central plains, eastern forests, the Appalachian Mountains, and southeastern swamps can be found coexisting in close proximity. The preserve comprises twelve widely separated units north, northwest, and northeast of the city of Beaumont, Texas. The Information Station is on FM 420, 7 miles north of Kountze. Big Thicket is also designated a Man and the Biosphere Reserve by the United Nations Educational, Scientific, and Cultural Organization (UNESCO).

Big Thicket is unique because of the abundance of diverse plant life coexisting in a small remnant of what was once a combination of virgin pine and bald cypress forest, hardwood forest, meadow, and blackwater swamp. The area features eighty-five tree species, more than sixty species of shrubs, and nearly 1,000 other flowering plants, including twenty orchids and four carnivorous plants. Wildlife thrives in the diverse habitats, although many animals come out only at night. During annual migrations nearly 214 kinds of birds have been sighted. Big Thicket is home to a few threatened or endangered species, including the red-cockaded woodpecker, American alligator, and paddlefish.

The Information Station is scheduled to open daily from 10:30 A.M. to 5:00 P.M. but frequently opens at 9:00 A.M. The preserve's twelve units are open to the public, and four have developed hiking trails. Two trails are wheelchair accessible. The best way to explore the Big Thicket is to hike a trail or to boat or canoe the river corridors and backwater sloughs. Few roads enter the preserve, limiting visitors from seeing the woods from their cars. Ranger-led programs for groups and individuals are available by reservation only. Contact the Information Station at (409) 246–2337 for information and reservations.

ENTRANCE FEE: No charge.

FACILITIES: No lodging or food service is available in the park, but both are available in the nearby communities of Woodville, Kountze, Silsbee, and Beaumont. Rest rooms and drinking water are located at the Information Station.

CAMPING: There are no developed camping facilities, although backcountry camping is permitted in designated areas of the preserve. A backcountry permit is required. Campgrounds with flush toilets and showers are located at Martin Dies Jr. State Park, 13 miles west of Jasper on U.S. 190 and at Village Creek State Park, east of Lumberton. Another campground, operated by the U.S. Army Corps of Engineers, is located nearby on B. A. Steinhagen Lake. Contact the preserve for a listing of nearby private campgrounds.

FISHING: Opportunities for bass, catfish, and carp are available in the preserve. A Texas fishing license is required.

HUNTING: Hunting is allowed in certain units of the preserve with an annual permit. These free permits are issued during July on a first-come, first-served basis. Contact the preserve for permit information.

CHAMIZAL NATIONAL MEMORIAL

800 South San Marcial Street
El Paso, TX 79905-4123
(915) 532–7273
cham_interpretation@nps.gov
www.nps.gov/cham

The histories of the United States and Mexico meet at Chamizal National Memorial, where the Chamizal Treaty is commemorated—a treaty resulting from the determined goodwill of two nations striving peacefully to resolve a persistent border dispute. The fifty-five-acre memorial was authorized by Congress in 1966. The park is located in south-central metropolitan El Paso, next to the international border. Entrances to the park are from Paisano Avenue or Delta Drive to South San Marcial Street.

The first commission to survey the international boundary between the United States and Mexico was established in 1849 after the signing of the Treaty of Guadalupe Hidalgo. The survey disclosed that 1,248 miles of the border was formed by the Rio Grande/Bravo, and an additional 23 miles was defined by the Colorado River. These river boundaries created difficulties because the rivers tended to change courses with each flood season. In an 1884 treaty both

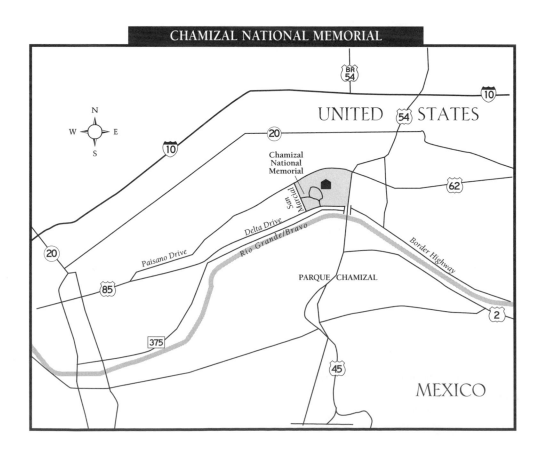

nations agreed to the principle that if a river changed course by a slow process of erosion, the boundary moved with the deepest channel. Conversely, if the river changed its course suddenly, the boundary remained in the old channel.

The settlement of the boundary dispute involved the moving of a railroad, a school, and a bridge; the displacement of more than 5,000 individuals; and the relocation of the river itself. Today Chamizal, situated on land acquired in the agreement, celebrates the goodwill inherent in the treaty through the performing, visual, and literary arts. Graced with an indoor and outdoor theater, an art gallery, and exhibition areas, Chamizal National Memorial Visitor Center is open daily from 8:00 A.M. to 5:00 P.M., except Thanksgiving, Christmas, and New Year's Day. The memorial grounds are open daily from 5:00 A.M. to 10:00 P.M. Special programs in the 500-seat indoor theater and outdoor amphitheater take place throughout the year. One of these events is Siglo de Oro Drama Festival, which takes place in late February and early March. The Music Under the Stars concert series is held every Sunday evening June through August. The Chamizal Festival, held the first weekend in October, features traditional music, crafts, demonstrations, dance, and visual art forms.

ENTRANCE FEE: No charge.

FACILITIES: No food or lodging is available at the memorial, but both are available nearby.

FORT DAVIS NATIONAL HISTORIC SITE

P.O. Box 1379
Fort Davis, TX 79734
(432) 426–3224, ext. 20
foda_superintendent@nps.gov
www.nps.gov/foda

Soldiers from Fort Davis helped open the area to settlement and protected travelers and merchants along the San Antonio–El Paso Road from 1854 to 1891. Today the fort is regarded as one of the best preserved in the Southwest. The site, which comprises 474 acres, was authorized in 1961 and established in 1963. The site is located on the north edge of the town of Fort Davis on Highways 17 and 118. The site can be reached from the north on Interstate 10 and from the south on U.S. 90.

Fort Davis, named in honor of then Secretary of War Jefferson Davis, was established in 1854 to protect travelers and settlers in the West Texas region. The first structures consisted of pine-slab *jacales* with thatched grass or canvas. By 1856 six stone barracks had been built to house enlisted men. During this period, the soldiers of Fort Davis spent most of their time escorting mail and freight trains and patrolling this sector of the Southwest.

With the beginning of the Civil War, Union troops abandoned the fort, which then became occupied by Confederate forces for over a year. After Fort Davis was abandoned by the Southern troops, many buildings collapsed and others were burned by Apaches. The fort then lay deserted for five years. In 1867 federal troops returned to rebuild the fort, and by the 1880s Fort Davis had become a major installation, with more than 100 structures and over 400 soldiers. Because Indian raiding had come to an end, the fort became an unnecessary expense and was finally abandoned in 1891.

Of the more than one hundred buildings that formed the second fort, twenty-one remain standing. Five of these (a shared lieutenants' quarters, the commanding officer's quarters, an enlisted men's barracks, the post commissary, and an officers' kitchen/servants' quarters) have been restored and furnished to the period of the 1880s. These five buildings and the post hospital are open to the public on a self-guided basis. During summer months, many of the buildings are staffed with interpreters dressed in period clothing.

The visitor center, located in one of the two restored enlisted men's barracks, is open daily from 8:00 A.M. to 5:00 P.M. (6:00 P.M. from Memorial Day to Labor Day). A video may be seen in the auditorium, and audio (bugle call and retreat dress parade) programs can be heard at scheduled times throughout the day

ENTRANCE FEE: $3.00 per person; good for seven days. Children ages sixteen and under are free.

FACILITIES: Food and lodging are not available at the site but can be found in the town of Fort Davis. Water and rest rooms are located in the visitor center. A picnic area is located on the grounds. Many of the buildings are equipped with ramps for visitors in wheelchairs, and an electric cart is available for the physically disabled.

CAMPING: No camping is permitted in the park. Camping facilities are available in the town of Fort Davis and in Davis Mountains State Park (432–426–3337), 4 miles to the northwest. The state park offers eighty-eight sites with tables, grills, water, flush toilets, and showers. Some sites in the town and the state park offer full hookups.

GUADALUPE MOUNTAINS NATIONAL PARK

HC 60, Box 400
Salt Flat, TX 79847-9400
(915) 828–3251
GUMO_Superintendent@nps.gov
www.nps.gov/gumo

Guadalupe Mountains National Park, established in 1972, comprises 86,416 acres of mountain and desert landscape, including the most extensive exposed fossil reef on Earth. The park is located in western Texas, 55 miles southwest of Carlsbad, New Mexico, and 110 miles east of El Paso via U.S. 62/180. It is 65 miles north of Van Horn, Texas, via SR 54.

The Guadalupe Mountains began to form nearly 250 million years ago, when this region was covered by a great inland sea. Near the shoreline, a reef grew from lime-secreting organisms and precipitates from the water. At the end of the Permian period, the reef died, and layers of sediment buried the entire area. Much later, a general uplifting raised the region several thousand feet and allowed the shaping of today's mountain range through erosion by wind and water. Today only a small portion of the 350-mile horseshoe-shaped reef is not buried beneath the ground. The most outstanding exposure is included in this park.

A variety of people have passed through and lived in this arid region. Hunter-gatherers, including the Mescalero Apache, made this their homeland. Spanish conquistadors passed the range on their explorations north from Mexico. Don Diego de Vargas, a colonizer of New Mexico, made a trip to the nearby Salt Flats and the Guadalupes in 1692. Military surveyors

GUADALUPE MOUNTAINS NATIONAL PARK

mapped the pass, and their route was used by settlers and forty-niners headed for the western gold strikes. The route was also used by the Butterfield Overland Mail in the late 1850s. The remains of The Pinery, a horse-changing stop, are marked and accessed via a trail from the Headquarters Visitor Center.

The Headquarters Visitor Center at Pine Springs is open daily from 8:00 A.M. to 4:30 P.M. (6:00 P.M. during summer). The visitor center offers exhibits, audiovisual programs, a bookstore, and maps. Frijole Ranch, a cultural history site, is 1½ miles north of Pine Springs and features exhibits on Native Americans, Spanish exploration, the Overland Mail, the U.S. Cavalry, and early ranching activities. Visitors may also secure a free permit at the visitor center giving them access to Williams Ranch Historic Site via an 8-mile (four-wheel-drive) road.

McKittrick Canyon Visitor Center, with exhibits on the canyon and the Permian Reef, is a trailhead for the spectacular canyon. The road to the canyon is 7 miles east of Pine Springs on U.S. 62/180. With 80 miles of hiking trails and no road bisecting Guadalupe Mountains National Park, backcountry hiking is one of the primary activities. Overnight permits are available at Pine Springs and Dog Canyon.

ENTRANCE FEE: $3.00 per adult; children ages fifteen and under are free.

FACILITIES: Water, rest rooms, and picnic areas are provided at the visitor centers and campgrounds. No food, commercial lodging, or fuel is available at the park.

CAMPING: Pine Springs Campground has twenty tent and nineteen RV sites with tables but no hookups or showers. Two group sites are available. Water, rest rooms, and a service sink are provided. Dog Canyon Campground has nine tent and four RV sites, none with hookups. One group site is available. Tables, rest rooms, and water are available. No fires are permitted at any of the campsites. Dog Canyon is accessed via New Mexico Highway 137 from Carlsbad, New Mexico, or via the state and county road through Dell City, Texas.

LAKE MEREDITH NATIONAL RECREATION AREA

P.O. Box 1460
Fritch, TX 79036-1460
(806) 857–3151
LAMR_Interpretation@nps.gov
www.nps.gov/lamr

Lake Meredith National Recreation Area (formerly Sanford Recreation Area) encompasses nearly 45,000 acres. The park is a popular spot for all types of water activities. It is located in the Texas Panhandle, 33 miles northeast of Amarillo via State Highway 136.

Lake Meredith is an oasis located in the high, flat, and dry plains area of north Texas. Formed by Sanford Dam on the Canadian River, the resulting body of water is used by eleven cities as a municipal water supply. The 200-foot canyon walls with white limestone caps and red-brown coves present an attractive contrast to the blue waters. A variety of wildlife inhabits the area, including bald eagles, golden eagles, hawks, mule deer, and white-tailed deer.

Typical activities at Lake Meredith National Recreation Area include waterskiing, sailing, swimming, scuba diving, fishing, and hunting. Boat-launching ramps are located at Harbor Bay,

Blue West, Sanford-Yake, Cedar Canyon, and Fritch Fortress. A marina is located at Sanford-Yake. Off-road vehicle trails are available at Rosita and Blue Creek Bridge. Swimming is recommended at Spring Canyon, below Sanford Dam and at Cedar Canyon in the lake proper. (Swim at your own risk—no lifeguards.)

ENTRANCE FEE: No charge. There is a boat launch fee of $4.00 (one day), $10.00 (three days), or $40.00 (annual pass).

FACILITIES: At Sanford-Yake, a concessioner provides a snack bar, a marina, small boat and houseboat rentals, a convenience store, and an enclosed fish house for year-round fishing (806–865–3391; www.marinaatlakemeredith.com). Lodging and food are available in nearby towns. Drinking water and rest rooms are available April through September at Fritch Fortress, Cedar Canyon, and Sanford-Yake. Chemical toilets are also provided at most of the other locations.

CAMPING: Campgrounds with tables, grills, water, and flush toilets are located at Sanford-Yake (fifty-three spaces, dump station) and Fritch Fortress (ten spaces). Campgrounds with chemical toilets but no water are located at Blue West (forty spaces), McBride Canyon (ten spaces), and Plum Creek (fifteen spaces). These sites are open year-round. No camping is permitted at the launching areas or the parking lots.

FISHING: The lake provides opportunities to fish for largemouth, smallmouth, and white bass, four species of catfish, crappie, sunfish, carp, and the only naturally reproducing walleye in Texas. A Texas fishing license is required.

LYNDON B. JOHNSON NATIONAL HISTORICAL PARK

P.O. Box 329
Johnson City, TX 78636-0329
(830) 868–7128
lyjo_superintendent@nps.gov
www.nps.gov/lyjo

Lyndon B. Johnson National Historical Park was authorized in 1969 to preserve the birthplace, boyhood home, and ranch of the thirty-sixth president of the United States. Johnson's grandparents' cattle-droving headquarters is also included in the park. The park comprises two areas. One district is located in Johnson City, Texas, 48 miles west of Austin via U.S. 290. The LBJ Ranch district is located 14 miles west of Johnson City, on the same highway.

Lyndon Baines Johnson was born and raised in the Hill Country of Texas. After serving as U.S. congressman from 1937 to 1948, U.S. senator from 1948 to 1960, vice president from 1960 to 1963, and U.S. president from 1963 to 1968, Johnson returned to Texas and lived there from 1969 until his death in 1973. He is buried in the family cemetery near his birthplace on the Pedernales River.

The Johnson City District includes a visitor center, LBJ's boyhood home, and the Johnson Settlement. The visitor center has an exhibit gallery, two films, one covering LBJ's presidency, the other a biography of Lady Bird Johnson, a children's activity room, a bookstore, and visitor facilities. Park staff provide tours of Johnson's boyhood home. A tour of the Johnson Settlement, accessible by a walking trail, begins at the exhibit center, which contains photographs, text, artifacts, graphics, and audiovisuals that introduce visitors to the history of the Johnson Settlement and the area. The Johnson Settlement area deals with two historical time periods (1867–1872 and 1872–1900). Park rangers in period costume demonstrate heritage skills of the Texas frontier six months of the year.

Bus tours of the LBJ Ranch depart from the Lyndon B. Johnson State Historical Park Visitor Center, located on Highway 290, 14 miles west of Johnson City. The tours include the Junction School, LBJ's Birthplace, Johnson Family Cemetery, Sam Ealy Johnson's Farmhouse, Texas White House exterior, LBJ Ranch lands, the show barn, and the Pedernales River. At the state park's visitor center, visitors are given an orientation to the state and national historical parks. The former serves as a day-use area for picnicking, interpretation of natural and cultural history (Sauer-Beckmann Living History Farmstead), hiking, swimming, and other recreation activities.

ENTRANCE FEE: No charge for visiting the Johnson City District; $3.00 fee for the bus tour of the LBJ Ranch. Children ages six and under are free.

FACILITIES: No food or lodging is available in either district of the park. Both can be found nearby. Drinking water and rest rooms are provided in both visitor centers.

CAMPING: No camping is permitted in the Lyndon B. Johnson National and State Historical Parks. Pedernales Falls State Park provides camping facilities east of Johnson City. Lady Bird Johnson Municipal Park, in the town of Fredericksburg, has an attractive campground. Other commercial sites providing camping facilities are available throughout the area.

FISHING: Fishing is permitted on the south side of the Pedernales River with a Texas fishing license.

PADRE ISLAND NATIONAL SEASHORE

20420 Park Road 22
Corpus Christi, TX 78418
(361) 949–8068
PAIS_Visitor_Center@nps.gov
www.nps.gov/pais

Padre Island National Seashore, authorized in 1962 and established in 1968, comprises more than 130,000 acres of wide sand beaches on a grass-covered barrier island that stretches for 113 miles, 70 miles of which are in the park. The park is located along the Gulf Coast in southern Texas. It is accessible via State Highway 358 and Park Road 22 from Corpus Christi or by State Highway 361 from Port Aransas.

Padre Island has been built by a combination of wave action and winds off the Gulf of Mexico. This long barrier island, from a few hundred yards to 3 miles in width, is continually changing as grassy interior sections are gradually covered by windblown sand. In some areas the sands have become stabilized by grasses and shrubs that have long, binding roots. Between the island and the mainland lies Laguna Madre, a shallow body of water with a maximum width of 10 miles.

PADRE ISLAND NATIONAL SEASHORE

Bus. 35

181

37

181

Free Ferry

Port Aransas

Corpus Christi

361

37

77

22

Kingsville

Bird Island Basin

Malaquite Beach

771

Baffin Bay

Four-wheel drive

Gulf of Mexico

Sarita

Yarborough Pass

77

N
W   E
S

Wreck of the *Nicaragua*

Mansfield Channel

Port Mansfield

186

Raymondville

Laguna Madre

Harlingen

83

South Padre Island

100

Port Isabel

UNITED STATES

77

MEXICO

48

Rio Grande

Brownsville

Life on the island is difficult for plant life, which must constantly battle the sand and wind to gain a foothold. Common mammals living here include coyotes, spotted ground squirrels, and white-tailed deer. More than 350 species of birds are year-round residents or seasonal visitors passing through on their migration routes. Reptiles that may be seen in the area include two species of rattlesnakes.

Vehicle access to Padre Island is only on the north end of the island via a bridge from Corpus Christi or a ferry from Port Aransas. Five miles inside the park boundary via a paved road is the Malaquite Visitor Center, with exhibits, an audiovisual presentation, and brochures. This should be your first stop. You will also find rest rooms, a small store, and a concession that rents beach chairs, umbrellas, inner tubes, and body boards. The paved road terminates at the beach approximately 1 mile south of the visitor center. Four-wheel drive is recommended beyond the first mile or two of generally firm sand. The sand becomes continually softer from about the 7-mile marker and reaches its deepest at Big Shell Beach from about the 18-mile marker to the 38-mile marker. A variety of hazards await newcomers wishing to drive on the beach, so it is worthwhile to ask at the visitor center for the brochure that provides advice for traveling down island.

For visitors without four-wheel drive or an interest in driving to the beach, the gradual slope and warm water along the Gulf make swimming a popular activity. Nearly all the beaches are open to hikers, and a short self-guided nature trail begins near the entrance station. The Bird Island Basin area, which lies between the entrance station and the visitor center on the western side of the island, is one of the top spots in the nation for windsurfing. A windsurfing concession operates here from March 1 through midsummer. Primitive camping and boat-launching ramps are also available in this area. An additional fee is charged for using this area of the national seashore.

ENTRANCE FEE: $10.00 per vehicle or $5.00 per person; good for seven days. Bird Island has a day-use fee of $5.00 (annual pass $10.00).

FACILITIES: No lodging facilities and very limited food service are within the national seashore, although hotels, motels, restaurants, and convenience stores are on the island several miles north of the entrance station. Many motels and a large grocery store are on the west side of the bridge leading from Corpus Christi to Padre Island. Limited camper supplies, free cold-water showers, and rental equipment for beach use are available at Malaquite Beach during summer months. Boating supplies and launching ramps are along the John F. Kennedy Memorial Causeway.

CAMPING: Malaquite Beach Campground (forty-six spaces) provides tables, water, flush toilets, cold-water showers, and a dump station. Primitive camping is permitted along 61 miles of the 65½ miles of Gulf beach. Primitive camping is also available on the Laguna Madre at Yarborough Pass and Bird Island Basin. Public campgrounds with hookups are located in Nueces County Park north of the seashore boundary and in Cameron County Park at the south end of the island near Port Isabel.

FISHING: Fishing is available year-round in Laguna Madre and the Gulf. Some fish that may be caught, with the respective best seasons, are pompano (April and October), redfish (fall), drum (December–April), red snapper (October–March), and tarpon (October and November). Snapper and tarpon are normally deepwater fish rarely caught from the beaches. Sharks and rays are occasionally caught in the surf. A Texas fishing license is required, as well as a saltwater stamp.

PALO ALTO BATTLEFIELD NATIONAL HISTORIC SITE

1623 Central Boulevard, Suite 213
Brownsville, TX 78520-8326
(956) 541–2785
paal_interpretation@nps.gov
www.nps.gov/paal

Palo Alto Battlefield National Historic Site comprises 3,357 acres and was established in 1991 to preserve a large battlefield on which the initial battle of the 1846–48 Mexican War took place. The historic site also interprets the war and its consequences from the perspectives of both countries. The historic site is located in the southern tip of Texas, approximately 5 miles north of downtown Brownsville. It is at the intersection of FM 1847 and FM 511.

Disputes regarding land ownership and the boundaries of Texas resulted in a two-year war between the United States and Mexico. The Battle of Palo Alto was the first major battle in a series of engagements along the Rio Grande. The Palo Alto battle ensued when Mexican forces decided to overtake Fort Texas, a U.S. base constructed on disputed territory. General Zachary Taylor's 2,300 U.S. troops, sent to stop the bombardment of the fort, encountered 3,400 men under Mexican General Mariano Arista. The resulting cannon battle produced 52 U.S. and 325 Mexican casualties. The battle demonstrated the superior strength of American firepower and the value of academy-educated U.S. military leaders. At the same time, it caused despair among Mexican troops, who had felt they could meet the enemy on even terms.

As a relative newcomer to the National Park Service, Palo Alto Battlefield National Historic Site is still under development. A visitor center that opened in late 2003 near the battle site offers exhibits and brochures to help interpret the importance of the battle and the history of the Mexican War. A fifteen-minute audiovisual presentation provides an overview of the battle. A 1/2-mile trail leads from the visitor center to an overlook of the battlefield. Daily ranger-led programs are offered seasonally, with schedules available at the visitor center. The remains of the original Fort Texas, later named Fort Brown, are on the bank of the Rio Grande near the University of Texas at Brownsville.

ENTRANCE FEE: No charge.

FACILITIES: The visitor center offers rest rooms and drinking water. Food service and lodging are nearby the historic site.

CAMPING: Numerous private campgrounds are in the Brownsville area.

SAN ANTONIO MISSIONS
NATIONAL HISTORICAL PARK

2202 Roosevelt Avenue
San Antonio, TX 78210-4919
(210) 534–8833 Headquarters
(210) 932–1001 Visitor Center
saan_superintendent@nps.gov
www.nps.gov/saan

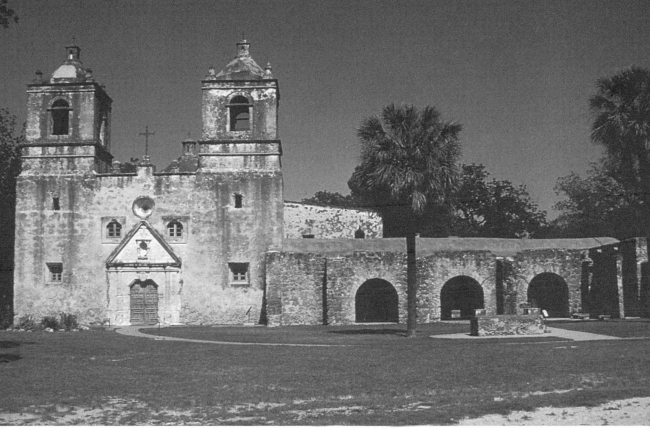

Mission Concepción, San Antonio Missions National Historical Park

San Antonio Missions National Historical Park comprises 835 acres and was authorized in 1978 to preserve four Spanish frontier missions that were part of a colonization system stretching across the Spanish Southwest in the eighteenth century. The park also includes a historic dam and aqueduct and the ranch associated with Mission Espada (Rancho de las Cabras) near Floresville, Texas. The missions are in south San Antonio along the San Antonio River.

To extend the Spanish culture and propagate the Catholic faith, in the seventeenth, eighteenth, and nineteenth centuries Spain introduced missions from California to Florida. Included in this expansion was a chain of missions established in the eighteenth century along the San Antonio River. These missions provided a link between the missions of East Texas and other Franciscan missions in Mexico. The missions served primarily as religious centers and training grounds for Indians to learn the Spanish culture. Indians who lived at the missions came from a number of hunting and gathering bands. These missions flourished in the mid-1700s, but by the end of the century, the Franciscans had opted to secularize them, turning them over to the local community. The combination of acculturation, intermarriage, and the impact of European diseases had reduced the need for the missions. By 1824 secularization was complete, with mission lands distributed among the mission Indians and the churches transferred to the secular clergy.

The historical park includes four missions along the San Antonio River, south of the city of San Antonio. Except for Mission Espada, which lies just south of I–410, the missions are located between city center and Interstate 410, which loops around San Antonio. A marked driving trail to all of the areas begins in downtown San Antonio at Mission San Antonio de Valero (the

SAN ANTONIO MISSIONS NATIONAL HISTORICAL PARK

Alamo). Tour buses with "hop on, hop off" service are available from downtown (near the Alamo) to Missions Concepción and San José. The missions are open daily from 9:00 A.M. to 5:00 P.M., except Thanksgiving, Christmas, and New Year's Day. A wheelchair is available at each mission, but mobility-impaired visitors may have some difficulty with accessibility at Mission San Juan and Mission Espada.

North of Mission Espada is an acequia system that provided irrigation water to crops that were grown at the mission. The system consists of a dam, gravity-flow ditches, and one of the oldest arched Spanish aqueducts in the United States. The system continues to provide water to nearby farms.

ENTRANCE FEE: No charge.

FACILITIES: The park visitor center is at Mission San José. Restaurants, lodging, and picnic facilities are available near the historical park. Rest rooms and drinking water are available in the missions. Each of the major sites in the park is wheelchair accessible, and a wheelchair is available for loan at each site.

CAMPING: No camping is available in the park, although commercial camping facilities are located nearby.

UTAH

STATE TOURIST INFORMATION
(800) 200–1160
www.utah.com

ARCHES NATIONAL PARK
P.O. Box 907
Moab, UT 84532-0907
(435) 719–2299
(435) 719–2319 (TTY)
archinfo@nps.gov
www.nps.gov/arch

Arches National Park was established as a national monument in 1929 (changed to a national park in 1971) to preserve 76,519 acres encompassing the country's largest collection of brilliantly colored natural stone arches, spires, windows, and pinnacles. The park is in southeast Utah on U.S. 191, 5 miles northwest of Moab or 28 miles southeast of I–70.

The rock that now presents such beautiful scenery was originally deposited as sand nearly 150 million years ago. This 300-foot layer was eventually formed into rock after being buried by even more sand. Later, the hardened layers of rock were uplifted and cracked. The top stone eroded away, and exposed Entrada Sandstone began to form into shapes that can be seen today. Carved out of red rock by years of rain, frost, and running water, the resulting shapes resemble nearly any fantasy a visitor can imagine. In some areas, the stone is softer and the weathering is more rapid. This results in shallow canyons and fins (freestanding sandstone walls). Arches is particularly spectacular after a summer shower, when streams turn into waterfalls.

The visitor center, located at the main entrance in the southern end of the park, is a recommended stop for the museum and slide program it provides. In addition, visitors may obtain information on activities such as guided walks, sight-seeing, and hiking. A road guide is available.

N
W · E
S

Devils Garden

Klondike Bluffs

(2-wheel drive)

Salt Valley

(4-wheel drive)

Fiery Furnace Viewpoint

Salt Valley Overlook

Wolfe Ranch

Delicate Arch

Delicate Arch Viewpoint

Panorama Point

To 191

Willow Flats (4-wheel drive)

Balanced Rock

The Windows Section

The Great Wall

Petrified Dunes

Courthouse Towers

To 70

Park Ave. Trail

La Sal Mountains Viewpoint

Visitor Center

Colorado River

128

To Fisher Towers

191

279

To Potash Mine

191

To Moab

Twenty-three miles of paved roads permit visitors to see much of Arches by car. A paved road begins at the visitor center and ends in the north part of the park. An 8-mile dirt road then continues to Klondike Bluffs in the northwest corner. Klondike Bluffs offers a moderate half-day hike into a remote backcountry area of fins, which features the massive Tower Arch. Paved roads run to the Windows Section in the east-central part of the park and to Delicate Arch trail-head and viewpoint. The Windows Section is an amazing spectacle of arches, offering close-up views from the road and easy 1-mile round-trip walks for closer viewing. A few unimproved roads for four-wheel-drive vehicles are located throughout the park.

Outside the park, State Highway 128 between the park entrance and Moab takes the motorist in a northeasterly direction along the Colorado River toward I–70. If time permits, be sure to take this drive as it presents some beautiful scenery.

Hiking trails leave from various points along the main road. The most popular for visitors with only a short time to spare is the leisurely 1-mile walk (each way) through Park Avenue. This worthwhile hike goes through a narrow corridor surrounded by high red-rock walls. Parking lots are located at each end of the trail. The Devils Garden Trail provides access to Landscape Arch, one of the longest natural arches in the world. This trail is a well-maintained gravel path for 1 mile, then becomes primitive for a moderate 7-mile round-trip hike through fins and canyons. Hikers should be aware that daytime temperatures during the summer may reach more than 100 degrees Fahrenheit. High temperatures and low humidity make it necessary for hikers to carry a minimum of 1 gallon of water per person for the full hike.

Perhaps the single most scenic and best-known feature of Arches National Park is Delicate Arch. This isolated formation is located amid bowls and domes. Also within view are the top of canyon walls of the Colorado River and the peaks of the La Sal Mountains. Delicate Arch is reached by means of a 1.2-mile paved road and a 1.5-mile foot trail. A drive on the paved road to Delicate Arch Viewpoint provides a look across a canyon for a distant view of the arch.

Naturalist-guided walks are made regularly through the Fiery Furnace area (three hours, 2 miles) from mid-March through October, when nightly campfire programs are also presented. The Fiery Furnace walk takes hikers through a labyrinth of red-rock fins leading deep into the Furnace, where a surprise arch may wait. On these walks the park naturalists share their knowledge of the wildlife and natural features that make Arches a unique national park. Visitors should be prepared with good walking shoes, a hat, and water. Reservations and a fee are required for joining the guided walks and must be made at the visitor center.

ENTRANCE FEE: $10.00 per vehicle or $5.00 per person; good for seven days.

FACILITIES: No food service or lodging is available within the park. Grocery stores, restaurants, service stations, and motels are available a few miles south of the park in Moab. Modern rest rooms and drinking water are provided at both the visitor center and the campground year-round. Picnic areas are located at the visitor center, Balanced Rock, and Devils Garden.

CAMPING: A single improved campground (fifty-two spaces) is located 18 miles north of the park entrance in the Devils Garden area. Tables, grills, and flush toilets (no dump station) are available. Both short and longer hiking trails originate at the campground.

BRYCE CANYON NATIONAL PARK

P.O. Box 170001
Bryce Canyon, UT 84717-0001
(435) 834–5322
brca_reception_area@nps.gov
www.nps.gov/brca

Bryce Canyon National Park comprises 35,835 acres. It was authorized as a national monument in 1923 and changed to a national park in 1928. Bryce contains numerous alcoves cut into cliffs along the eastern edge of the Paunsaugunt Plateau. Bordering this winding cliff line is a badlands of vivid colors and fragile forms. The park is located in southwestern Utah and is most easily reached via U.S. 89. Turn east on Utah 12, 7 miles south of Panguitch and drive 17 miles to Utah 63 and the park entrance.

Bryce Canyon is a high section of the Colorado Plateau containing rock strata from the Tertiary and Quaternary chapters of geologic history. Formed from compacted sediments, this area caps a sequence of rock layers—the most ancient of which are seen in the Grand Canyon. The massive sandstone boulders that represent the middle history may be seen in nearby Zion National Park. At Bryce these earlier rock formations remain buried.

The cliffs in the park are the result of an accumulation of sand, silt, and lime washed into inland lakes and compacted into layers of rock. Later, the lands were uplifted to mountainous heights, and persistent erosion widened gaps and fractures. The resulting color and shapes of the rock formations are Bryce's most outstanding sights.

A visitor center near the entrance provides a slide program and exhibits to help explain the history and geology of the area. A schedule of the park's various programs is posted at the visitor center.

For those with a limited amount of time, a short tour of four excellent viewpoints may be completed within one hour. Sunset Point, Inspiration Point, Bryce Point, and Paria View form a scenic concentration of sculptured red rocks. Trailers should be unhooked and parked at the parking area outside the park or at your campsite prior to the tour.

A variety of hiking trails is available for visitors. These include the Navajo Loop Trail (1½ miles, one and a half hours) and the Navajo and Peekaboo Loops combined (5 miles, three to four hours) starting at Sunset Point; the Queens Garden Trail (1.7 miles, one and a half hours) beginning at Sunrise Point; Tower Bridge Trail (3 miles, three hours) starting north of Sunrise Point; and the Fairyland Loop Trail (8 miles, four to five hours) beginning at Fairyland or north of Sunrise Point. For the hardy, the Under-the-Rim Trail extends from Bryce Point to Rainbow Point (23 miles). During the summer, ranger-guided programs are offered daily at various points in the park. Activities include geology talks, a Rim Walk near the lodge, and evening campfire programs. A schedule of conducted activities is posted at the visitor center. Morning and afternoon horseback trips are available from a concessioner and begin at the corral near the lodge. For information, call (435) 679–8665 or (435) 834–5500.

ENTRANCE FEE: $20.00 per vehicle; good for seven days. A $5.00 permit is required for anyone planning to stay overnight in the backcountry (good for fourteen days).

FACILITIES: Bryce Canyon Lodge, near the rim of Bryce amphitheater, offers three types of sleeping accommodations from April 1 through November 1. Most of the rooms are in cabins or motel-type buildings, with a few suites on the second floor of the attractive main lodge. For information or reservations, write Xanterra Parks and Resorts, 14001 East Iliff Avenue, Suite 600,

BRYCE CANYON NATIONAL PARK

To 89

12

12

Shakespear Point

63

N
W   E
S

Visitor Center

Fairland Point

North

Sunrise Point Overlook

Sunset

Sunset Point Overlook

To Tropic

Inspiration Point

Bryce Point

Swamp Canyon

Paria View

Piracy Point

Farview Point

Under-the-Rim Trail

Natural Bridge

Agua Canyon

Ponderosa Point

Black Birch Canyon

Rainbow Point

Yovimpa Point

Aurora, CO 80014. Call (303) 297–2757, or check out the Web site at www.brycecanyonlodge. com. The main lodge building has a dining room, post office, and gift shop. A store near the Sunrise Point parking area sells groceries and offers pay showers and a laundromat. The nearest hospital is in Panguitch, 26 miles away.

CAMPING: North Campground (109 spaces) is immediately east of the visitor center, and Sunset Campground (109 spaces, one group camp) is 2 miles south. Both provide tables, grills, and flush toilets. The North Campground has a dump station, is closer to the park's developed facilities, and generally fills first.

CANYONLANDS NATIONAL PARK

2282 South West Resource Boulevard
Moab, UT 84532
(435) 719–2313
canyinfo@nps.gov
www.nps.gov/cany

Canyonlands National Park comprises 337,598 acres and was established in 1964 to protect a geological wonderland of rocks, spires, and mesas. The park is located in east central Utah and is reached via Utah 191 and its paved extensions.

Canyonlands is an outstanding and unique national park. Its incredible sandstone landscape has been shaped over a period of 300 million years by oceans, winds, and floods. A portion of the park is built on a 1-mile-thick layer of rock and sand covering 3,000 feet of pure salt. The salt was left after the outlet of an inland salt sea was blocked by mountains, and evaporation concentrated the brine into layers of salt. As the salt dissolved and was carried away by underground water, the surface sandstone slowly settled and formed long, narrow, straight canyons (the Needles District).

One of the many spectacular sights in the park is the merging of the Colorado and Green Rivers at the confluence. Commercially operated float trips, led by licensed guides, are available down either river. Write the park for a list of available concession trips. Private groups with proper equipment and experience may attempt the trip upon obtaining a permit (fee charged) from the superintendent.

The Needles District in the southern portion of the park contains a "forest" of rock spires. Within the district, Salt Creek and Horse Canyon expose graceful walls and glimpses of past ancestral Puebloan history in the form of rock art and ruins. You must travel 35 miles on a paved road through magnificent canyon country to reach this area. All passenger cars must stop at Elephant Hill, a 40 percent grade traversed only by high-clearance, four-wheel-drive vehicles. Tours can be obtained or jeeps may be rented in nearby communities. Be sure to stop at Newspaper Rock Recreation Site when entering this area on Highway 211.

The Maze District, lying west of the Green and lower Colorado Rivers, is the least accessible portion of the park. Non-four-wheel-drive vehicles can reach the ranger station at Hans Flat most of the time, but the backcountry must be approached by four-wheel-drive vehicles or on foot. Much of the area that is accessible only on foot has sheer-walled canyons that twist and

View from Inspiration Point, Bryce Canyon National Park (opposite page)

CANYONLANDS NATIONAL PARK

To Moab ↑
313
To Moab ↗

Mineral Bottom
Mineral Rd. (Horsethief Trail)

HORSESHOE CANYON UNIT

Dead Horse Point State Park
Potash Rd.

ISLAND IN THE SKY

Whale Rock

Shafer Trail Rd.

N
W — E
S

Willow Flat

Green River Overlook

White Rim Rd.

Colorado River

Glen Canyon National Recreation Area

Grand View Point Overlook

Green River

To 24

Hans Flat Ranger Station

Colorado River Overlook

Maze Overlook

THE MAZE

Big Spring Canyon Overlook

Needles Outpost

Standing Rocks

Devil's Lane

Squaw Flat

Salt Creek

211

The Fins

THE NEEDLES

Colorado River

Lake Powell

Salt Creek

To Hite Marina

For some dirt roads, use 4-wheel drive only

wind in a wild manner. Some outstanding pictograph panels are found here. Contact park headquarters for information before visiting the Maze District.

In the north district of the park, Island in the Sky overlooks the remarkable array of landforms to the south that encompass the 40-mile-wide erosional basin of the Green and Colorado Rivers. A paved road makes this area completely accessible year-round. From overlooks, visitors can view the White Rim formation, 1,000 feet below, and catch glimpses of the Colorado and Green Rivers 1,000 feet below the White Rim. The White Rim Road offers more than 100 miles of four-wheel-drive or mountain bike travel into the backcountry. Shafer Trail Road, for which a four-wheel-drive vehicle is advised, is a thrilling route involving some "testy" driving.

The Horseshoe Canyon Unit is 32 miles east of Utah Highway 24 via a graded dirt road. This area includes sheer sandstone walls, cottonwood groves, and what is considered by many to be some of the most significant rock art in North America. The most spectacular panel, The Great Gallery, includes life sized figures with intricate designs. There are no roads into this part of the park, but there is a trailhead just outside the park on land administered by the Bureau of Land Management. Visitors may camp at the trailhead, which has vault toilets but no water.

ENTRANCE FEE: $10.00 per vehicle or $5.00 per person; good for seven days. Permits must be purchased for four-wheel-drive day trips into Horse Canyon, Salt Creek to Peekaboo, and Lavender Canyon, overnight backcountry trips, and overnight trips on the rivers.

FACILITIES: No overnight accommodations or food services are available within the park. Monticello, Moab, Green River, and Hanksville are the nearest towns providing a full range of services. Rest rooms are available in the Needles District at the visitor center and Squaw Flat Campground.

CAMPING: Squaw Flat Campground (twenty-six spaces, three group sites, fee) in the Needles District provides tables, grills, vault toilets, and water. Willow Flat Campground at Island in the Sky (twelve sites) has picnic tables, grills, and toilets, but no water. Primitive campsites without water are located in four-wheel-drive areas.

CAPITOL REEF NATIONAL PARK

HC 70, Box 15
Torrey, UT 84775-9602
(435) 425–3791
CARE_Interpretation@nps.gov
www.nps.gov/care

Capitol Reef National Park comprises 241,904 acres and was established to protect one of the largest exposed monoclines in North America. Here narrow, highwalled gorges cut through a 100-mile uplift of sandstone cliffs with highly colored sedimentary formations. Capitol Reef remains one of the undiscovered treasures of the National Park System. The park is located in south-central Utah, with the visitor center 37 miles west of Hanksville on Utah 24.

CAPITOL REEF NATIONAL PARK

The geology of this high-desert land is derived from millions of years of wind and water erosion. Millions of years ago this part of the country was covered by a shallow sea. As the sea gradually retreated, the land changed to a floodplain and then a desert. The alternation between shallow sea and desert occurred many times during ensuing centuries. Water- and wind-borne sediments deposited during these periods slowly hardened into rock layers of varying color, composition, and thickness. Immense geological forces buckled and tilted the rocks into an upwarp called the Waterpocket Fold. Erosional forces have subsequently dissected and sculptured the Fold. Steeply pitching rock layers spring out of the ground across the breadth of the Fold. The normally horizontal geologic column has been tipped nearly on end, allowing park visitors to drive through 200 million years of geologic history in a relatively short distance.

Perhaps the biggest surprise a visitor will encounter is the oasislike nature of the historic Fruita District, the park's headquarters area. The sagebrush flats and desert stand in stark contrast to the lush vegetation made possible by irrigation from the Fremont River and Sulphur Creek. Away from the river the land returns to its true desert state.

Capitol Reef National Park was named, in part, because of the resemblance of its rounded white Navajo sandstone to the Capitol Building in Washington, D.C. The second half of the name originates from a term used by early prospectors to describe a natural barrier to travel. The area was home to Indians and later to Mormon settlers. The first permanent settlement here occurred at Fruita in 1880. This small community supported up to ten families at one time.

Most of the activity at Capitol Reef is located along or near Highway 24, which cuts through the park in an east-west direction. The visitor center offers a slide program and exhibits to help interpret the area. One mile east is the old Fruita schoolhouse, which has been restored and is open to the public on a limited basis. Ancient Fremont Indian petroglyphs can be found ¼ mile east of the school and also about 12 miles south of the visitor center in Capitol Gorge. Interpretive programs take place daily during spring, summer, and fall. Visitors may pick fruit from orchards maintained by the Park Service. Depending on the season, cherries, apricots, apples, pears, and peaches are available. A paved 10-mile scenic drive heads south from the visitor center. A free pamphlet is provided at the fee station.

ENTRANCE FEE: There is a $5.00 fee per vehicle for traveling Scenic Drive beyond the campground.

FACILITIES: No food or lodging is available in the park. Both may be found in the town of Torrey, 11 miles west of the visitor center on Utah 24. A beautiful, shaded picnic area with picnic tables, grills, and drinking water is located just north of the campground. Rest rooms are available at the visitor center, campground, and picnic area.

CAMPING: The park's developed campground (seventy spaces) is 1 mile south of the visitor center. The campground is surrounded by fruit trees and backs up to the Fremont River. Staying there is one of life's great pleasures. The campsites generally fill every night. Primitive campgrounds (no water) are located approximately 35 miles from the visitor center via dirt roads. Inquire at the visitor center for road conditions and directions.

FISHING: Fishing is available at Capitol Reef National Park. A state fishing license is required and may be purchased locally.

CEDAR BREAKS NATIONAL MONUMENT

2390 West Highway 56 #11
Cedar City, UT 84720-4151
(435) 586–9451
cebr_superintendent@nps.gov
www.nps.gov/cebr

Cedar Breaks National Monument, comprising 6,155 acres, was established in 1933 to preserve a huge multicolored amphitheater that is eroding into the 2,000-foot-thick Pink Cliffs. The park is located in southwestern Utah and can be reached via Utah 14, 27 miles from U.S. 89 at Long Valley Junction, and 23 miles from Interstate 15 at Cedar City. It can also be reached from the north via Utah 143 and Parowan (22 miles) or from U.S. 89 at Panguitch via Utah 143 (36 miles). Zion National Park and Bryce Canyon National Park are 73 and 65 miles away, respectively.

The rock layers that form the amphitheater walls at Cedar Breaks were deposited nearly fifty-five million years ago as a limey ooze in shallow freshwater lakes. Later, as the area was uplifted from near sea level to more than 10,000 feet, the westward-facing limestone wall was exposed to the elements. The softer parts of the limestone have been eroded by centuries of rain, wind, snow, and ice, leaving spires and ridges of spectacular shapes. The period of uplifting was accompanied by volcanic eruptions, and lava may be seen along the road between Cedar Breaks and U.S. 89. The colors of the breaks stem from the oxidation of impurities (mainly iron and manganese) contained in the white limestone.

Commonly seen wildlife in the monument includes mule deer, marmots, pikas, red squirrels, and chipmunks. Birds include the Clark's nutcracker, violet-green swallow, white-throated swift, blue grouse, and golden eagle. Wildflowers begin blooming as the snow melts, and the blooms reach a peak during late July. Bristlecone pines up to 1,650 years old grow within the monument.

Depending upon the weather, the season at Cedar Breaks extends from early June to late October. The visitor center, 1 mile inside the south entrance, houses exhibits on geology and life within the park. The visitor center is open from early June through September and into October, depending on the weather. Interpretive presentations are offered daily from late June to Labor Day. Much of the monument may be seen from a 6-mile paved road running north and south along Cedar Breaks Rim. Viewpoints with parking areas are located along the road. A number of trails are scattered along 6-mile Rim Drive. Ramparts Trail (2 miles) begins near the visitor center and leads through forests and meadows to a stand of bristlecone pine on Spectra Point (1 mile from the visitor center). Alpine Pond Trail, a self-guided nature trail, leads to an area containing a pond and many wildflowers. Bristlecone Pine Trail is a short walk at Chessmen Ridge Overlook that takes visitors to a stand of bristlecone and limber pine on the rim. At 11,315 feet above sea level, Brian Head Peak, 2½ miles north of the north entrance in Dixie National Forest, offers an impressive view of the area.

ENTRANCE FEE: $3.00 per person; good for seven days.

FACILITIES: No food service or overnight lodging is available in the park, but both are found in Cedar City (23 miles southwest), Parowan (19 miles north), and Brian Head (8 miles north). Drinking water and flush toilets are available at the visitor center and the campground.

CEDAR BREAKS NATIONAL MONUMENT

To Parowan,
Brian Head, and (15)

(143)

North View

(143)

To (89)

ADAMS BARRIER

ADAMS CANYON

CEDAR BREAKS RIM

Alpine Pond
Trail

THE MEADOWS

Chessmen
Ridge
Overlook

Dixie

National

Forest

CRESCENT HOLLOW

AMPHITHEATER

Sunset
View

THE
BARTIZAN

Point
Supreme

Visitor
Center

Spectra
Point

N

W   E

S

Ramparts
Trail

Point
Supreme
Campground

(148)

To (14) and Cedar City

CAMPING: Point Supreme Campground (thirty spaces) provides tables, grills, water, and flush toilets. The campground is usually open from June 15 to September 15. A number of Forest Service campgrounds are located southeast of Cedar City along Utah Highway 14. There is one Forest Service campground 4 miles south of Parowan off Highway 143.

GOLDEN SPIKE NATIONAL HISTORIC SITE

P.O. Box 897
Brigham City, UT 84302-0897
(435) 471–2209
gosp_superintendent@nps.gov
www.nps.gov/gosp/home.html

Golden Spike National Historic Site comprises 2,200 acres and was authorized by Congress in 1965 to commemorate the joining of the Union Pacific and Central Pacific Railroads on May 10, 1869, to form the first transcontinental railroad. The historic site is located 84 miles northwest of Salt Lake City and 32 miles west of Brigham City.

Although many individuals saw the benefits of a railroad from the Atlantic to the Pacific soon after the development of the steam locomotive, years of debate over the amount of federal financing and the location of an eastern terminus kept the project from commencing. The Pacific Railroad Act, initially signed by President Abraham Lincoln in 1862 and revised two years later, provided that the Union Pacific was to build westward and the Central Pacific eastward. The railroads were given a 400-foot right-of-way through the public domain, twenty sections of land for each mile of completed track, and the loan of government bonds to use as collateral for issuing their own bonds.

The Central Pacific broke ground in January 1863 and the Union Pacific at Omaha in December of the same year. Both railroads experienced manpower shortages until the end of the Civil War, when veterans could be recruited. The Central Pacific helped resolve its labor shortages by hiring Chinese, while the Union Pacific employed European immigrants. It was Congress's intent that the Central Pacific lay track to the California–Nevada border, a point that was later moved 150 miles to the east. Both railroad companies built as fast as possible, which resulted in wasteful parallel grades until it was decided in the spring of 1869 that Ogden, Utah, would be the final junction point. On May 10, 1869, the final section of track was laid, and four precious-metal spikes from California, Nevada, and Arizona were symbolically driven with a silver-plated spike maul. Promontory Summit was the temporary junction until early January 1870, when the deal was completed and the junction moved.

By 1904 a shorter route was completed across Great Salt Lake by the Southern Pacific (which had absorbed the Central Pacific), and little traffic was routed through Promontory. In 1942 the rails were pulled and relaid in military depots such as Defense Depot Ogden, Utah, and the Naval Yards in Hawthorne, Nevada.

A visitor center at the park is open daily from May 1 to September 30 and Wednesday to Sunday, October 1 to April 30. It offers exhibits, slide presentations, and films. Nearly 2 miles of track have been relaid on the original roadbed where the rails were joined in 1869. Two operating replica steam locomotives are in operation from the first weekend in May to Labor Day. Visitor activities include ranger programs, reenactments, the Big Fill Walk, and auto tours.

Several special events take place at the historic site, including the annual May 10 anniversary celebration, the Railroaders Festival (second Saturday in August), and the Railroaders Film Festival and Winter Steam Demonstration (weekend after Christmas).

ENTRANCE FEE: Off-season, $5.00 per vehicle or $3.00 per person; summer (May 1–Labor Day), $7.00 and $4.00; good for seven days.

FACILITIES: No overnight accommodations or food services are available in the park, but both are found in Brigham City and Tremonton. The nearest available gasoline is in Corinne, 26 miles from the site. Water and modern rest rooms are located in the visitor center.

CAMPING: No camping is permitted at the site. Hyrum Lake State Park (thirty-five spaces with flush toilets) is located approximately 14 miles northeast of Brigham City on U.S. Highways 89 and 91. USDA Forest Service Box Elder Campground (pit toilets) is 1 mile east of Brigham City on U.S. 89. Willard Bay State Park and a private campground are located about 5 miles south of Brigham City, and Crystal Springs Resort is approximately 12 miles to the north.

NATURAL BRIDGES NATIONAL MONUMENT

HC 60, Box 1
Lake Powell, UT 84533-0101
(435) 692-1234
nabrinfo@nps.gov
www.nps.gov/nabr

Natural Bridges National Monument comprises approximately 7,500 acres. It was established in 1908 to protect three natural bridges carved from sandstone. The monument is in the southeastern corner of Utah, approximately 4 miles off State Highway 95. Natural Bridges is approached from the east via Highway 95 from Blanding or from the south via Mexican Hat and Highway 261 or from the west via Highway 95 from Hanksville and Hite Crossing.

The making of a natural bridge requires a proper stone with joints or fractures and a desert-type stream with a head of water and sand. In the United States such conditions are most favorable in the Four Corners region of the Southwest. As streams gradually entrench themselves in deep, meandering channels and canyons, they constantly attempt to straighten their courses. During heavy rainstorms, the sand-filled waters batter against the walls in the streambeds. In several places the rock around which a stream winds is so thin that over many centuries a hole is gradually bored through. The result is a natural bridge.

Three natural bridges are highlighted in the monument. Sipapu Bridge (220 feet high, 268-foot span, 31-foot width, 53-foot thickness) has a graceful and symmetrical span with its abutments now far enough from the streambed that the river has little or no cutting effect. Kachina Bridge (210 feet high, 204-foot span, 44-foot width, 93-foot thickness) is the youngest of the three. Its bulk is still being eroded by flood waters in White Canyon. Numerous prehistoric pictographs may be seen on one of its abutments. Owachomo Bridge (106 feet high, 180-foot span, 27-foot width, 9-foot thickness) is the oldest bridge and is no longer eroded by a stream.

A visitor center is located just inside the monument's boundary. A ranger is on duty to answer questions, and a video program is presented upon request. Evening ranger talks are given at the campground during the summer when staffing permits. A paved 9-mile loop road links the trailheads to the three bridges.

ENTRANCE FEE: $6.00 per vehicle or $3.00 per person; good for seven days.

FACILITIES: No food service or lodging is available at the monument. Drinking water and rest rooms are located at the visitor center. The nearest source of gasoline and food is at Blanding, 40 miles away. The nearest overnight accommodations and year-round services are at Blanding and Mexican Hat (45 miles).

CAMPING: A single campground (thirteen sites) is located near the visitor center. There is a combined length limit of 26 feet (including trailers and two vehicles), and only one vehicle per site is permitted. Grills, tables, and pit toilets are available, and rest rooms at the visitor center remain unlocked at night. The campground usually fills in the early afternoon during summer months.

RAINBOW BRIDGE NATIONAL MONUMENT

c/o Glen Canyon National Recreation Area
Box 1507
Page, AZ 86040-1507
(928) 608–6404
Betsy_Scroggs@nps.gov
www.nps.gov/rabr

Rainbow Bridge National Monument was established in 1910 and comprises 160 acres, including the world's largest known natural bridge. Rainbow Bridge is as high as the nation's Capitol and thicker at the top than a three-story building is tall. The monument is located in south-central Utah on the south edge of Glen Canyon National Recreation Area. It is reached only by a 13-mile trail (one-way) from Navajo Mountain Trading Post, a 13-mile trail (one-way) from abandoned Rainbow Lodge, or by boat on Lake Powell. The hiking trails are located on Navajo Reservation land. Permits are required from the Navajo Nation and may be obtained by writing Navajo Nation, Parks & Recreation Department, Box 9000, Window Rock, AZ 86515.

Millions of years ago slow streams flowed south and west across a broad floodplain in this region. Sand and mud were deposited in thin beds that eventually consolidated to form the reddish brown layer that is now exposed beneath Rainbow Bridge. Much later, a change in the climate brought winds that deposited great quantities of sand. The resulting pale orange to reddish brown rock called Navajo sandstone is the material from which Rainbow Bridge and Bridge Canyon have been carved.

Following this period, the next hundred million years saw the area change from desert to swamp to lakes, and the Navajo sandstone was buried under more than 5,000 feet of strata. Approximately sixty million years ago, the region was gradually uplifted, and streams began cutting into the rock layers. Rainbow Bridge was formed during this period by Bridge Creek, which flows today from Navajo Mountain northwest to Lake Powell. (For a short description of the formation of a natural bridge, see the narrative on Natural Bridges National Monument.)

Water dripping into pools near the bottom of Rainbow Bridge Canyon comes from rainwater seeping through the porous Navajo sandstone. Once it reaches the underlying impervious rock layers, it accumulates and eventually seeps out along the walls of the canyon as springs. Rainwater also causes dark streaks on the side of the arch by washing iron oxide down from the top.

Most visitors to Rainbow Bridge National Monument take the water route of approximately 50 miles from Wahweap, Bullfrog, or Halls Crossing to the landing in Bridge Canyon, then walk about ½ mile (depending on the fluctuating lake level) up the canyon to the bridge. For visitors bringing their own boats, launching ramps are available at Wahweap, Halls Crossing, Bullfrog, and Hite. For visitors interested in the trail trip, inquiry should be made as to trail conditions and availability of water and supplies before beginning. This is a difficult hike, and the roadway leading to the trail is only accessed by high-clearance vehicles.

ENTRANCE FEE: $10.00 per vehicle or $3.00 per person, which includes Glen Canyon National Recreation Area.

FACILITIES: There are no facilities within the monument. The nearest town with complete facilities is Page, Arizona, on U.S. 89. Concessioners at Wahweap, Halls Crossing, Bullfrog, Dangling Rope, and Hite sell boating and camping supplies. Tour-boat trips are provided at Halls Crossing, Bullfrog, and Wahweap. A floating complex anchored in Dangling Rope Canyon contains a refueling station, a small store for camping supplies, and a ranger station.

CAMPING: Although picnicking is permitted at Rainbow Bridge, there is no camping within the monument and no picnic area located within the monument boundary. No water is available. Modern National Park Service campgrounds are located at Wahweap, Bullfrog, and Halls Crossing as part of the Glen Canyon National Recreation Area.

FISHING: Fishing is prohibited within the monument. Striped, largemouth, and smallmouth bass, black crappie, and catfish are caught in Lake Powell. A Utah and/or Arizona fishing license is required.

TIMPANOGOS CAVE NATIONAL MONUMENT

R.R. 3, Box 200
American Fork, UT 84003
(801) 756–5239
tica_ranger_activities@nps.gov
www.nps.gov/tica

The Timpanogos Cave System was set aside as a national monument in 1922 to preserve a unique limestone cave system. The caves are known for their unusual origin, rare formations, beautiful coloration, and rich human history. The monument is near Utah's two largest population centers—Salt Lake City to the north and Provo/Orem to the south—9 miles east of I–15 on State Route 92.

It is theorized that the caves in the Timpanogos system were dissolved by a weak acid that was created by rising thermal water mixing with the water table. As the Wasatch Mountains rose, the caves drained and calcite formations began to be deposited. The caves are now located more than 1,000 feet above the current water table.

The caves can be reached by hiking on a beautiful 1½-mile paved trail that climbs 1,065 feet. The average round-trip takes about three hours and offers some outstanding views of American Fork Canyon and Utah Valley. The cave system consists of three caves connected by two constructed tunnels. The first, Hansen Cave, was discovered by Martin Hansen in 1887 when he followed cougar tracks to its entrance. Timpanogos Cave was discovered in 1914 by two fourteen-year-old boys, James Gough and Frank Johnson. Finally, Middle Cave was spotted from across the canyon in 1921 by Wayne and Heber Hansen.

The caves are profusely decorated with forty-two different types of cave formations. These formations are highlighted by many natural colors, including purples, greens, and yellows. Small lakes reflect the beauty of these exquisite caves.

A visitor center, located near the parking lot and trailhead, explains the origin and history of the caves. The caves are open from 7:00 A.M. to 5:30 P.M. daily, mid-May to late October, weather permitting. The Introduction to Caving tour takes visitors to a section of Hansen Cave that has been closed to the public since 1924. Between Memorial Day and Labor Day cave tours are frequently sold out by early afternoon. To avoid problems, arrive early in the day or purchase tickets in advance. Beginning each May tour tickets can be purchased in advance by calling (801) 756–5238.

ENTRANCE FEE: American Fork Canyon, $3.00; good for three days. Cave tour fees are $6.00 for adults; children ages six to fifteen, $5.00; ages three to five, $3.00; ages two and younger, free.

FACILITIES: There are two picnic areas with water, tables, grills, and rest rooms. A concession sells food and souvenirs.

CAMPING: No camping facilities are available in the monument, but the USDA Forest Service provides a number of campgrounds nearby in the Uinta National Forest.

FISHING: Fishing is permitted in the American Fork River. A Utah fishing license is required.

ZION NATIONAL PARK
Springdale, UT 84767-1099
(435) 772-3256
zion_park_information@nps.gov
www.nps.gov/zion

Zion National Park boasts nearly 147,000 acres of colorful canyons and mesas that create phenomenal shapes and landscapes. Zion is located in southwestern Utah, with the south entrance approximately 150 miles northwest of Las Vegas, Nevada, via I–15 and Utah 9. The southern section of the park is accessed by Utah Highway 9, while access to the northern section is by paved road (Exit 40) off I–15.

Zion National Park formed through millions of years of erosion from water, gravity, and the persistent force of the Virgin River. Scenic drives and trails provide spectacular vistas of canyons, sculptured rocks, cliffs, and rivers. The park is one of the most beautiful in the National Park system and is Utah's oldest national park (established in 1909).

The park's main road, the scenic Zion–Mt. Carmel Highway, passes through two tunnels as it winds between the park's south and east entrances. This road is open to private vehicles year-round, although oversize vehicle restrictions apply for the narrow, 1-mile-long tunnel. Tunnel height at the east entrance is 11 feet 4 inches. The 6-mile Zion Canyon Scenic Drive leads north through Zion Canyon and past Zion Lodge. Scenic points from the road are The Sentinel, Court of the Patriarchs, Mountain of the Sun, and Great White Throne. This road is closed to private vehicles from early April to the end of October, when a free public tram operates. The park transportation system incorporates two loops, one from the south end of Springdale to the park entrance and another from the new Zion Canyon Visitor Center at the south end of the park to the end of the scenic drive. Both routes include scheduled stops at various points. Parking at the Zion Canyon Visitor Center is often full from 10:00 A.M. to 3:00 P.M., when visitors will need to park in Springdale and ride the free town shuttle to the park. The park entrance fee includes use of the transportation system. In the park's northwest section, Kolob Canyons Road is a 5.2-mile paved road originating from I–15. This road may be closed by winter snows. A paved road

To Cedar City and
Salt Lake City

14

EXIT 40

KOLOB
CANYONS
SECTION

N
W E
S

Lava
Point

15

ZION
CANYON SECTION

Kolob Road

Zion Canyon
Scenic Drive

9

Mt. Carmel
Junction

17

Museum
South
Entrance
Springdale

South
Watchman

East
Entrance

89

Virgin

9

Hurricane

9

59

(closed during winter) connects the town of Virgin with the Kolob Canyons Section to the north. The narrow road leads to Lava Point and includes steep grades.

One of Zion's most popular visitor activities is hiking, and a great variety of trails wander through this scenic park. The trails range in difficulty from paved loops that can be easily walked in a half hour to strenuous routes that require a full day to traverse steep grades with sharp drop-offs. It is important to evaluate your physical condition as well as the time available before starting out on a hike. Also remember that summer days are often quite hot. Rangers can recommend trails that are most likely to be compatible with your time and abilities. Two popular paved trails can be walked in an hour or less: One leads to Weeping Rock (round trip: ½ mile, half hour) and begins at the Weeping Rock parking lot; the other goes to Lower Emerald Pools (round trip: 1.2 mile, one hour) and begins across the road from Zion Lodge. A longer trail (round trip: 2 miles, two hours) to Middle Emerald Pools begins at the same location. Riverside Walk (round trip: 2 miles, ninety minutes) is a paved trail that begins at the Temple of Sinawava and follows the Virgin River along the bottom of a narrow canyon. This walk provides views of hanging gardens, one of the park's most popular attractions. Longer trails begin at the Weeping Rock parking lot and the Grotto picnic area. The park's northwest Kolob Canyons Section also offers trails. All overnight hikes and hikes through Zion Narrows and other narrow canyons require a permit.

The Zion Canyon Visitor Center, near the south entrance, has exhibits and information on the park's natural history and geology. In addition, a schedule of events and orientation programs is available. The Zion Human History Museum has exhibits on how humans have interacted with Zion and a film orienting visitors to the park. Evening talks are given spring through fall at the lodge and campgrounds. Ranger-guided walks and hikes originate at various points around the park. Reservations for horseback trips within the park may be made at the corrals near the Zion Lodge or by calling (435) 679–8665.

ENTRANCE FEE: $20 per vehicle or $10 per person; good for seven days. Backcountry permits are $10 to $20, depending on the size of the group. A "tunnel escort" is required for all vehicles and trailers 7 feet 10 inches wide and/or 11 feet 4 inches tall. The fee for this is $10.

FACILITIES: Zion Lodge has cabin and motel accommodations and is open all year. For information or reservations, write Xanterra Park and Resorts, 14001 East Iliff Avenue, Suite 300, Aurora, CO 80014. Call (303) 297–2757; fax (303) 297–3175; www.zionlodge.com. A dining room and a cafe are also available at the lodge. Additional food service and accommodations are located in nearby communities. Because of high demand and limited space, reservations are strongly encouraged for facilities within 25 miles of the park. Rest rooms and drinking water are available at the lodge, visitor centers, and both campgrounds. Picnic sites are located at the Zion Canyon Visitor Center, the Grotto in Zion Canyon, and at the end of the Kolob Canyons Road in the northwest section of the park.

CAMPING: The two major campgrounds at Zion are near the south entrance. Watchman (160 spaces, some electrical hookups, and seven group campsites) and South (128 spaces) each have tables, grills, flush toilets, and dump stations. Both border the Virgin River. In addition, both are near a private store lying just outside the park. Watchman camping sites can be reserved (800–365–2267; reservations.nps.gov). Lava Point (six spaces) is a primitive campground off the Kolob Canyons Road and near the West Rim Trail that has pit toilets and no water.

FISHING: Fishing is allowed year-round in the Virgin River below Zion Narrows but is poor because of frequent flooding and seasonal fluctuations in water levels. The river is not stocked, and fishing success is very low. A Utah fishing license is required.

WASHINGTON

STATE TOURIST INFORMATION
(800) 544–1800
www.tourism.wa.gov

EBEY'S LANDING NATIONAL HISTORICAL RESERVE

908 NW Alexander Street
P.O. Box 774
Coupeville, WA 98239-0774
(360) 678–6084
ebla_administration@nps.gov
www.nps.gov/ebla

Ebey's Landing comprises more than 17,000 acres, including the waters of Penn Cove. It was established as the first national historical reserve in 1978 to preserve a rural community providing a historical record of Puget Sound from its nineteenth-century exploration and settlement to the present. The reserve is located in northwestern Washington on Whidbey Island, about a two-hour drive from Seattle. It is reached from Mount Vernon via the town of Oak Harbor and State Highway 20. The reserve may also be reached by ferry from either Port Townsend or Mukilteo (via Highway 525).

Whidbey Island is the largest of more than 600 islands in Puget Sound. The island was named by Captain George Vancouver, who, while exploring this region in 1792, wrote of the beautiful, open, fertile lands. Subsequent years saw the Hudson's Bay Company established near present-day Olympia, but English rule came to an end with the Treaty of 1846, which gave the Oregon Territory to the United States. This treaty opened the Pacific Northwest to settlement. Settlers in wagon trains soon followed the Oregon Trail west and established homesteads, then farms and communities, around Puget Sound. People also arrived by sailing ship, as did most early settlers of central Whidbey Island.

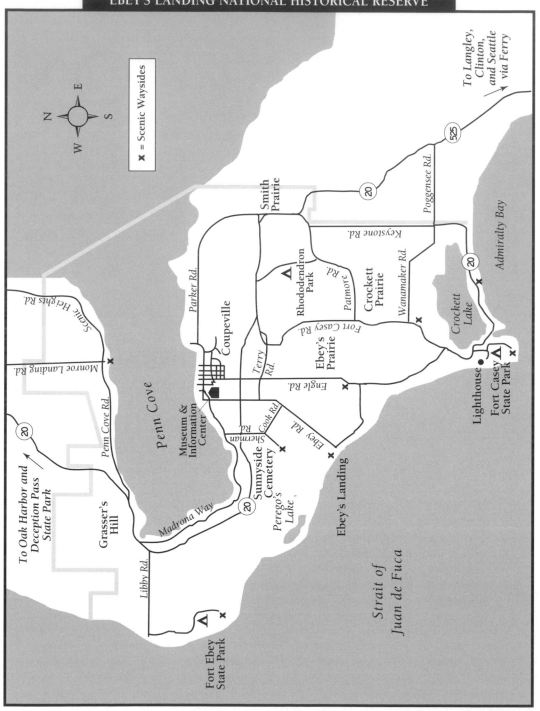

Ebey's Landing National Historical Reserve provides a glimpse of this early settlement. The town of Coupeville was settled by New England sea captains. There are forty-eight historic structures, including many of the sea captains' homes, in the town. An additional fifty structures on the National Register are outside Coupeville but within the reserve. The Historical Society maintains a museum of settler life, and there is National Park Service information in the museum.

Ebey's Landing, where the island's first European settler landed, is near Coupeville. The beach and a bluff hiking trail are part of the Washington state park system. There are spectacular views of the Olympic Mountains and Puget Sound from the beach and the trail. Several scenic waysides offer beautiful views of open waters, farmland, and historic structures.

The open fields between Coupeville and Ebey's Landing are natural prairies that were created and maintained over many centuries by Native Americans who harvested plants important to their diet. The farmers who live here today, many themselves descendants of early settlers, continue to plow land claims established by their families in the 1800s. Many of the farmhouses that dot the prairie are the original homes or are built on the foundations of the homes of the first settlers.

There are two state parks within the reserve. Fort Casey, an early-twentieth-century coastal-defense fort, has a lighthouse (with interpretive center), gun emplacements, and a beach to explore. Fort Ebey, established during World War II, offers beach hiking, picnicking, and exploration of World War II gun emplacements.

ENTRANCE FEE: No charge.

FACILITIES: Food and lodging are available in Coupeville.

CAMPING: Fort Casey State Park (360–678–4519) has thirty-five sites with tables, grills, and flush toilets, but no showers. Fort Ebey State Park (360–678–4636) has fifty sites and one group camp with tables, grills, flush toilets, and showers. Both parks offer fishing and swimming. Camping is also available at Rhododendron Park.

FISHING: Surf fishing and a boat ramp are available at Fort Casey State Park. A boat ramp is at Coupeville.

FORT VANCOUVER NATIONAL HISTORIC SITE

612 East Reserve Street
Vancouver, WA 98661-3811
(360) 696–7655
fava_superintendent@nps.gov
www.nps.gov/fova

Fort Vancouver National Historic Site was authorized as part of the National Park Service in 1948. It comprises 175 acres commemorating what was the economic, political, social, and cultural hub of the Pacific Northwest. Fort Vancouver is located within the city limits of Vancouver, Washington, and is reached by exiting east off I–5 at the Mill Plain Boulevard interchange and then following signs to the visitor center on East Evergreen. From I–205, exit on Washington 14, drive west 6 miles, then take I–5 north and exit at Mill Plain.

After 1800, traders from Canada, England, the United States, and several European countries were competing for the fur resources of the Pacific Northwest. After years of struggle a British firm, Hudson's Bay Company, gained supremacy in the region. In an attempt to strengthen its claim to the territory, in 1824 the company decided to move its western headquarters from a location at the mouth of the Columbia River to a site about 100 miles upstream. It was here that Fort Vancouver was built.

The fort became the center of activity in the Pacific Northwest. Not only did it serve as the headquarters to a huge commercial empire, it was also the center of a farming and manufacturing community and provided much of the cultural and social life for the Oregon Country. At the height of its importance (1840–1846), the fort included twenty-two major structures within a palisade of upright logs. In addition, thirty to fifty wooden dwellings were located on the plain to the west and southwest of the stockade.

The Treaty of 1846 between the United States and Great Britain established the forty-ninth parallel as the southern boundary of Canada and placed Fort Vancouver on American soil. A U.S. Army camp was established nearby in 1849, and in 1860 the fort was abandoned by the Hudson's Bay Company. Over the next six years, the palisade and the structures within were torn down and burned.

The historic site is open daily from 10:00 A.M. to 6:00 P.M. Monday to Thursday, and until 8:00 P.M. on Friday, Saturday, and Sunday from Memorial Day Weekend through Labor Day. The remainder of the year it is open daily from 9:30 A.M. to 4:00 P.M., except Thanksgiving, December 24 and 25, and New Year's Day. The visitor center contains a museum and a small store and offers three different audiovisual presentations, including a fifteen-minute presentation specifically about the fort, a twenty-minute presentation about Lewis and Clark in Washington, and a twenty-three-minute presentation about the Vancouver National Historic Reserve (which includes Fort Vancouver). The National Park Service has reconstructed the palisade and some of its buildings. Guides are available to take visitors through the reconstructed chief factor's house, kitchen, bakehouse, blacksmith shop, Indian trade shop, carpenter shop, fur store, dispensary, and bastion. Additionally, there is an 1845 period garden in the adjacent Kanaka Village area that has signage telling the stories of the labors of the original fort.

ENTRANCE FEE: $5.00 per family or $3.00 per adult; children ages sixteen and under are free; good for seven days.

FACILITIES: No food or lodging is provided by the Park Service, but both are available nearby. Rest rooms and drinking water are available in both the visitor center and the fort. A picnic shelter is next to the visitor center.

CAMPING: No camping is permitted at the site. Battleground Lake State Park (thirty-five regular sites, fifteen walk-in tent sites) provides tables, grills, flush toilets, showers, swimming, and fishing, but no hookups. To reach the state park, drive 20 miles northwest of Vancouver via I–5 and State Highway 502. Directions are available at the Fort Vancouver Visitor Center.

KLONDIKE GOLD RUSH NATIONAL HISTORICAL PARK

117 South Main Street
Seattle, WA 98104-2540
(206) 553–7220
KLSE_Ranger_Activities@nps.gov
www.nps.gov/klse

Klondike Gold Rush National Historical Park was established in 1979 to commemorate the 1897 gold rush to the Yukon. The park is divided into two sections, with the main area in Skagway, Alaska (see Klondike Gold Rush National Historical Park in the Alaska section of this book), and an interpretive center in Seattle. The Seattle visitor center is downtown at 117 South Main Street, two blocks north of Seahawks Stadium. From I–5, take Exit 164 (northbound) or Exit 165 (southbound). Parking is available on the street and at several private lots near the visitor center.

Attempting to recover from the national financial panic of 1893, Seattle aggressively competed with Portland, Tacoma, and Vancouver to secure a position as the main portal through which thousands of gold seekers would pour on their way to the Yukon, where gold had been discovered in July 1897. Through promotion and a location at the terminus of three transcontinental railroads, Seattle proved successful in its quest and became the chief outfitting and transportation center for the miners and others who sought riches in the Yukon. Most took steamers north from Seattle to Skagway, Alaska, where they were required to climb the coastal mountains along the famous Chilkoot Trail on their way to the goldfields near Dawson City, Canada. Those with greater wealth took the all-water route from Seattle to St. Michaels and the Yukon River. Successful miners often returned to Seattle, where they sold their gold and spent their riches. Others were attracted to this busy center to sell goods and services to the miners. The population of Seattle nearly doubled, from 42,000 to 80,000 people, during the decade from 1890 to 1900 as the city became the financial and commercial hub for the Northwest.

Consisting of a visitor center in the city's Pioneer Square Preservation District, the Seattle unit of the Klondike Gold Rush National Historical Park is one of the smallest areas managed by the National Park Service. The interpretive center offers photos, books, exhibits, and a variety of films and slide presentations explaining the gold rush and Seattle's role in the historic event. Films and slide presentations are offered on a request basis from mid-September through mid-June. From mid-June to early September, ranger-led tours, mining demonstrations, films, slide presentations, and ranger talks are offered on a scheduled basis. Call or write the park for details. The center is open daily from 9:00 A.M. to 5:00 P.M. except on Thanksgiving, Christmas, and New Year's Day. Union Trust Annex is within the Pioneer Square Preservation District, an area of the city that has been restored. Pioneer Square includes a number of gold rush–era buildings and many unique shops, restaurants, and antiques dealers.

ENTRANCE FEE: No charge.

FACILITIES: The visitor center offers drinking water and rest rooms. Lodging and numerous interesting food establishments are within walking distance. Pike Place Market, 10 blocks northwest via First Avenue S, is a great place to find fruits, vegetables, and seafood.

CAMPING: The nearest public camping is at Saltwater State Park (fifty-two spaces), 2 miles south of Des Moines on Highway 509. The park has hiking trails and a concession stand.

LAKE ROOSEVELT NATIONAL RECREATION AREA

1008 Crest Drive
Coulee Dam, WA 99116
(509) 633–9441, ext. 110
laro_web_master@nps.gov
www.nps.gov/laro/home.htm

Lake Roosevelt National Recreation Area (renamed from Coulee Dam NRA in 1997) was added to the National Park System in 1946. The area's principal feature is 151-mile-long Franklin D. Roosevelt Lake, which was formed by Grand Coulee Dam. Approximately 55,000 acres of the lake and its shoreline lie within the NRA. The remainder is within the Colville and Spokane Indian Reservations and is managed by the respective tribes. The park is located in northeastern Washington, and its eastern side is bordered by Washington Highway 25.

Millions of years ago this region was the scene of successive volcanic lava floods that filled the Columbia Basin and pressed against the granite mountains to the north. As the Columbia River was forced into new channels by each additional flow, it eventually made a large westward bend. During the last Ice Age, catastrophic floods with ten times the flow of all the rivers on earth raged through this area, carving the spectacular canyon of the Grand Coulee.

Grand Coulee Dam is the largest hydroelectric dam on the Columbia River. Excellent views of the structure may be obtained from the canal headworks, above the west end, or from Crown Point, 2½ miles north on Washington 174. Behind the dam, Franklin D. Roosevelt Lake stretches nearly to the Canadian border.

Driving northward by way of Fort Spokane, the road passes through the rolling wheatlands of eastern Washington before nearing the lake and plunging into evergreen forests. A museum and self-guided trail at Fort Spokane tell the story of the frontier period of the American West. From Fort Spokane, Highway 25 winds northward in the narrow valley between the Huckleberry and Kettle River Mountains. The Gifford ferry provides access to the lake's west side and a different type of scenery. For another scenic drive, cross the lake on the Keller ferry and follow the Sanpoil River north to the old mining town of Republic. From there a drive east over Sherman Pass goes past numerous spots for camping, fishing, picnicking, or relaxing. St. Paul's Mission, located 57 miles north of Fort Spokane, is the oldest existing Catholic mission in Washington. A reconstruction stands today as a testament to the trappers, missionaries and settlers who came to the area in the early 1800s.

Most of the activity in Lake Roosevelt NRA is water-related. Waterskiing is popular within the shelter of larger tributaries such as the Spokane, Kettle, and Colville Rivers and Sanpoil Bay. Sailing is excellent because a breeze usually blows on the lake from the surrounding hills.

ENTRANCE FEE: No charge. There is a $6.00 boat launch fee; good for seven days.

FACILITIES: Food, lodging, groceries, gasoline, and other services are available in Grand Coulee, Coulee Dam, and other nearby towns. Similar services are provided at Colville, Kettle Falls, and Northport on the northern portion of the lake. Small stores with groceries are located at Seven Bays and McCoys marinas, and at marinas at Keller Ferry, Kettle Falls, Two Rivers, and Daisy. Snack bars are available at Keller Ferry, Kettle Falls, and Spring Canyon. Smaller towns and nearby Indian reservations usually sell gasoline, groceries, and snacks.

LAKE ROOSEVELT NATIONAL RECREATION AREA

CAMPING: Thirty-five campgrounds surround Franklin D. Roosevelt Lake. Those with tables, grills, water, and flush toilets are Spring Canyon (seventy-eight spaces, one group camp, dump station), Keller Ferry (fifty-five spaces, one group camp, dump station), Fort Spokane (sixty-seven spaces, one group camp, dump station), Porcupine Bay (thirty-one spaces, dump station), Hunters (thirty-nine spaces), Kettle Falls (eighty-nine spaces, one group camp, dump station), and Evans (forty-six spaces). The six campgrounds listed above are open year-round, but drinking water and flush toilets are not available during the winter season. Other campgrounds are less developed: some can be reached by auto, others by boat only. Campgrounds on the west arm of the lake are on open terraces where shade is limited, while those on the north arm are generally in forested areas.

FISHING: More than thirty species of fish make fishing one of the most popular activities in the park. Common catches include walleye (1 to 4 pounds), rainbow trout (1 to 3 pounds), yellow perch (3 to 5 pounds), lake whitefish (2 to 3 pounds), and kokanee salmon (1 to 3 pounds). Other fish present are cutthroat trout, bass, carp, pike, white perch, and sunfish. Trolling is a popular method of fishing these waters, with dawn and dusk being the best times.

MOUNT RAINIER NATIONAL PARK

Tahoma Woods Star Route
Ashford, WA 98304
(360) 569–2211
MORAinfo@nps.gov
www.nps.gov/mora

Mount Rainier National Park was established in 1899 and comprises 368 square miles, including the greatest single-peak glacial system in the contiguous United States. The summit and slopes of the volcano are surrounded by glaciers, dense forests, and subalpine flowered meadows. The park is located in southwestern Washington, 80 miles south of Seattle via I–5 and Highways 512, 7, and 706 or I–5 and Highways 161, 7, and 706, and 64 miles west of Yakima via U.S. 12 or 410.

Mount Rainier National Park was named for what has become one of the most-photographed mountains in the United States. The 14,410-foot peak collects snowfall in large quantities as the wet Pacific air flows eastward; it is not unusual to have the three-story Paradise Inn on the park's south side covered up to its roofline during winter. The mountain's two craters and general shape betray its life as an active volcano. Some experts believe Rainier is a likely candidate for an eruption because steam from within the mountain continues to carve tunnels in the summit ice cap.

Mount Rainier is best known for the numerous glaciers that flow down its slopes. Thirty-five square miles of ice are contained in twenty-six named glaciers. These ice flows have carved deep valleys into the mountain's sides. The huge quantities of ice and snow create dangers that are unique to this type of mountain including mudflows, snow and ice avalanches, and rock slides.

Mount Rainier National Park (opposite page)

N

W **E**

S

↑ *To Tacoma*

Carbon River Entrance

To Tacoma via (165)

(Road subject to flooding)

Ipsut Creek

410

Mowich Lake

To (165)

Sunrise

White River

White River Entrance

Mather Memorial Parkway

Mather Memorial Parkway

410

To Yakima

MOUNT RAINIER

(Road closed due to flooding)

123

Paradise

Cougar Rock

To Tacoma

Sunshine Point

706

Nisqually Entrance

Longmire

Stevens Canyon Entrance

Ohanapecosh

123

↓ *To Yakima and Packwood*

The most popular activities at Mount Rainier are scenic drives, hiking, and climbing. The ultimate is a climb to the summit of Mount Rainier. A guide service at Paradise offers one-day snow-and-ice climbing seminars and rents climbing equipment. The summit trip is a two-day affair. Two hundred and forty miles of maintained trails, both short and long, begin at various locations around the mountain. Trail guides and maps are sold at visitor centers. The Longmire Museum is open all year; the visitor centers at Sunrise and Ohanapecosh are open in summer only. Paradise is open year-round but only on weekends and holidays from mid-October through April.

Self-guided nature trails are located at Carbon River, Sunrise, Longmire, Ohanapecosh, and Paradise. Naturalist-guided walks and evening programs are available during summer months. Weekly schedules are posted in the park newspaper and at campgrounds and visitor centers. The Carbon River Road is subject to being washed out for long periods. Check for current road conditions.

During winter, food, lodging, gifts, and recreation equipment are available at Longmire. Inner tubes and platters may be used only in the designated snow-play area at Paradise. Information about cross-country ski routes and snow conditions is available from rangers. Except for the road from the Nisqually entrance to Paradise, park roads are usually closed from late November to June.

ENTRANCE FEE: $10.00 per vehicle or $5.00 per person; good for seven days. There is an annual climbing cost recovery fee of $30.00 per person.

FACILITIES: As one of the country's older and more popular areas administered by the National Park Service, Mount Rainier National Park offers a wide variety of facilities for visitors. Overnight accommodations are available at the National Park Inn at Longmire (year-round) and Paradise Inn (late May–early October). For reservations and rates, write Mount Rainier Guest Services, P.O. Box 108, Ashford, WA 94304 (360-569-2275; www.guestservices.com/rainer). Outside the park, accommodations are available at Ashford, Packwood, White Pass, Crystal Mountain, and Enumclaw.

Fast-food service is available in the visitor center at Paradise; restaurant service is provided all year at Longmire and at Paradise Inn during its season of operation. A snack bar is available at Sunrise. Limited groceries are sold at Sunrise and Paradise during summer and at Longmire year-round. Gas is not available in the park.

CAMPING: Improved campgrounds with grills, tables, flush toilets, and drinking water are located at Cougar Rock (200 spaces, dump station), Ohanapecosh (205 spaces, dump station), and White River (117 spaces). Campgrounds without flush toilets are located at Ipsut Creek (twenty-nine spaces, no potable water), Mowich Lake (thirty undesignated sites, no potable water, walk-in only), and Sunshine Point (eighteen spaces). The latter is the only campground open all year. Reservations are required for Cougar Rock and Ohanapecosh from July through Labor Day. During the reservation period visitors can make reservations at the respective campground offices on the day they wish to camp as long as space is available. This is especially important on weekends during this time. Call (800) 365–CAMP, or visit reservations.nps.gov.

FISHING: Fishing is permitted all year without a license. Most lakes melt by early to mid-July. Fishing through ice is not permitted, but alpine lakes and streams contain cutthroat, rainbow, brown, and brook trout. The Ohanapecosh River and its tributaries are open to fly-fishing only. For up-to-date information on fishing, call (360) 569–2211, extension 3314, or visit the park's Web site.

NORTH CASCADES NATIONAL PARK
LAKE CHELAN NATIONAL RECREATION AREA
ROSS LAKE NATIONAL RECREATION AREA

810 State Route 20
Sedro-Woolley, WA 98284
(360) 856–5700
noca_interpretation@nps.gov
www.nps.gov/noca

The North Cascades National Park Service Complex, established in 1968, comprises 1,069 square miles of magnificent scenery. Here high peaks intercept moisture-laden winds, producing glaciers, icefalls, and waterfalls in a wild alpine region where lush forests and meadows thrive. The park is located in

northern Washington—the north boundary borders on Canada. Access to the area is gained via State Route 20, which bisects the park through Ross Lake National Recreation Area. Hiking access and roadside views of the northwest corner are available from State Route 542 east from Bellingham. Access to Stehekin Valley in Lake Chelan National Recreation Area is by boat, float plane, or trail. Vehicle access to Ross Lake is by graded gravel road from Canada.

The North Cascades National Park Complex is comprised of three distinct sections jointly administered from park headquarters in the town of Sedro-Woolley, Washington. The complex is relatively uncrowded, and many visitors consider its alpine scenery to be unmatched in the continental United States. The area's heavy precipitation has produced alpine lakes, snow-covered peaks, snowfields, glacier-carved canyons, and glaciers. With more than 300 glaciers, this complex comprises the most heavily glaciated area in the United States outside Alaska. About 386 miles of hiking and horse trails wind and climb throughout the three sections of the complex. Permits required for backcountry camping are issued on a first-come, first-served basis. Horses and mules can be rented in nearby communities. Hiking and boating maps and guides are available at the visitor center. Professional guide and pack train services are available. The park is open year-round, but access is limited by snow in winter.

The largest and least accessible portions of the complex are the two sections of North Cascades National Park that sandwich Ross Lake National Recreation Area. These rugged areas are accessible via hiking trails that begin at various points inside and outside the complex. Cascade Pass Trailhead in the south unit of North Cascades National Park can be reached via Cascade River Road, a 23-mile improved dirt and gravel road that begins at Stehekin Landing in Lake Chelan National Recreation Area. The most accessible portion of the complex is the boot-shaped middle section of Ross Lake National Recreation Area that has vehicle access via North Cascades Highway (State Highway 20). The highway is partially closed from approximately mid-November to mid-April, depending on weather, snow depths, and avalanche hazards. This route provides outstanding vistas and allows access to the park's main visitor center in the small town of Newhalem. The visitor center, with exhibits, a bookstore, and an audiovisual presentation, is open daily from spring to fall and on weekends during the winter. A short hiking trail begins here. Scheduled commercial boat service including transportation to Ross Lake Resort is available near the dam on Diablo Lake. Additional boat service at the resort offers transportation on Ross Lake. Vehicle access to the north end of the lake is via a dirt-and-gravel road from Canada. Ross Lake is 24 miles long and 2 miles across at its widest point. Diablo Lake and George Lake occupy 910 acres and 210 acres, respectively. Three dams impounding Ross, Diablo, and George Lakes provide electric power for the city of Seattle.

Lake Chelan National Recreation Area at the south end of the complex encompasses the northern section of 55-mile-long Lake Chelan. This beautiful lake is from 1 to 2 miles wide and occupies a glacial trough exceeding 8,500 feet in depth from lake bottom to valley crest. Three classes of boat transportation are offered from the town of Chelan and Field's Point Landing to the tiny village of Stehekin at the north end of the lake. A National Park Service visitor center, restaurant, and lodging facility are at Stehekin. Call the Lake Chelan Boat Company (509–682–2224) for schedule information and prices. Floatplanes also provide public transportation to Stehekin. The National Park Service operates a seasonally scheduled shuttle service from Stehekin Landing to scenic Rainbow Falls and up-valley trailheads and campgrounds in Lake Chelan NRA and North Cascades National Park.

North Cascades National Park (opposite page)

**NORTH CASCADES NATIONAL PARK;
LAKE CHELAN NATIONAL RECREATION AREA;
ROSS LAKE NATIONAL RECREATION AREA**

ENTRANCE FEE: No charge. A $5.00 dock permit is required to use the docks between May 1 and October 31. A $5.00 Northwest Forest Pass is required for parking anywhere along the North Cascades National Park portion of the Cascade River Road or at trailheads. The National Park and Golden Age passes are also honored for parking.

FACILITIES: Guest accommodations are available in the recreation areas and in local communities near the park. For information or reservations, write North Cascades Stehekin Lodge, P.O. Box 457, Chelan, WA 98816 (509–682–4494, www.stehekin.com); Stehekin Valley Ranch, P.O. Box 36, Stehekin, WA 98852 (800–536–0745, www.courtneycountry.com); Ross Lake Resort, Rockport, WA 98283 (206–386–4437).

CAMPING: Three developed campgrounds with vehicle access are located along State Route 20 in Ross Lake NRA. Colonial Creek (164 spaces) has tables, grills, flush toilets, and a dump station. Goodell Creek (twenty-two sites and three group camps) provides tables, grills, water, and pit toilets, and is open all year, although during winter there are no services, no water, and no fee. Only group camps can be reserved. Newhalem Creek (119 spaces and 3 group camps) offers flush toilets and a dump station. Hozomeen Campground (122 spaces) in Ross Lake NRA is reached via a 40-mile gravel road from Hope, British Columbia. This campground is less developed but has water and pit toilets.

In the Lake Chelan National Recreation Area, Purple Point at Stehekin is within walking distance of the boat landing. It has drinking water and pit toilets. Access to all campgrounds in the Lake Chelan National Recreation Area is by boat, shuttle bus, float plane, or trail only. No outside roads connect to this area.

FISHING: The principal game fish are trout—rainbow, brook, cutthroat, and Dolly Varden char/bull trout. Lake Chelan offers fishing for kokanee salmon. In addition to the two big lakes, there are many small mountain and valley lakes and countless streams. A Washington state fishing license is required.

OLYMPIC NATIONAL PARK

600 East Park Avenue
Port Angeles, WA 98362-6757
(360) 565-3130
Olym_visitor_center@nps.gov
www.nps.gov/olym

Olympic National Park is a 922,651-acre diverse wilderness that has mountains, active glaciers, Roosevelt elk, more than 60 miles of wild, scenic ocean shore, and one of the finest remnants of undisturbed temperate rain forest in North America. The park's two sections are located in the northwestern corner of Washington. Main access is via U.S. 101 and its numerous side roads. Roads penetrate only the perimeter of the park. Information on Washington State ferry schedules is available by calling (800) 843-3779 or on the Internet at www.wsdot.wa.gov/ferries/current/. Information on private ferries operated by Black Ball Transportation may be obtained by calling (360) 457-4491. The Black Ball Ferry goes between Port Angeles and Victoria, British Columbia.

The Olympic Mountains are composed partially of sedimentary rocks, such as sandstone and shale, formed from sand and silt deposited in the sea that covered this region millions of years ago. These rocks were later uplifted and carved by erosion and glaciers. There are currently more than sixty active glaciers in the Olympic Mountains; the three largest are found on 7,980-foot Mount Olympus. The strip of park along the Pacific contains some of the most primitive coastline to be found in the continental U.S. The rocky shoreline is the home of birds, seals, and other marine wildlife.

The park has three visitor centers—Olympic National Park Visitor Center near Port Angeles (open all year), the Hoh Rain Forest Visitor Center, and Hurricane Ridge Visitor Center. Each contains exhibits and slide programs. Self-guided nature trails are available throughout the

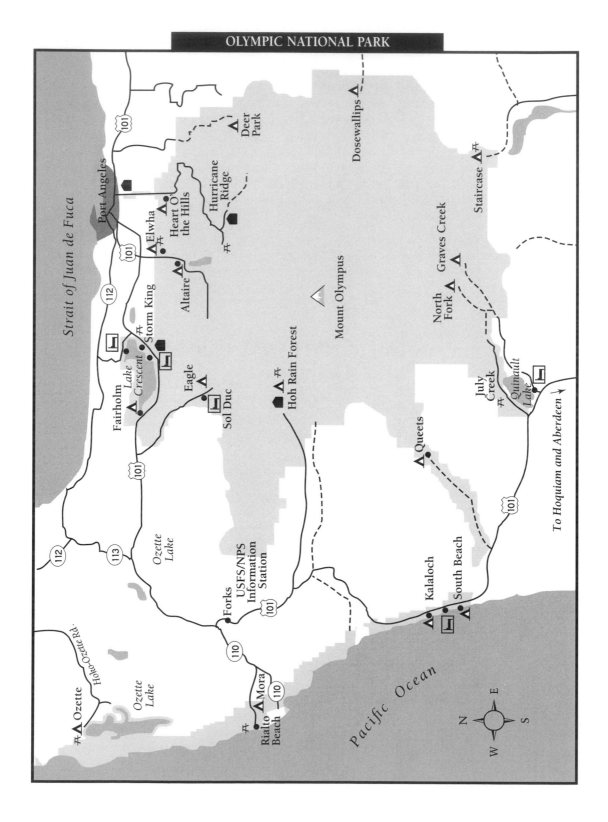

Strait of Juan de Fuca

Port Angeles

Deer Park

Dosewallips

Hurricane Ridge

Elwha

Heart O' the Hills

Staircase

Altaire

Storm King

Graves Creek

Mount Olympus

North Fork

Fairholm

Lake Crescent

Eagle

Hoh Rain Forest

July Creek

Quinault Lake

Sol Duc

To Hoquiam and Aberdeen

Ozette Lake

Queets

Forks

USFS/NPS Information Station

Kalaloch

South Beach

Ozette Lake

Hoko-Ozette Rd.

Ozette

Mora

Rialto Beach

Pacific Ocean

N
E
S
W

101

112

113

110

110

park including Hoh, Ozette, Staircase, Elwha, Quinault, Sol Duc, and Lake Crescent. During summer months park rangers lead guided walks and present evening campfire programs. Six hundred miles of trails wander throughout the park.

The west side of the Olympic Peninsula has the wettest winter climate in the continental United States, with annual precipitation of more than 160 inches in some sections. Easy access to the rain forest is available at Hoh and Quinault.

The park's high country is most easily reached from the park's north side at Heart O' the Hills. Hurricane Ridge provides excellent views of Mount Olympus and subalpine meadows. Winter activities at Olympic National Park include cross-country skiing and snowshoe walks along open subalpine ridge tops.

ENTRANCE FEE: $10.00 per vehicle or $5.00 per person, good for seven days. There is a $1.00 parking fee at Ozette. There is a $5.00 fee to register for a permit to camp overnight in the wilderness (for groups up to twelve people), plus $2.00 per person per night.

FACILITIES: Four overnight lodging facilities are located within the borders of Olympic National Park. Three lodges are situated on the north end of the park. Lake Crescent Lodge on the southeast shore of Lake Crescent, offers a main lodge with rooms, cabins, and motor lodge rooms. All facilities are closed in winter, with the exception of twenty one- and two-bedroom cabins (360–928–3211; www.lakecrescentlodge.com). Log Cabin Resort provides lodge rooms, cabins, and chalets on the north side of Lake Crescent. It is closed during the winter (360–928–3325; www.logcabinresort.net). Sol Duc Hot Springs Resort, which also closes in the winter, has cabins with or without kitchen near a hot mineral spring (360–327–3583; www.northolympic.com/solduc). Kalaloch Lodge, with cabins and rooms in the main lodge, is directly on the Pacific Ocean and is open year-round (360–962–2271 or www.visitkalaloch.com). Restaurants are located at each of the four lodges, and there is a cafeteria at Hurricane Ridge Visitor Center during summer months and on weekends in winter. A snack bar is located at the Fairholm General Store.

Limited groceries and gasoline are sold at the Fairholm General Store, which is closed in the winter. Limited groceries only are sold at Sol Duc Hot Springs, Kalaloch Lodge, and Log Cabin Resort. Boat rentals are provided at Fairholm, Lake Crescent Lodge, and Log Cabin Resort.

CAMPING: Campgrounds with tables, grills, water, and flush toilets include Altaire (30 spaces, summer only, no large trailers), Dosewallips (30 spaces, summer only, no trailers), Elwha (40 spaces, no large trailers), Fairholm (88 spaces, dump station), Graves Creek (30 spaces, summer only), Heart O' the Hills (105 spaces), Hoh (88 spaces, dump station), Kalaloch (175 spaces, dump station), Mora (94 spaces; dump station), Sol Duc (82 spaces, summer only, dump station), and Staircase (56 spaces). Limited spaces at each of these campgrounds will accommodate larger RVs. All other sites are recommended to a maximum of 21 feet.

Campgrounds with tables, grills, and pit toilets include Deer Park (fourteen spaces, summer only, no trailers), North Fork Quinault (seven spaces summer only, no trailers), Ozette (thirteen spaces, dirt road access), and Queets (twenty spaces, no trailers).

FISHING: Olympic's streams and lakes contain cutthroat, rainbow, Dolly Varden, and brook trout and several species of salmon. Large rivers are noted for steelhead trout. No license is required except when fishing in the Pacific Ocean from shore. Steelhead and salmon punchcards are required. Some park waters are closed to fishing. Check at a ranger station before fishing within the park.

SAN JUAN ISLAND NATIONAL HISTORICAL PARK

P.O. Box 429
Friday Harbor, WA 98250-0429
(360) 378–2240
sajh_administration@nps.gov
www.nps.gov/sajh

San Juan Island Historical Park encompasses 1,752 acres on San Juan Island, the second largest island in the San Juan archipelago. The park became part of the National Park system in 1966 to commemorate the peaceful resolution of the boundary dispute of 1859, better known as the Pig War. English Camp is located on the island's northwest shoreline, while American Camp occupies a windswept prairie on the southern end of the island. San Juan Island is accessible via Washington State Ferries from Anacortes, Washington, about 83 miles north of Seattle, and Sidney, British Columbia, 15 miles north of Victoria on Vancouver Island. Good docking facilities for private craft are available in Friday Harbor and Roche Harbor.

San Juan Island was the scene of a confrontation and then relatively peaceful coexistence between American and British forces during the 1800s. The Oregon Treaty of 1846 between Great Britain and the United States settled the larger land disputes by giving the United States undisputed possession of the Pacific Northwest below the forty-ninth parallel, extending the boundary to the middle of the channel separating the mainland from Vancouver Island. But the treaty's wording left unclear who owned San Juan Island. Both sides declared the island as its possession, and in 1859 an insignificant event caused a confrontation between the two powers. After a series of threats, both sides agreed to withdraw all but token military forces and negotiate a settlement. The Americans remained in place in what is now called American Camp, while the British landed a detachment of royal marines at today's English Camp. San Juan Island remained under peaceful joint military occupation for the next twelve years. In 1871 the two sides signed the Treaty of Washington and submitted the San Juan question to Kaiser Wilhelm I of Germany for settlement. In 1872 the Kaiser ruled in favor of the United States.

Park headquarters, at First and Spring Streets in Friday Harbor, serves as an information station. It is open seven days a week from 8:30 A.M. to 4:30 P.M. At English Camp four historic buildings and a small formal garden have been restored. Several buildings are open in the summer. A self-guided historical walking trail is available, and the barracks offers a slide program explaining the territorial dispute. At American Camp two historic buildings and the remains of an earthwork gun emplacement survive. An exhibit/information center and a self-guided historical walking trail are located here. South and Fourth of July beaches, which flank the Cattle Point peninsula, offer splendid areas for picnicking, walking, and watching wildlife. The Jakle's Lagoon trail network features a variety of woodland and saltwater lagoon hikes.

ENTRANCE FEE: No charge.

FACILITIES: A number of motels, lodges, and bed-and-breakfast facilities are available on the island. A listing is at the visitor center. Picnic areas and accessible rest rooms are located at both American Camp and English Camp. Water is available only at American Camp.

CAMPING: No camping is provided by the National Park Service. Limited camping facilities (with flush toilets) are available at San Juan County Park (eighteen sites). For reservations, write 380 West Side Road No., Friday Harbor, WA 98250 (360–378–1842). A small commercial trailer park (twenty sites, hookups) is located 1 mile from the ferry landing on Roche Harbor Road (360–378–4717), and three private campgrounds are available on the island.

FISHING: Fishing in bays surrounding the island and in San Juan Channel is available at various locations.

WHITMAN MISSION NATIONAL HISTORIC SITE

328 Whitman Mission Road
Walla Walla, WA 99362
(509) 522–6360
whmi_interpretation@nps.gov
www.nps.gov/whmi

Whitman Mission National Historic Site was authorized in 1936 to commemorate a landmark on the Oregon Trail where Dr. and Mrs. Marcus Whitman ministered to the spiritual and physical needs of Indians. The site is located in southeastern Washington, 7 miles west of Walla Walla and 4 miles west of College Place. A short connecting road leads south from U.S. 12 to the park.

Marcus Whitman was sent west in 1835 by a Protestant church society to carry out missionary work among the Indians. After returning east to recruit workers, Whitman and his wife crossed the continent in 1836 via steamboat, wagon, two-wheeled cart, and horseback. His mission was established among the Cayuse Indians at Waiilatpu. The Indians remained nomadic and were generally apathetic to spiritual matters, so the society considered closing the mission in 1842. Whitman was able to convince his superiors of the mission's value, and it continued to provide shelter to both the Indians and settlers traveling the Oregon Trail. In 1847 measles came into the area, creating an epidemic that killed half the Cayuse tribe. In the same year, a small group of Cayuse attacked the mission and killed Marcus Whitman, his wife, and eleven others. The mission buildings were also destroyed. The tragedy spurred Congress to create the Territory of Oregon in August 1848.

The visitor center contains exhibits on Whitman Mission and the Oregon Trail, and a slide show on the establishment of the mission is presented hourly. Self-guided walks lead past the Whitman Memorial and the Great Grave, where the remains of those killed in the massacre are buried. Visitors may also walk around the old mission grounds, where recorded messages and building outlines help interpret the site. A restored section of the old Oregon Trail is available to walk. The mission is open daily except Thanksgiving, Christmas, and New Year's Day.

ENTRANCE FEE: $3.00 per person; with a maximum of $5.00 per family; good for seven days. Children ages sixteen and under are free.

FACILITIES: No food service or lodging is available at the site. Water and rest rooms are provided at the visitor center. A shaded picnic area with tables and drinking water (no grills) is located north of the visitor center near the parking area. Full facilities are located 7 miles east in Walla Walla.

CAMPING: No camping is permitted in the park. A campground with hookups is located 7 miles east in Walla Walla on Dalles Military Road, and a map showing directions to the campground may be obtained at the Whitman Mission Visitor Center.

WYOMING

STATE TOURIST INFORMATION
(800) 225–5996
www.wyomingtourism.org

DEVILS TOWER NATIONAL MONUMENT

P.O. Box 10
Devils Tower, WY 82714
(307) 467–5283
deto_interpretation@nps.gov
www.nps.gov/deto

Devils Tower National Monument comprises 1,347 acres and was established in 1906 as the country's first national monument. The monument features a spectacular stump-shaped cluster of rock columns rising 867 feet above its base (featured in the movie *Close Encounters of the Third Kind*). Devils Tower is located in extreme northeastern Wyoming, 29 miles northwest of Sundance. The entrance is off Wyoming Highways 24 and 110, 7 miles north of U.S. 14. The drive over paved Wyoming Highway 24 (South Dakota Highway 34) connecting Belle Fourche, South Dakota, and the monument is quite scenic.

Devils Tower was formed millions of years ago when molten materials originating from within the earth cooled and crystallized. Joints in the columns were established when the hot rock cooled and contracted. Some of the columns have since fallen as the joints enlarged by the freezing and thawing of water. These broken columns may be seen piled around the base of the tower. The remainder of the monument is composed of rocks formed through the accumulation of materials on the floors of ancient seas. The prominence of Devils Tower is due to the more rapid erosion of the surrounding rock and to the color difference between the tower's core and base.

Devils Tower National Monument (opposite page)

For centuries the butte was and still is a sacred site of worship to several Plains tribes. It is also the focus of Indian legends. As explorers and pioneers moved westward, it became one of their landmarks. The naming of Devils Tower is generally credited to Colonel Richard Dodge, who was the commander of a military escort for a U.S. Geological Survey party.

The monument's visitor center contains exhibits explaining the history and geology of the area. During the summer fifteen- to twenty-minute interpretive talks are presented in front of the visitor center. The 3-mile paved road to the visitor center passes through a prairie-dog town approximately ½ mile from the east entrance. The monument has 7 miles of hiking trails, including an easy self-guided nature trail (1¼ miles, one hour) that circles the tower and begins at the visitor center. Here the visitor may see a wide variety of animals and birds. The 2¾-mile Red Beds Trail is quite scenic and is easiest to hike in a clockwise fashion. A picnic area is located near the campground.

ENTRANCE FEE: $8.00 per vehicle or $3.00 per walk-in; good for seven days.

FACILITIES: Three general stores, restaurants, and a post office are located just outside the monument, approximately 2 miles from the campground. Rest rooms and drinking water are available in the visitor center area and at the campground.

CAMPING: A pleasant campground (fifty spaces), located in a grove of cottonwood trees, provides tables, grills, water, and flush toilets. Depending upon the weather, the campground is open, with water and rest rooms available, from approximately May 1 through October. A large private campground with hookups and showers is located just outside the park entrance.

FISHING: Fishing is permitted in the Belle Fourche River, which cuts through the park and borders the campground. Catches include catfish, suckers, and carp. A Wyoming fishing license is required.

FORT LARAMIE NATIONAL HISTORIC SITE

HC 72 Box 389
Fort Laramie, WY 82212
(307) 837–2221
fola_superintendent@nps.gov
www.nps.gov/fola

Fort Laramie National Historic Site comprises 832 acres and was added to the National Park Service in 1938 to preserve the site and remaining buildings of an important fur trading and military post of the 1800s. The park is located in eastern Wyoming, 3 miles southwest of the town of Fort Laramie on County Road 160. It is approximately 95 miles from Cheyenne.

The original stockade, called Fort William, was constructed by fur traders in 1834. Two years later it was purchased by a large fur company and soon became one of the major trading centers in the Rockies. By the 1840s the fur trade had declined, but the fort's location on one of the main routes west gave it renewed importance.

In 1849 the post was purchased by the U.S. government for use as an Army post to protect travelers along the Oregon Trail. Subsequently, Fort Laramie was used as a station for the Pony Express and the Cheyenne–Deadwood Stagecoach and as a staging area for military campaigns against the Plains Indians. By the late 1800s the importance of the fort had waned, and by 1890 it was abandoned.

The National Park Service has restored a number of the fort's standing buildings—eleven have been historically furnished and are open to visitors. The park is open year-round. A visitor center in the commissary storehouse is open from 8:00 A.M. until 7:00 P.M. during summer. Exhibits and a film on the post's history are provided, and park personnel are on hand to answer visitors' questions. Talks on historic subjects are offered daily during June, July, and August. The park presents an excellent living-history program.

ENTRANCE FEE: $3.00 per person; children ages sixteen and under are free.

FACILITIES: No food service or lodging is available in the park. Both can be found in the town of Fort Laramie. Cold soft drinks are sold during the summer in the soldiers' bar. Water and rest rooms are located in the visitor center and the cavalry barracks.

CAMPING: No camping is permitted in the historic site. The town of Fort Laramie has camping facilities with tables, grills, water, and flush toilets at a small but nice municipal park. Thirteen miles west of Fort Laramie on Highway 26, the town of Gurnsey provides campsites in a city park south of town. Water, electrical hookups, grills, tables, and hot showers are available.

FISHING: Fishing is permitted in the Laramie River outside the fort's historic zone with a Wyoming fishing license. Catches include catfish, carp, and some trout.

FOSSIL BUTTE NATIONAL MONUMENT

P.O. Box 592
Kemmerer, WY 83101-0592
(307) 877–4455
fobu_superintendent@nps.gov
www.nps.gov/fobu

Fossil Butte National Monument comprises nearly 8,200 acres. It was established as part of the National Park Service in 1972 to preserve the nation's most extensive concentration of fossilized freshwater fish. Fossil Butte is located in southwestern Wyoming, 11 miles west of Kemmerer via U.S. 30.

For much of geologic time, most of Wyoming was either underwater or beachfront property. Then, seventy million to eighty million years ago, the Rocky Mountains began to form, creating intermountain basins. Fossil Lake, a subtropical freshwater lake, formed in one of these basins.

Fifty-million-year-old fossils found within the butte and surrounding sediments are among the most perfectly preserved remains of ancient plant and animal life in the world. Fish abounded in the lake; palms, ferns, and reeds grew along the shores. Fossils show that floodplain forests were inhabited by horses the size of dogs and by lemurs, while the streams around the lake contained crocodiles and turtles.

Several theories are advanced for the exquisite fossilization conditions over the life of the lake. One theory attributes the abundance of fish fossils, which are actually found in several layers of sediments, to the stratified nature of the large lakes. The temperate climate created surface waters that were warmer and lighter than the deeper waters. Winds blowing across the lakes created well-oxygenated surface layers that acted as seals for the dense bottom waters that became stagnant and void of oxygen. When the fish that thrived in the warm surface water died and sank to the lake bottoms, there were no scavengers to bother their remains, and the fish were buried by limestone precipitating out of the water.

The visitor center, located 1 mile north on the park road, provides numerous examples of fossils and information about them. Two videos are offered. One presents an orientation to the Fossil Lake deposits, and a second displays how fossils are quarried and prepared. A preparation lab permits the visitor to observe fossil preparation. Personnel in the visitor center provide assistance and hiking information. A trail leads to a historic quarry on Fossil Butte. Wayside exhibits describe some of the natural and cultural features of the area. The 1½-mile Fossil Lake Trail begins at the picnic area and winds through aspen groves and meadows.

ENTRANCE FEE: No charge.

FACILITIES: No food or lodging is available at the monument, but both are found at Kemmerer and Cokeville. Rest rooms and drinking water are available at the visitor center. Vault toilets are found near the trailheads. A picnic area is located 2½ miles beyond the visitor center.

GRAND TETON NATIONAL PARK
JOHN D. ROCKEFELLER JR. MEMORIAL PARKWAY

P.O. Drawer 170
Moose, WY 83012-0170
(307) 739–3300
grte_info@nps.gov
www.nps.gov/grte
www.nps.gov/jodr

Grand Teton National Park was established in 1929 and expanded in 1950. The park comprises nearly 310,000 acres of some of America's most impressive mountain landscape. The John D. Rockefeller Jr. Memorial Parkway covers nearly 24,000 acres and provides a resource link between Grand Teton and Yellowstone. The parks are located in northwestern Wyoming. From Yellowstone and the north, access is via U.S. 89/287/191 and from the south via U.S. 26/89/191. This road parallels the Teton Range. From the east (Casper and Riverton), the park is entered on U.S. 26/287.

The Teton Range rises nearly 7,000 feet above the valley called Jackson Hole. The steep eastern front is the result of an uplifting that occurred along a fault zone in the earth's crust. As the

GRAND TETON NATIONAL PARK;
JOHN D. ROCKEFELLER JR. MEMORIAL PARKWAY

Yellowstone National Park

Grassy Lake Road

Flagg Ranch

John D.
Rockefeller Jr.
Memorial
Parkway

89

191
287

Lizard Creek

GRAND TETON
NATIONAL
PARK

Jackson Lake

Two Ocean Lake

Leeks
Marina

Jackson
Lake
Lodge

Emma Matilda Lake

To Dubois, Wyoming

Colter Bay
Village

Signal
Mountain
Lodge

26   287

Moran
Junction

Leigh Lake

Cunningham
Cabin Historic Site

String Lake
Jenny Lake

Jenny
Lake
Lodge

Triangle X Dude Ranch

GRAND
TETON

Bradley Lake
Taggart Lake

Moose

Dornan's

Teton Science School

Phelps Lake

Gros Ventre Road

Snake River

Kelly

Gros
Ventre

Teton
Village

Jackson Hole
Airport

Gros
Ventre
Junction

26

89

N
W   E
S

22

191

To Jackson, Wyoming

uplifting progressed, the mountains were eroded by wind and water. Later glaciers carved the gullies into U-shaped valleys. The rock debris carried down by the glaciers (now melted) resulted in natural dams for lakes at the base of the range.

This spectacular park offers visitors a wide variety of outdoor activities. Moose Visitor Center (307–739–3399), at the park's south end, is open all year, and park personnel are on hand to answer questions. At the north end of the park, the Colter Bay Visitor Center and Indian Arts Museum (307–739–3594) is open from mid-May through September and offers audiovisual presentations, map and publication sales, and an American Indian art collection. The Jenny Lake Visitor Center is open from early June through late September and houses geology exhibits in the historic Crandall Studio.

Some of the more popular activities are boating, fishing, hiking, and mountaineering. The Snake River diagonally bisects the valley portion of the park. A float trip with your own boat (permit required) or on one of the many concessioner-operated rafts is an exciting experience. No motors are allowed on the Snake. Hand-propelled boats are permitted on Emma Matilda, Two Ocean, Bradley, Taggart, Leigh, Bearpaw, and String Lakes. Motors of up to 10 h.p. are allowed on Jenny Lake and Phelps Lake. All types of boats are permitted on Jackson Lake, and concessioner boat tours operate daily during the summer. Boat shuttle transportation across the lake is available at Jenny Lake.

Grand Teton contains more than 250 miles of trails (horses allowed on many miles of these), including access to the high country. One of the more popular hikes near Jenny Lake is a half-day trip to Hidden Falls. Self-guided trails are located at Taggart and Bradley Lakes, Cascade Canyon, Colter Bay, Cunningham Cabin, and historic Menors Ferry. Frequent ranger-guided hikes are available in the summer, with schedules posted in the park newspaper. For visitors interested in mountaineering, instruction and guide service are available during summer months.

Two other relatively popular activities are horseback riding and swimming. Horses may be rented at Colter Bay and Jackson Lake Lodge. Swimming is possible during late summer in shallow areas of String, Leigh, and Jackson Lakes. Most lakes are quite cold, and no lifeguards are on duty.

During winter months, ranger-conducted snowshoe hikes are available (snowshoes provided), and snowmobiles may be operated in designated areas. Although no downhill skiing is available in the park, three private ski developments are located nearby.

ENTRANCE FEE: $20 per vehicle, $15 per motorcycle, or $10 per person; good for seven days in Grand Teton and Yellowstone National Parks and the John D. Rockefeller Jr. Memorial Parkway.

LODGING: Seven lodging facilities are in Grand Teton National Park and the John D. Rockefeller Jr. Memorial Parkway. Accommodations range from cabins at Triangle X Dude Ranch, the only working dude ranch in a national park, to cozy cabins at four-star Jenny Lake Lodge. Other lodging includes panoramic Jackson Lake Lodge, cabins and lakefront apartments at Signal Mountain, Flagg Ranch in John D. Rockefeller Jr. Memorial Parkway, and cabins and tents at Colter Bay. Dornan's Spur Ranch near Moose offers modern log cabins near a gourmet food store.

FACILITIES: A wide assortment of facilities may be found throughout Grand Teton and Rockefeller Parkway. A summary by location is:

Colter Bay: Lodging (cabins, RV park, tent village), food (grill, restaurant, snack bar), laundry, showers, service stations, general store, groceries, and marina. Write Grand Teton Lodge Co., Box 250, Moran, WY 83013 (307–543–3100; www.gtlc.com).

Flagg Ranch (John D. Rockefeller Jr., Memorial Parkway): Lodging (cabins), food (restaurant, deli), package store, service station, gift shop, grocery, float trips, cross-country skiing, and snowmobile rentals. Write Flagg Ranch Village, Box 187, Moran, WY 83013 (800–443–2311, 307–543–2861; www.flagranch.com).

Jackson Lake: Hotel, grill, restaurant, beauty shop, package store, service station, gift shop, swimming pool. Write Grand Teton Lodge Co., Box 250, Moran, WY 83013 (800–628–9988 or 307–543–3100; www.gtlc.com).

Jenny Lake: Cabins, dining room, boat rentals and cruises, grocery, gift shop. Write Grand Teton Lodge Co., Box 250, Moran, WY 83013 (800–628–9988 or 307–733–4647; www.gtlc.com).

Moose: Housekeeping cabins, food (restaurant, snack bar), package store, laundry, service station, canoe rental, grocery store, sporting-goods store, fishing shop, float trips. Write Dornan's Spur Ranch Log Cabins, Box 39, Moose, WY 83012 (307–733–2522; www.dornans.com).

Signal Mountain: Lodging (log cabins, motel units, housekeeping apartments), food (coffee shop, restaurant), service station, gift shop, marina, grocery store, float trips. Write Signal Mountain Lodge, Box 50, Moran, WY 83013 (307–543–2831; www.signalmtnlodge.com).

CAMPING: In Grand Teton National Park, campgrounds with tables, grills, water, and flush toilets are at Colter Bay (350 spaces, nine group camps, dump station, a concessioner-operated 111-site trailer village, showers, laundry), Gros Ventre (360 spaces, dump station), Jenny Lake (44 spaces for tents only), Lizard Creek (60 spaces), and Signal Mountain (86 spaces, dump station). Jenny Lake and Signal Mountain generally fill first; Gros Ventre fills last.

In John D. Rockefeller Jr. Memorial Parkway, a concessioner campground with 175 spaces is located at Flagg Ranch.

FISHING: Jackson Lake has cutthroat and lake trout. A number of other lakes and many streams have whitefish and cutthroat, brook, and rainbow trout. Ice fishing is permitted on Jackson, Leigh, and Jenny Lakes, and the Snake River is open only for whitefish in winter. A Wyoming fishing license is required.

YELLOWSTONE NATIONAL PARK

P.O. Box 168
Yellowstone National Park, WY 82190-0168
(307) 344–7381
yell_visitor_services@nps.gov
www.nps.gov/yell

Yellowstone was established in 1872 as America's first national park. It comprises 3,472 square miles of lakes, waterfalls, and mountains and more than 10,000 hydrothermal features, including geysers and hot springs. The majority of the park is located in the northwestern corner of Wyoming, with overlapping areas in Montana and Idaho. Access is available from all four major directions.

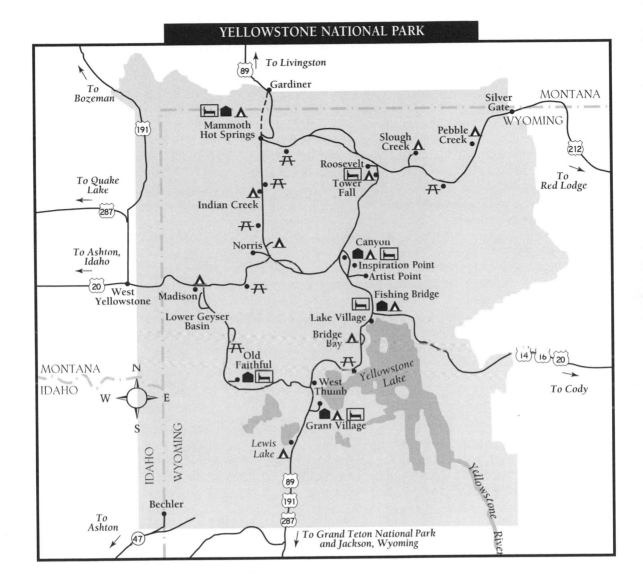

The central portion of Yellowstone is a volcanic plateau with an average elevation of approximately 8,000 feet. On the northwest, north, east, and south, this table is surrounded by mountain ranges rising from 2,000 to 4,000 feet above the plateau. The region has been shaped by volcanoes and ice. The volcanic activity began fifty million to fifty-five million years ago and is still evident in the geysers and hot springs drawing heat from the earth's interior. Ice has moved through the park at least three times. In each case, permanent ice on mountains to the north and east quarried rocks and debris as it flowed into the valleys. As the climate warmed and the ice melted, lakes and piles of debris were left.

The park contains nearly 310 miles of paved/primary roads leading to a seemingly endless supply of scenic areas. Many major attractions are found near the Grand Loop Road, which makes a figure eight in the park's central area. The road's east side provides access to canyons, mountains, and waterfalls, while the west side leads to areas of thermal activity. The most popular of these latter attractions is Old Faithful. Numerous other geysers have predictable eruption times that are posted at Old Faithful Visitor Center and Norris Museum. Norris Geyser Basin is the park's most active thermal area—it has numerous steam vents and hot springs. At Mammoth Hot Springs, hot waters cascade over colored limestone pools. In Lower Geyser Basin, Fountain Paint Pots Trail provides access to more varied hot-water phenomena in a concentrated area than any other trail in the park.

Some of Yellowstone's most scenic areas lie along the Yellowstone River. Near Canyon, there are spectacular views of the Grand Canyon of the Yellowstone from Artist Point and Inspiration Point. North of here, a hike to the top of Mount Washburn ends with a view of the entire park.

Other activities in Yellowstone include horseback trips from Canyon, Tower-Roosevelt, and Mammoth and stagecoach rides on a regular schedule at Roosevelt. Bus tours leave from hotels and lodges, and boat tours leave regularly from Bridge Bay. Power boating is permitted only on open areas of Yellowstone Lake and on Lewis Lake (includes boat launch). All boaters are required to purchase permits for motorized and nonmotorized boats. For most, swimming is an uncomfortable experience because of Yellowstone's cold lakes and streams.

Winter activities are concentrated at Mammoth and Old Faithful, and U.S. 89 to the north entrance is open year-round for automobiles. Several trails are available for cross-country skiing, and major roadways are open to snowmobiles from mid-December through early March. Snowmobiles may be rented at Mammoth, Gardiner, West Yellowstone, and Flagg Ranch. Tours in enclosed snowcoaches are available via Xanterra Parks and Resorts. No downhill skiing is possible in the park, but several ski developments are located nearby.

ENTRANCE FEE: $20 per vehicle; $15 per motorcycle; or $10 per person; good for seven days in Yellowstone and Grand Teton National Parks and John D. Rockefeller Jr. Memorial Parkway.

LODGING: Nine separate lodging facilities are located within Yellowstone National Park. The busy Old Faithful area has three lodging facilities, including famous Old Faithful Inn. Other accommodations are at Grant Village, Mammoth Hot Springs, Roosevelt, Canyon Village, and Lake Village. The facilities range from a wonderful hundred-year-old hotel on the banks of Yellowstone Lake to rustic cabins at several locations. Not all rooms or cabins have private bathrooms. All nine lodges are operated by the same firm. For reservations or information, write Xanterra Parks and Resorts, Reservations Office, P.O. Box 165, Yellowstone National Park, WY 82190 (307–344–7311; www.travelyellowstone.com).

FACILITIES: Yellowstone is one of the more developed parks administered by the National Park Service. Visitors can find nearly anything at some location inside its borders.

Bridge Bay: Boat rental.

Canyon: Food service, gasoline station, grocery, laundry, lodging, photo shop, post office, visitor center.

Fishing Bridge/Lake Area: Food service, gasoline station, grocery, hospital (summer only), laundry, lodging, marina, photo shop, post office, propane service, visitor center.

Grant: Food service, gasoline station, laundry, lodging, post office, propane service, visitor center.

Mammoth: Food service, gasoline station, grocery, lodging, medical clinic, photo shop, post office, visitor center.

View from Artist Point in Yellowstone National Park (opposite page)

Old Faithful: Food service, gasoline station, grocery, lodging, photo shop, medical clinic (summer only), post office, propane service, visitor center.

Tower-Roosevelt: Food service, gasoline, grocery, lodging.

CAMPING: Campgrounds with tables, fireplaces, dump stations, and flush toilets are located at Bridge Bay (430 spaces, showers), Canyon (272 spaces, showers), Grant Village (425 spaces, showers), Madison (280 spaces, no showers), Mammoth (85 spaces, no dump station, no showers), and Norris (116 spaces, no dump station, no showers). Less-developed campgrounds are located at Indian Creek (seventy-five spaces), Lewis Lake (eighty-five spaces), Pebble Creek (thirty-two spaces), Slough Creek (twenty-nine spaces), and Tower Falls (thirty-two spaces). Only Mammoth is open all year. Campsites at Bridge Bay, Canyon, Grant Village, and Madison may be reserved through Xanterra Parks and Resorts, Box 165, Yellowstone National Park, WY 82190 (307–344–7311). The other campgrounds do not accept reservations.

A concessioner-operated trailer park at Fishing Bridge offers hookups and is open from mid-June to early September.

FISHING: Yellowstone Lake is noted for its native Yellowstone cutthroat trout. Other park streams and lakes contain rainbow, brook, brown, cutthroat, and lake trout, grayling, and whitefish. Fishing regulations vary widely throughout the park—some waters are closed, others are restricted to fly-fishing, and some are open only for catch and release. Anglers twelve to fifteen years of age are required to obtain a free park fishing permit that is available at all ranger stations and visitor centers. Individuals over fifteen years old must purchase a permit. Children ages eleven and younger may fish without a permit but must be supervised by an adult who knows the regulations. No state fishing license is required for fishing in the park.

NATIONAL PARK AREAS FACILITIES AND ACTIVITIES CHART

The following chart presents current information on visitor services in the areas described in this book. Generally, the services listed are those in the parks themselves. Additional services are usually available in nearby cities. Parks permitting activities such as horseback riding and boating do not necessarily rent equipment. Many parks curtail service in their off-seasons. A few park areas are not listed here or their entries are blank because they do not have the visitor services listed here.

ALASKA

	Fees	Visitor Center	Programs/Tours	Self-guided Tour/Trail	Guide for Hire	Picnic Area	Campground	Group Camp Site	Backcountry Permits	Hiking	Mountain Climbing	Horse Trail	Swimming	Bathhouse	Boating	Boat Rental	Boat Ramp	Fishing	Hunting	Bicycle Trail	Snowmobile Route	Crosscountry Ski Trail	Cabin Rental	Hotel, Motel, Lodge	Groceries, Ice	Restaurant, Snacks	Campsites	Activities/Service	Visitor Center
Aniakchak Natl. Monument and Preserve, P.O. Box 7, King Salmon, AK 99613	●	●	●			●	●		●	●								●	●								●	●	●
Bering Land Bridge Natl. Preserve, P.O. Box 220, Nome, AK 99762			●		●				●	●					●			●	●										●
Cape Krusenstern Natl. Monument, P.O. Box 1029, Kotzebue, AK 99752		●	●		●				●	●								●	●										●
Denali Natl. Park and Preserve, P.O. Box 9, Denali Park, AK 99755	●	●	●	●		●	●		●	●	●										●						●	●	●
Gates of the Arctic Natl. Park and Preserve, 201 First Ave., Doyon Building, Fairbanks, AK 99701		●	●		●				●	●	●				●			●	●										●
Glacier Bay Natl. Park and Preserve, P.O. Box 140, Gustavus, AK 99826		●	●	●		●	●		●	●	●				●		●	●						●	●	●		●	●
Katmai Natl. Park and Preserve, P.O. Box 7, King Salmon, AK 99613	●	●	●		●				●	●					●		●	●						●	●	●			●
Kenai Fjords Natl. Park, P.O. Box 1727, Seward, AK 99664	●	●	●		●		●		●	●					●			●				●	●						●
Klondike Gold Rush Natl. Historical Park, P.O. Box 517, Skagway, AK 99840 (See also Washington)		●	●						●	●												●					●		●
Kobuk Valley Natl. Park, P.O. Box 1029, Kotzebue, AK 99752									●	●								●	●										●
Lake Clark Natl. Park and Preserve, 4230 University Drive, Anchorage, AK 99508		●	●		●				●	●	●				●			●	●									●	●
Noatak Natl. Preserve, P.O. Box 1029, Kotzebue, AK 99752					●	●			●	●		●			●			●	●	●									●
Sitka Natl. Historical Park, P.O. Box 738, Sitka, AK 99835	●	●	●	●		●				●																		●	●
Wrangell–St. Elias Natl. Park and Preserve, P.O. Box 439, Copper Center, AK 99573		●	●		●	●	●		●	●	●				●	●		●	●					●	●	●		●	●
Yukon–Charley Rivers Natl. Preserve, 201 First Ave., Doyon Building, Fairbanks, AK 99701		●							●	●																			●

AMERICAN SAMOA

	Fees	Visitor Center	Programs/Tours	Self-guided Tour/Trail	Guide for Hire	Picnic Area	Campground	Group Camp Site	Backcountry Permits	Hiking	Mountain Climbing	Horse Trail	Swimming	Bathhouse	Boating	Boat Rental	Boat Ramp	Fishing	Hunting	Bicycle Trail	Snowmobile Route	Crosscountry Ski Trail	Cabin Rental	Hotel, Motel, Lodge	Groceries, Ice	Restaurant, Snacks	Campsites	Activities/Service	Visitor Center
Natl. Park of American Samoa, Pago Pago, AS 96799-0001		●	●		●					●			●		●			●										●	●

ARIZONA

	Fees	Visitor Center	Programs/Tours	Self-guided Tour/Trail	Guide for Hire	Picnic Area	Campground	Group Camp Site	Backcountry Permits	Hiking	Mountain Climbing	Horse Trail	Swimming	Bathhouse	Boating	Boat Rental	Boat Ramp	Fishing	Hunting	Bicycle Trail	Snowmobile Route	Crosscountry Ski Trail	Cabin Rental	Hotel, Motel, Lodge	Groceries, Ice	Restaurant, Snacks	Campsites	Activities/Service	Visitor Center
Canyon de Chelly Natl. Monument, P.O. Box 588, Chinle, AZ 86503	●	●	●	●	●	●	●	●	●	●		●																●	●
Casa Grande Ruins Natl. Monument, 1100 Ruins Drive, Coolidge, AZ 85228	●	●	●	●		●																						●	●
Chiricahua Natl. Monument, 13063 E. Bonita Canyon Road, Willcox, AZ 85643	●	●	●	●		●	●			●																		●	●
Coronado Natl. Memorial, 4101 E. Montezuma Canyon Road, Hereford, AZ 85615		●	●	●		●				●																		●	●
Fort Bowie Natl. Historic Site, P.O. Box 158, Bowie, AZ 85605		●	●	●						●																		●	●
Glen Canyon Natl. Rcreation Area, P.O. Box 1507, Page, AZ 86040 (See also Utah)	●	●	●			●	●	●	●	●			●		●	●	●	●					●	●	●	●	●	●	●
Grand Canyon Natl. Park, P.O. Box 129, Grand Canyon, AZ 86023	●	●	●	●	●	●	●	●	●	●		●						●		●		●		●	●	●	●	●	●
Hubbell Trading Post Natl. Historic Site, P.O. Box 150, Ganado, AZ 86505	●	●	●	●		●																						●	●
Montezuma Castle Natl. Monument, P.O. Box 219, Camp Verde, AZ 86322	●	●	●	●		●																				●		●	●
Navajo Natl. Monument, HC 71 Box 3, Tonalea, AZ 86044		●	●	●	●	●	●		●	●																			●

ARIZONA *(continued)*

Organ Pipe Cactus Natl. Monument, Route 1, Box 100, Ajo, AZ 85321

Petrified Forest Natl. Park, P.O. Box 2217, Petrified Forest Natl. Park, AZ 86028

Pipe Spring Natl. Monument, HC 65 Box 5, Fredonia, AZ 86022

Saguaro Natl. Park, 3693 S. Old Spanish Trail, Tucson, AZ 85730

Sunset Crater Volcano Natl. Monument, 6400 N. Highway 89, Flagstaff, AZ 86004

Tonto Natl. Monument, HC 02 Box 4602, Roosevelt, AZ 85545

Tumacácori Natl. Historical Park, Box 67, Tumacacori, AZ 85640

Tuzigoot Natl. Monument, P.O. Box 219, Camp Verde, AZ 86322

Walnut Canyon Natl. Monument, 6400 N. Highway 89, Flagstaff, AZ 86004

Wupatki Natl. Monument, 6400 N. Highway 89, Flagstaff, AZ 86004

ARKANSAS

Arkansas Post Natl. Memorial, 1741 Old Post Road, Gillett, AR 72055

Buffalo Natl. River, 402 N. Walnut, Suite 136, Harrison, AR 72601

Central High School Natl. Historic Site

Fort Smith Natl. Historic Site, P.O. Box 1406, Fort Smith, AR 72902

Hot Springs Natl. Park, P.O. Box 1860, Hot Springs, AR 71902

Pea Ridge Natl. Military Park, P.O. Box 700, Pea Ridge, AR 72751

CALIFORNIA

Cabrillo Natl. Monument, 1800 Cabrillo Memorial Dr., San Diego, CA 92106

Channel Islands Natl. Park, 1901 Spinnaker Dr., Ventura, CA 93001

Death Valley Natl. Park, P.O. Box 579, Death Valley, CA 92328 (See also Nevada)

Devils Postpile Natl. Monument, 47050 Generals Highway, Three Rivers, CA 93271

Eugene O'Neill Natl. Historic Site, P.O. Box 280, Danville, CA 94526

Fort Point Natl. Historic Site, P.O. Box 29333, Presidio of San Francisco, CA 94129

Golden Gate Natl. Recreation Area, Fort Mason, Building 201, San Francisco, CA 94123

John Muir Natl. Historic Site, 4202 Alhambra Ave., Martinez, CA 94553

Joshua Tree Natl. Park, 74485 National Park Dr., Twentynine Palms, CA 92277

Kings Canyon Natl. Park, 47050 Generals Highway, Three Rivers, CA 93271

Lassen Volcanic Natl. Park, P.O. Box 100, Mineral, CA 96063

Lava Beds Natl. Monument, P.O. Box 867, Tulelake, CA 96134

Manzanar Natl. Historic Site, P.O. Box 426, Independence, CA 93526

Mojave Natl. Preserve, 222 E. Main St., Suite 202, Barstow, CA 92311–2366

Muir Woods Natl. Monument, Mill Valley, CA 94941

Natl. AIDS Memorial Grove, 856 Stanyan St., San Francisco, CA 94117

Pinnacles Natl. Monument, 5000 Highway 146, Paicines, CA 95043

Point Reyes Natl. Seashore, Point Reyes, CA 94956

Port Chicago Naval Magazine Natl. Memorial, c/o Eugene O'Neill NHS, P.O. Box 28, Danville, CA 94526

Redwood Natl. Park and State Parks, 1111 Second St., Crescent City, CA 95531

San Francisco Maritime Natl. Historical Park, Fort Mason, San Francisco, CA 94123

Facilities and Activities Chart — Wheelchair Access: Activities/Service, Visitor Center

	Fees	Visitor Center	Programs/Tours	Self-guided Tour/Trail	Guide for Hire	Picnic Area	Campground	Group Camp Site	Backcountry Permits	Hiking	Mountain Climbing	Horse Trail	Swimming	Bathhouse	Boating	Boat Rental	Boat Ramp	Fishing	Hunting	Bicycle Trail	Snowmobile Route	Crosscountry Ski Trail	Cabin Rental	Hotel, Motel, Lodge	Groceries, Ice	Restaurant, Snacks	Campsites	Wheelchair: Activities/Service	Wheelchair: Visitor Center
CALIFORNIA (continued)																													
Santa Monica Mountains Natl. Recreation Area, 401 W. Hillcrest Dr., Thousand Oaks, CA 91360		●	●	●		●				●		●								●						●		●	●
Sequoia Natl. Park, 47050 Generals Highway, Three Rivers, CA 93271	●	●	●	●		●	●	●	●	●	●	●						●		●		●		●	●	●	●	●	●
Whiskeytown Natl. Recreation Area, P.O. Box 188, Whiskeytown, CA 96095	●	●	●	●		●	●	●		●		●	●		●	●	●	●								●	●	●	●
Yosemite Natl. Park, P.O. Box 577, Yosemite Natl. Park, CA 95389	●	●	●	●		●	●	●	●	●	●	●	●					●		●		●	●	●	●	●	●	●	●
COLORADO																													
Bent's Old Fort Natl. Historic Site, 35110 Highway 194 East, La Junta, CO 81050-9523	●	●	●	●	●	●																						●	●
Black Canyon of the Gunnison Natl. Park, 102 Elk Creek, Gunnison, CO 81230	●	●	●	●		●	●		●	●	●							●									●	●	●
Colorado Natl. Monument, Fruita, CO 81521	●	●	●	●		●	●		●	●										●							●	●	●
Curecanti Natl. Recreation Area, 102 Elk Creek, Gunnison, CO 81230	●	●	●	●		●	●	●		●		●	●		●	●	●	●								●	●	●	●
Dinosaur Natl. Monument, 4545 E. Highway 40, Dinosaur, CO 81610 (See also Utah)	●	●	●	●		●	●	●	●	●				●	●			●									●	●	●
Florissant Fossil Beds Natl. Monument, P.O. Box 185, Florissant, CO 80816	●	●	●	●		●			●	●		●										●						●	●
Great Sand Dunes Natl. Monument and Preserve, 11500 Highway 150, Mosca, CO 81146	●	●	●	●		●	●	●	●	●																	●	●	●
Hovenweep Natl. Monument, McElmo Route, Cortez, Co 81321 (See also Utah)	●	●	●	●		●	●			●																	●		●
Mesa Verde Natl. Park, P.O. Box 8, Mesa Verde, CO 81330	●	●	●	●	●	●	●			●														●	●	●	●	●	●
Rocky Mountain Natl. Park, Estes Park, CO 80517	●	●	●	●		●	●	●	●	●	●	●						●				●					●	●	●
GUAM																													
War in the Pacific Natl. Historical Park, 115 Marine Dr., Haloda Building, Piti, Guam 96915	●	●	●	●		●				●			●		●			●		●						●		●	●
HAWAII																													
Haleakala Natl. Park, P.O. Box 369, Makawao, Maui, HI 96768	●	●	●	●		●	●	●	●	●		●											●				●	●	●
Hawaii Volcanoes Natl. Park, P.O. Box 52, Hawaii Natl. Park, HI 96718	●	●	●	●		●	●	●	●	●													●	●	●	●	●	●	●
Kalaupapa Natl. Historical Park, P.O. Box 2222, Kalaupapa, HI 96742		●			●					●																			
Kaloko–Honokohau Natl. Historical Park, 73-4786 Kanalani St. #14, Kailua-Kono, HI 96740-2600		●	●	●						●			●					●										●	●
Pu'uhonua o Honaunau Natl. Historical Park, P.O. Box 129, Honaunau, Kona, HI 96726	●	●	●	●		●				●								●										●	●
Pu'ukoholā Heiau Natl. Historic Site, P.O. Box 44340, Kawaihae, HI 96743		●	●	●																								●	●
USS Arizona Memorial, 1 Arizona Memorial Place, Honolulu, HI 96818		●																								●		●	●
IDAHO																													
City of Rocks Natl. Reserve, P.O. Box 169, Almo, ID 83312	●	●	●	●		●	●	●		●	●							●	●	●		●					●	●	●
Craters of the Moon Natl. Monument and Preserve, P.O. Box 29, Arco, ID 83213	●	●	●	●		●	●		●	●										●		●					●	●	●
Hagerman Fossil Beds Natl. Monument and Preserve, 221 N. State St., P.O. Box 570, Hagerman, ID 83332	●	●		●						●								●										●	●
Nez Perce Natl. Historical Park, Route 1, Box 100, Spalding, ID 83540		●	●	●		●				●																		●	●

IOWA

Effigy Mounds Natl. Monument, 151 Highway 76, Harpers Ferry, IA 52146

Herbert Hoover Natl. Historic Site, P.O. Box 607, West Branch, IA 52358

KANSAS

Brown v. Board of Education Natl. Historic Site, 424 S. Kansas Ave., Suite 220, Topeka, KS 66603

Fort Larned Natl. Historic Site, Route 3, Box 69, Larned, KS 67550

Fort Scott Natl. Historic Site, Old Fort Blvd., Fort Scott, KS 66701

Nicodemus Natl. Historic Site, 304 Washington Ave., Bogue, KS 67625

Tallgrass Prairie Natl. Preserve, Route 1, Box 14, Strong City, KS 66869

LOUISIANA

Cane River Creole Natl. Historical Park, 400 Rapids Ave., Natchitoches, LA 71457

Jean Lafitte Natl. Historical Park and Preserve

Poverty Point Natl. Monument, c/o Poverty Point State Historic Site, P.O. Box 276, Epps, LA 71237

MINNESOTA

Grand Portage Natl. Monument, P.O. Box 668, Grand Marais, MN 55604

Mississippi Natl. River and Recreation Area, 111 E. Kellogg Blvd., St. Paul, MN 55101

Pipestone Natl. Monument, 36 Reservation Ave., Pipestone, MN 56164

St. Croix Natl. Scenic Riverway, P.O. Box 708, St. Croix Falls, WI 54024

Voyageurs Natl. Park, 3131 Highway 53, International Falls, MN 56649

MISSOURI

George Washington Carver Natl. Monument, 5646 Carver Road, Diamond, MO 64840

Harry S Truman Natl. Historic Site, 223 N. Main St., Independence, MO 64050

Jefferson Natl. Expansion Memorial, 11 N. Fourth St., St. Louis, MO 63102

Ozark Natl. Scenic Riverways, P.O. Box 490, Van Buren, MO 63965

Ulysses S. Grant Natl. Historic Site, 7400 Grant St., St. Louis, MO 63123

Wilson's Creek Natl. Battlefield, 6424 W. Farm Road 182, Republic, MO 65738

MONTANA

Big Hole Natl. Battlefield, P.O. Box 237, Wisdom, MT 59761

Bighorn Canyon Natl. Recreation Area, P.O. Box 7458, Fort Smith, MT 59035 (See also Wyoming)

Glacier Natl. Park, West Glacier, MT 59936

Grant-Kohrs Ranch Natl. Historic Site, P.O. Box 790, Deer Lodge, MT 59722

Little Bighorn Battlefield, Natl. Monument, P.O. Box 39, Crow Agency, MT 59022

NEBRASKA

Agate Fossil Beds Natl. Monument, 301 River Road, Harrison, NE 69346

Chimney Rock Natl. Historic Site, P.O. Box 27, Gering, NE 69341

Homestead Natl. Monument of America, 8523 W. State Highway 4, Beatrice, NE 68310

Missouri Natl. Recreational River, P.O. Box 591, O'Neill, NE 68763

Niobrara Natl. Scenic River, P.O. Box 591, O'Neill, NE 68763

Scotts Bluff Natl. Monument, P.O. Box 27, Gering, NE 69341

NEVADA

Park	Fees	Visitor Center	Programs/Tours	Self-guided Tour/Trail	Guide for Hire	Picnic Area	Campground	Group Camp Site	Backcountry Use Permits	Hiking	Mountain Climbing	Horse Trail	Swimming	Bathhouse	Boating	Boat Rental	Boat Ramp	Fishing	Hunting	Bicycle Trail	Snowmobile Route	Crosscountry Ski Trail	Cabin Rental	Hotel, Motel, Lodge	Groceries, Ice	Restaurant, Snacks	Campsites	Activities/Service	Wheelchair Access: Visitor Center
Death Valley Natl. Park, P.O. Box 579, Death Valley, CA 92328 (See also California)	●	●	●	●	●	●	●	●	●	●	●	●	●										●	●	●	●	●	●	●
Great Basin Natl. Park, Baker, NV 89311	●	●	●	●		●	●		●	●								●			●						●	●	●
Lake Mead Natl. Recreation Area	●	●	●	●		●	●	●	●	●			●		●	●	●	●						●	●	●	●	●	●

NEW MEXICO

Park	Fees	Visitor Center	Programs/Tours	Self-guided Tour/Trail	Guide for Hire	Picnic Area	Campground	Group Camp Site	Backcountry Use Permits	Hiking	Mountain Climbing	Horse Trail	Swimming	Bathhouse	Boating	Boat Rental	Boat Ramp	Fishing	Hunting	Bicycle Trail	Snowmobile Route	Crosscountry Ski Trail	Cabin Rental	Hotel, Motel, Lodge	Groceries, Ice	Restaurant, Snacks	Campsites	Activities/Service	Wheelchair Access: Visitor Center
Aztec Ruins Natl. Monument, 84 CR 2900, Aztec, NM 87410	●	●	●	●						●																			●
Bandelier Natl. Monument, HCR I Box 1, Suite 15, Los Alamos, NM 87544	●	●	●	●		●	●	●	●	●																		●	●
Capulin Volcano Natl. Monument, P.O. Box 40, Capulin, NM 88414	●	●	●	●		●				●																		●	●
Carlsbad Caverns Natl. Park, 3225 National Parks Highway, Carlsbad, NM 88220	●	●	●	●					●	●															●	●		●	●
Chaco Culture Natl. Historical Park, Box 220, Nageezi, NM 87037	●	●	●	●		●	●	●	●	●	●								●										
El Malpais Natl. Monument, 123 E. Roosevelt, Grants, NM 87020	●	●	●	●		●		●	●	●									●										
El Morro Natl. Monument, Route 2, Box 43, Ramah, NM 87321	●	●	●	●		●	●			●																			●
Fort Union Natl. Monument, Watrous, NM 87753	●	●	●	●						●																			●
Gila Cliff Dwellings Natl. Monument, HC 68 Box 100, Silver City, NM 88061	●	●	●	●		●			●	●	●							●											●
Pecos Natl. Historical Park, P.O. Box 418, Pecos, NM 87552	●	●	●	●						●																		●	●
Petroglyph Natl. Monument, 6001 Unser Blvd. NW, Albuquerque, NM 87120	●	●	●	●		●				●	●																		●
Salinas Pueblo Missions Natl. Monument, Box 517, Mountainair, NM 87036	●	●	●	●		●				●																			●
White Sands Natl. Monument, P.O. Box 1086, Holloman AFB, NM 88330	●	●	●	●		●			●	●	●														●			●	●

NORTH DAKOTA

Park	Fees	Visitor Center	Programs/Tours	Self-guided Tour/Trail	Guide for Hire	Picnic Area	Campground	Group Camp Site	Backcountry Use Permits	Hiking	Mountain Climbing	Horse Trail	Swimming	Bathhouse	Boating	Boat Rental	Boat Ramp	Fishing	Hunting	Bicycle Trail	Snowmobile Route	Crosscountry Ski Trail	Cabin Rental	Hotel, Motel, Lodge	Groceries, Ice	Restaurant, Snacks	Campsites	Activities/Service	Wheelchair Access: Visitor Center
Fort Union Trading Post Natl. Historic Site, 15550 Highway 1804, Williston, ND 58801	●	●	●	●		●				●								●										●	●
International Peace Garden, Route 1, Box 116, Dunseith, ND 58329	●	●				●																			●			●	
Knife River Indian Villages Natl. Historic Site, P.O. Box 9, Stanton, ND 58571		●	●	●						●								●			●							●	●
Theodore Roosevelt Natl. Park, P.O. Box 7, Medora, ND 58645	●	●	●	●		●	●		●	●		●			●			●									●	●	●

OKLAHOMA

Park	Fees	Visitor Center	Programs/Tours	Self-guided Tour/Trail	Guide for Hire	Picnic Area	Campground	Group Camp Site	Backcountry Use Permits	Hiking	Mountain Climbing	Horse Trail	Swimming	Bathhouse	Boating	Boat Rental	Boat Ramp	Fishing	Hunting	Bicycle Trail	Snowmobile Route	Crosscountry Ski Trail	Cabin Rental	Hotel, Motel, Lodge	Groceries, Ice	Restaurant, Snacks	Campsites	Activities/Service	Wheelchair Access: Visitor Center
Chickasaw Natl. Recreation Area, P.O. Box 201, Sulphur, OK 73086		●	●	●		●	●	●	●	●		●	●		●			●	●								●	●	●
Oklahoma City Natl. Memorial	●	●																											
Washita Battlefield Natl. Historic Site, P.O. Box 890, Cheyenne, OK 73628-0890						●																							

OREGON

Park	Fees	Visitor Center	Programs/Tours	Self-guided Tour/Trail	Guide for Hire	Picnic Area	Campground	Group Camp Site	Backcountry Use Permits	Hiking	Mountain Climbing	Horse Trail	Swimming	Bathhouse	Boating	Boat Rental	Boat Ramp	Fishing	Hunting	Bicycle Trail	Snowmobile Route	Crosscountry Ski Trail	Cabin Rental	Hotel, Motel, Lodge	Groceries, Ice	Restaurant, Snacks	Campsites	Activities/Service	Wheelchair Access: Visitor Center
Crater Lake Natl. Park, P.O. Box 7, Crater Lake, OR 97604	●	●	●	●		●	●		●	●		●						●			●	●		●	●	●	●	●	●
Fort Clatsop Natl. Memorial, 92343 Fort Clatsop Road, Astoria, OR 97103	●	●	●	●		●				●												●						●	●
John Day Fossil Beds Natl. Monument, HCR 82 Box 126, Kimberly, OR 97848		●	●	●		●				●								●										●	●
McLoughlin House Natl. Historic Site, 713 Center St., Oregon City, OR 97045	●	●	●	●																								●	●

OREGON (continued)

Oregon Caves Natl. Monument, 19000 Caves Highway, Cave Junction, OR 97523

SAIPAN

American Memorial Park, P.O. Box 5189-CHRB, Saipan, MP 96950

SOUTH DAKOTA

Badlands Natl. Park, P.O. Box 6, Interior, SD 57750

Jewel Cave Natl. Monument, R.R. 1, Box 60AA, Custer, SD 57730

Mount Rushmore Natl. Memorial, P.O. Box 268, Keystone, SD 57751

Wind Cave Natl. Park, R.R. 1, Box 190, Hot Springs, SD 57747

TEXAS

Alibates Flint Quarries Natl. Monument, Box 1460, Fritch, TX 79036

Amistad Natl. Recreation Area, HCR-3 Box 5J, Del Rio, TX 78840

Big Bend Natl. Park, P.O. Box 129, Big Bend Natl. Park, TX 79834

Big Thicket Natl. Preserve, 3785 Milam, Beaumont, TX 77701

Chamizal Natl. Memorial, 800 S. San Marcial St., El Paso, TX 79905

Fort Davis Natl. Historic Site, P.O. Box 1456, Fort Davis, TX 79734

Guadalupe Mountains Natl. Park, HC 60 Box 400, Salt Flat, TX 79847

Lake Meredith Natl. Recreation Area, P.O. Box 1460, Fritch, TX 79036

Lyndon B. Johnson Natl. Historical Park, P.O. Box 329, Johnson City, TX 78636

Padre Island Natl. Seashore, 20420 Park Road 22, Corpus Christi, TX 78418

Palo Alto Battlefield Natl. Historic Site, 1623 Central Blvd., Suite 213, Brownsville, TX 78520

San Antonio Missions Natl. Historical Park, 2202 Roosevelt Ave., San Antonio, TX 78210-4919

UTAH

Arches Natl. Park, P.O. Box 907, Moab, UT 84532

Bryce Canyon Natl. Park, Bryce Canyon, UT 84717

Canyonlands Natl. Park, 2282 S. West Resource Blvd., Moab, UT 84532

Capitol Reef Natl. Park, Torrey, UT 84775

Cedar Breaks Natl. Monument, 2390 W. Highway 56 #11, Cedar City, UT 84720

Dinosaur Natl. Monument, 4545 Highway 40, Dinosaur, CO 81610 (See also Colorado)

Glen Canyon Natl. Recreation Area, P.O. Box 1507, Page, AZ 86040 (See also Arizona)

Golden Spike Natl. Historic Site, P.O. Box 897, Brigham City, UT 84302

Hovenweep Natl. Monument, McElmo Route, Cortez, CO 81321 (See also Colorado)

Natural Bridges Natl. Monument, HC 60 Box 1, Lake Powell, UT 84533

Rainbow Bridge Natl. Monument, c/o Glen Canyon Natl. Recreation Area, Box 1507, Page, AZ 86040

Timpanogos Cave Natl. Monument, R.R. 3, Box 200, American Fork, UT 84003

Zion Natl. Park, Springdale, UT 84767-1099

WASHINGTON

Site	Fees	Visitor Center	Programs/Tours	Self-guided Tour/Trail	Guide for Hire	Picnic Area	Campground	Group Camp Site	Backcountry Permits	Hiking	Mountain Climbing	Horse Trail	Swimming	Bathhouse	Boating	Boat Rental	Boat Ramp	Fishing	Hunting	Bicycle Trail	Snowmobile Route	Crosscountry Ski Trail	Cabin Rental	Hotel, Motel, Lodge	Groceries, Ice	Restaurant, Snacks	Campsites	Activities/Service	Visitor Center (Wheelchair Access)
Ebey's Landing Natl. Historical Reserve, P.O. Box 774, Coupeville, WA 98239	•	•	•	•		•				•																		•	•
Fort Vancouver Natl. Historic Site, 612 E. Reserve St., Vancouver, WA 98661-3811	•	•	•	•	•	•																						•	•
Klondike Gold Rush Natl. Historical Park, 117 S. Main St., Seattle, WA 98104 (See also Alaska)		•	•	•																								•	•
Lake Chelan Natl. Recreation Area, 810 State Route 20, Sedro-Woolley, WA 98284	•	•	•	•	•	•	•	•		•			•		•	•	•	•						•	•	•	•	•	•
Lake Roosevelt Natl. Recreation Area, 1008 Crest Dr., Coulee Dam, WA 99116	•	•	•	•	•	•	•	•		•			•	•	•	•	•	•					•	•	•		•	•	•
Mount Rainier Natl. Park, Tahoma Woods Star Route, Ashford, WA 98304	•	•	•	•	•	•	•		•	•	•	•						•				•	•	•	•	•	•	•	•
North Cascades Natl. Park, 810 State Route 20, Sedro-Woolley, WA 98284		•	•	•		•	•		•	•	•	•						•									•	•	•
Olympic Natl. Park, 600 E. Park Ave., Port Angeles, WA 98362	•	•	•	•	•	•	•		•	•	•	•	•		•	•	•	•		•	•	•	•	•	•	•	•	•	•
Ross Lake Natl. Recreation Area, 810 State Route 20, Sedro-Woolley, WA 98284	•	•	•	•		•	•		•	•	•	•			•	•	•	•									•	•	•
San Juan Island Natl. Historical Park, P.O. Box 429, Friday Harbor, WA 98250		•	•	•		•			•	•																		•	•
Whitman Mission Natl. Historic Site, 328 Whitman Mission Road, Walla Walla, WA 99362	•	•	•	•		•																						•	•

WYOMING

Site	Fees	Visitor Center	Programs/Tours	Self-guided Tour/Trail	Guide for Hire	Picnic Area	Campground	Group Camp Site	Backcountry Permits	Hiking	Mountain Climbing	Horse Trail	Swimming	Bathhouse	Boating	Boat Rental	Boat Ramp	Fishing	Hunting	Bicycle Trail	Snowmobile Route	Crosscountry Ski Trail	Cabin Rental	Hotel, Motel, Lodge	Groceries, Ice	Restaurant, Snacks	Campsites	Activities/Service	Visitor Center (Wheelchair Access)
Bighorn Canyon Natl. Recreation Area, P.O. Box 7458, Fort Smith, MT 59035 (See also Montana)	•	•	•	•		•	•		•	•		•	•		•	•	•	•	•								•	•	•
Devils Tower Natl. Monument, P.O. Box 10, Devils Tower, WY 82714	•	•	•	•		•	•			•	•															•		•	•
Fort Laramie Natl. Historic Site, HC 72 Box 389, Fort Laramie, WY 82212	•	•	•	•		•				•							•	•										•	•
Fossil Butte Natl. Monument, P.O. Box 592, Kemmerer, WY 83101		•	•	•		•			•	•																	•	•	•
Grand Teton Natl. Park, P.O. Drawer 170, Moose, WY 83012	•	•	•	•	•	•	•	•	•	•	•	•	•		•	•	•	•		•		•	•	•	•	•	•	•	•
John D. Rockefeller Jr. Memorial Parkway, c/o Grand Teton Natl. Park, P.O. Drawer 170, Moose, WY 83012	•	•	•	•		•	•		•	•	•	•			•	•	•	•	•	•		•	•	•	•	•	•	•	•
Yellowstone Natl. Park, P.O. Box 168, Yellowstone Natl. Park, WY 82190	•	•	•	•	•	•	•	•	•	•	•	•	•		•	•	•	•			•	•	•	•	•	•	•	•	•

ABOUT THE AUTHORS

DAVID AND KAY SCOTT reside in Valdosta, Georgia, where the winters are mild, the humidity is high, and the people are friendly. They have spent twenty-seven summers touring the United States and Canada in a series of Volkswagen campers. The first VW bus they owned was a 1967 model that looked like a relic from World War II. During its first cross-country trip, in 1970, the VW was barely able to make headway against the wind blowing across a Wyoming interstate. Their two- and three-month trips have taken the couple through all the states, the Canadian provinces, and to nearly all the areas administered by the National Park Service. The Scotts drove from Georgia to Alaska and back during the summer of 1983. David and Kay have appeared live from Yellowstone National Park and Grand Canyon National Park on NBC's *Today* show, offering tips on visiting the national parks. In addition to their domestic travels, the Scotts spent five summers carrying backpacks while riding trains through Europe.

David Scott was born in Rushville, Indiana, attended Purdue University and Florida State University, and received a Ph.D. in economics from the University of Arkansas. During most of the year, he is a professor of accounting and finance at Valdosta State University. He has written numerous books on accounting and finance. In addition to travel, he is interested in amateur radio, computers, and the Atlanta Braves. His e-mail address is dlscott@valdosta.edu.

Kay Woelfel Scott was born in Austin, Minnesota, and was raised in Yankton, South Dakota. She graduated from Clearwater (Florida) High School and earned degrees at Florida Southern College and the University of Arkansas. After working thirty-one years in education, she retired from her position as an elementary school administrator in 1999. She is interested in a wide variety of crafts, including working with stained glass and making flags.